Incorporating Architects

The publisher and the University of California Press Foundation gratefully acknowledge the generous support of the Richard and Harriett Gold Endowment Fund in Arts and Humanities.

Incorporating Architects
HOW AMERICAN ARCHITECTURE BECAME A PRACTICE OF EMPIRE

Aaron Cayer

UNIVERSITY OF CALIFORNIA PRESS

University of California Press
Oakland, California

© 2025 by Aaron Cayer

All rights reserved.

Library of Congress Cataloging-in-Publication Data

Names: Cayer, Aaron, author.
Title: Incorporating architects : how American architecture became a practice of empire / Aaron Cayer.
Description: Oakland, California : University of California Press, [2025] | Includes bibliographical references and index.
Identifiers: LCCN 2024044766 (print) | LCCN 2024044767 (ebook) | ISBN 9780520400863 (cloth) | ISBN 9780520400870 (paperback) | ISBN 9780520400887 (ebook)
Subjects: LCSH: AECOM (Firm)—History—20th century. | Architecture—Political aspects—United States—History—20th century.
Classification: LCC NA2543.I47 C39 2025 (print) | LCC NA2543 .I47 (ebook) | DDC 338.7/61720973—dc23/eng/20250122
LC record available at https://lccn.loc.gov/2024044766
LC ebook record available at https://lccn.loc.gov/2024044767

GPSR Authorized Representative: Easy Access System Europe, Mustamäe tee 50, 10621 Tallinn, Estonia, gpsr.requests@easproject.com

34 33 32 31 30 29 28 27 26 25
10 9 8 7 6 5 4 3 2 1

To my mother
and to the memory of my father.

Contents

Acknowledgments   *ix*

Introduction   *1*

1. Profession: Shattering Tradition   *25*
2. Firm: Corporate Conglomeration   *64*
3. Building: Enclosing Indeterminacy   *110*
4. Contract: Developing Architects   *142*
5. Portfolio: Valuing Practice   *184*
6. Vault: Keeping Secrets   *201*

   Conclusion   *232*

   Appendix   *239*
   Notes   *245*
   Bibliography   *295*
   Index   *335*

Acknowledgments

This project would not have been possible without the support, guidance, and labor of many people. What began as a dissertation at UCLA has become so much more than I could have ever imagined. This was due, in large part, to the formative brilliance of my dissertation committee: Dana Cuff, Michael Osman, Sylvia Lavin, and Sherry Ortner. I am particularly grateful to Dana for her support in the years following UCLA: checking in, writing letters, and demonstrating, through her own tireless work, how architecture scholarship can, indeed, make the world a better place.

While in graduate school, I was fortunate to study alongside many selfless and dedicated scholars, both at UCLA and at institutions across the country, who have become lifelong friends. Their continued willingness to discuss and read drafts, even when conclusions were premature or lacked coherence, provided inspiration and clarity. These include Yang Yang, Veronica Giordano, Maria Francesca Piazzoni, KT Bender, Robert Farley, Deepa Ramaswamy, Susila Gurusami, William Davis, Rebecca Choi, Mohamed Monkez, Hogan Lee, and Kimberly Serrano. I have learned so much from each of them, as well as from a growing community of scholars interested in architectural work who have challenged me and sharpened my focus at various points, including Peggy Deamer, Magali Sarfatti Larson,

Michael Kubo, Claire Zimmerman, Bryan Norwood, Michael Abrahamson, Aaron Tobey, and many members of The Architecture Lobby.

Equally central to my growth as a writer and teacher has been the support of my partners-in-academic-arms at the University of New Mexico and Cal Poly Pomona. At UNM, I am particularly grateful to Nora Wendl, whose incessant optimism, generosity, and sincerity make me not only a better teacher and researcher, but also a better human. I am thankful to the ever-sharp and supportive Albert Lopez, Cesar Lopez, Gabriel Fries-Briggs, Georgiann Davis, Ranita Ray, Kathy Kambic, Michaele Pride, Kuppu Iyengar, Renia Ehrenfeucht, Katya Crawford, Karen King, Sasha Ortenberg, and Lauren Bricker for always helping me find light in a seemingly endless tunnel of corporate and bureaucratic darkness. The support of my department chairs, including John Quale, Chris Cornelius, and George Proctor, through letters and release time, provided essential support to complete the manuscript. I am thankful to my graduate and undergraduate students whose eagerness to learn and curiosity about this project provided me both a refreshing source of energy and productive distraction as I finished writing. Rahul Balla at UNM and Ayana Johnson at CPP provided critical graphical expertise at different points in the book's development.

I am eternally grateful to Kim Robinson at UC Press for trusting my vision for the book and supporting it with openness, Aline Dolinh and Jeff Anderson for moving the manuscript along with patience, Richard Earles for his excellent copyedits, and to the press's unique and generous support of first-gen writers like me. I thank the many people who have carefully reviewed or offered thoughts or comments on this project at various stages, at conferences or elsewhere, including Meredith TenHoor, Joy Knobluach, John Harwood, Daniel Paul, and Helena McDermott, as well as three exceptionally generous reviewers of the manuscript: Arindam Dutta, Sara Stevens, and one anonymous reader. I am also indebted to Lisa Fetchko, who pushed me to polish the text and tighten its arguments in the manuscript's final stage.

I am thankful to the many archivists, librarians, and research assistants who have helped me uncover archival material that, at first glance, seemed hopelessly inaccessible, including those at the Huntington Library, Cal State University Northridge, Cal State University Dominguez Hills, Yale University, the City of LA Bureau of Engineering, the Air Force Historical Research Agency at Maxwell Air Force Base, the CIA Archives and Special Collections, Vandenberg Air Force Base, the Tillman Water Reclamation Plant, Ashland Oil, the Lumsden family, and AECOM.

Beyond archival material, this book would not have been possible without the dozens of architects, engineers, business executives, managers, draftspersons, and their families, who generously offered their time, their homes, and their offices to share their stories, family histories, insights, and reflections. These perspectives add an essential voice to documents, buildings, and drawings that otherwise would remain voiceless—as "things."

My research and writing was supported by a postdoctoral fellowship at the Huntington Library, research grants at the University of New Mexico, the International Archive of Women in Architecture, the Texas State Historical Association, and a production grant from the Graham Foundation. I was most fortunate to finish writing this manuscript while a Fellow at the American Academy in Rome, where I was surrounded by yet another lifelong family of brilliant minds and generous spirits.

Finally, I thank my close circle of family and friends for their patience, love, and gentle querying about what seemed like a never-ending project. I am grateful beyond measure to Fernando for his steady love and for encouraging me even during the most selfish moments of research and writing. Above all, this book is dedicated to my mother and to the memory of my father. I was reminded throughout this project that, if not for the many rural papermill towns like the one in which we grew up and where they worked to support me, there would be no architectural documents, drawings, or books to study, nor pages upon which to write. They taught me the meaning of work, dedication, and love in ways that no book or university could; this work is for them.

Introduction

Surrounded by Northern California's towering redwoods, architect Stanley Smith was reminiscing with Michael Deaver, President Ronald Reagan's chief of staff, as they waited for dinner on the open-air deck of their camp, the "Sahara." A beer and a vodka-and-soda within reach, they were nearing the end of a two-week retreat of the Bohemian Club, an exclusive gentlemen's club, at Bohemian Grove—where Robert Oppenheimer once discussed the atomic bomb and Henry Kissinger frequently lectured about foreign policy.[1] It was a late July evening in 1982. The country was in a recession, and some of the world's most prominent men were socializing "off the record" at this campground of themed camps and clubhouses, as they have each summer since 1872.[2]

"I've . . . tried to recapture that feeling of relaxation and friendship," Deaver wrote to Smith on White House letterhead a few months later. "I certainly look forward to another trip."[3] It was not surprising to find Deaver, as chief draftsman of Reagan's press releases and policies, at the Grove. And the same was true for the hundreds of invited politicians, professors, and industrialists. Former CIA chief John McCone from California and German chancellor Helmut Schmidt attended that year.[4] But who was Smith, and why was he, an architect, among them? He was no "bohemian"—a title reserved for artists and musicians hired to entertain the Grove's members.[5]

Smith was known neither for the artistry of his drawings nor for the ingenuity of his buildings; it was his firm, where he worked as vice president, and its political power, that earned him his seat. The firm was Daniel, Mann, Johnson, and Mendenhall, or DMJM (affectionately pronounced "Dim-Jim"), a Los Angeles–based architecture and engineering company known for its managerial efficiency and a web of clients that included politicians and corporate executives, bankers and military commanders, city councils and federal governments.

Smith and Deaver's casual conversation was hinting at a deeper relationship between architecture firms and the federal government—one that was challenging the traditional image of a "professional architect" in the United States. Beginning in the late nineteenth century, architects, like doctors, had pledged to shield their work from political pressure and the sway of economic markets for the public's safety. Most were working alone or in small firms for private patrons, grumbling about their low wages and limited social impact.

However, there were lesser-known architects—more like Smith— who, after World War II, began to weave themselves into the operations of the government and military. By the century's end, these architects were designing nearly every part of urban environments within US cities and those abroad: schools, housing, offices, and infrastructure, as well as the weapons, military bases, and legal codes through which they were governed. No longer fixed to their drafting tables or working alone in artist-like studios, they were designing an inscrutable and sometimes violent system of public-private exchange behind the closed doors of their private offices, boardrooms, clubhouses, and hotel rooms.

As testament to these architects' influences on the post–World War II economy, Smith's firm became the largest publicly traded company in Los Angeles. Formed in 1946 by three young architects who were struggling to make ends meet as a small partnership, DMJM ballooned into a multinational corporate "conglomerate" by the end of the twentieth century—a firm with dozens of corporate subsidiaries spanning more than sixteen sectors and a hundred cities worldwide. By then—in 1990—the firm had been renamed AECOM, a firm with services that ranged from architecture to data processing to diplomacy. And by 2020, AECOM's revenue rivaled only that of the Walt Disney Company, based next door in Burbank. With more capital than ninety-seven countries, and offices in as many nations as the United Nations, more people worked there than lived in 98 percent of American cities.[6]

What follows is a story about how, over the course of the twentieth century, architects slowly incorporated the terms, tools, and techniques of the US government as they formed mutual dependencies. What began as a practice of architecture—architects designing local schools, shops, and grocery stores—transformed into a practice of empire as architects expanded and reproduced the imperial acts of the government through the legal and organizational tools of their businesses and profession. This is a story about how architecture firms had, by century's end, become political-economic bellwethers not only for the cities and states in which they operated but for the country as well.

. . .

Like many young students hoping to become architects, I entered college in 2007 with the impression that architects impacted the world with the creativity of their designs, the clarity of their drawings, and the imagination of their buildings. Darkening the already-dark clouds of the Great Recession hovering above us, we learned that architects earned relatively low wages, that large firms—which offered the most jobs—were few and unremarkable, and that a good professional architect sheltered her work from political and economic influence.

At the time, we were reading ethnographies, manuals, and histories of architects' "practices" written during the 1970s and 1980s that have remained required texts for students of architecture today—Dana Cuff's ethnography of architects, Judith Blau's analysis of firms, Robert Gutman's demographic study, and Mary Woods's later history of the profession.[7] These books were inspired by stories of economic downturns and political concerns that mirrored ours: architects and interns trying to stay afloat during a recession, a profession defined by structural contradictions and inequity, and lessons about work and culture that were missing from most textbooks. Their authors often cited Ayn Rand's *The Fountainhead* in their introductions, with its romantic depiction of an architect-as-hero, Howard Roark, who set his own interests above those of others despite society's woes.[8] In the shared stories, architects were beginning to work collaboratively and in corporate offices, standing out against the individualist character of Roark—a character who, despite mild critiques, still seemed alive and well across the profession. However, while architecture had become the work of many, increasingly defined by bureaucracy, most scholarship and academic institutions have, up to today, remained focused on the creative work of individuals and that of small design firms.

When I moved to Los Angeles five years later, news was stirring about AECOM. The company had recently moved into One California Plaza in Downtown—a forty-two-story mirror-glass tower surrounded by offices of financial institutions, including Union Bank and U.S. Bank. AECOM's name prominently crowned its tower, visible for miles from the surrounding freeways and hills. Despite this publicity, within the city and on the stock market, the reflective surface of California Plaza was deflecting views inside the building, much like the armed security guards turning away visitors in the ground-floor lobby. Its mystique stymied local critics: it was a 1980s story of postmodern opacity that appeared to be replaying again in the early 2000s. A "quiet giant," as one newspaper described it.[9]

I found myself fascinated by the widespread curiosity about AECOM, especially since I had grown up in a rural New England town without architects, let alone a company with thousands of them. And also because contemporary magazines at the time were, despite AECOM's significance, emphasizing the fact that only 5 percent of buildings globally were designed by licensed architects.[10] Equally curious to me was the way that journalists and scholars were portraying AECOM as a radically new kind of "Leviathan" that seemed to have hatched overnight. The firm was luring in critics, trapping them within the feedback loops of its mirror-glass façade, reflecting and re-reflecting. Was it trapping me, too? How, I began to wonder, had the firm come to be? What work went on there? Were there other firms like it? As it turns out, the work that architects do there is quite different from what I had read about in school.

My first research step was a cursory search online for details about AECOM's history, which only heightened the firm's obscurity. Anonymous bureaucrats—"directors" and "presidents," "managers" and "heads"—led the firm, rather than architects or engineers. Its chief executive officer earned a staggering $15.6 million that year, compared to the average worker's $78,500.[11] And AECOM's website listed twenty-eight services, each more abstract than the last: "Architecture and Design," "IT and Cybersecurity," "Finance," "Government Relations," "Public-Private Partnerships," "Strategy Plus."

In one division of the firm, architects had recently designed a new headquarters for the Los Angeles Police Department; in another, architects were helping to train Afghans for combat; in yet another, architects were writing legal code as part of a new master plan for Kigali, Rwanda. How had architects developed these remarkably different muscles of colonial-capitalist governance? What were the global consequences of their work? As I would soon learn, AECOM's rise was not an isolated phenomenon. It was a beacon, hinting at more significant shifts and cycles of change within the history of business, professions, and the political economy during the twentieth century that were structuring—if not replaying in—the present.

This book looks backward to consider how and why postwar anxieties and concerns about loss and instability made corporate and, ultimately, "conglomerate" practices in architecture both possible and desirable. It also looks forward to consider what happens to labor, firms, cities, professions, and the political economy when architects form them. While the work of architects was once bound by an ethical code and defined primarily through the labor of drawings, architecture had, by the end of the twentieth century, expanded to include virtually anything, placing the practice of architecture at odds with the history of its own profession. "We are AECOM," one senior vice president proclaimed in 2010. "We can do anything."[12] Indeed, architects were not only producing drawings; they were preparing income statements and corporate charters, surveillance reports and financial spreadsheets, land surveys and weapons assessments. The profession of architecture, as a result, was set free from any standard definition.

Rather than weave together the materials of many businesses to produce an abstract history that mirrors the very logics of corporate conglomeration examined within it, and rather than present a static view of a particular moment—an approach that, business historians point out, undermines our ability to explain changes over extended periods or see how transitions, shifts, or cycles of booms and busts were designed—I consider, instead, AECOM's emergence, transformation, and effects as a single case.[13] The history I trace, of AECOM's rise and its associated changes within the profession—how a small architecture firm produced an elaborate system of urban governance—might be considered inevitable. It was in the US, and in California more specifically, that architects produced a military-industrial-entertainment-education complex during the twentieth century and drafted the plans, designed the infrastructures, and produced the urban inequities that have since come to define neoliberalism. If Illinois, New York, Pennsylvania, and Washington, DC, were where the architecture profession was assembled during the nineteenth century, California was where it landed in the twentieth century and where it was, for better or for worse, ripped apart.

. . .

Until recently, it was common for scholars to skirt the work of architects within large architecture and engineering firms.[14] It is true: such firms were and remain politically controversial and structurally contradictory, their immense sizes and tangled webs of bureaucracies overwhelming. These are the types of firms that, during the first half of the twentieth century (and ever since), designed mile-long factories for the mass production of cars and facilities for battle tanks and missiles, as well as housing for vulnerable communities at the same time as prisons and barracks for concentration camps.

This relative lack of attention to the collective enterprise of architecture and engineering is ironic, however, since it is at this scale that architects have most impacted everyday public life. As recent scholars have pointed out, the perpetual eclipsing of such firms, and of the labor conditions and cultures within them, not only has perpetuated long-standing myths about architecture as an act of "creative genius" within universities and the public imagination, but also has limited the ways in which architects have seen themselves as part of broader political and economic systems.[15]

To be sure, many of the young architects who founded the soon-to-be-large architecture and engineering firms after World War II were contending with very real hardships. Following the double-strike of the war and the Great Depression preceding it, they, like many, saw work as a form of freedom—as a new bourgeois sense of morality that could be extracted from a postwar capitalist state in search of global hegemony.[16] Architecture offered unique liberating possibilities that, in some ways, aligned with the contradictions embedded in a two-party political system: it was helpful for envisioning alternative futures while at the same time for guarding against change. Yet in this otherwise familiar story of rags to riches, architects began to interpret the tools offered by the state as tools for the business of architecture. As their businesses grew, so too did their sense of safety and stability, and with that stability came a greater sense of authority. In turn, these architects slowly and unabashedly gripped the reins of their profession—the very terms of licensure, membership, training, and awards—to defend their livelihoods and secure their place within history.[17]

It would be inaccurate to suggest that big businesses in architecture first formed during the twentieth century. The view of the architect as a businessman was codified during the era of monopoly capitalism of the late nineteenth century, when industrial organizations consolidated and merged into increasingly larger ones. As architecture historian Mary Woods has argued, in order to establish firms that could endure, architects in the US were—unlike architects in places like Europe, where sustained public patronage was historically more common—required to actively tune the structures of their private practices to the market economy, adapting them according to the shifting means of capital accumulation.[18] At the turn of the twentieth century, one New Jersey architect writing to a broad professional audience concluded that "the architectural opportunities fall to those who are preeminent for business rather than artistic ability, and thus it is they who build the architecture of the country, good, bad or indifferent. The architect must be a business man first and an artist afterwards."[19]

In New York City, George B. Post's small, debt-laden and student-dependent practice, formed in 1867, transformed a sole proprietorship into a partnership, complete with a "modern office" with sixty people and a clear division of labor that allowed architects and draftsmen to work more efficiently on multiple commissions simultaneously.[20] McKim, Mead & White, also in New York, surged to an exceptionally large firm of 110 by the panic of 1893; meanwhile, in Chicago, William Holabird and Martin Roche's 1880 partnership, Holabird and Roche, swelled to forty by 1890, and Daniel Burnham & Co. grew to 180 by 1912.[21] However, such partnerships were then largely driven by private commissions, companies, and wealthy industrialists rather than by the state. And they were rare even after World War I, as less than 0.1 percent of US firms by 1920 employed more than eighty people.[22]

At the start of the twentieth century, architecture firms were considered "large" if they employed fifty people; by mid-century, that threshold was one thousand.[23] The settings, spaces, and procedures of their work were distinct, most argued, from those of artist-architects, who, more like Rand's Howard Roark, worked alone in their studios or in small groups.[24] In 1947, the year after DMJM formed, Henry-Russell Hitchcock notably described this split—between creative authors known for their expressive, imaginative designs on the one hand, and large anonymous bureaucracies known for their precision and organizational efficiency on the other.[25] What Hitchcock could not have predicted, however, was the sheer impact such bureaucracies would have on the arc and architecture of the twentieth-century political economy, or the ways that small firms of creative authors, too, would come to embrace the tools of big business as industrialization waned and as size-based distinctions became less meaningful.[26]

Today, many architecture firms in the US can be considered bureaucracies or even complex corporate conglomerates akin to

AECOM—as firms with many firms within them. Architecture firm Albert Kahn, born as a partnership in Detroit in 1895 alongside the rise of the auto industry, now defines itself as a corporate "family" of seven "multi-disciplinary" firms that comprise the "Albert Kahn Family of Companies."[27] Perkins & Will, founded in Chicago in 1935, describes itself since 1986 as part of a "family of partner companies" named the Dar Group, owned by the Lebanese conglomerate Dar Al-Handasah.[28]

Even firms for which high design and cultural capital, rather than economic capital, were once understood to be primary motivating forces began adopting the protocols, organizational structures, and lessons of big business—most in order to weather downturns in the economy—at the end of the twentieth century. A design firm such as Gehry Partners in Los Angeles can be considered a corporate conglomerate: despite publicizing itself as a partnership, the firm is a corporation that includes six subsidiaries in California alone. Some Gehry subsidiaries offer textiles, furniture, materials, and proprietary technology, while others define a particular nation or region *as* an economic offering—Gehry Technologies Middle East, Mexico, Brazil, and the Netherlands.[29] SHoP Architects, a younger yet equally notable design firm, comprises more than twenty companies linked to its New York office that capitalize on geographic and economic breadth, including Shop Africa, which supports construction in Botswana, and 30littleramisland, through which the firm's principals have acquired private property.[30]

Despite the expanded size and scope of architecture firms such as DMJM (and later AECOM), it is true that most architects in the US work in small firms with fewer than twenty employees. By 1972, for instance, only fifty-four architecture firms—0.5 percent of all firms—employed more than one hundred people, while 93 percent were smaller than twenty people.[31] At the same time, large firms accounted for 14 percent of the field's total revenue, leaving smaller firms to compete for an even smaller share of projects. While the profession has remained consistently stratified by firm size, large firms nearly doubled their control of total revenue by 1992 (to 21 percent) and tripled it by 1997 (to 40 percent).[32] Beyond this redistribution of capital, it is worth remembering that smaller firms at varying stages of development have also adopted the organizational strategies of large firms. Therefore, the influence of the large firms' all-out pursuits of capital is even more profound than the category "large" suggests.

. . .

The stake of AECOM's history was palpable during my first attempt to meet with architects at the firm. After emailing a "general.inquiries" address posted on the firm's website with no luck, I tried reaching the firm's leaders directly. One problem: their addresses were not publicized. I attempted various configurations—first initial <dot> last name <at> aecom <dot> com; last name <dot> first name <at> aecom <dot> com; first name <dot> last name <at> aecom <dot> com. Most of my messages bounced back, but the last configuration worked. "Thanks for your interest and we would be happy to help," wrote the firm's second-in-charge. "The best is actually yet to come for AECOM as we reinvigorate our architecture practice. I am copying our head of buildings and places . . . to make sure you get access to what you need. Thanks again. Good stuff."[33]

After passing by the security guards in the first-floor lobby and presenting my ID at the front desk, I was escorted to the elevators and up to AECOM's office. There, I checked in with the receptionist, a young woman whose entire body was blocked by a computer screen, her neck wrapped with a cord to her microphoned headset. I met with an executive vice president, who had worked at the firm less than three months, to discuss the firm's history. While I was introducing myself as an architectural historian, she immediately interrupted. "*Architecture history?*" she asked. "Why research *us?*" Her question caught me off guard. By that point, I knew that the A in AECOM stood for "architecture" and that the firm began as a small "architecture-only" partnership named DMJM, so the unfamiliarity with AECOM's roots in architecture, even among its senior personnel, was surprising. They preferred the more general descriptors "contractor" and "consultancy," she told me, since they did "*so much more*" than architecture.

Returning home, I downloaded the firm's recent annual report, a document necessary for maintaining good standing with the government and shareholders, in which I could see that the economic status of architecture within the firm was quite minimal. By 2016, only 1,491 of the company's ninety thousand employees—less than 2 percent—were architects. And architectural work accounted for even less of the firm's revenue: two-tenths of a percent, or $320 million of the firm's $18.2 billion.[34] What were the historical conditions that led to the displacement of architects within the firm? How did this trend compare with others across the profession? And what was the *so much more?*

A month after my visit, one of the firm's directors emailed me a five-part autobiography of the firm in lieu of records: a scanned, low-resolution PDF of the "legacy" days of the firm, which I later learned was written by one of the first women architects to work at the company. Accessing documents in AECOM's archives, the firm's executive vice president explained, would require special approval from the firm's legal counsel. While I waited, hoping to be allowed access to any drawings, photographs, business documents, or contracts that might explain the firm's history or projects in greater detail, I visited public archives and libraries in Southern California where the firm had left substantial paper trails.

AECOM, the autobiography explained, was formed in 1990 as "AECOM Technology Corporation," an outgrowth of DMJM. As with many large postwar firms, DMJM was formed by three young architects who were united by military service, Depression-era degrees, and a Cold War–era concern about loss that echoed the feeling of many in government: concerns about the nation's sovereignty, authority, and control over narratives of its past and future. Drawing from the lessons of business partnerships from the late nineteenth century, architects Phillip Daniel, Arthur Mann, and S. Kenneth Johnson formed Daniel, Mann, and Johnson Architects (initially DM&J, later DMJM) as a partnership in 1946. While cautiously optimistic about architectural work during a postwar construction boom as a trio, rather than sole practitioners, they knew very little about running a business. By the end of the 1940s, despite steady work, stacks of unpaid bills were teetering on the architects' desks, and they were returning home at the end of each week with less than fifty dollars in their pockets. As the editor of one business magazine recalled, the architects believed it was only a matter of time before the "profit-sapping" partnership would "explode apart."[35]

Instead of giving up, the architects hired management consultants—professionals unfamiliar to most architects at the time—who were advocating corporate structure, diversification, and government alliances. Encouraged to adopt a new business model, they began to use the legal, technological, and administrative tools of the corporation to consolidate their business, limit their risk, and expand their services internationally by following postwar funding wherever it could be found: in local communities, the federal government, aid organizations, the military, and expanding business enterprises.

Building intimate friendships and aligning themselves with those in power—politicians and military leaders, corporate executives and policymakers—architects began to internalize and reproduce the terms, tools, and techniques of their clients: most often, the state. By the 1970s, architecture firms were acquired and merged, fractured and sold, transforming into "corporate conglomerates," and they wielded new power over the cities they were serving and the professions within which they worked. By the end of the twentieth century, architecture and engineering conglomerates such as DMJM were being studied not only by small architecture firms, but also by governments, oil companies, accounting and law firms, and even the US military itself.

. . .

Given its use across time, industry, and geography, the term *conglomerate* in relation to corporations warrants a preliminary working definition. The US Federal Trade Commission defined conglomerates in the 1950s through three practices. These included (1) market extensions, wherein firms acquire similar companies but in different geographies; (2) product extensions, wherein firms acquire others that are similar in work but do not directly compete; and (3) "pure" conglomerates, wherein firms acquire others that are disparate in service, product, function, or geography.[36] More conceptually, though, conglomerates can be defined as firms with many firms within them—as social, physical, economic, political, and technological infrastructures through which land, money, people, resources, materials, or businesses flow in or out and change over time. Despite the various "posts" that have been attributed to their urban and architectural effects (postmodern architecture, for example), business historians such as Alfred D. Chandler Jr. argued that conglomerates were extreme outgrowths of diversified modern business enterprises.[37] Unlike the Great Merger Movement of the late twentieth century, when single-industry organizations merged with or acquired similar firms to increase their market power within a single industry, conglomerates maximized their profits during the 1960s and 1970s by acquiring, developing, or exploiting businesses or geographies at their so-called *periphery*—a term that has become central to, and problematized by, theories of postcolonialism.[38]

In theory, conglomerates were like any modern firm, since they were motivated by profit, united by management, and defined by contracts.[39] In practice, however, they were known for a culture of hostility—"takeovers," "acquisitions," and "genocide," to cite one architect at the Houston-based architecture firm Caudill Rowlett Scott.[40] Or, in the words of an economist and business school dean in 1970, as the "kind of business that service[d] industry the way Bonnie and Clyde serviced banks."[41]

Within histories of political economy, the act of acquiring—land, people, buildings, and corporations—has indicated a shift from individual to imperial pursuits and a most advanced stage of capitalism.[42] Historians and political leaders used the term *conglomerate* during the early twentieth century to describe greedy empires "with no racial, geographic, or linguistic reasons for their association" beyond power, ranging in time and scale, including the Roman Empire, China, Russia, and the United States, among others.[43] The US Senate, too, has debated associations with the term *conglomerate* in an attempt to distance themselves from it.[44]

By the start of the Cold War, US military installations abroad began to mask these underlying motives by investing in national and international infrastructures, directing attention to "generous" development aid and modernizing construction projects. However, as the government and military hired architecture and engineering firms to design their installations at home and abroad, conglomeration-as-empire slowly drifted toward private business enterprises. While adopting the terms, tools, and techniques of the state, architecture and engineering firms produced and made visible the stages of capitalist development through the design of their firms and of everyday urban infrastructure.

While the general rise (1960s) and fall (1980s) of conglomerates has been the subject of a number of business histories, the impacts of conglomeration on cultural production have only recently been explored.[45] In architecture, this oversight is due, in part, to a modernist tendency to focus on a single moment or system (such as capitalism), rather than the transitions between systems over time that could explain rises and falls, booms and busts, and transformations. In film studies, Tom Schatz has studied conglomerates such as the Walt Disney Company, tracing its evolution from "Disney Brothers Cartoon Studio" to "Walt Disney Productions" in 1929 to a more general "Walt Disney Company" in 1986, which acquired and established a "system" of studios that combined film, music, books, television, and theme parks.[46] In literary studies, Dan Sinykin has investigated the historical impacts of conglomerates on publishing and literature by tracing the media conglomerate Time Inc.'s "network" of subsidiary organizations, through which it produced not only magazines and books but cable television and telephone services—while catapulting writers into the fiercely competitive economic market.[47]

These cultural histories map onto architecture's history, not only through the similar changes in business structures and rhetoric, but also through their impacts on discourse. The publishing houses of the professional magazines that produce architectural discourse, such as *Architectural Record*, *Progressive Architecture*, and *Architectural Forum*, were acquired by a cross section of conglomerates during the 1960s and 1970s, revealing the economic and political stakes of architecture—a tool for public diversification, if not distraction from corporate empire-building. The publishing company McGraw Hill acquired *Architectural Record* in 1961, defense contractor Litton Industries acquired *Progressive Architecture* in 1968, and the entertainment giant Billboard acquired *Architectural Forum* in 1972.[48]

With each company acquired, corporation formed, or redefinition of work implemented, however, the history of single enterprises becomes increasingly difficult to trace and study. Indeed, studying the history of a corporate conglomerate such as AECOM has proved methodologically challenging. While AECOM's leaders responded to my initial questions and requests for access to the firm's archives with enthusiasm and interest, after fourteen months of meetings and negotiations, the firm's legal counsel denied my access beyond the emailed autobiography. The firm's attorneys argued that public access—even if only to study the firm's past—could ostensibly expose the firm as well as its current and former clients (such as the US government) to liability. Rightfully so. In the past ten years alone, AECOM has been the subject of more than ninety-five lawsuits alleging wage, work-hour, and workplace safety violations; it has been sued for submitting fraudulent timesheets to clients (including the federal government), overcharging taxpayers, and falsifying documents on behalf of clients for federal emergency relief funding.[49]

In many of AECOM's enterprises, the firm has followed the script of other government contractors (as described by Naomi Klein in her book *The Shock Doctrine*), which simultaneously participate in the construction of weapons and infrastructure for war and descend on communities disoriented by conflict and disaster to procure massive construction contracts.[50] Yet in masking its expansionary acts, tools, and historical ambitions by restricting access to its archives, AECOM reveals just how fully architecture firms have embedded themselves in the operations of the state.

In response to AECOM's decision to restrict my access to its records, I decided to draw from archives, sources, and methods as fragmented and scattered as the firm itself. One day, I was flying to Washington, DC, to examine a three-page letter in the Watergate files that referenced an architect at DMJM. Another day, I was sitting across from gloved scholars who were examining Renaissance manuscripts and medieval drawings in a public archive while I thumbed through photocopied business memos and letters from the 1970s, marked as "rare" simply because of the firm's association with the government. Other days, I was meeting with eighty- and ninety-year-old architects who shared intimate details of their careers while combing through old photographs and documents. More often, I was sitting at my computer until 2:00 or 3:00 a.m., returning emails to FOIA (Freedom of Information Act) officers about drawings or contracts held by the US Army or Air Force and arguing with researchers, such as those at the CIA, who claimed to have no records of their own buildings or their designers. Perhaps most helpful, though, were the family members of some of the earliest architects, engineers, clerical workers, and draftspersons who worked at DMJM. Their boxes of forgotten paperwork in attics, closets, garages, and basements, as well as their vivid stories of their parents and relatives at work, helped to fill in gaps and contextualize dates, names, and data.

While the lack of unrestricted access to AECOM's archives was disappointing—and a case could be made for studying the firm's history in the future, if and when its protocols change—I argue that gaps in our knowledge are inevitable, and there may never be an ideal time to examine practices entangled with state operations. As Alex Wellerstein argues in his history of US nuclear secrecy, "archival sources never tell the full story, because not everything is written down, and not everything written down is complete, and not everything written down is truthful."[51] While buildings and the process of their design and construction can sometimes stand in for gaps in historical records of practice, they similarly do not reveal complete stories. This became clear to me as I began to find torn handwritten letters taped together, articles and photographs scanned from clipped newspapers, and business data without context.

As it turns out, despite their public image of organizational efficiency and order, much about the politics and business of architects involved in state operations was loose and informal. I wondered how newspaper clippings might relate to spiral-bound business manuals, scribbled memos to computational organization charts, family photographs to legal contracts. Rather than focus on each type of document and risk reifying them as static objects or overstating the significance of a select few workers (white men as "founders"), I have attempted to highlight, where possible, the work of those whose labors produced no material records and who, despite their significant contributions, have been historically considered "temporary" or "peripheral" to the work that architects defined as their own through their business and profession. Recognizing that gaps in historical records can be reconciled and enriched by lived histories, I include oral histories of architects, engineers, draftspersons, interns, librarians, and business leaders. While some requested anonymity due to the controversial details they shared, others are named with permission. In some cases, these individuals were workers who felt as though their voices were never heard in the office or that they were marginalized or exploited. In other cases, these were business leaders who were proud to claim ownership of the firm. For instance, in the first three oral histories I conducted, each architect I spoke with claimed that he "founded" AECOM—a product of the collective nature of corporate practice. Therefore, as I reconcile these sometimes contradictory narratives and archival documents, I hope to make clear that this is only one story—not *the* story—of AECOM, and only one story—not *the* story—of architectural practice.

In relating oral histories to historical documents, I borrow from the many methodological lessons of scholars writing historical ethnographies, and especially those examining state archives and struggling within and against practices of colonial concealment, secrecy, corruption, redaction, and shadows. From Ann Stoler's *Along the Archival Grain* and Mary Des Chene's "Locating the Past" to Samia Henni's more recent *Colonial Toxicity* and Tara Dudley's *Building Antebellum New Orleans*, these recent works about colonial architecture and resistance offer detailed methodological maps for scholars studying these dense webs.[52] They teach us how to resist the overwhelming temptation to see architecture only as itself—to look further, as scholars Aimé Césaire and James Scott suggest, at the ways that colonized subjects, lands, and cultures are more than simply representational "things," more than "official" documents, pixelated photographs, detailed computer drawings, or machine-made buildings.[53] The interlacing of material conditions, history, and ethnography, historian Hayden White has argued, can serve as a foundation of a "theatre of 'practical reason' . . . in which human agency [is] displayed in the activity of making a world rather than simply inhabiting one."[54]

While the study of history may indeed rattle the age-old epistemological credo of ethnography that "seeing is believing," it also offers a reminder that ethnography does not represent an objective "translation" of culture; instead, it represents a "historically situated mode of understanding historically situated contexts, each with its own, perhaps radically different, kinds of subjects and subjectivities, objects and objectives."[55] Whether removed in time or in space, ethnography and historical analyses constitute unique epistemologies; but they are united in their ability to extend beyond the immediate site of a practice as it unfolds or unfolded, in order to better understand the ways that power operates.[56]

A final note about the book's tone and point of view: while the use of third person has long served as a cardinal rule of modern historiography, it would be disingenuous to pen a narrative about the architectural strategies of corporate concealment without shedding light on the ways that this story came to be—its archival dead ends and breakthroughs and the difficulties encountered when trying to connect obscure or contradictory rhetoric to practices "on-the-ground." As historian Enzo Traverso has recently reminded us, the conventions of historiography, including the use of a scientific and impersonal tone, were intended to serve the nation-state—to provide "objective" documents with verifiable events and chronologies of the past for use in the future. In many instances, he writes, such as in Western Germany during World War II, the myth of scientific objectivity camouflaged the subjectivity of scholars who were themselves involved in war or totalitarian regimes.[57]

At the same time that architecture scholars became interested in issues of "practice" during the neoconservative turn of the 1980s, historians began writing history as first-person investigations. They have continued to do so more recently, sometimes revealing emotional ties to their subjects and presenting worldviews that allow them to identify with and connect with others. Wary, still, of the "illusory character of historiographical positivism," Traverso writes, historians are now challenged to recognize the links between themselves and their subjects, taking care to not blur personal memories with history, or center themselves in their stories as "ego-histories."[58] Following Traverso's recommendations, I aim in this book to navigate between self and collectivity by presenting a history of architecture produced by the labors of many, akin to the practice of architecture itself. "To be fruitful scholars," Traverso argues elsewhere, "we must be open to the societies surrounding us."[59]

. . .

Each of this book's six chapters focuses on a particular structure of architectural governance, tracing how they came to be after World War II and their shared effects on the political economy. The first chapter, "Profession: Shattering Tradition," begins at the macro scale with the profession itself, providing a broad overview of the major changes within architecture firms after World War II that enabled architects to build big businesses, intervene in politics, and ultimately liberalize their profession by the 1970s. It offers an outline of how architecture and engineering conglomerates "shattered" professional tradition and expanded the scope and possibility of architectural work through political lobbying, by means of quid pro quo, and by advocating the liberalization of "design" in the federal government.

The second chapter, "Firm: Corporate Conglomeration," begins with DMJM's particular history as an architecture firm, including how its three founding architects formed the business and how it changed in legal, organizational, and service definitions that led to AECOM—an architecture, engineering, construction, operations, and management conglomerate. The chapter traces the histories of DMJM's founding architects, from their early postwar partnership to a managerial corporation in the 1950s and to a corporate conglomerate in the 1970s. Connecting the ebb and flow of the founders' postwar careers to the ebb and flow of the political economy itself, the chapter reveals how corporations and, ultimately, corporate conglomerates were intimately tied to and fueled by urban renewals and shifts in the urban forms of Los Angeles, producing and making visible various urban "posts"—post-Fordism, postmodernism, postcolonialism.

The third chapter, "Building: Enclosing Indeterminacy," focuses on the ways in which the discourse of business conglomeration influenced the aesthetic theories and formal composition of architecture that came to define postmodernism. Not only was the term *conglomerate* used to describe the structure of businesses during the 1960s and 1970s, but it also came to describe the aesthetic and material conditions of those enterprises, including laboratories and office spaces of conglomerate organizations. This chapter examines the theories of aesthetics developed by architects at DMJM, such as Cesar Pelli and Anthony Lumsden, which were direct responses to the demands for efficiency, flexibility, and profitability by DMJM's conglomerate clients. While many of the buildings produced by Pelli and Lumsden came to be characterized by their reflective, increasingly thin, hermetic surfaces, which scholars have defined as products of late capitalism, the chapter reveals how it was through the infrastructures of conglomerate business, and a collaborative approach to design, that the speculative affinities of the 1970s–80s and, ultimately, the concepts of postmodernism were made visible.

The fourth chapter, "Contract: Developing Architects," dives more deeply into the prehistory of corporate conglomeration by tracing how military and government aid commissions after World War II provided the terms, tools, and techniques that came to be associated with conglomeration, thereby showing its imperialist undercurrents. It traces a social history of DMJM's earliest projects, following procurement processes and terms of government contracts during the 1950s and 1960s. As this chapter demonstrates, the government and military not only encouraged architecture firms to establish a global presence; the scale and complexity of military projects made joint ventures, multi-firm practices, and conglomerate structures necessary.

The fifth chapter, "Portfolio: Valuing Practice," traces a history of architecture through the types, formats, and contents of books about architecture as a "practice" during the twentieth century as they were revised, updated, and republished in response to the boom-and-bust cycles of the economy. It follows the evolution of the 1920s single-volume "handbook," published by the American Institute of Architects, which became, by the 1960s, a three-ring "portfolio" that coincided with the conglomerate-as-portfolio theory of businesses, as well as emerging theories of investment portfolios for the stock market. Woven into this history were academic books about architects' "practices," which were commonly published during economic recessions. Through a macrohistory of these two types of books about architectural practice, I argue, it is possible to see how the cyclical woes of the profession began to fuel a new kind of economy of book-writing within the discipline, and vice versa, during the twentieth century.

The final chapter, "Vault: Keeping Secrets," examines the ways in which the archives of large corporate firms were changing in tune with new layers of government classification, new archival protocols, and new types of architectural workers during the Cold War, as part of a broader regime of "secrecy." This chapter reveals how the contemporary difficulties of accessing archival records were traceable to a heightened sense of fear of loss—both of colonial and authorial tradition and of life, legacy, and sovereignty. Secondly, it demonstrates how the rise of secrecy corresponded with a disproportionate increase in the number of historically marginalized architectural workers within large firms by the 1970s, including women and people of color. It was these workers (and their families) who, despite being left out of "official" histories of architecture firms such as DMJM and AECOM, have been central to the social reproduction of architecture firms and the country itself. It was only through their collective power, their careful records management and organization, and their continued willingness to share their stories, today, that such a history of DMJM and AECOM could be written.

1 *Profession*
Shattering Tradition

In his 1977 study of corporate management, *The Visible Hand*, historian Alfred D. Chandler Jr. argued that large multinational firms in the US had grown more economically powerful than nation-states.[1] At the time it was published, architecture firms were still relatively small by comparison; the vast majority—95 percent—employed fewer than twenty people.[2] While this stratification continued well into the twenty-first century, scholars in architecture had grown concerned by the late 1970s about large firms and their impact on the profession. "The issue that inevitably arises in any revelation of the dominance of architectural practice by the large firm," sociologist Robert Gutman cautioned in 1977, "is how far it will go, and [whether it will] swallow the offices made up of two or three partners and a professional staff of a couple of other architects working full- or part-time."[3] Latent in Gutman's apprehension was a deeper unease about what could happen to the profession after architects met the limits of expansion made possible by a single firm, since acquisitions—of land, bodies, buildings, and businesses—characterized a historical jump from an individualist to an imperialist pursuit.[4] However, evading Gutman's watchful eye were architecture firms that had been diversifying their services and acquiring firms for nearly a decade in order to build stability into their firms and protect their authority—all while pressing the profession to follow their expansionary lead.

We begin there, in the 1970s, recounting the ways in which rapid internationalization and extraordinary postwar economic growth in the US were blanketed by an avalanche of crises: the end of the Bretton Woods compact, OPEC's oil embargo, back-to-back recessions, antitrust sanctions, and, as will be discussed in the following pages, an architecture profession overrun by state interest. By the end of the decade, architectural work was defined as many things: designing buildings, processing data, surveilling communities—ethical and jurisdictional standards were shattered. As a symptom of this shattering, firms were fractured, sold, acquired, and merged; secure salaries and careers were replaced by project-based jobs; and consultants were all the rage as capital and labor were spread across space, time, and geography through "subsidiary" firms and "subsidiary" workers. Yet, as this chapter explores, not all architects and architecture firms were passive victims of the political and economic shifts of the 1970s. Some firms had increased in size and diversified so widely after World War II that they had internalized the construction market, gripped the reins of their profession, and transformed into systems of governance.

While these postwar systems had material and spatial effects on the shapes and structures of cities—effects that urban geographers and historians have used to illustrate a series of interrelated "posts" (post-Fordism, postindustrialization, postcolonialization, and postmodernism)—a history of architecture firms reveals how such "posts" were initially and slowly designed within business itself. In short, architecture firms not only challenged the professed traditions of architectural work by surpassing the limits imposed by the project of professionalization, but they also marked and made visible otherwise hidden shifts and cycles of twentieth-century political economy.[5]

Political Architects

In a 1971 issue of *Fortune*, editor Gurney Breckenfeld made a bold assertion that the profession of architecture was on the brink of "obsolescence."[6] In an article about architects and large-scale urban development in which he suggested that the field needed radical reform not just in design, but also in business, Breckenfeld called on architects to take desperate measures to keep their profession alive: to "shatter professional tradition." For Breckenfeld, shattering tradition meant abandoning nineteenth-century firm structures, such as sole proprietorships or partnerships, which were commonly organized around named authors, a single service, or a specific project type. He encouraged them to embrace multi-firm corporate conglomerates that could expand the scope of architectural work beyond building design and help firms live on past the individuals who founded them. He pointed to architects like those working at DMJM or Caudill Rowlett Scott (CRS) who were incorporating their firms, crossing geographies, and merging with others to expand their services—from architecture to real estate to construction management.

However, Breckenfeld's recommendations contradicted a long-standing definition of architectural work and the guiding tenets of the so-called "gentleman's profession." Since 1909, the American Institute of Architects (AIA) had defined the work of architects in its Code of Ethics—a twentieth-century hallmark of organized professions—as designers of buildings, not builders or developers. Neither were they permitted to compete on the basis of price.[7] As it was imported from Europe during the early nineteenth century, the profession was intended to sustain the work of "gentlemen" architects whose exclusive obligations to their clients meant that they were to be "disinterested" in the political economy.[8] They were expected to offer impartial advice, unswayed by politics or market pressures, so they would be valued and trusted by the public and their potential clients. "By contrast with business," sociologist Talcott Parsons asserted more broadly about professions in the 1930s, "the professions are marked by 'disinterestedness.' The professional man is not thought of as engaged in the pursuit of his personal profit, but in performing services to his patients or clients, or to impersonal values like the advancement of science."[9]

Nevertheless, Breckenfeld's recommendations in 1971 echoed a rising tide of liberal economic concern in Washington, DC, that fractured the antimarket foundation of the architecture profession the same year. Yet these abrupt shifts were neither a direct result of top-down government sanctions, as recent historians of this period have suggested, nor a general result of abstract shifts within the nature of global capitalism.[10] Architects leveraged the economic and political weight of their firms to lobby and influence politicians in order to socially control the profession—using it to set their firms free from ethical, and thus legal and regulatory, constraint. But how did these architects begin to amass such power in the first place, and how did they use it to deregulate the profession? One way to begin answering these questions is by pairing histories of the postwar architecture profession with histories of postwar business.

At a general level, the global exchanges of resources and expertise by the 1960s were challenging country-specific ethics that bound architects to their profession.[11] If US architects were working in Japan or Venezuela or France or Sudan, were they to carry their professional ethics with them? At a more specific economic level, postwar government spending in the US had resulted in massive national deficits, inflation, and surging unemployment, eclipsing what business historian Mark Levinson has described as an "extraordinary time" of postwar economic growth or what Diane Coyle has called the "Golden Age" of gross domestic product.[12] This led to a sharp political debate: continue with the Fordist-Keynesian compact that had guided recovery efforts or turn to supply-side economics—a descendant of nineteenth-century classical economics.[13] Those who followed Keynes believed that creating demand for goods and services through state intervention was the key to a strong and stable economy, while those in opposition advocated renewed liberal economic freedom and less government intervention.[14]

In architecture, debates about regulation were not new. The earliest professional associations struggled to take hold during the antebellum period because of contradictory ideals: expand, yet contract; be popular yet exclusive.[15] As economic depression curtailed post–Civil War reconstruction during the late nineteenth century, the first iteration of the AIA, then a regional association based in the Northeast, advocated an exclusive definition of architecture and opposed state regulation through licensure. They believed that licensure would restrict the creative liberties of architects. The Western Association of Architects, led by a group of Chicago architects with clients in railroad, insurance, retail, and real estate industries, stood in opposition and foreshadowed the ideals that would formalize during the twentieth century within private businesses. It advocated a *broad* definition of architectural work and supported regulation through licensure to try to boost architects' "public authority."[16] When the associations merged in 1889, they compromised by promoting licensure and a narrow definition of architectural service.

However, courts viewed licensure in architecture as an attempt to restrict competition. It was only after several failed attempts in New York and Illinois during the 1890s, efforts led by Dankmar Adler in Chicago—and, crucially, by an insider architect-cum-legislator, C.W. Nothnagel, who introduced a bill in the state legislature—that the first licensing laws passed in 1897 in Illinois.[17] Thus, while the architects based their final arguments in favor of licensure on the safety of builders and the general public—since construction was becoming more complex and deaths of builders more common—it was not coincidental that the drive for licensure was led primarily by those in the most prosperous firms and with the assistance of political insiders. This loose marriage of the architecture profession and politics would only strengthen during the twentieth century.

Between the 1890s and 1960s, the federal government largely held that professions were exempt from pro-competition antitrust law since they were not "trades."[18] This began to change during the late 1960s, as professions were pulled under the microscopes of the Department of Justice (DOJ) and the Federal Trade Commission (FTC) during Nixon's presidency (1969–74). But rather than focus on licensure, regulations, or practices, the government focused on rhetoric: in the case of the AIA, its stated "rules, bylaws, resolutions," and "policy statements."[19] Peggy Deamer and Jay Wickersham have described the arguments of the DOJ and FTC during this period in detail. In short, those leading the government's efforts, including legal scholar Robert Bork, Nixon's solicitor general, suggested that professions could no longer be considered exempt from antitrust sanctions because their codes of ethics shielded businesses from competition and impeded marketplace freedoms.[20] In December 1971, the DOJ used the 1890 Sherman Antitrust Act, written to prevent and break up monopolies, to threaten a lawsuit against the AIA, among other professional organizations. The AIA agreed to a consent decree in 1972, pledging to change.

Following the sanctions by the DOJ, the AIA *encouraged* architects to compete on the basis of price and to significantly expand the scope of architectural work. Architects could, by the mid-1970s, ethically offer construction management services, participate in design-build teams, and own or develop property so long as they disclosed such services to their clients.[21] Yet who was to say that one was *required* to follow the code of the AIA, a membership club (in fact, a corporation with little legal difference from most architecture firms) of twenty-three thousand architects, representing fewer than half the architects in the United States by 1970?[22] After all, architects had skirted professional ethics long before the changes in the AIA in the 1970s. As soon as the AIA was formed in 1857, for instance, architects were forced to tune their businesses to the market in order to survive, which caused many to engage in work and politics in ways that contradicted the definition of a *professional architect*.[23]

Some architects in the late nineteenth and early twentieth centuries quietly ventured into real estate.[24] Chicago and New York architects Stanford White, Daniel Burnham, William Holabird, and Martin Roche invested in their clients' projects in exchange for stocks, which, as Mary Woods has argued, demonstrated the reality of architectural work within a capitalist society and laid bare architecture's fragility as a profession in the US.[25] The 1970s represented a pivotal moment within the history of the profession, however, with the first effort to formally impose such practices—the desires of big business—upon the profession as a whole, with the endorsement of the federal government.

Despite the inscrutability of large architecture and engineering firms and their (often) inaccessible archives, it is in records of public controversy—public speeches, court records, and trade journals—about the profession's near-death and means of survival that it is possible to trace how large firms took control of the profession and the structural links between the market and jurisdiction on which it depended. Take, for example, a speech made to Congress in 1971 by the president of the AIA, Robert F. Hastings, former president of the Detroit-based architecture and engineering firm Smith, Hinchman & Grylls, one of the largest firms in the US at the time. In the speech, he offered support for a new bill that would form a National Institute of Building Sciences to develop standard criteria for building codes, and he shared his views about the duty of an architect to serve the moment, arguing: "The architect today, and the Institute he directs, must now plunge actively into political life, enlist allies, swing votes, mobilize community action and take positions on issues that once were thought to be outside our rightful area of concern. . . . [We] can have anything we want that we are willing to work and pay for, [but] we must strike a balance between our aspirations and our resources."[26]

Such a statement was perhaps easy, if not necessary, for an AIA president hailing from one of the largest architecture and engineering firms in the US to make. Smith, Hinchman & Grylls owed its financial success to federal contracts, including for military bases, weaponry, and urban infrastructure projects during World War II and the Cold War.[27] In effect, Hastings's advocacy for political interference was challenging the profession's long-standing mechanisms of social control, as well as neoliberal ideology taking shape more broadly, wherein businesses were ostensibly "set free" from government intervention. Set free? Yes. But only after they were built up by the state. Architecture and engineering firms during the twentieth century were therefore both participating in and benefiting from shifting government policy and deregulation—a pattern of influence that demonstrated how architecture could be instrumentalized particularly during low points in the economy, such as after wars and natural disasters, when communities were most vulnerable.[28] This is what Naomi Klein has described as "disaster capitalism."[29]

As a case in point, architecture firms such as DMJM had, by the 1970s, amassed significant economic and political power in California and in Washington, DC, due to their military and foreign aid contracts during the 1950s and 1960s.[30] As a testament to the firm's political importance, DMJM's president and cofounder S. Kenneth Johnson was nominated as architect of the US Capitol in 1970. Although Johnson was not ultimately voted in, his nominating letter was written by one of DMJM's vice presidents, Barry Mountain, based in Washington, DC, who served as the deputy chairman of the Republican National Committee's Administration Committee during the late 1960s—the same committee working tirelessly to elect and reelect President Nixon. "Even though there was an understanding that you would not serve even if selected," Mountain wrote, "this, nevertheless, by the fact that you were identified, gives greater credit to the importance of DMJM with the administration."[31]

At the same time, quid pro quo was common between architects in large firms and political campaign organizations. In 1980, for instance, the State of Massachusetts exposed a pattern of architects bribing officials during the early 1970s with campaign contributions in exchange for public design work. A state commission reported that DMJM, among other "political architects," contributed to the Republican National Committee in exchange for design and construction contracts. One of DMJM's contracts was for the design of Holyoke Community College, built in 1975 in Massachusetts—a $2 million contract.[32] Not only was the college built and DMJM paid; the building won an AIA Design Award in 1976 and was featured in many professional journals, including *Architectural Record*, then owned by McGraw Hill. The project was celebrated for its formal composition, aesthetics, and material challenge to college-as-"type."[33] Ironically, in the award announcements, one writer highlighted that the profession was celebrating architecture that questioned the "rules" and broke from "convention."[34]

Diving further into this case, if only to better illustrate the webs of architecture and bureaucracy that had been woven by the 1970s, the quid pro quo scheme at DMJM was so complex that it required an architecture of agreement that was negotiated over buffet lunches, ice cream, and open bars. This included DMJM vice presidents Barry Mountain and Stanley Smith, CEO Albert Dorman, an architect-friend in Massachusetts with strong ties to a lead banker, and another friend, Albert Manzi, who worked at the Massachusetts Turnpike Authority and was involved in campaign fundraising. After DMJM made campaign contributions, money traveled from the State of Massachusetts back to DMJM, including funds earmarked for architect-negotiators or for political campaigns, delivered in hotels in installments that were not traceable—as cashier's checks and cash—and deposited as campaign contributions by individuals with made-up names. "Mountain opened his briefcase and showed Manzi the money," reads the state committee's report, continuing: "The briefcase was a slim, dark, attache case with a handle on top and snaps on each side of it. The money was banded with bank wrappers. When he saw the denomination, Manzi said, 'What in hell am I going to do with five-dollar bills?' . . . The money had come from DMJM's office in Seoul, Korea because it was difficult to get cash out of the company's US bank accounts. He said he felt the small denominations allowed DMJM 'to get the money into the country without raising any eyebrows.'"[35]

The court ultimately concluded that "the [state] Designer Selection Board system could be, and was, successfully manipulated by design firms knowledgeable about state bureaucracy."[36] The result was not only a closed cycle of capital flow that kept architects in business and the politicians who supported them in office, but also, as the report describes, buildings that were often "shoddily" constructed because they were built too rapidly and had dangerous structural defects. Political skill, rather than professional expertise, was therefore not only undermining the professional duty of "gentleman" architects—to shelter themselves from politics and the economy and to protect the public—but also off-loading personal risk onto the shoulders of the public through architecture. This was precisely the kind of danger on which architects based their arguments to the state for regulating the profession through licensure during the nineteenth century: an enduring contradiction-turned-feedback-loop that had become essential to businesses' and the profession's survival.

Through the self-serving eyes of free-market economics, however, these all-out pursuits of capital and political advantage should not be considered surprising. Nor should they be considered exclusive to the US. As scholars such as Amy Thomas, Albert López, Charlie Xue, and Guanghui Ding have shown, architects were, in radically different political contexts yet around the same time, forming enduring relationships with states in many countries—from Britain to Mexico to China.[37]

Justifying these actions within the US, classical liberal economist Milton Friedman wrote: "As a believer in the pursuit of self-interest in a competitive capitalist system, I can't blame a businessman who goes to Washington and tries to get special privileges for his company. He has been hired by the stockholders to make as much money for them as he can within the rules of the game. And if the rules of the game are that you go to Washington to get a special privilege, I can't blame him for doing that. Blame the rest of us for being so foolish as to let him get away with it."[38]

Similarly, at Skidmore, Owings & Merrill (SOM) in Chicago, Nathaniel Owings influenced Washington, DC, during the Kennedy and Nixon presidencies. SOM opened an office there when Kennedy appointed SOM architect Gordon Bunshaft to the National Fine Arts Commission in 1963—a year after Owings was selected by Kennedy to devise plans for a "grand vision" of Pennsylvania Avenue as the chairman of the President's Commission on Pennsylvania Avenue.[39] Owings seemed proud to lodge himself into a history of neoclassicism—an architecture of "nationalism," as historian Mitchell Schwarzer describes it, that was defined more by the relationships between presidents and architects than by the visual language of classical architecture they espoused.[40] He seemed proud to represent and reproduce the republican and patriarchal legacy of the nation's Founding Fathers while acknowledging its imperial roots: "All through those years my real collaborators, friends and advisers were ghosts turned flesh and blood—the triad of George Washington, L'Enfant and Thomas Jefferson; crotchety Andrew Jackson and his displaced Treasury building; the surprisingly effective short-term

Chester Arthur and his landscape architect Andrew Jackson Downing, whose death when Fulton's steamship blew up was the only thing that saved the Mall from becoming an English garden; Teddy Roosevelt, Daniel Burnham, and Frederick Law Olmsted needing only Roman togas to crown their misdirected, compulsive drive for an Augustinian Roman plan."[41]

These forays into national politics were led by a generation of architects educated during the Great Depression whose careers were throttled by war and who were beginning to reach the age of retirement. Their firms had grown too large to be effectively managed, and they were forced to plan for a next generation of leadership to safeguard their legacies—concerns that, as Albena Yaneva has described in her study of architects' legacy-making during this period, mirrored the concerns of the Cold War more broadly.[42] During the 1970s, when new types of urban professionals, such as the real estate developer, were positioning themselves as public experts, architects were decrying that they no longer had "leverage," "influence," or "control" over the terms of urbanization.[43] They blamed this on a number of factors: a historically narrow definition of the "professional" architect, zoning restrictions limiting urban growth, and new environmental and energy conservation efforts that they "were not trained to consider."[44]

In Los Angeles, the president of Charles Luckman Associates, architect-cum-businessman James Luckman (Charles's son), argued that "the profession hurt itself by pushing the idea that architecture is only design. . . . They convinced the public that the architect is interested only in how a building looks on the outside. But if it doesn't work on the inside it is lousy architecture. And all the students want to be designers only."[45]

These sentiments were echoed by architects on the political left and right. Those on the left blasted the academy and the profession for their long-standing disregard for the environment as well as socioeconomic, racial, and gender inequities. They sought to "expand" the discipline and the membership of the profession by tearing down the barriers of entry for those who had been historically marginalized.[46] Using similar rhetoric, those on the right focused on "expanding" the scope of architectural work, rather than the profession's demographics, while doubling down on the need for licensure. They often joined examinations boards or the boards of professional organizations, including the AIA.[47] The right-leaning influence of large firms within this political spectrum was evident in a parallel shift in the type of architect serving as AIA president. Immediately following World War II, AIA presidents were commonly the leaders of small businesses with wartime projects: work on the Manhattan Project (Raymond Ashton, 1943-45), on memorials and memorial churches (Douglas Orr, 1947-49), or on wartime "housing," such as that built for the Minidoka concentration camp in Idaho (Glenn Stanton, 1951-53). Beginning in the mid-1950s, AIA presidents were more commonly (though not as an absolute rule) leaders of large, corporate firms: Leon Chatelain of Chatelain, Gauger & Nolan in 1956; Philip Will of Perkins & Will in 1960; George Kassabaum of HOK in 1968; Robert Hastings of Smith, Hinchman & Grylls in 1971; Archibald Rogers of RTKL in 1974.

Recalling the recommendations of Breckenfeld's *Fortune* article to earn "relevance" and control through corporate mergers and acquisitions, Charles Luckman Associates was acquired in 1968 by the massive New York-based conglomerate Ogden Corporation—a firm with interests ranging from shipbuilding to restaurants to savings and loans—by swapping stocks to form the Ogden Development Corporation. The acquisition, which caught the attention of architects and leaders of the AIA, demonstrated that a managerially strong architecture firm—especially if coupled with real estate—was worth more on the stock market than in the "books."[48] In other words, firms were considered valuable because of their *potential* earning power over time, rather than their material assets in the present. This served as a wake-up call for architects, since they had, for more than a hundred years, earned their livelihoods in the US primarily by designing and producing material assets.

In a 1969 *New York Times* article about the Ogden-Luckman acquisition, California's AIA president, Cabell Gwathmey, a former Army Corps of Engineers colonel and director of the Department of Licenses and Inspections in Washington, argued that "we should welcome such efforts as those of Charles Luckman Associates to increase the scope of the architect's service and his influence on the final product."[49] New York's AIA president similarly suggested that architects were "kidding themselves" if they did not make similar moves. The acquisition added pressure to the AIA to remove from its Code of Ethics the portions of text that prohibited architects from working as builders or developers. The AIA circulated drafts of a new code of ethics in a 1969 Standards of Professional Practice—two years before the DOJ formally sanctioned them.

Other firms were following suit. Between 1966 and 1976, more than two hundred architecture firms acquired or merged with other organizations, and the AIA published "marriage manuals" to aid them.[50] The DC-based federal contractor and computer company Planning Research Corporation acquired engineering firms through stock-for-stock transactions similar to Ogden's; the architecture firm Rogers, Taliaferro, Kostritsky and Lamb (RTKL) in Baltimore merged with the engineering, research, and computer software firm URS Systems of San Mateo, California, in 1971; Caudill Rowlett Scott (CRS) in Houston acquired nearly thirty firms between 1970 and 1990; and DMJM's earliest acquisitions were in the mid-1960s.[51]

Amid recessions and the antitrust sanctions, architecture caught the attention of sociologists including Robert Gutman (studying architecture's demographics), Judith Blau (studying firms), and Magali Sarfatti Larson (studying the profession).[52] Theorizing professions more generally, Larson emphasized that professions such as architecture were defined by structural links between certified knowledge, standardized training, and protected positions in the social division of labor. With structural links that were rationalized either through ideology (following Max Weber) or through economic institutions (following Adam Smith), members of a profession were, in theory, to be sheltered from the pulls of the market in order to earn public trust, and they borrowed monopoly practices to do so: "standardizing" competencies and excluding those considered "untrained" through licenses, degrees, and permits.[53] To be sure, the project of professionalization, as Larson described, was born in the US at the end of the nineteenth century as political capitalism morphed into corporate capitalism and as close partnerships formed between business leaders and the state.[54] Indeed, the expansion of bureaucratic apparatuses of the state *produced* professions such as architecture.

Architecture was considered an "exceptional" profession in the United States, since its members could not, like practitioners of law or medicine, establish full jurisdictional control over their work.[55] Most states did not (and still do not) require someone to hire a licensed architect to design small residential structures—a fact that has led to a continuous concentration of architects in major cities, where permitting and licensing regulations are considered most necessary.[56] This trend, beginning in the nineteenth century, was unlike those experienced by other professionals, including doctors and lawyers.[57] Yet this exceptionalism did not seem to matter to the federal government.

So how did these lobbying efforts and antitrust sanctions affect the profession? Sociologist Eliot Freidson argued in the 1980s that they weakened architecture's ability to self-regulate and protect itself from competition, shifting the tools of social control from schools and professional associations, such as the AIA, to large, private businesses whose capital power enabled them to control each.[58]

Some sociologists declared that the profession was eroding, due to deprofessionalization on the one hand (a loss of control over the rules and criteria of good architecture) or proletarianization on the other (the Marxian idea that professionals were increasingly employees rather than employers, thereby losing their capacity to control the terms of their labor).[59] However, both Larson and Friedman argued that, in the long run, prestige, public trust, and the structural links more or less endured, as did the relative distribution of architects in large and small firms.

While the relative number of firm owners remained stable since mid-century (a trend that continues to this day), the distribution of capital and workers within firms shifted significantly. By 1972, approximately 55 percent of employees across the profession worked at firms with fewer than twenty people, which accounted for 59 percent of the profession's total revenue.[60] By contrast, only 15 percent worked at firms with more than one hundred people, contributing only 14 percent of revenue. However, between 1972 and 2017, the proportion of employees at small firms dropped by 11 percent, with 7 percent redistributed to medium-sized firms and 4 percent to large firms. Small firms' revenue declined during this period by 20 percent—a drop twice as large as their decrease in workers—while medium- and large-sized firms boosted their revenues by 12 percent and 8 percent, respectively.[61]

This redistribution of workers and capital had profound implications. What this meant for small firms was that they earned more per worker during the twentieth century than large firms, while this was reversed by the 2010s.[62] At the same time, the number of architects in urban areas across the US more than doubled (while the numbers of lawyers and doctors declined) from roughly four architects per ten thousand people in 1970 to eight in 2020. A jump of this size had not occurred since the birth of the profession during the mid-nineteenth century, when the number of architects per ten thousand people went from two architects in 1850 to four in 1910.[63]

Therefore, the redistribution of capital, obvious proletarianization, and the oversaturation of architects (driven by both the politicization and corporatization of firms) were diluting, if not dissolving, the nineteenth-century standards of a "gentleman's" profession. And in this "race to the bottom" or "hollowing out of the core," as sociologists of professions have described, the functions and aims that were once considered central to the "gentleman's" profession of architecture—public good, safety, and well-being—were relegated to nonprofits and the public sector as "extracurriculars."[64]

Manfredo Tafuri's observations in 1969 provide one possible reading of these changes. He argued that the *fear* of proletarianization was felt not only by architects who were reconstructing their own image of a profession, but also by the scholars who, bestowing upon architects an eternal status, discouraged a broader class of architectural workers from organizing or making demands to effect social change.[65]

If, as Larson argued, the public trust of professions depended on a sheltered position within the market, then the profession of architecture by the end of the 1970s could exist only in theory—subject to the same controls and hierarchies as other occupations.[66] Or, at best, architecture had transformed into what she called a "techno-bureaucratic" profession akin to engineering, with firms, rather than the state, controlling the distances between professional jurisdictions and the standards within them.[67]

Further, considering the roles that large firms played in lobbying for licensure in the 1890s and later in loosening the rules and terms of practice in the 1970s, architects at large firms wanted to have their cake and eat it too. They wanted licensure and standardized training, enforced by the state, but they also wanted to be sure they were the ones to enforce the profession's terms of exclusion—especially during downturns in the economy—as part of broader twentieth-century consequences of the military-industrial-education-entertainment complex: urban discipline and control through private capital.

. . .

We have seen how the end of postwar growth contributed to conglomeration and the consequent shattering of professional tradition during the 1960s and 1970s. As architects were adding services and acquiring businesses in the name of "expansion," they were producing and claiming new types of work as part of an integrated and technocratic system of architecture and engineering. Such claims, however, depended on the construction of spatial and jurisdictional distinctions to make clear who or what could be "acquired"—distinctions not only between architecture and non-architecture, but also between inside and outside, center and periphery, manual and nonmanual labor, and urban and nonurban. Yet as the histories of these jurisdictional distinctions reveal, conglomerates were referencing an imperialist vocabulary that had historically justified the acquisition or death of "others"—lands, peoples, objects—in the name of self-preservation, self-renewal, and natural right.

This adoption of imperialist terms, tools, and techniques during the twentieth century, and the possibility of conglomeration in architecture more particularly, corresponded with a series of shifts that have been associated with the rise of neoliberalism between the 1930s and 1970s.[68] Before exploring in the following chapters how these shifts were produced within a single firm (DMJM into AECOM), I introduce three broad shifts here to illustrate the structural relationships between architects, their labor, their firms, their profession, and the cities and nation-states for which they worked.

First was a designed and deliberate shift in the definitions of architectural labor and its relationship to capital: conglomerate architecture and engineering firms created new sectors, redefined and reorganized architectural work, and thus produced and publicized a shift from a so-called Fordist economy to a post-Fordist economy. Architects engaged in work less directly correlated with capital output as the firms they worked for acquired subsidiaries and created new services they claimed were "peripheral" to the historical labor of architects, including drawing. Second was a related and designed shift in the legal organization of work and a new relationship with the state: architects incorporated their firms using state charters, rather than maintain the sole proprietorships or partnerships popularized during the nineteenth century. Incorporation enabled architects to shield themselves from liability and boost their income, but also to acquire and merge with businesses in other industries and geographies. Third was an emerging dependency of the state and military on private industry as the US sought to defend its sovereignty within a postwar and postcolonial global political economy. As architecture, engineering, and construction firms were hired to design both defense and development infrastructures abroad, architecture firms and architectural work were internationalized.

Post-Fordism

Under Fordism of the late nineteenth and early twentieth centuries, architectural work was defined by economies of manual production. Manual labor inputs were directly correlated with profit outputs, and work that was highly regulated, well organized, and internally focused generally yielded better pay and job security. Put another way, in order to earn more, one had to produce more, which often meant procuring more projects and hiring more manual laborers, such as draftsmen.[69]

Fordist labor was also defined by the organization of the work itself; large-scale industrial organizations, including architecture firms, adopted the standardized assembly-line processes of Henry Ford's factories, for instance, and they broke work into repetitive, specialized tasks to ensure efficiency, speed, and volume.[70] During the industrial resurgence of the 1930s, firms like Albert Kahn Associates, which was founded in Detroit in 1895 and produced Ford's factories, and SOM, founded in Chicago in 1936, embraced Fordism in both practice and design philosophy. The factories produced by Kahn's firm and the office buildings by SOM emphasized volume and standardization, rather than diversity and difference. Reflecting the organization of these factories, Kahn's firm was a "unitary" or "U-form" organization, comprising departments that were coordinated much like an assembly line: work moved from "design" to "architecture" to "structure" to "mechanics." Speed, volume, and efficiency were valued above all else, and architects turned to standardized systems wherever possible to simplify coordination across departments and support rapid construction.[71] Similarly, at SOM, cofounding architect Nathaniel Owings declared that "to work, we must have volume.... Volume meant power."[72]

Organization charts—nineteenth-century inventions that Matthew Allen has shown were modeled on tree diagrams and that architects used to reinforce industrial processes and hierarchies of capital, labor, and resources—were themselves architectural drawings.[73] While they were ambiguous, often used to assert administrative power more than anything else, they documented changes in the designs of businesses and in their methods of production before they materialized in the built environment. SOM's organization chart from 1957 (drawn at the firm), not unlike Kahn's, typified a Fordist model of architectural work (figure 1).[74] Drawings moved across well-coordinated assembly lines, passing from administration to design and drawing to engineering and construction.

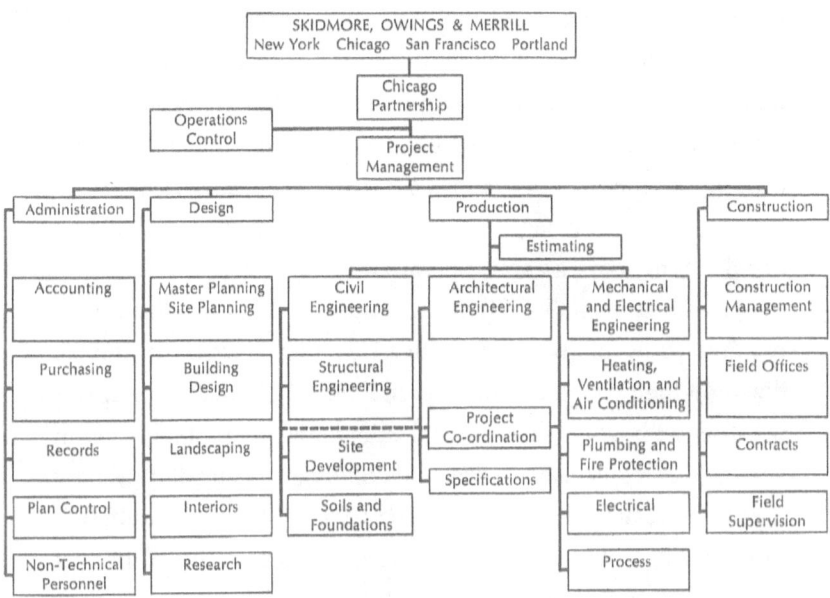

FIGURE 1. Firm organization chart, Skidmore, Owings & Merrill, 1957. © SOM.

By the 1970s, to accommodate new forms of labor, Fordist economies and work processes broke down to promote more flexible, fragmented, and varied means of production.[75] Under post-Fordism, the direct correlation between labor input and capital output was disconnected; workers could begin to yield profits without expending manual labor, and work was set free from the demands of consumers. In the words of Italian sociologist Maurizio Lazzarato, this included "immaterial" labor: "labor that produces the informational and cultural content of the commodity"—from marketing to real estate—and that could yield a higher capital return.[76]

In 1972, management consultant and sociologist Peter Drucker argued that industrial organizations such as General Motors (which he had described in his 1946 book *Concept of the Corporation*) had become outmoded by "post-Fordist" organization.[77] He wrote: "The essence of this [post-Fordist] large-scale organization of the late twentieth century is that within it people of very diverse skills and knowledges work together. Today we do it—or at least try—with very large numbers—thousands of people with different knowledges, coming together in a business, a government agency, or an armed service—under a management with specific knowledge of building and directing the large-scale organization."[78]

As with many industrial organizations, architecture firms were required to decide whether to diversify their practices or double down on their siloed means of production. Historical accounts of SOM reveal how the firm's organization grew increasingly rigid in structure as it increased in size, and buildings remained its primary objects of focus.[79] Other firms adopted an "M-Form" (multidivisional form), embraced as early as the 1920s by some of the first conglomerate companies, such as DuPont, which created semiautonomous operating divisions and differentiated work not by individual tasks, but by service, product, brand, or geography.[80] Without a single specialization or reproducible aesthetic logic, multidivisional firms were positioned more favorably toward growth in a number of industries and geographies, not just architecture.[81]

As evidence of this shift, architectural and engineering firms were subjected, during the 1960s, to new measures of evaluation based on profit, rather than on symbolic, cultural, or aesthetic merit. A 1961 issue of *Engineering News-Record* (*ENR*), for instance, described design firms as either "winners" or "losers" principally on the basis of their ability to be "money-makers."[82] The editors of *ENR* noted that many firms "beat the market with profitable sidelines" by forming "capital-heavy" supplemental practices that could support those that were more traditionally "labor-heavy."[83] In other words, the "winners" were those with subsidiaries or affiliated organizations engaged in work not traditionally associated with the history of manual labor. In 1964, a decade after *Fortune* published its first list of firms based on revenue, *ENR* published the first of its annual rankings of "Top 500" design firms based on revenue. Firms ranked at the top of the revenue-based listings were increasingly defined as firms with multiple firms within them, including subsidiaries and affiliated companies that *ENR* described as "profitable sidelines." Throughout the 1970s, there were few subsidiaries in architecture and engineering, and they could be listed as footnotes in annual *ENR* listings. By the 1980s, however, several pages of appendices were dedicated to "designer affiliates and subsidiaries."[84]

As capital outputs were disconnected from manual labor inputs, it became increasingly difficult to diagram the flow of capital using a top-down chart with lines connecting to each department. In contrast to the linear organization charts of Fordist firms, post-Fordist organizations were commonly depicted through radial diagrams with "subsidiary" workers or "subsidiary" firms drawn outside the firm. Such drawings were also outsourced, drawn by precariously employed, contracted illustrators outside of firms or the publishing houses of professional journals.

As these distinctions between manual and nonmanual labors emerged, so did new distinctions between "inside" and "outside," and "core" and "periphery." One example (among many others) is a radial diagram, from 1961, of John B. Parkin Associates, a Canadian architecture and engineering firm that followed and then departed from the historical trajectory of Kahn's firm, demonstrating the broad influence of American architecture firms (figure 2).[85] Drawn by contracted illustrators for *Canadian Builder*, the diagram de-emphasized a top-down approach to management. Its centripetal arrangement placed clients and administration at the center, emphasizing the "inside" and the "outside" or "periphery" of the firm. Further from the center were less protected positions, including draftsmen and clerical workers, while consultants and subsidiary

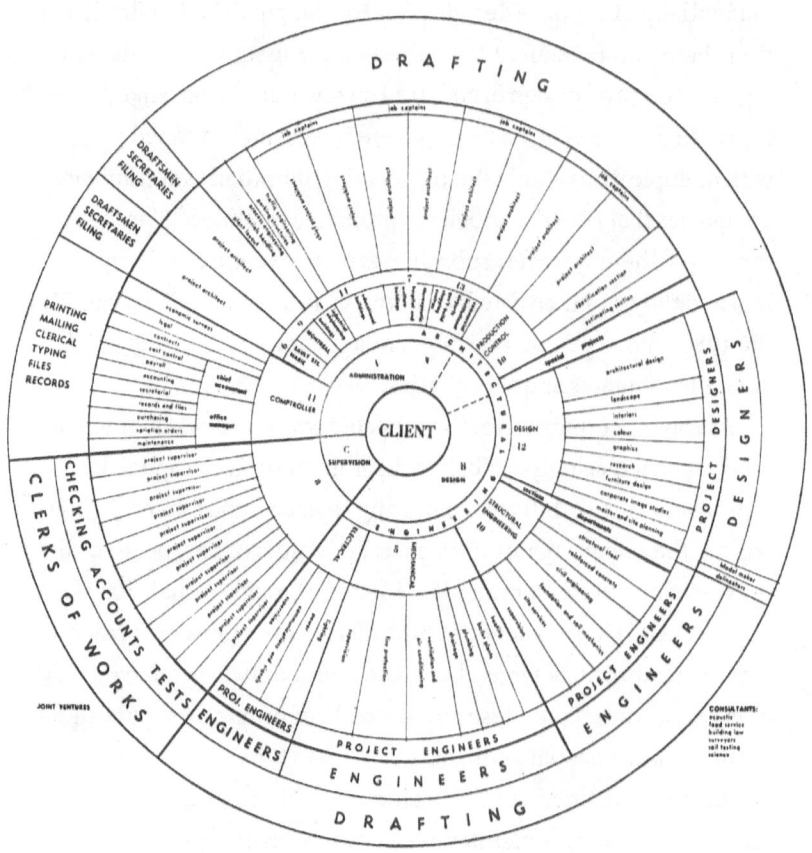

FIGURE 2. Firm organization chart, John B. Parkin Associates, 1961. From *Canadian Builder*, April 1961, 32. John B. Parkin Associates fonds, accession 88A/80.23, box 3, file 4, Canadian Architectural Archives, Libraries and Cultural Resources, University of Calgary.

firms—those deemed "capital-heavy"—were outside the diagram, though still connected to the firm through capital flows.

While the core-periphery concept belonged to a view of the world as a capitalist system—described most notably by Immanuel Wallerstein in 1974—in which high-capital, industrial "core" countries colonized, exploited, and extracted surplus capital from "peripheral" or "undeveloped" countries, the longevity of twentieth-century capitalism was predicated on geographic differentials and the reification of boundaries such as "core" and "periphery," or "first" and "third" worlds, as theorized by Marx and Lenin.[86] While applying these theories might risk oversimplification (of one class or region exploiting the other, or as a general theory of linear expansion), their distinctions—even if anachronistic—are useful here to better understand the role that architecture firms played in translating imperial motivations into spatial and material conditions that came to be known as post-Fordist. Rather than abolishing such distinctions as "core/periphery," as Marxian scholars advocated, those at the helm of large organizations viewed them as an opportunity for management.[87]

In the face of antitrust pressures during the 1960s, for instance, large firms diversified their companies through acquisitions and mergers to evade antitrust sanctions, since entering other sectors was not initially considered monopolistic and therefore could not easily be regulated. As a case in point, the president of the defense conglomerate Litton Industries, which acquired the publishing house that produced *Progressive Architecture* in 1968, argued in a speech to Congress in 1967 that "the application of the antitrust laws, particularly in cases of conglomerate mergers, seems to be aimed directly at making sure that a minimum number of bridges are built between different industries and the technologies that they employ."[88] Yet bridges, as both conceptual and physical structures, redistributed resources and power. While bridges, like railroads and highways, have served within histories of architecture as infrastructures for connecting land and people as part of larger nation-building efforts, they also maintained differentials between people, places, and professions for spatial and jurisdictional control, including the separation of "architecture" from "engineering" during the eighteenth century.[89] As one former DMJM CEO, an engineer turned architect, argued,

"I observed that around the world, many cities were connected by bridges. As I went around the world, I found that they didn't bring cities together; rather, they separated them. San Francisco and Oakland were totally different. St. Louis and East St. Louis, or Philadelphia and Camden. One was upper class, and one was a lower class. How do you make Oakland not lesser to San Francisco?"[90]

And while the core/periphery focus of architectural practice coincided with post-Fordist urbanization, with development occurring more in suburbs than in urban centers (a history explored in the following chapters), the term *periphery* also implied a rise in the precarity of work itself. Well-compensated work was replaced by work that was temporary, flexible, subcontracted and sub-owned; stable careers were replaced by project-based jobs; and entire groups of workers were viewed as dispensable.[91] As business historian Louis Hayman has described, work, business, and the American Dream all came to be viewed as "temporary" by the end of the 1960s.[92] The merging and acquiring of firms was exacerbated by the ease of purchasing, selling, subcontracting, and outsourcing.[93] Similarly, geographer Edward Soja argued that conglomeration processes went further than the horizontal mergers of the late nineteenth century and challenged the state-sponsored monopolies that were central to the rise of Fordism.[94] Firms often initiated these processes by first subcontracting between firms, continuing to joint ventures, and then establishing holding companies that expanded work beyond the bounds of traditional firms and ownership structures. Business gurus such as Alvin Toffler predicted that new "flexible" organizations of the future would be characterized by "ad-hocracy," rather than bureaucracy and organization, and his 1971 book *Future Shock* became a playbook for the gig economy that would later define twenty-first-century work.[95]

These shifts were summarized within a number of texts that offered a diagram of a "flexible firm"—an illustration first produced in

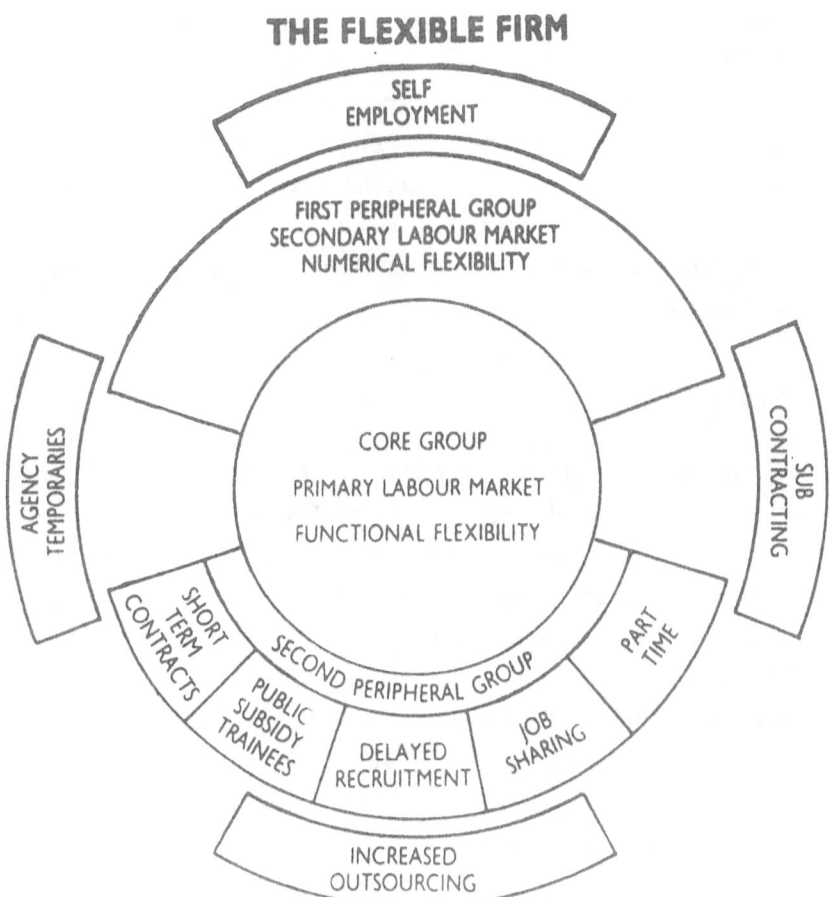

FIGURE 3. Diagram of labor market structures within "flexible accumulation." From *Flexible Patterns of Work*, edited by Chris Curson (London: Institute of Personnel Management, 1986). © Institute for Employment Studies.

1984 by John Atkinson, a research fellow at the British Institute of Manpower Studies (today the Institute for Employment Studies) for a conference about the future of work and its organization (figure 3).[96] The diagram included a "core group" of workers in the center, a "first peripheral group" and "second peripheral group" arranged

Profession: Shattering Tradition [51]

around it, and a detached outer ring comprising four quadrants: "self employment," "sub contracting," "increased outsourcing," and "agency temporaries." Perceived, in many scholarly circles, as a graphical epitome of late capitalist or post-Fordist work, the diagram went on to be republished and recirculated several times, including in the London-based Institute of Personnel Management's book *Flexible Patterns of Work* (1986) and in David Harvey's *The Condition of Postmodernity* (1989).[97]

Incorporation

Connected to the shift from Fordism to post-Fordism was a shift in the legal structures of architectural work. To thrive within and protect themselves against the instabilities of a Cold War economy, architects abandoned nineteenth-century partnerships and sole proprietorships and incorporated their firms. Conceptually, as sociologists Bruno Latour and Pierre Bourdieu described, among many theorists of "practice," *incorporation* could be considered a sociocultural process through which skills, knowledge, or dispositions are embodied or written into the body—including those of a client—such that "written instructions [about how to act or what to believe] are useless."[98] More pragmatically, as a legal form of practice authorized and protected by the state itself, corporations not only offered architects liability protections through law, but they also saved them money and helped boost profits. Corporations also encouraged architects to work collectively, across sectors and geographies, and to acquire land, people, business, or things.[99]

Incorporation represented an important step toward supporting multiple economic functions, since corporations were relatively anonymous enterprises structured for maximum efficiency and expansion. Led by a board of directors, rather than individual partners, they were based on a model of shared governance and constituted a new relationship with the state. As described in a 1980 issue of *AIA Journal*, corporations were particularly advantageous because they offered greater tax benefits than partnerships or sole proprietorships, since after-tax dollars traditionally set aside for boosting a firm could be reported and taxed as corporate income, which was taxed at a lower rate than personal income.[100] Expenses could also be expensed and deducted by the corporation; profit-sharing trusts permitted the distribution of profits to employees in proportion to their salaries; and finally, they offered architects more effective means by which to transfer ownership of their firms beyond the founding individuals through the transfer of stock.

While a few large architecture firms incorporated during the first half of the twentieth century to mitigate risks primarily associated with international work, most remained as sole proprietorships until the 1960s.[101] This slow transition was due, in part, to states that were slow to adopt laws permitting architects to incorporate, along with a hesitancy of architects to embrace the anonymity associated with the corporation, since it also challenged the age-old tradition of the architect-as-identifiable-genius.[102] By 1969, twenty-five states allowed architects to form corporations, including California, Massachusetts, and Illinois, while four states, including New York, prohibited architects from forming them.[103] Many of these changes came by lawsuit: in California, for example, architects were permitted to practice as corporations in 1927 after the state attempted to prohibit a firm of eight architects, Allied Architects Association of Los Angeles, from operating as a corporation.[104] The state argued that individual architects, like lawyers, held unique and intimate relationships with their clients based on confidence and trust, and that by working "cooperatively," architects would be unable to maintain one-on-one trust not only with their clients, but also with the public, since they would be degrading the standards of their profession and putting communities at risk. The Supreme Court of California ruled in favor of the architects, however, suggesting that the comparison to law was inappropriate and stating that so long as architects held individual licenses, they could practice together as a corporation.

By the late 1970s, architecture corporations surpassed partnerships in number, and by the 1980s, corporations surpassed even the number of sole proprietorships. Nearly 60 percent of architecture firms had adopted corporate structures by 1982—a trend that continued into the twenty-first century, with 80 percent of firms having adopted such structures by 2012.[105]

As architectural work slowed with the retirement of Depression-era architects and the end of post–World War II reconstruction, incorporation was followed by conglomeration. Through the legal tools of the corporation, architects could use surplus capital to acquire other companies, often those at risk of bankruptcy or collapse, since the corporation as a legal entity functioned much like an individual. Needing new expertise, corporate firms increasingly acquired entire companies and their assets, thereby helping to fuel capital's constant thirst for expansion. Architects' incorporation of new markets, geographies, laborers, and their histories demonstrated, as Michael Hardt and Antonio Negri notably described in their book *Empire*, how capital expansion inevitably took on the political form of imperialism.[106] American graphic designer S. Neil Fujita captured the omnidirectional and expansionary thrust of corporations in a diagram used by Drucker for the cover of *Concept of the Corporation*: a black circle of radiating rings on which eight arrows point outward, an industrial city at the center.

During the mid-1980s, architecture firms either continued as partnerships or quickly restructured as corporations; those with economic woes were often taken over by larger firms—sometimes by firms outside the United States. Perkins & Will, for example, on the verge of bankruptcy in 1985, was swallowed up the next year by the Dar Group, whose services ranged from "retail" and "transportation planning" to "hospitality design." The Dar Group acquired the two-hundred-person firm in order to "build a global portfolio of premium engineering and design brands."[107] In his memoir *Out of the Middle East*, the founder of Dar Al-Handasah, Jordanian businessman-cum-politician Kamal Shair, wrote: "I knew all along that if I was to build Dar Al-Handasah into a truly global business, sooner or later we would have to take on the United States . . . the mightiest market in the world. It has the biggest economy and the largest and most prosperous customers. But it is also the hardest market of all to crack—a tough no-nonsense free-enterprise system where winners take all and losers are allowed to go to the wall."[108] Arguing that Perkins & Will was in the "corporate sick-room" due to "poor management," Shair purchased the company for $700,000 and acquired other firms on the verge of collapse over the next four years.[109] The firm's acquisitions included, among others, the Atlanta-based architectural consultancy Nix Mann and T. Y. Lin International, which was known for specialized structural engineering.[110]

In his description of Dar Al-Handasah, Shair positioned the global architecture and engineering firm at the end of the twentieth century as yet another kind of bridge: a "technological bridge" between developed and "developing" nations in ways that seemed to reflect the work of the World Bank or the United Nations more than an architecture or engineering firm.[111] Shair explained his belief that the work of a global architecture-and-engineering conglomerate was to reorganize the flow of values and materials from one country to another:

> In a sense, I feel that we at Dar Al-Handasah have played a small part in reversing a pernicious feature of history. From the seventeenth to the twentieth centuries, colonizers from Europe exploited their overseas possessions for the value they could extract from them—whether that value flowed in gold, groundnuts or, most evil of all,

slaves. Building a company that acts as a kind of technology bridge from the developed to the developing world reverses the flow of value. We are now bringing new technologies to the developing world—helping to build up their industries and infrastructure and improve the quality of life for their people. I do not want to give the impression we are philanthropists. We do this because it is our business and we do it for a profit.[112]

Despite Shair's emphatic claim that the firm was reversing the colonial flow of "value" and redistributing material resources (to build infrastructure, for example) from one place to another, the flow of capital in fact moved from governments, multinational aid organizations, and militaries to private enterprises. In other words, Dar Al-Handasah was reproducing and maintaining the socioeconomic, geographic, and political differentials between the developed and developing nations, as well as those between businesses that thrived on instability and war and those who suffered their effects.[113] Indeed, the company has been widely critiqued for its colonizing imprints in its pursuit of profit. In the late 1980s, for example, the firm specified lighting at the Holy Mosque in Makkah that turned it into a "daylight stadium" more suited to soccer than to prayer, according to one geographer, while also demolishing homes to introduce piazzas in "alien patterns" around it—which, as one urban historian has argued, foreshadowed the kind of "postmodern" speculative developments that would emerge at the mosque's periphery in the decade ahead.[114] And in Beirut, for another example, the company's "profit-oriented urban planning" in 1991 was met with strong public protest.[115]

Unlike Perkins & Will, whose architects were open to structurally reinventing their firm and its work, many postwar architecture corporations were less open to change—and they collapsed. At CRS in Texas, incorporated in 1958, profit-motivated acquisitions were supported by the firm's public listing on the New York Stock Exchange in

1971. However, these business practices clashed with the conservative cultural ideals of the firm's founding architects, who fought to foreground building design above all else. An architect at CRS used the phrase "cultural genocide" to describe the process by which an acquired company (often not an architecture firm) would be merged with—"flattened"—within the "architecture" culture of CRS.[116] This violent language explains not only the dispositions of big business in the US, but also the immense effort required to maintain a white-majority, labor-intensive, male-dominated architectural practice.[117] The thirst for expansion and greater profit, understood in the embrace of the corporate form and public listing, clashed with the simultaneous desire of CRS's senior architects to stay focused on building design and drawings even as the firm's work began to skew heavily toward engineering and construction management. The firm splintered into several commodifiable parts during the early 1990s.[118] Its architecture group was sold to Missouri-based Helmuth, Obata + Kassabaum (HOK); its engineering and construction groups were sold to California-based Jacobs Engineering; and its cogeneration group, CRSS Capital, was sold to the engineering firm Tractebel. Another such example was The Architects Collaborative (TAC), based in Massachusetts, an obstinately architects-only firm known for its postwar collaborative and "team"-based approach to practice. Incorporated in 1963, it was no longer able to pay its expenses by the end of the 1980s and was bankrupt by 1995.[119] At the core of these fractures was a clash of cultural ideals, between the expansionary thrust of capital accumulation embodied by the corporate form and a contradictory desire to control production by guarding against political-economic change.

Internationalization

As Dar Al-Handasah's history reveals, the legal tools of incorporation coincided with the internationalization of architecture firms after

World War II. While many US enterprises were exporting expertise prior to the war, very few had branches or subsidiaries abroad by then; the oil industry was considered exceptional because of its early international footprint and influence on global policy.[120] Between the 1940s and 1970s, however, the shocks of the Great Depression, World War II, and the political shifts accompanying the purported end of nation-based colonial empires restructured the global political economy.[121] After the war, the US federal government and military began to rely heavily on the private sector to produce infrastructure—such as highways and electrical grids, some facilitated by international aid organizations—as well as weapons, including the atomic bomb and ballistic missile systems, to defend the sovereignty of the US and preserve its position within the new global order.[122] Architecture and engineering firms had important roles designing and building these new global infrastructures, and in turn these projects restructured firms and, consequently, professions. In practice, the federal government encouraged firms working abroad to incorporate their international enterprises due to the many financial and physical risks involved; many did so before incorporating their firms domestically. This general trend was aligned with the basic vision of incorporation established by Adam Smith in his *Wealth of Nations*. He argued that incorporation tended to confer monopolistic powers upon an enterprise and thus should be reserved for businesses working on high-risk, large-scale projects abroad on behalf of the state.[123]

While many of these infrastructural projects have been described within the history of architecture as part of a broader history of "exporting" Western expertise, including the stylistic preferences or managerial efficiency of architects and engineers, these development and defense projects also influenced the practices of architects, not only by facilitating their internationalization and boosting their financial footing, but by offering insights into international governance. Once the military and international organizations made visible the effectiveness of their own tools—from computers to military airplanes—for managing and disciplining geographic footholds abroad, architects and engineers also saw how they could manage and control larger sets of business activity beyond drawing. At the end of the 1960s, economist Neil Jacoby argued, this migration of tools from military to private industry carried with it the possibility of conglomeration in private industry.[124]

Outside of architecture, the Delaware chemical conglomerate DuPont, for instance, shifted its offerings depending on wartime need, from gunpowder for World War I to neoprene, nylon, tires, and plutonium for World War II, to ballistic body armor during the Cold War, to gasoline following the OPEC crisis during the late 1970s. The Beverly Hills electronics company Litton Industries boasted product lines ranging from navigation technology to microwave ovens. New York's Sperry Rand conglomerate sold computers, office furniture, hay balers, gyroscopes, and electric razors. And the Boston-based textile company Textron manufactured synthetic yarns, parachutes, and aircraft. Architecture and engineering firms were equally wide-ranging, offering aerial surveillance and survey services with warplanes, and data processing with new military computers.

Yet how were large firms able to procure such projects, while other, smaller firms were not? Prior to the 1970s, the criteria for selecting architects and engineers for federal government projects were not required to be publicly announced; selections were determined primarily on the basis of price, loose friendships, and the geographic proximities of a firm, rather than by competency, experience, and qualifications.[125] Therefore, while architects did not initially need to have an excessively large firm with broad experience in order to compete for and win defense or development contracts during much of the Cold War, having friends in high places was paramount. This changed in 1972 with the Brooks Act, which required government briefs to be publicly released and decisions to be based on a firm's prior experience. However, this merely rewarded firms that had already been built up by the state and had earned the kind of broad expertise and experience that now had to be formally demonstrated.

Beyond procurement, though, it was the terms of government contracts that enabled firms to both earn large profits and establish long-term state patronage. In 1940–41, for instance, appropriations for the War Department ballooned, and contractors were paid using full costs plus a fixed fee, rather than sealed bids. The government was friendly to these burgeoning businesses, often paying more when a firm or project was poorly managed, or allowing firms to keep excess funding even if projects came in under budget, which was less risky and financially rewarding. As Henry Stimson, US secretary of state, said in 1941, "If you are going to try to go to war, or to prepare for war, in a capitalistic country, you have got to let business make money out of the process or business won't work."[126]

City

While conglomerate business practices grew in popularity during the 1960s and fell out of favor by the 1980s, large conglomerate architecture firms helped to deinstitutionalize firms as bounded organizational bodies and naturalize, instead, a logic of practice defined by contracts and coordination across otherwise unrelated geographies, markets, and professional lines.[127] Economist Oliver Williamson developed a broad theory of the firm in the 1970s by returning to Ronald Coase's seminal 1937 essay "The Nature of a Firm," which anticipated the economic limitations to vertical integration.[128] Williamson suggested that, as firms adapt, expand, and disintegrate—as they become so complex that no individual can manage all of their parts—the firm itself evolves into a structure of governance fueled by adaptation and coordination through contracts, rather than human managers. "The firm as a production function," Williamson argued, "needs to make way for the view of the *firm as governance structure*."[129]

These changes to the architecture firm redefined not only the profession, but also the shape and organization of the cities they served. David Harvey attributes this relationship—between late capital accumulation and the imposing of order by architects onto entire urban economies—to post-Fordism and the accumulation of profit.[130] While the history of capitalism has largely followed the history of urban development, from the rise of the mercantilist city to the industrial city and the Keynesian and post-Keynesian city, postwar urbanization presented a spatiotemporal solution to the crisis of surplus. However, the presence of surplus also risked overaccumulation, which posed a potential contradiction to capitalist accumulation, since it could result in excess commodities, falling rates of profit, or idle money. To avert and delay such a crisis, architects could invest in the process of urbanization itself: "It is through urbanization," Harvey argued, "that the surpluses are mobilized, produced, absorbed, and appropriated," and thus architecture firms themselves took the very shape of the urban economies in which they were investing.[131]

In the 1960s, Southern California was the epicenter of aerospace development and Cold War manufacturing; by no coincidence, it was also a hatchery for large, international architecture and engineering firms. By 1970, 12 percent of the fifty largest design firms in the US, ranked by revenue, were based in Southern California; by 1990, the region was home to 18 percent of those firms.[132] In comparison, only 8 percent were based in Chicago and 4 percent in New York.

While only 1 percent of all architecture firms across the US have, steadily since the 1970s, employed more than one hundred people, they were and continue to be concentrated in postindustrial cities such as Los Angeles. By 2020, for instance, 5 percent of all architecture firms in Los Angeles had, on average, more than a hundred people—significantly higher than the national average of 1 percent.[133]

In Los Angeles during the Cold War, firms like DMJM and Charles Luckman Associates were emerging just as craft forms of production were declining—industries such as film production were vertically disintegrating, and subcontracting companies absorbed the more generic tasks.[134] As manufacturing jobs plummeted and industrial zones were vacated in cities across the country, Los Angeles marked its exceptionality by reindustrializing in aerospace and electronics—establishing what historian Allen Scott referred to as a "technopolis" by reimagining the "periphery" of the city.[135] Geographers who formed the so-called "Los Angeles School of Urbanism" during the mid-1980s positioned Los Angeles as a decentralized and prototypical "post-Fordist" city with segmented labor markets and "peripheral urban concentrations" of high technology at the city's edges.[136] It is not surprising, then, that firms such as DMJM emerged as models of diversified multi-firm practice just as American cities like Los Angeles were being described as fragmented and polycentric palimpsests whose development occurred on the "periphery" rather than in traditionally concentric industrial zones.

In the early 1990s, architecture critic Charles Jencks argued that postwar Los Angeles architects were "separate and independent" from the "Los Angeles School," since they saw themselves as individual "mavericks" who challenged the disciplinary establishment of architecture through material innovations characterized by "heterogeneity" and "informality."[137] However, by comparing the structures of architecture firms, rather than the rhetoric of design by individual architects, it is possible to see how architects were indeed part of, and responsible for, the post-Fordist city and the defining tenets of the Los Angeles School. Even further, large architecture and engineering firms had spatialized these urban arrangements in practice before they were visible in built form. Conglomerate firms such as DMJM, though overlooked—except for "noteworthy" individual architects such as Cesar Pelli and Anthony Lumsden—by Los Angeles School urbanists, emerged as political-economic barometers for Los Angeles. DMJM was awarded by the Los Angeles City Council for its "substantial contributions made to the city's growth" in 1958—the same year that President Eisenhower noted, in a celebration of the profession of architecture's one hundredth year, that it had, from the "earliest days of our Republic . . . contributed to the growing industry of our land, to the development of our public buildings and to raising in form and fabric the aspirations of our people."[138] This trend continued in 1980, as Mayor Tom Bradley argued that "DMJM seems to be on the wave of the future" of Los Angeles, and again over thirty years later, as Mayor Eric Garcetti argued in 2014 that the firm, as the largest publicly traded revenue generator in the city, was an urban force that represented "a strong signal of confidence in LA's economy."[139]

In other words, by the end of the twentieth century, one looked to an architecture firm, not the buildings it produced, to understand the economic strength and political structure of a city. Moreover, because the conglomerate architectural firm served to produce and reproduce the state, to look at such a firm is to look at how cities have served as consolidations of capital and material instruments by which multinational businesses-as-oligarchs, in the words of Hardt and Negri, reproduce and reinforce global order.

2 *Firm*

Corporate Conglomeration

I started as a structural engineer and was subsidiary to the architect, so I thought I better become an architect. Then I thought architects were subsidiary to owners, so I became an owner. Then I realized that owners were subsidiary to financial institutions, and the only way to get something built was if someone was willing to finance it. So I started a savings and loan. My history is one of always expanding. Mechanical, civil, structural, architecture, ownership, finance, and then community-shaping policy.

ALBERT DORMAN, former CEO of DMJM and cofounder of AECOM

At age ninety, retired architect and engineer Albert Dorman was still going to the office. One day, sitting behind his desk with his hands tightly clasped, he began sharing stories about his life's work and his cofounding of AECOM. "I started as a one-man office in Hanford, California," he explained hesitatingly, seemingly unsure about what I wanted to know or what I might later write about him. "And I have lived to see the firms I headed grow to be the biggest in the world."[1]

Dorman's use of the term *subsidiary* in the initial outline of his career hinted at the ways in which social, economic, and political hierarchies of labor lay hidden beneath the built environment. It also revealed how individual ambitions in the postwar period evolved, even if unintentionally, into imperial pursuits through the design and redesign of firms: from personal accumulation to collective governance; from production to politics; from partnership to corporate conglomerate; from architecture and engineering to policy and regulation.²

As they were attempting to carve out a safe space in which to work after World War II, architects such as those at DMJM were treating their businesses as if they were architecture: their firms' legal structures protected them from personal injury; strong management and diverse offerings helped them weather cycles of boom and bust; and, eventually, mergers and acquisitions shielded them from unpredictable markets when one sector or region collapsed. Yet as their businesses grew and their practices reified, they began to contribute to and capitalize on the very cycles of development and destruction, boom and bust, and life and death against which they had once braced themselves—bombs and genocides, strokes and heart attacks, depressions and corporate acquisitions.

This chapter considers how the structure and scope of architects' firms evolved over the course of the twentieth century through DMJM and AECOM's particular history. By tracing a history of coordinated changes to the company's services, workers, organization, geographic reach, and legal definition, it reveals how the conditions of postindustrialization and urban inequity that were surfacing at the end of the twentieth century were first taking shape within architects' firms.

· • ·

It was the first year of the postwar baby boom. The construction of Levittown was set to begin, and the United Nations had just convened its first session. Alfred Hitchcock's spy film *Notorious* was hitting the screens and Louis Réard unveiled a two-piece swimsuit in

Paris named the "bikini." Congress established the Atomic Energy Commission. The Philippines gained independence. And the US Army formally announced its first computer, developed at the University of Pennsylvania to calculate artillery firing tables.[3]

These were the events recorded in DMJM's autobiography as political-economic markers of the year 1946, the year the company was born. The events capture some of the contradictions that defined the postwar US, demonstrating the architects' attentiveness to the dualities that structured the cycles of the economy. In global politics? Invasions as business opportunities, celebrated as liberations. In technological advancements? Bombs and computers. In cultural production? Drab news and blockbuster films. The events foreshadowed a new reality for the country, whose economic sovereignty would depend on private-sector companies—including those of architects and engineers—using their managerial expertise and productive capacities to both manage and maintain that sovereignty while hedging against postwar instability in an internationalized world. Only one year later, historian Henry-Russell Hitchcock predicted this: that large, anonymous, bureaucratic architecture firms would prove crucial to the postwar global economy; valued for their expertise in mechanical precision and their ability to rapidly produce drawings for construction. These firms' collective organizational genius, he wrote, would soon supplant the individual architectural genius.[4]

Ten years earlier, twenty-five-year-old Phillip Daniel had set out to find his first job as a draftsman. He had recently graduated from the University of Southern California (USC) with a bachelor's degree in architecture. The country was facing its second economic recession since the Great Depression, which had already grayed his childhood. Like many universities formed after the Long Depression of the 1870s, USC was born as a private institution with donations from disparate sources.[5] While not central to this story, the economic details of the school's founding sponsors are important because architectural work was and continues to be conditioned by the histories of the schools that architects attended, which are themselves shaped and constrained by the values, anxieties, and ambitions of their donors.[6]

Only twelve years old when Daniel graduated, the USC School of Architecture was led by Dean Arthur C. Weatherhead—an architect committed to turning life into capital: pushing architectural education beyond Beaux Arts traditions to focus instead on simulations of "real life," including "specific sites," "real problems," and "planning principles."[7] Weatherhead argued that "architecture must grow out of the conditions existing in the civilization which it serves," pointing to the "theatrical realism" of both Hollywood and spectacular displays of military might across Southern California, where he urged students to find work.[8] "The architect in many respects," he argued, "along with the engineer and the scientist, [is] one of the ultimate governors of our lives in this urban age in which we are living."[9]

Weatherhead's vision left a lasting impression on Daniel. After graduating, he traveled northward to Santa Maria, California—a booming seven-thousand-person oil town soon to be overshadowed by an army training installation, Camp Cooke (later Vandenberg Air Force Base). There, he found a position with engineer-cum-architect Louis Crawford, a beloved local designer of schools and public buildings and vice president of the California State Association of Architects.[10] When Crawford suffered a stroke in 1940, Daniel found himself leading the firm, Crawford & Daniel Architects, at age twenty-seven, and he called on his friends to help.

Enter S. Kenneth Johnson, Daniel's fellow USC classmate, who had a penchant for the dramatic. He was not only a budding architect; he was a former child actor who had graced film screens in *Our Gang*, the popular comedy series that chronicled the adventures of a group of "real" working-class children.[11] In the 1930s, it was not uncommon for USC architecture graduates to work in film and government.[12] Johnson worked in the art department of MGM Studios during his studies, as did several of his classmates who would become award-winning set designers and art directors, including fraternity-mate Hilyard Brown (*Citizen Kane*, 1941; *Cleopatra*, 1963), Henry Bumstead (*To Kill a Mockingbird*, 1962; *The Sting*, 1973), and Jack Martin Smith (*The Wizard of Oz*, 1939; *Cleopatra*, 1963; *Fantastic Voyage*, 1966; *Hello, Dolly!*, 1969).[13]

Crawford & Daniel quickly became a family affair. In addition to Johnson, Daniel hired his soon-to-be brother-in-law, structural engineer Irvan Mendenhall, as a consultant, and Mendenhall's soon-to-be wife, Margaret Peterson, as a secretary.[14] However, construction slowed due to material shortages with the onset of World War II, and the office closed in 1942.

During the interlude between the office closure and the war, Daniel found short-term defense employment at Kaiser Engineering, where he worked on steel mills in Fontana and met architect Arthur Mann, chief architect and assistant engineer at D. R. Warren Structural Engineers. Mann's résumé typified the instability of the profession during the 1930s. Work was difficult to come by, and jobs were often brief and poorly paid, if paid at all. Mann had twenty-five different jobs in twelve years, most lasting no more than two months, although he "moved up" from an unpaid "office boy" in 1930 to a licensed chief architect by 1942 as wartime construction work accelerated.[15] Daniel and Mann immediately bonded, and they began envisioning a future firm of their own—one that could thrive during an inevitable postwar construction boom and, more importantly, provide each architect a level of socioeconomic stability and protection that neither had ever experienced.

Unlike Daniel and Johnson, Mann had attended the Chouinard Art Institute across town, which predated USC's architecture school by four years. Like USC, the institute had connections to private industry. It was championed by Walt Disney, who supported the school financially and administratively when its founder suffered a stroke in the 1950s and who hoped to turn it into a "City of the Arts." In 1961, however, the Chouinard Art Institute merged with the Los Angeles Conservatory of Music to become the California Institute of the Arts. The institute's trajectory exemplifies how cultural producers, such as Weatherhead at USC, established links between academia, private industry, the city, and the state—to form the "culture industry," as Adorno and Horkheimer described it.[16]

Daniel and Mann's plans came to a halt when they were drafted. During the war, Daniel served as a navy radar officer, Mann worked in intelligence and construction in the army air corps, Mendenhall served in a naval construction battalion, and Johnson worked at the Pollack Shipyard in Stockton, California, as a civilian. Nonetheless, the instability of war only fueled those plans—for Daniel and Mann, planning their future world of work and imagining their postwar routines was, in some ways, an exercise in liberation.[17] They had turned to architecture not only to dream up war-free homes and schools and cities, but also because they considered architectural work itself a collective endeavor that required the labor and coordination of many. Echoing the military, practicing architecture was considered a form of security.

It was during one of the deadliest battles of the war that they solidified their firm of the future: "I was in Saipan with the 20th Air Force when Phil's ship came into the harbor with a load of wounded from Iwo Jima," Mann recalled in a letter to a coworker, referring to the same Twentieth Air Force that was responsible for dropping atomic bombs on Nagasaki and Hiroshima. "Phil came ashore and found me, and we sat on the beach looking at Tinian and sealed the deal. Then we went aboard his ship and got a little high on torpedo juice [the popular Navy cocktail made by mixing pineapple juice with the 180-proof grain-alcohol fuel used in torpedo

FIGURE 4. The four founding partners of DMJM (left to right): Phillip Daniel, Arthur Mann, S. Kenneth Johnson, and Irvan Mendenhall. From *DMJM: Four Decades of Excellence*, 1986. Courtesy of William Coburn.

motors]."[18] Following the war, Daniel, Mann, and Johnson began breathing life into a new partnership in Santa Maria: Daniel, Mann & Johnson Architects (DM&J), with Mendenhall continuing as their trusted consulting engineer (figure 4).

. . .

After visiting AECOM and exchanging introductory emails with the firm's executives in 2015, I had only learned a few general details about DMJM and AECOM's origins. I began working backward, writing to the most recent CEO and cofounder, engineer Richard Newman, who had left the company in 2010 but remained as a "non-executive chairman of the board." Since employee emails were not published online, I continued by guessing "first name <dot> last name" addresses. Newman was still checking his; he was then working for AECOM as a consultant. Newman shared my address with AECOM's other cofounder, Albert Dorman, and a web of CEOs began to emerge—one that, unsurprisingly, began to resemble the familiar family trees of white male architects I had studied in college. How, I wondered, could I reach those *not* "at the top"—the draftspeople, interns, project managers, and secretaries? Surely their stories would be different.

In the meantime, Dorman and Newman met with me and shared my name with yet another generation of architects and the family members of DMJM's founders. Most were excited to contribute: Daniel's son shared PDFs of 1960s magazine articles and newspaper clippings by email; Mann's daughter welcomed me to her home to sift through boxes of brochures, photographs, and letters; architect Tef Kutay's son and daughter mailed a package; Mendenhall's son and granddaughter chatted with me by phone; and architect Stanley Moe's daughter invited me to unpack boxes of paperwork, newspapers, and photographs before she donated them to public libraries across the country.

Stories about the company's history began to repeat themselves as I moved from house to house, email to phone call, and details emerged about everyday work routines, travels, conflicts at work, and lifelong friendships. "An exceptional place to work, he says," I wrote in my first notebook entry. "Reunions and rituals continue today."

As if I were digging through a family's photo album or memory box, I tried to imagine *why* specific documents were saved or written in the first place: announcements of new hires and promotions; marriages and birth certificates; retirements and death notices. The stories of endings were bringing DMJM to life while they were also beginning to explain the supposed death of the profession.

At the top of most boxes were photocopied résumés, reunion brochures, and obituaries—usually the most recent additions before the boxes were covered and shelved. Layered beneath these were corporate charters, company brochures, and an occasional financial record lodged between pages, out of place. Further down were periodicals, essays, and newspaper clippings. It was clear that some clippings were saved because of a project that won an award or because a mayor or diplomat had visited the office and caused a stir. Others offered frozen frames of global news during the Cold War—some about the Soviets' testing of ballistic missiles and many others about the prospects of "development" work in Southeast Asia, Africa, or the Middle East.

A 1967 issue of *Time* magazine was stored in a box with Stanley Moe's papers. One bookmarked article was "On Being an American Parent," which offered stark advice: "Listen." "Spend time, not money." "Discipline." While at first I set the magazine aside, since it seemed unrelated to the history of an architecture firm, the terms *parent* and *child* surfaced repeatedly during my conversations, sometimes referring to the architects and their children who were open to sharing stories in order to keep the legacies of their parents alive, and other times referring to subsidiary companies as "children" owned or managed by "parents"—a dual familial order.

While much still seemed to be missing—drawings, explanations about who did what, how the office functioned—these newspapers, obituaries, and corporate charters, as records of public memory, were providing details not only about each architect's personal life, but also about their careers, details that outlined DMJM's history as a social organization, as a firm. "Daniel was a founding partner and senior vice president of Daniel, Mann, Johnson, and Mendenhall," his obituary explains. "Licensed in 15 states and winner of numerous awards for his design of residential facilities . . . he directed DMJM's systems division, led the firm into new computer applications for architectural, engineering and economics work, and sparked his firm's involvement in the nation's missile-space programs."[19]

The same language was used in corporate charters—the corporation, too, a body that lives and dies. According to DMJM's first articles of incorporation, the company was born as an international corporation in California in 1952, its charter was amended in 1960, the company was killed by "dissolve" in 1962, it was revived in 1975, killed again by "acquisition" in 1984, revived in 1990, and "dissolved" again in 2008. Other companies with ties to DMJM were listed in the charters and paperwork, their names unfamiliar: "Logicomp," "Design Methods," "Realtech," "TMSI." What were these companies? How did they relate to DMJM? Despite my lack of access to official records, these questions would be answerable thanks to contemporary search databases, social media, career-networking websites, and public stewards. But it would take time and patience.

Partnership

With a construction backlog stretching back to the Great Depression, and with careers stunted by war, many young architects chose to face the postwar period in partnership, rather than alone as sole proprietors. Among many others, The Architects Collaborative (TAC) formed as a partnership in Cambridge, Massachusetts, in 1945; Caudill Rowlett Scott (CRS) in Houston in 1946; and Austin, Field & Fry in 1946 in Los Angeles, the same year as DMJM (then DM&J).

As discussed in chapter 1, partnerships offered architects who were scarred by economic depression a better chance at long-term economic success, since they could join with others with complementary skills and brace themselves against inevitable recessions or slowdowns. During the nineteenth century, the architects who embraced partnerships became "big businesses" because they were able to combine the efforts of many and thereby complete multiple projects simultaneously.

Back from the war, the DM&J partners opened a one-room office in 1946 within the Motta Building in Santa Maria, California, where they focused exclusively on "architecture"—designing new schools, grocery stores, and a few local shops. As was common for partnerships, the three architects and one engineer divided the work by their complementary skills: Daniel the marketer, Mann the designer, Johnson the technical expert, and Mendenhall the consulting engineer.[20] Within the first year of opening its doors in Santa Maria, DM&J opened a second office in Los Angeles—in a sixteen-hundred-square-foot space in the Spanish-style Granada Buildings on La Fayette Park Place near Wilshire Boulevard (figure 5).[21] The Granada

FIGURE 5. Franklin Harper, The Granada Buildings [Granada Shoppes and Studios], La Fayette Park Place, Los Angeles, 1927. Security Pacific National Bank Collection, Los Angeles Public Library.

Buildings, built in 1927 and intended for both living and working, were designed by a speculative journalist-turned-developer/architect named Franklin Harper, whose financial and architectural risks foreshadowed DMJM's in the 1960s.[22]

During the late 1940s, the partners were procuring more work than the firm could handle.[23] Their early projects included a new Alvin Avenue Elementary School in Santa Maria and grocery stores for Safeway, then the largest national chain, in Los Angeles. Still, despite the steady flow of work, the first three years were financially turbulent, and the partners were struggling to stay afloat.[24] Fears of loss surfaced yet again. By the end of 1949, DM&J employed forty people, and the inability of the partners to make a living—let alone a profit—

challenged the viability of an informally organized, architecture-only partnership. While the architects claimed to be decent "salesmen," Daniel argued that "what we knew about running a business you could stick in your ear."[25] He and Johnson took turns in the hospital with stress-induced stomach ulcers. Johnson's wife, Kathy, captured the bewilderment: "This is awful," she said. "We've got four kids, a big house, and no income. We never know when the money is coming in. The company's so busy, so, how come?"[26] A retrospective issue of *Management Methods* in 1957 described the partnership as "sagging," with each partner blaming the others for the firm's "profit-sapping problems."[27] The incredible pressures of running a profitable partnership led to sharp disagreements about the direction of the firm, which spiraled into animosity.[28]

At first, the trio resorted to psychological tests to try to understand the sources of their personal friction, and they shared frank assessments of each other's strengths and weaknesses, a practice that continued for years. They wrote things like "Phil: Fine clarity of vision; exhibits and uses authority properly; [but] conceals from people; resists change." Or "Art: fine administration; excellent in current role; [but] stubborn, impatient with others." And "Ken: fine organizer; high standards for personnel; [but] ruthless with incompetent people" (figure 6). In the end, they concluded that there were deeper, structural problems with the business.[29] Grappling with a firm that had grown so large so quickly, better business and personality management would be key, they thought. But whom could they hire?

Johnson learned that Chicago-based architectural firm Perkins & Will, which was formed a decade earlier than DM&J, was also struggling with waning school commissions as the postwar demand for them quickly faded. In response, Perkins & Will had hired the management consultant firm Booz Allen Hamilton (BAH). Management consultants such as BAH and McKinsey were incredibly useful to firms that had grown large very quickly, offering financial planning

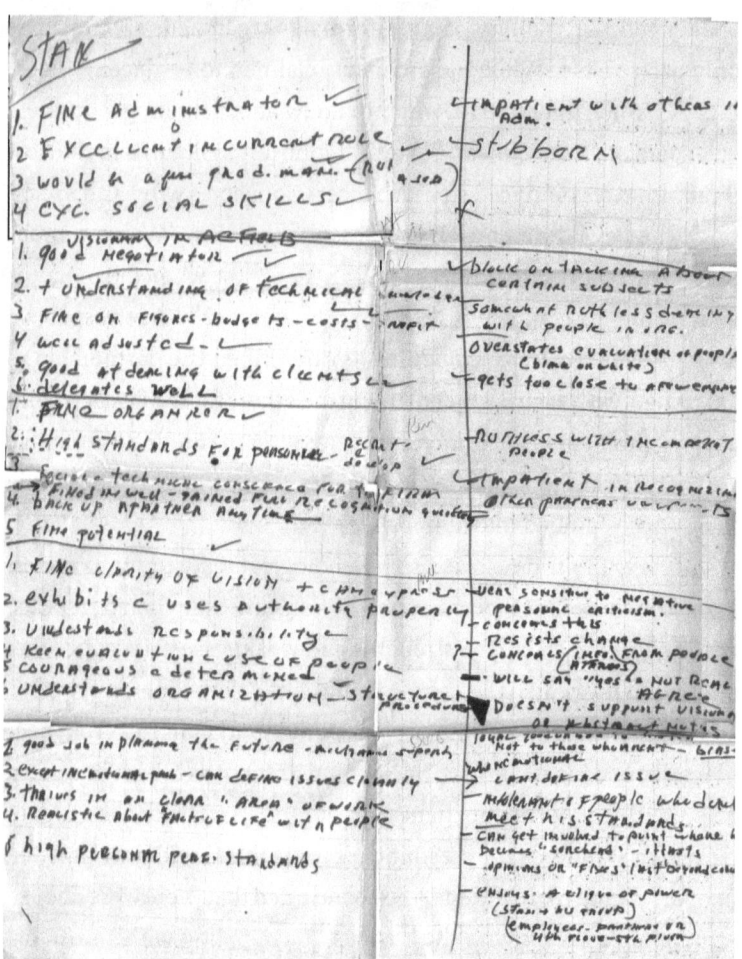

FIGURE 6. DMJM corporate retreat notes by Stanley Moe. Papers of Stanley Moe. Private collection. Courtesy of Billie Moe Crouse.

guidance for businesses in a range of industries, from oil to publishing to architecture and engineering. As some historians have suggested, it was management consultants who directly influenced the merger and acquisition boom of the 1960s, sparking the so-called conglomerate era.[30]

In the eyes of the DM&J partners, BAH seemed to help Perkins & Will yield "wholesome profits" and enabled its partners to spend "more time on the golf course than in the office."[31] DM&J followed suit and hired BAH in 1949 to help identify inefficiencies in the business as well as to develop long-term management procedures and economic goals. Managerial expertise, they hoped, would become a key to economic success. As it turned out, management would inform not only their business decisions, but also their views about the role and regulation of professional associations.

Upon his arrival at DM&J, BAH consultant Douglas Russell found work unbilled, bills unpaid, and no business plan in sight. After an initial six-week survey, he drafted a new structure for DM&J that was based on the business structure of BAH itself.[32] In his final report, Russell argued that the architecture firms most likely to thrive after the war would be those that (1) recognized each contributing professional as social and economic equals; (2) fully integrated architecture and engineering services; (3) diversified their project types—from school and military to commercial and industrial projects—since specialization subjected the firm to peaks and valleys of business; and (4) incorporated, to provide architects with liability protections and to facilitate expansion from one sector or geography to another.

Putting his words into action, Russell first insisted on a new "ethics" that encouraged the partners to approach business "dispassionately"—removing any sense of personality that could interfere with management or capital flow—and to consider each other strictly as social and economic counterparts. Russell demanded that each partner learn all aspects of the practice through a five-year rotation, taking turns in each role of the firm. Additionally, each partner was to be paid the same weekly salary of seventy-five dollars (a yearly salary of $48,000 in 2023 dollars), though they were permitted to bring only half of that home. The remaining half was partially held for their individual taxes, while the rest was kept for "plowing back into the business."[33]

Following Russell's second recommendation to integrate architecture and engineering as a hedge against a possible economic downturn, DM&J acquired Irv Mendenhall's engineering firm and he became a full partner. DM&J was already outsourcing nearly 50 percent of its engineering work to his office. "We realized that either straight architecture or engineering would not fit the pattern and need of future professional services," Mann recalled. "In order to service our clientele, we must diversify and develop other disciplines into the firm. As the A&E business is quite cyclical, we figured that the peaks and valleys would even out more as the two disciplines did not necessarily coincide."[34] In 1950, Mendenhall's addition as partner resulted in a new firm name: Daniel, Mann, Johnson, and Mendenhall, Architects and Engineers (DMJM). Russell, too, was named a partner and general manager of the firm in 1950, though his name, ironically, did not make its way into the firm's—suggesting that, despite the rhetoric of equivalency, managerial labor was not yet viewed as socially comparable to architecture and engineering. Or, put another way, management was private coordination's "visible hand" (to cite Alfred Chandler again), though it was still unnamed in public.

The rhetoric of equivalency embedded in the integration of architecture and engineering represented a particular characteristic of modern architecture-and-engineering firms such as Albert Kahn Associates; The Austin Company, based in Cleveland; Skidmore, Owings & Merrill; and Allied Engineers. The latter was a joint venture in Los Angeles comprising architects Paul Williams and Adrian Wilson and engineer Donald R. Warren, for which Mann had worked prior to World War II. However, the social leveling of architects, engineers, and business managers did not occur until after the war.[35] When engineer John Merrill first joined SOM in 1939, for instance, he was only a limited partner, even though his name was equally represented in the firm's title. Even after he became a full partner, historians have argued, SOM remained focused exclusively on architecture as a Fordist economy of work that prioritized scale, rather than diversity.[36]

Architects, engineers, and business managers described the integrated partnership of DMJM in sharp contrast to SOM, as an economy of means rather than scale—with a fully integrated, multidivisional structure meeting the demands of a dubious postwar economy. At DMJM, architects and engineers worked in semiautonomous divisions and were responsible for their own projects. With no particular project specialization or reproducible aesthetic logic, multidivisional firms such as DMJM were positioned more favorably toward growth in a number of industries and geographies, not just architecture. Albert Dorman explained the firm in contrast to other large architecture firms: "The single most important difference about DMJM was that architecture and engineering was under one roof. There was no other firm—SOM or others—that incorporated engineering as an equal part of the firm. . . . DMJM represented the concept of a multidisciplinary firm in which all of the disciplines were equal, whether it was the economist, urban planner, architect, mechanical engineer, structural engineer, financial people, or marketing."[37] With architecture and engineering services both completed in house, the architects and engineers maintained independent responsibility for their own streams of revenue. As a testament to their approach, the engineers generated as much revenue as the architects well into the 1970s, and drawings were often produced over the same desks—with architects and engineers filtering in and out as needed, rather than the drawings moving from one table to the next.[38]

Incorporation

With integration came a newly unified view of the firm. The founding partners began working on Russell's third and fourth recommendations: find new projects abroad to pad the firm's bank accounts, and incorporate the firm to protect the founders from individual loss. By the 1950s, management consultants were advocating incorporation. The BAH consultants were promoting, in the firms for which they worked, ideas developed by business guru Peter Drucker, whose book *Concept of the Corporation* was published the same year that DM&J was formed, 1946.[39] As the US government became dependent on private enterprises to assist with postwar redevelopment as well as to build up a global military infrastructure, it offered legal protections through incorporation to those willing to take such risks. As mentioned earlier, incorporation provided liability benefits to individuals, enabled companies to expand abroad, and boosted profits. The Revenue Act of 1945 set corporate income tax rates below individual rates, which made corporations more financially advantageous than partnerships or sole proprietorships, wherein architects filed taxes individually.[40]

Following Russell's final recommendations, the DMJM partners pressed forward by cautiously incorporating the firm in 1952, according to the corporate charter filed with the California secretary of state (figure 7). DMJM's internal records indicate that the firm was first incorporated as "DMJM International" to facilitate the designing of military bases and infrastructure abroad, prior to the incorporation of the US-based firm "DMJM Architects and Engineers" in 1960, soon before nearly a hundred military bases would be closed in a cost-cutting plan and military work shifted back to the US.[41]

While only partially explaining how this work came to be and how it impacted the trajectory of the firm, this logic—to incorporate an international company before a domestic office—was aligned with the vision of incorporation established by Adam Smith in his *Wealth of Nations*, discussed in chapter 1. To recall, he believed that incorporation should be reserved for businesses working on high-risk, large-scale projects abroad on behalf of the state.[42] In Smith's view, incorporation at home should be reserved for enterprises

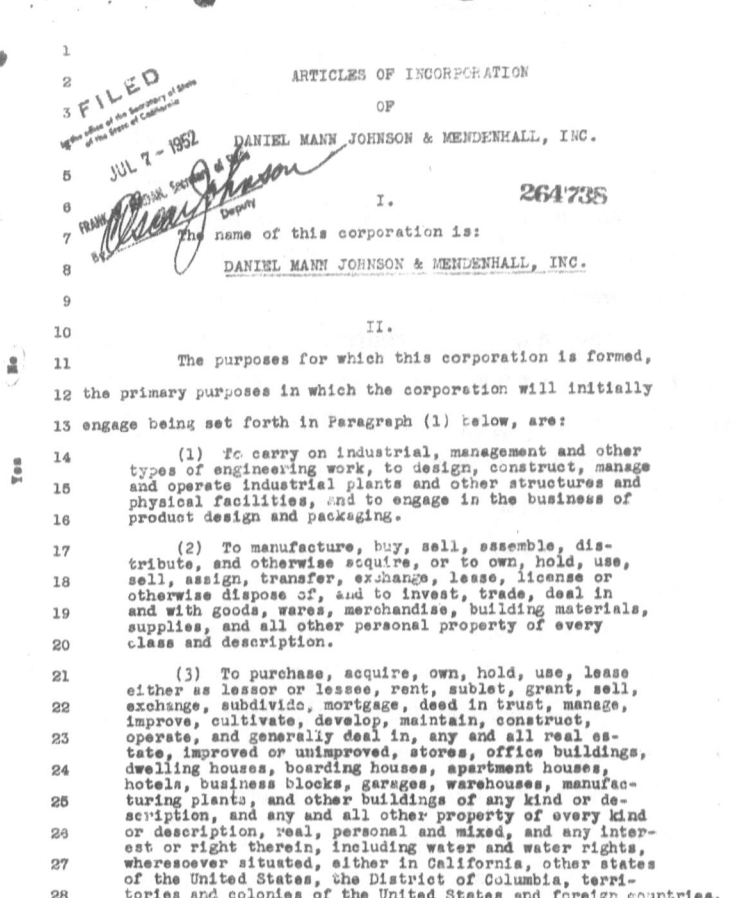

FIGURE 7. DMJM's articles of incorporation, 1952. California Secretary of State.

providing public services, such as the construction of bridges, highways, and schools. All others should be organized as partnerships. For architects, incorporation provided a legal means of financial protection, but it did so through the construction of material "bridges"—infrastructure—through which capital, labor, and resources could flow between "developing" and developed regions, as well as between states and private enterprises.

When DMJM was incorporated in 1952, Mendenhall assumed the position of president. Above him was a newly formed board of directors, which advised the firm and shielded the partners from individual liability. Stanley Moe, the sixth partner, was also hired, as well as an additional principal, Tevfik "Tef" Kutay, who oversaw business development. By 1960, the firm offered six services—master planning, architectural planning and design, engineering planning and design, systems engineering, construction management and supervision, and process engineering—and the firm's employees were described as wide-ranging in their skills, which enabled the firm to compete for projects with greater complexity. The firm employed not only architects and structural engineers, but also nuclear engineers, physicists, mathematicians, microwave engineers, surveyors, and statisticians.[43]

By the time of incorporation, DMJM had moved offices again, from the Sunset Boulevard office to a third and larger Los Angeles office at 3325 Wilshire Boulevard in 1956, where they remained until 1971. In striking contrast to the messiness of unpaid bills and stacks of paperwork that had typified the firm a decade earlier, drafting tables were now rigidly organized in long rows unobstructed by walls or columns, at which (mostly) men in button-down shirts and black ties worked (figure 8). Thus, incorporation ushered in a clean, white, and orderly image of work for architecture firms such as DMJM, as captured by Los Angeles–based photographer Julius Shulman in 1963.

As DMJM formalized its corporate identity, architecture journals were following a similar path, merging into larger publishing conglomerates. As previously mentioned, the diversifying publishing company McGraw Hill acquired *Architectural Record* in 1961, and the entertainment giant Billboard acquired *Architectural Forum* in 1972, after it had passed through the hands of Time Inc. (1932–64), Urban

FIGURE 8. DMJM's office at 3325 Wilshire Boulevard, Los Angeles, 1963. Photo by Julius Shulman. © J. Paul Getty Trust. Getty Research Institute, Los Angeles (2004.R.10).

America Inc. (1964–69), and Whitney Publications (1970–74). These acquisitions were marking a broader trend in which even the narratives of architectural practice were subsumed under corporate frameworks, focusing the public's attention on revenue and organization.

In 1958, when *Architectural Forum* was still owned by Time Inc., DMJM was ranked as the second "biggest" architectural firm in the US, measured by the dollar value of construction, in a listing akin to the Fortune 500 by no coincidence: *Time* and *Fortune* shared a founder.[44] By then, DMJM employed 480 people and had surpassed Perkins & Will, Albert Kahn Associates, and SOM in revenue, though still not in size. This suggested that profit, rather than size, had become a new metric of power and merit in architectural practice.

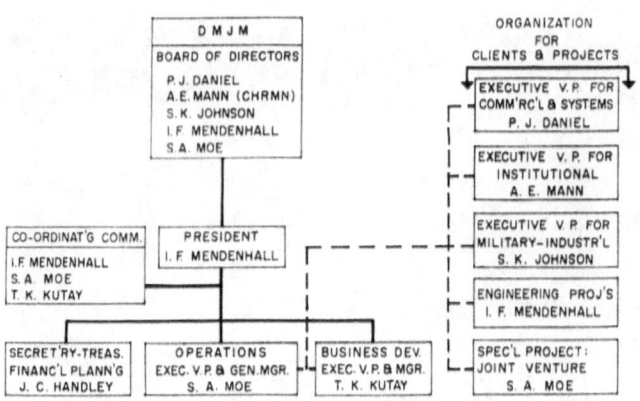

FIGURE 9. Firm organization chart, DMJM, 1960. From *Architectural Record*, June 1960, 190. © Architectural Record.

Perkins & Will, Albert Kahn Associates, and SOM employed 180, 200, and 1,060 people, respectively, though they began to fall in revenue-based rankings between 1957 and 1958.[45] In 1958, DMJM was also recognized by the Los Angeles City Council for its revenue, as well as for its contributions to the city's business growth.[46]

Finally, incorporation meant a reorganization of work. Organizational diagrams and flow charts, produced at companies like DMJM during the 1950s and published in journals such as *Architectural Record*, revealed not only a shift away from nineteenth-century partnerships centered around individuals, but also a shift away from a Fordist economy of work. *Architectural Record*, founded in 1891 by Clinton W. Sweet, the publisher of the *Real Estate Record and Builders' Guide*, was then owned by the F.W. Dodge Corporation (though acquired a year later)—an architecture and engineering firm interested in promoting its work as well as broader construction trends in professional journals. The firm's organization chart was published in a 1960 issue, and it reflected an overarching attention to administration and business development rather than to design work, as well as an emerging distinction between manual and nonmanual architectural labor (figure 9).

Within the *Architectural Record* organization chart, the firm's founders were named executive vice presidents and were responsible both for duties on the corporation's governing board of directors and for the marketing of new work in respect to each partner's individual interests. The tasks of marketing and procuring new work, however, were diagrammed as part of a semiautonomous subsection, the "Organization for Clients & Projects." More tellingly, this work was connected to the firm only by dashed lines that connected at the midpoint between "Operations" and "Business Development." The dashed line exemplified a distinction between manual drawing labor and business labor, though both were done by architects; therefore, the corporate organization chart made visible an early shift from Fordist to post-Fordist practice, since "Operations"—which encompassed the production of drawings—was now understood to be only indirectly connected to the marketing, supervision, and overseeing of the firm's business development.

These external relationships provided both stability and a steady stream of diversified projects to the office, but they also suggested that DMJM was as focused on the organization of the firm as it was on the opportunities at its disciplinary and geographic "periphery." The term *periphery* peppered the firm's *Standard Practices Manual*, first outlined in 1964, which included the firm's goals as well as diagrams of firm hierarchies, standard contract forms, purchase orders, and specific protocols and procedures for conducting business.[47] A section titled "Intra-company Relationships," added in 1969, described the firm as nonhierarchical in its social structure and explicitly oriented "outward"—attuned to the political and economic conditions "outside" the firm. Two of the clearest intra-company goals were outlined as (1) "avoidance of status levels, one organizational unit relative to another"; and (2) "emphasis on the *peripheral* organization elements which constitute our primary relationships to the outside world and clientele."⁴⁸ In a 1960 article in *Architectural Record*, the editors described DMJM as a firm that explicitly emphasized its "Extra-professional Activities":

> Growth of the DMJM practice has brought with it an increasing awareness of, and participation in outside activities by the firm members and employees. Increasingly, it has become apparent that the progress of the organization, dependent as it is on efficient service to its client is almost equally dependent on the outside activities of the firm. So DMJM gets itself involved (as a firm and individually) in a great number of civic and other peripheral pursuits.... In this way, the firm and its members become more important and integral members of their communities and of society than would be possible within the strict confines of professional practice.⁴⁹

Conglomeration

While the shift from a partnership to a corporation provided DMJM with legal benefits related primarily to liability and taxes, it also reinforced the firm itself as an irreducible and commodifiable unit of capitalist development. DMJM's articles of incorporation rid it of any remnant of individuality except in its name, defining the company as a human-like body able to "acquire, by purchase or otherwise, the goodwill, business, property rights, franchises and assets of every kind ... of any person, firm, association or corporation."⁵⁰ As new expertise was needed, DMJM could acquire entire companies and their assets, rather than merely hiring the chief laborer himself, which was a strategy for expanding into new markets and geographies and for mitigating competition.

An early acquisition occurred in 1965, when the engineering division of a small architecture and engineering office, Alexander & Dorman Architect/Engineer of Hanford, California, was acquired so that its founder, Albert Dorman, could work for DMJM as engineering project director. By 1970, Dorman had been elevated to oversee all corporate development, and he was named president and then chief executive officer in 1977, following Phillip Daniel's abrupt death from a heart attack at work in 1972 at age sixty and Johnson's death in 1974 at age sixty-two. It was immediately after Daniel's and Johnson's deaths that acquisitions of additional companies under Dorman's leadership ramped up. While these deaths were no doubt tragic, the firm was not only prepared to manage the cycles of life and death, it was financially fueled by them. For one seemingly minor yet telling example, DMJM's *Standard Practices Manual* set a maximum age of employees (sixty-five years old) and maximum rates to spend on condolence gifts for important events in employees' families. Death was worth more than life: $10.00 in flowers for a funeral, $7.50 in flowers for a new baby. The careers of women workers also died when new life began: the manual set a mandatory maternity "termination" for women after their sixth month of pregnancy.[51]

As president, Dorman added to the firm's *Standard Practices Manual*, including a new section on "Corporate Objectives," which would become the founding text for AECOM in 1990. In it, he described the firm's long-term financial and professional goals, correlating profit with new subsidiaries and acquisitions: the firm's geographic span should be widened by acquiring firms in "international markets" and "new professional fields."[52]

A revised organization chart was published in a rare twelve-page colored feature on the firm's projects and business methods in an issue of *Progressive Architecture* (*P/A*) in 1972—the year Daniel died (figure 10). By the early 1970s, *P/A*, which began in 1920 as *Pencil Points*, was owned by the Reinhold Publishing Corporation. One part of a complex web of subsidiary organizations (not unlike DMJM itself), Reinhold was a subsidiary of Litton Publications—a division of

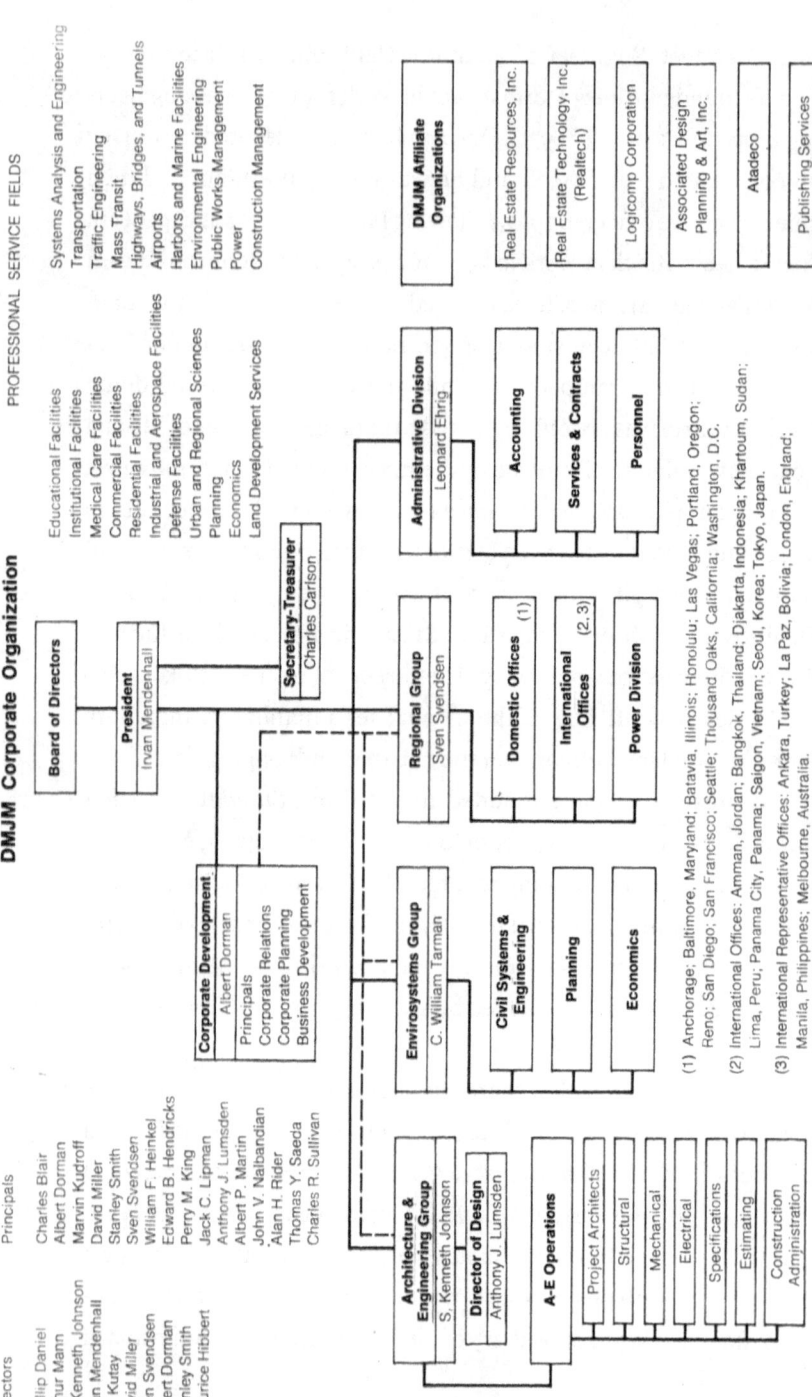

FIGURE 10. Corporate organization chart, DMJM, 1972. From *Progressive Architecture*, June 1972, 78. © Informa Group.

the large Cold War defense contractor Litton Industries, headquartered in Beverly Hills and one of the largest conglomerates in the US, which began to suffer financially during the 1970s before turning back to defense work in the 1980s.

Not only did the publication of the DMJM profile and revised organization chart immediately precede a sharp recession in building construction in 1973 and a surge in acquisitions in architecture, but it also coincided with the consent decree issued by the American Institute of Architects, under pressure from the Department of Justice. Further, it coincided with the publication of Peter Drucker's revised synthesis of the corporate form, in which he announced a post-Fordist turn.[53]

While DMJM's 1960 organization chart, published in *Architectural Record*, was shared openly with the publisher and reproduced as it appeared in DMJM's business manuals, the 1972 organization chart was provided to *P/A* and redrawn by a new class of contracted staff illustrators at the magazine, in its own established style and typeface—a tertiary representation of the firm's organization. As the pages were laid out, managing editor John Morris Dixon recalls, spaces were reserved for the diagrams and the published versions were fit to those spaces.[54]

The published chart presented the firm as a series of "groups" with divisions organized beneath them. In addition, six independent subsidiaries appeared on the chart as "DMJM Affiliate Organizations," emphasizing a more distinct separation between the firm and its "peripheral" or "subsidiary" organizations. These were organizations that had appeared in name only on the firm's detail-less brochures found in family archives—autonomous entities that, according to the *P/A* chart, were no longer physically attached to the firm in ways that could be represented by diagrammatic lines. Subsidiaries thus challenged the very function of an organization chart as a mechanism through which to understand an architectural firm. Lines that traditionally connected each of the firm's departments no longer applied, since the relationship between the affiliated companies to DMJM was primarily economic and contractual. As a further demonstration of labor's reconfigured relationship to capital, the drawing work—historically the focus of an architect's work—was described in the same *P/A* article as internally focused and "labor *intensive*," while its accumulated subsidiaries and affiliated companies—the so-called "profit centers"—were described as externally focused and "capital *extensive*."[55] The chart reproduced the center-periphery relationship by allowing a high-labor, low-profit center to exploit a high-profit, low-labor periphery.

By then, DMJM had surged to seven hundred employees, the number of the firm's services had increased from six in the 1960s to twenty-two, and the firm's services included "Planning, Architecture, Engineering, Systems, and Economics." Despite drastic reductions in the profits of many architecture and engineering practices as a result of a slowing economy during the recession of 1973, DMJM's gross revenue and profit were at an all-time high.

In 1966, DMJM was ranked within the *Engineering News-Record*'s "Top 500 Design Firms," the architectural equivalent to the Fortune 500, as the second largest architecture and engineering firm in the US in terms of revenue—second only to the engineering firm Giffels & Rosetti of Detroit.[56] By the 1980s, however, at a time when several pages of *ENR* listings were dedicated to subsidiary firms, there were only a few firms ranked above DMJM—such as the Planning Research Corporation, which was only years away from becoming part of DMJM.[57]

While the numerous revisions to the firm's organization charts were widely published in architecture and engineering journals, the company kept private a different kind of diagram—an "organizational concept" that was not publicized. In striking contrast to the vertically organized business charts, the organizational concept was instead a "circular diagram," first developed in 1968 and modified several times thereafter.[58] A radial distribution of employees promoted a greater expansion of services and better reflected the nonvertical hierarchical structure that the architects and engineers had espoused before incorporation. Besides de-emphasizing a top-down approach to management, the circular diagram also implied a spatial, centripetal arrangement with a clearly defined center, which added an inherent emphasis on the inside and the periphery of the firm. "The radial arrangement," the manual described, ensured that "no such organizational unit is further removed from central Company management than any other."[59] At the center was the corporate board of directors, farthest from the outer edge and therefore in the most secure of positions, while those closer to the circle's edge appeared less protected. This new arrangement was intended to help stimulate growth beyond architecture, as well as to provide an "appealing and workable framework for integration of other highly professional firms which wish to merge their interests with DMJM." Yet, as already discussed, circular organizational concepts—with the core group of workers in the center and with affiliates, associates, and subcontractors at the edge—were specifically used to illustrate the "flexible" means of accumulation under post-Fordism. Workers—subcontractors, consultants, freelancers, and temporary workers—and geographies on the "outside" were in the most precarious positions.[60]

One example of the "flexibility" and precarity of those working at the outer edge of the firm can be found in a DMJM subsidiary, Technical Management Services Inc. (TMSI). According to company brochures, the subsidiary was intended to perform "worldwide construction management, base operations and maintenance, and facilities management services."[61] As one architect described it, however, TMSI was a "rent-a-body-contractor" that facilitated the migration of temporary, non-salaried contract workers from developed to "developing" nations. In Saudi Arabia, for example, TMSI facilitated the travel of English-speaking professionals, such as engineers, architects, and nurses, from the US and the UK; these professionals were assigned to work for one to three years for companies such as the Saudi Arabian oil company ARAMCO, where they were provided housing as an incentive. At ARAMCO, DMJM completed many proposals for "new towns" and "satellite cities." Through TMSI, contractors also helped form and operate public organizations, such as the Saudi Arabia Public Transport Company (SAPTCO).[62]

By the mid-1970s, DMJM represented a corporate model of profitability that was attractive to a number of local companies in California, precisely because the firm had figured out how to absorb and manage what many within the office referred to as the hyperindividualistic architect. As Dorman later described, accounting and law firms in Southern California began to study DMJM, viewing it as a model for their own practices because their growth, and thus their longevity, was restrained by unrelenting individuality.[63]

Only in the mid-1970s did the firm's own publications begin to use the term *conglomerate* to describe DMJM. In a 1976 edition of the self-published journal *DMJM Review*, the vice president and manager of the Architecture and Engineering division asserted: "This professional conglomeration [DMJM] is called a 'multidisciplinary team'— and DMJM was one of the very first firms in the post–World War II era to assemble such an organization. That it has proven itself effective is evidenced by the fact that now many organizations are emulating the 'multidisciplinary' approach to building design."[64]

Importantly, however, despite the emphatic rhetoric of novelty, the term *conglomerate* was not universally accepted among all architects nor all the profession's business leaders.[65] Indeed, at DMJM, several architects vehemently denied such assertions, citing the fact that the subsidiaries and services of DMJM were all closely related to architecture. This revealed an anxiety about departing from modernist conceptions of architecture work: "DMJM was not a conglomerate," Dorman sharply disputed, "it was just an *extremely* diverse, modern firm."[66] Nonetheless, the inconsistent use of and debate about the term *conglomerate* was mirrored by increasingly broad definitions of the term developed by the federal government and signaled a new discursive formation within architectural practice by drawing particular attention to the boundary, scope, and value of architecture under late capitalism.[67]

In 1977, DMJM hired engineer-cum-businessman Richard Newman as deputy CEO, and Newman helped ramp up the firm's merger and acquisition activity, which was made apparent in DMJM's (and later AECOM's) chronology of acquired firms (figure 11). Prior to joining DMJM, Newman had served as president of Genge, one of the earliest architecture and engineering companies to be publicly listed on the stock market, which had grown by acquiring other companies. At Genge, Newman had acquired firms to establish a national network of subsidiaries, which *ENR* described in 1973 as a "stable of firms," implying that they could easily be purchased and sold, as needed, and Newman was featured on the cover of the magazine.[68]

Acquisitions ranged from Hilton Engineers of Portland, Oregon, in 1974, which formed DMJM-Hilton, to Curtis and Davis Architects and Engineers in 1976, which drew Arthur Q. Davis into the firm to provide a strong architectural presence in New Orleans. As one architect described, the strategy for acquiring and merging with firms was based on a hegemonic interest in reaching "beneath" other firms and geographies: "While this was much later, there were a couple acquisitions we did that really spoke to our strategy early on. There was a niche Chicago company that did foundation design for large state-of-the-art building towers like the Sears Tower. They were working with all of the big firms, like KPF and SOM and Foster. . . . The idea was that all of them [the big firms] would have to use our services. . . . It

FIGURE 11. Firms acquired, merged, or developed by DMJM (1946–1984), Ashland Technology (1985–1989), and AECOM (1990–2017). Drawn by Rahul Balla and Ayana Johnson.

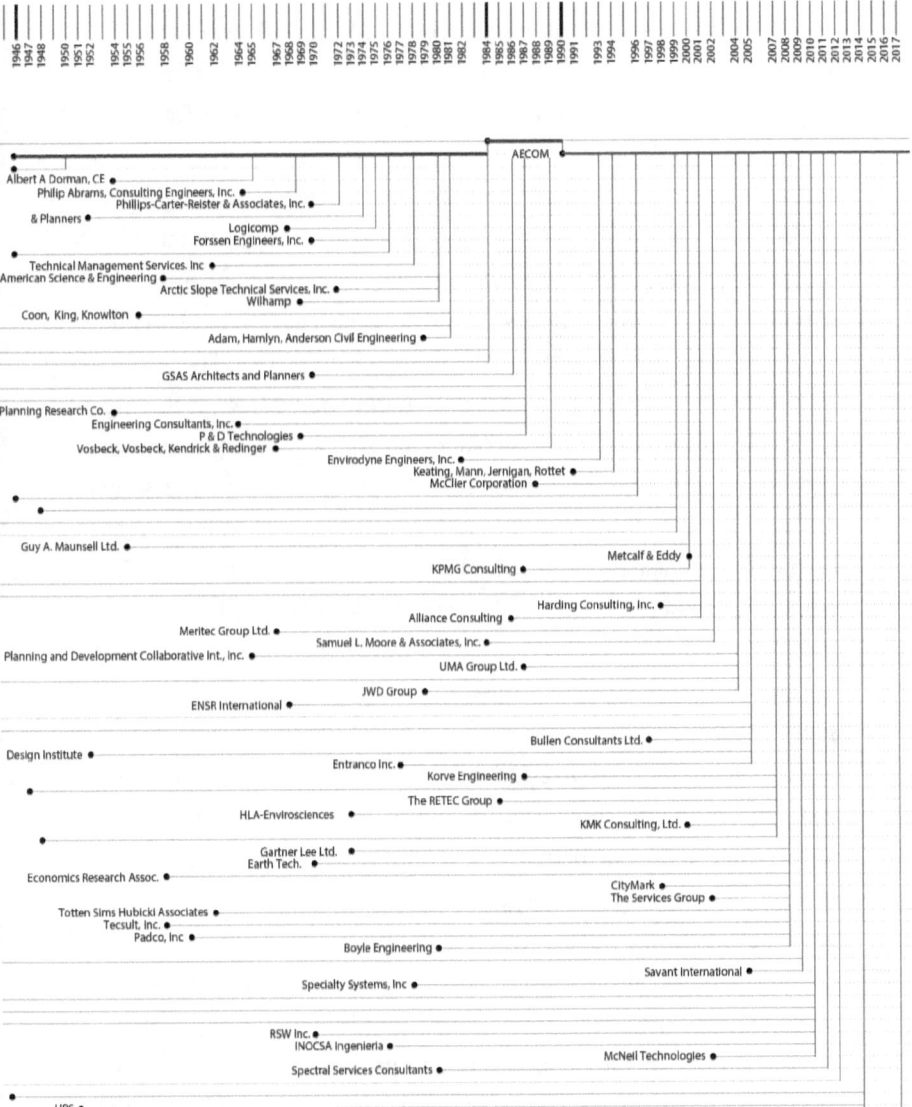

seemed to me that we were always trying to get beneath everyone else in one way or another with our M&As [mergers and acquisitions]."[69]

Another important subsidiary company was Logicomp, founded in 1971 by DMJM founding architect Phillip Daniel, which was an affiliated data-processing and computer-service firm formed initially at DMJM for the US Army Corps of Engineers research laboratory.[70] The company provided and maintained all computer and communication equipment and services for DMJM as well as other independent companies, installing and maintaining a Univac 9300 Data Communications System for data computation at DMJM, including a Univac 1108S that provided the "pulse" to the computation process.[71] The Univac computer system was operated primarily by women as part of secretarial work, which was still independent of drawing or business work. In addition to being hired for secretarial work, some women were hired as architects by DMJM throughout the 1970s, though very few made their way to the ranks of administration. Additional subsidiaries during the 1970s included a space-planning and interior-design affiliate company, Associated Design, Planning and Art (ADPA), as well as a loosely defined company, Atadeco, which was initially established as a shell within which architects and planners first worked on top-secret aerial surveillance projects for the government, using DMJM's company airplane; Atadeco was later used for construction contract management. Finally, DMJM's Economics Department operated independently, conducting financial analyses for a range of development projects, including office buildings, condominiums, apartments, and marinas. By the end of the 1970s, DMJM had become a bona fide corporate conglomerate that included a package of geographically diverse firms and multidisciplinary services, with fourteen subsidiaries listed in ENR, ranging from real estate to management to construction supervision to cosmic X-rays to computer data processing.[72]

Office

DMJM's own office was the result of a working relationship with some of the firm's more closely related subsidiaries. One such subsidiary was Real Estate Resources (RER), a development company co-owned by DMJM vice president Tef Kutay, which included its own subsidiary, Real Estate Technology Inc. (Realtech); DMJM's effective ownership of RER was 32 percent.[73] Realtech spun into one of the largest real estate development companies in Los Angeles, and during the 1970s served as a crucial vehicle for commercial investment for DMJM, since it could take greater financial risks as owner or co-owner for clients. A built illustration of their working relationship was a DMJM and Realtech collaboration in 1971, when Realtech acquired the land to develop a new office for DMJM in Los Angeles that could reflect its new structure; DMJM and Realtech co-owned the building.

Designed by DMJM architect Anthony Lumsden, the office building, named One Park Plaza, was constructed on Wilshire Boulevard. It comprised a twenty-two-story tower and a longer low-rise podium attached for parking and office space (figure 12). Clad in dark, earthy brown-tinted glass, a common material choice for Lumsden, the building caught the eye of Los Angeles critics as it joined a chorus of similarly clad office buildings rising in the 1970s. Critic John Pastier, for example, who titled a 1974 article "What's Brown—Brown All Over?" for the *Los Angeles Times*, wrote that there was nothing wrong with the buildings per se, but that there were simply "too many" of them and that they represented an "umber glut."[74]

Formally, One Park Plaza was notable because its tower had no base—the façade led directly to the ground—and thus the brown glass made for a visually seamless transition. Beyond material conditions, however, the tower was unique because it presented four corners that rounded and protruded outward—a technique similarly

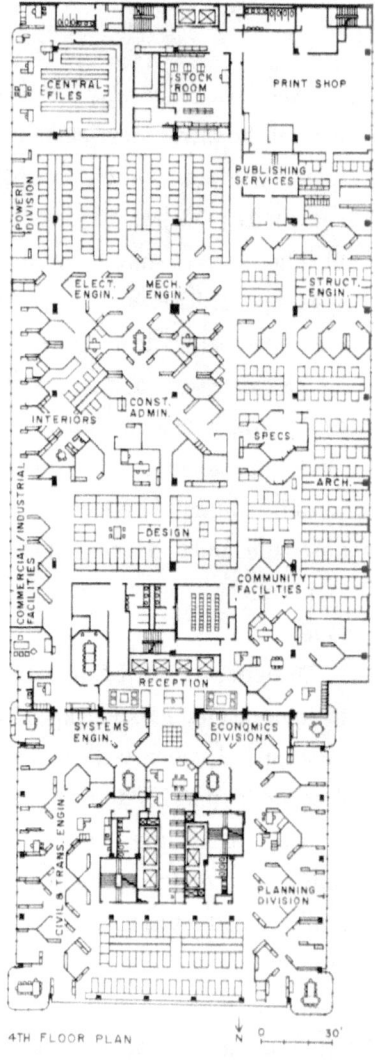

FIGURE 12. DMJM office building, One Park Plaza, Los Angeles, 1971. Photo by Wayne Thom. Wayne Thom Photography Collection, USC Digital Library.

FIGURE 13. Fourth-floor plan of DMJM's office in One Park Plaza, Los Angeles, 1971. From *Progressive Architecture*, June 1972, 82. © Informa Group.

used in the design of buildings at places like Disneyland—to humanize the otherwise sharp ninety-degree corners and thus make workers and passersby feel comfortable with the otherwise austere corporation.[75] On DMJM's floors, the four corners enclosed four offices of the firm's founders: Daniel, Mann, Johnson, and Mendenhall. From

FIGURE 14. DMJM office in One Park Plaza, Los Angeles, 1971. Papers of Arthur Mann. Private collection. Courtesy of Karen Letterman.

within them, the bulging corners offered 270-degree views of the city below.[76]

DMJM occupied the fourth and fifth floors of the building. On the fourth floor, codependent groups, such as "planning," "construction administration," "economics," and "planning," were organized on what was known as the main "production" area (figure 13). Rather than using a rigid grid of cubicles and corridors to organize desks, as was common in modernist architecture offices, employees were provided adjustable five-panel desk systems—systems introduced by Herman Miller only five years prior—that hinged at each joint, offering employees the option to customize the perimeter of the workspace with their office neighbors (figure 14).

As in the firm's organization chart, the "design" area was differentiated from the "architecture" area where most drawing and drafting were done, while engineering and "production" radiated outward.[77] The corporate offices—accounting, personnel, contracts, communications, and administrative—were lofted above, demonstrating that the freely disintegrated vertical relationships of the building's section were as important to DMJM as subjecting other firms, cities, and regions to horizontal control. To focus on the "periphery" was to focus not only on the façade, but also on the building's floors—as one related to another—and the radical span of companies that occupied them.

Since DMJM was involved as the building's co-owner in selecting its tenants, the building's renters were curated as part of the office's "design." DMJM's own subsidiaries, including Realtech and Logicomp, occupied spaces above and below the company's "official" floors. On the ground floor was ten thousand square feet of office space rented by the Bank of California; there was twenty-one thousand square feet for the Univac Computer Division of the Sperry Rand Corporation above and below DMJM's floors. The office building had thus become a vertical diagram of the economic interdependency espoused by the DMJM conglomerate and its friends. Above the first floor were offices for insurance companies, the Philippine Consulate, attorneys' offices, a tobacco boutique, travel agencies, a restaurant, and an advertising agency.[78]

This practice of vertically disintegrated organizing has more recently typified other architecture firms with subsidiaries that have organized entire corporations around a particular floor, rather than a particular identity of work. The example of SHoP Architects in New York makes this most clear, as some of the firm's floors have the same names as some of the firm's subsidiaries: Shopw25participant LLC, Shopw25thirdfloor LLC, Shopw25fourthfloor LLC.[79]

Urban System of Governance

Although the small, architect-only partnership of DM&J in 1946 was hardly recognizable within what the company had become, DMJM

CEO Albert Dorman argued that the emphasis after the 1970s would not be on the narrowly focused designing of buildings nor on the identification of specific building types, but rather on "the total social and environmental context of the project." The individual building, he argued, "will be viewed from this perspective. Since social and environmental issues are very complex, it will take complex interdisciplinary teams to approach them. Therefore, the firms of the future will be very large (by today's standards) to include the variety of disciplines required."[80] By emphasizing the context of a building, rather than the building itself, Dorman was shifting the role of architects and engineers from designers of buildings to designers of firms themselves. DMJM would not be wed strictly to a particular building type or to a region: "We were not going be a school firm like Perkins and Will. We were not going to be a high-rise firm like SOM. We were going to be everywhere. Because my own observation was that things went up and down due to funding. The Northeast [United States] might be dead, and the Southwest might be booming; schools [buildings] might be the biggest thing in the world, and then highways might be booming. It would cost us money. When a discipline or a region went down, we would pay a price for it. But overall, we would be steady."[81]

The synchronicity of the firm and the urban economy was made clear in a diagram for an experimental city developed by DMJM planners and architects.[82] Drawn as a circular "urban system" that directly echoed the work of DMJM, the hypothetical city comprised twelve "subsystems," each of which was outlined as a bounded component that neither touched nor overlapped the others (figure 15).[83] As for the services offered by DMJM, the "urban system" comprised social, economic, political, and physical subsystems. Architecture was designated as only part of the "physical" attributes of the city—not at all touching the political or economic components, and directly opposite to nonmaterial social and cultural subsystems. However, when considering the range of practices and the scope of work

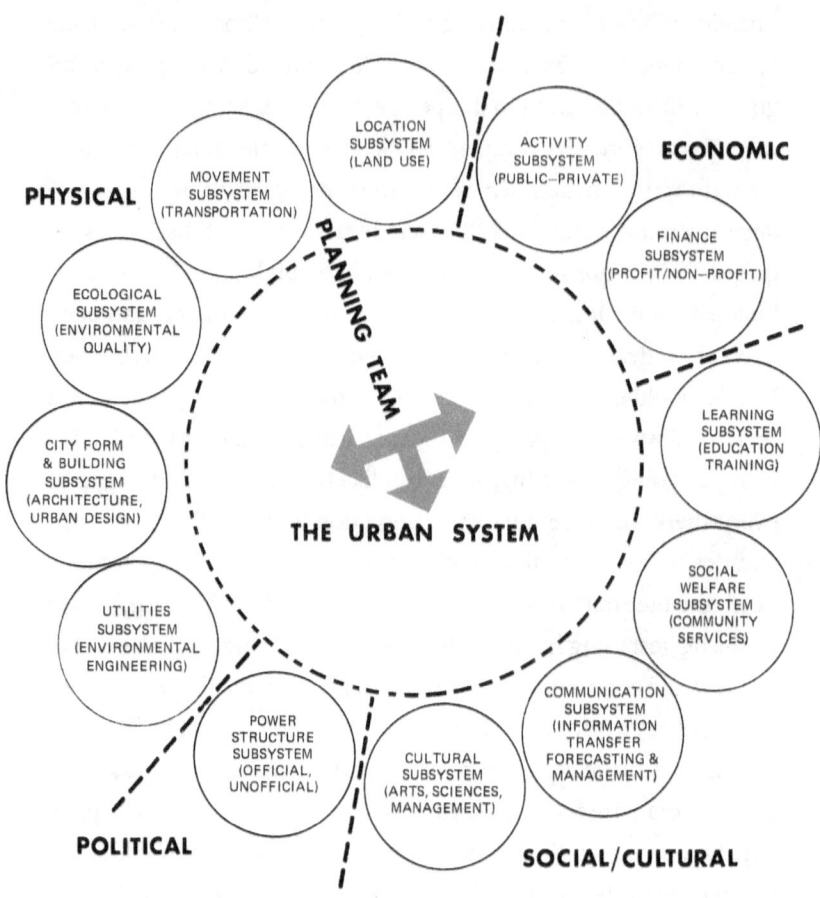

FIGURE 15. "The Urban System and Subsystems." From DMJM, *Proposal for an Experimental City*, 1968. California State University Dominguez Hills Special Collections, Dominguez Hills, California.

FIGURE 16. DMJM site development for Century City. Photo by Robert Earl Spence. From *A Presentation of the Work of Daniel, Mann, Johnson, & Mendenhall: Company General Brochure*, 1967. © AECOM. Stanley Moe Papers, Huntington Library, San Marino, California.

in which architects were actively engaged, through subsidiaries and affiliated companies, the field of architecture was much wider than the diagram reveals. Beyond merely the "City Form and Building" subsystem, DMJM's practices—from real estate to computer services to economic consulting—exemplified the economic, sociocultural, and political dimensions of the firm's imagined urban economy as well.

The slow process of designing a responsive architectural practice through corporate conglomeration, therefore, resulted in a precise attunement to the process of urbanization that yielded an urban system of governance. It was a response to the crisis of overaccumulation. Therefore, while DMJM itself was not directly investing in the built environment, the allocation of profits to the development and acquisition of new firms in tune with the shifting demands of urbanization enabled architectural practice not only to take the very shape of the urban economy in which the firm was embedded, but also to allow a wide-ranging and multinational conglomerate firm, such as DMJM, to produce, reproduce, and govern such economies. Beyond the abstracted diagrams of cities, Los Angeles itself made this clear. DMJM was carving out space for "total site development" during the middle of the 1950s on the city's edge, turning 180 acres of land, once used as a studio backlot for 20th Century Studios, into Century City—a $4.5 million subdivision for twelve thousand people, according to DMJM's company brochures, and "the largest earthmoving project ever completed in Southern California" (figure 16).[84]

AECOM

By the 1980s, conglomeration had expanded to oil companies, which diversified in response to unstable oil markets in the Middle East and antimonopoly efforts by the US Department of Justice. With its experience managing a wide spectrum of architectural and engineering services, DMJM was acquired in 1984 by a Kentucky-based oil company, Ashland Oil Inc.—a diversified corporation with operations ranging from petroleum to insurance and the parent of Valvoline Oil. Ashland's chief operating officer, John Hall, explained in a 1986 annual report that the company was forced to shift away from strictly oil refining and gasoline production, toward "high-technology" products and services. Hall noted that "back in the 1960s, our chief strategy was to push more oil through the refineries, make more gasoline, sell more gasoline. . . . It doesn't work like that anymore. The world has changed. You've got to have a different *twist*."[85] Unlike oil giants such as Exxon or Gulf, the smaller Ashland was required to think more broadly to maintain economic stability. Ashland acquired DMJM so that the latter's corporate leadership could manage previously acquired architecture and engineering companies. In 1985, Ashland Technology Corporation was formed as a subsidiary of Ashland Oil Inc., and Dorman was hired to take the reins of the new Ashland holding company, consisting of three architecture and engineering firms and their respective subsidiaries: DMJM, Holmes & Narver Inc., and Williams Brothers Engineering.[86]

Ashland Oil dipped into and out of the engineering and construction industry after its finances had strengthened by 1989. In 1990, Ashland withdrew from the engineering business, selling a majority interest in Ashland Technology, and Richard Newman initiated a $3 million employee stock ownership plan (an employee-led buyback) in April 1990, which resulted in an employee-owned multinational architecture and engineering firm, named AECOM Technology Corporation, which consisted of five so-called "legacy" companies that had been acquired during the five years of Ashland's holding: DMJM; Consoer, Townsend & Associates Inc.; Frederic R. Harris Inc.; Holmes & Narver Inc.; and P&D Technologies Inc.

While DMJM represented only one part of this new conglomerate of firms, its structures and ideals of practice were reproduced by AECOM, which named Dorman its first chairman of the board and CEO and Richard Newman its president.[87] AECOM's "Corporate Objectives" were nearly identical to DMJM's, written in 1974, including six potential areas of long-term professional, financial, and social goals. The objectives included an emphasis on the quality of work, professional standards, public reputation, and development of both individual employees and the firm.[88] However, the rhetoric of "growth" and "expansion" pervaded the objectives, as they had at DMJM, including an emphasis on change, adaptation, and an open-ended approach to practice. One of the six corporate objectives was "Growth in Services," which outlined the ways in which Dorman and Newman hoped to achieve 100 percent employee ownership, maintain strong profit margins, and plan for a "self-renewing" firm. Another was "Geographical Expansion," which described an effort to continue to diversify the corporation geographically (nationally and internationally) so that the firm was not wholly dependent on any single region. Yet another was "Expanded Activities"—the same phrase used by DMJM in the 1970s—which explicitly defined the firm's goals as expanding its technical, operational, maintenance, and managerial services and "merg[ing] into AECOM other related firms that would expand AECOM's range of services or geographic coverage."[89]

In a metaphoric nod to the thousands of employees that AECOM purported to unite under a new corporate identity, the annual report was sandwiched by pages of the individual names of thousands of "employee-stockholders," printed across several spreads in tiny font and in alphabetical order, with justified text that conformed to the margins of the page. In their first letter to the shareholders, Newman and Dorman argued that "in a literal as well as figurative sense, its employees *are* AECOM."[90] But the blocks of individual names could also be read as blocks of materials: embodiments of experience, capital, and labor, which demonstrated to the shareholders a sense of uniform, affective strength. The firm's new name, AECOM, no longer attached to the names of the founding partners, was reduced to its anonymized services. However, the name also provided for future flexibilities and open-ended possibilities. A and E were clear—architecture and engineering—yet the COM was left open-ended, a testament to the flexible and open-ended possibilities precipitated by late capitalist economics. It could be used to suggest Construction, Operations, and Management; or Contracts, Operations, and Maintenance; or Construction Management.[91]

Under a new generation of business management, AECOM was listed on the stock exchange in 2007, and the firm absorbed the individual names of its subsidiary companies, including DMJM—thus concealing the history of a firm that was fundamentally varied. Beyond "Architecture and Design," by 2017 AECOM included services as far-ranging as "IT and Cybersecurity," "Cost Management," and "Equity Investment," which enabled its practitioners not only to design buildings for their clients in ways that are familiar to histories of architectural practice, but also to build, finance, and operate them after they were constructed. The seemingly limitless scope of services offered by AECOM has enabled the firm to produce entire urban systems in ways that the founding architects at DMJM could only have imagined. As the senior vice president of AECOM asserted in 2010: "We are AECOM, we can do anything."[92]

The implications of this expanded scope of work were made visible by AECOM's new location in Los Angeles, as the firm moved its design offices in 2001 from DMJM's One Park Plaza on Wilshire Boulevard to the central business district of Downtown, embedding itself in a homogeneous sea of banks and financial institutions—a fitting juxtaposition for a firm that now offered financial services.[93] However, unlike financial institutions, which hold no inherent allegiance to the built environment, AECOM had become a direct conduit through which capital could be channeled into the built environment. The company's prominence was viewed as a barometer by which the strength of Los Angeles's urban economy could be measured. Despite this public recognition, the company had stretched itself so widely—no longer led by architects or engineers, but instead by accountants and attorneys—that in 2016 it allocated substantial funds to answering a profoundly paradoxical question: What is the role and value of the architect within such a firm? Though it may seem an AECOM-specific conundrum, the question reflects longstanding and recurring debates in architecture about the value of architects—both how they contribute to a large firm economically and how they influence economies more broadly. Indeed, it was precisely on the cyclical economy of fear—of loss—that the architecture business was based during the twentieth century.

The history of DMJM and AECOM begins to provide insight into this question. While one could argue that architects at DMJM helped expunge the historical role of the architect as they pursued growth and profit, I suggest instead that the rise and prominence of DMJM was predicated on the ability of its architects to elevate their own economic and political value, while also continually renewing their firms by expanding in accordance with anticipated shifts in the economy. By positioning themselves as equals—rather than superiors—to other urban practitioners, they demonstrated how architectural work could be lucrative within a post-Fordist economy. For better or worse, architects expanded the field of practice upon which they could operate.

However, the subsumption of the architect into capitalist trends does not come without caution or challenge. Like many large postwar architecture firms, DMJM peddled a predominantly white, male-dominated view of corporate practice, fueled by exploited and precarious labor and launched by government and military funding. The firm did not radically reimagine the labor traditionally associated with architectural production. The inability to *revise* or restructure in favor of addition demonstrates the uncritical and additive nature of capitalist production that defines not only business, but the built environment. Moreover, the infinite possibility of unrestrained neoliberal accumulation—fueled more recently by public finance capital and the ease of global circulation—poses an inherent ethical dilemma for professional architects. With a profession and political-economic policy moved by the momentum of corporations, the architect's geopolitical power appears limitless. As AECOM now lays the foundation—from material infrastructure to legal rights—for entire cities and urban regions, including those in developing regions across the world, the trajectory of corporate architectural practice may begin to evoke a wider range of architectural histories about discipline and governmentality.[94]

While a corporate firm such as DMJM may be an unexpected site upon which to launch a study about the values of architectural work, the firm's attunement to the inner workings of a capitalist economy is illuminating for a profession that has historically understood—especially in the United States—the pursuit of economic capital to be antithetical to architectural design. If histories of multinational conglomerates can offer views of architecture in which firms themselves, rather than merely the buildings they produce, are objects of design that reconcile capitalist possibility, urban imperatives, and architecture's disciplinarity, then such histories may also provide architects with models for expanding—or grounds for critiquing—the value of the architect within the profession and in the public sphere.

3 *Building*
Enclosing Indeterminacy

In 1959, *Architectural Forum* named corporate conglomerates as architects' "biggest clients." From AT&T and Teledyne to Union Carbide and DuPont, conglomerates were demanding new laboratories and office buildings to accommodate their new business structures.[1] However, the increasing diversity of subsidiaries within conglomerates and the unpredictability of their acquisitions presented a fundamental challenge to the organizational and aesthetic tendencies of modern architects: conglomerates defied standardization, reproducibility, and homogeneity, and thus indeterminacy was pitched to architects as a challenge for design. Those at firms such as DMJM, who had practice designing their own (similarly structured) businesses, were best prepared to turn this new architecture of business into the business of architecture.[2]

By the 1960s, architects were being hired to reconcile what seemed like an impossible contradiction. On the one hand, they were asked to design physical infrastructures that could support the open-ended interchange of subsidiaries within conglomerate businesses; on the other hand, they were asked to design façades to enclose them. This challenge reflected an intensification of what Louise Mozingo describes as *pastoral* capitalism, when corporations embraced suburban campuses after World War II to project ideals of control and tranquility while simultaneously housing increasingly fragmented business parts.³ The resulting buildings boasted highly reflective hermetic surfaces that protruded, curved, jogged, and folded in ways that expressed the mania for acquisitions within them. Critics, historians, and theorists of this period have described these enclosures as postmodern, given that they seemed to respond to underlying yet abstract shifts within the political economy; the façades, they argued, *represented* or *belonged to* "late capitalism."⁴ While these assertions may be true, to focus exclusively on the surface was to accept the concealing trap of conglomeration and skirt the attendant matters of businesses that explained their antagonistic strategies, power relationships, geopolitics, and effects.

Rather than retheorize these surface conditions, this chapter connects the enclosures of conglomerate buildings to the infrastructures of the businesses that made them necessary in order to more directly consider the antagonism of theory and practice that produced the very slow and subtle shifts from modernism to postmodernism as defined within urban and architectural discourse at the end of the twentieth century.

Conglomerate businesses, as Alfred Chandler described, were extreme outgrowths of *modern* firms; conglomerates emerged slowly and over an extended period.⁵ To this day, business historians regard conglomerates as diversified modern firms, though architectural historians and critics regard the surfaces that such businesses required as postmodern. Buildings, of course, are more than their enclosures. As this chapter will reveal, conglomerates, and thus the postmodern architecture they produced, were not derived from abstract socioeconomic relationships between capitalism and the built environment, nor were they reducible to surface conditions. Instead, they were designed by architects attuned to the geographical and political practices of profit- and power-seeking business that were wrapped up in the explosion of postwar growth and bracing for an inevitable economic downturn. More profoundly, this chapter documents how the term *conglomerate* transcended business and fully saturated discourse about form and aesthetics by the 1970s—what Sylvia Lavin has described as postmodernism's *effect*—in ways that were entirely removed from the term's meanings in business.[6] Not only used to describe the composition of advanced capitalist corporations, the term was used to describe the material and spatial ordering of postmodern buildings more generally. Architect Cesar Pelli, for instance, who worked at DMJM from 1964 to 1968, used the term *conglomerate* to describe projects with competing and seemingly divergent geometries, while architectural historian and theorist Charles Jencks used it in a similar manner to announce the arrival of postmodern architecture.[7]

Designers

The economic value of architectural design within DMJM had been called into question by 1960. With a growing portfolio of projects published in construction, engineering, and military journals, rather than in architecture journals, the firm's founding partners sought to balance DMJM's work by hiring reputable designers who were equally comfortable with bureaucracy to procure more traditionally "architectural" projects. Citing the firm's military work, Phillip Daniel argued that "we didn't want to be known only as industrial architects."[8] Moreover, the looming possibility that Cold War tensions would soon ease was coupled with technological advancements that threatened the future role of architects in military work more generally.

In order to avoid overdependence on military or engineering-dominant work, projects were distributed along the lines of the firm's divisions, such that each group (e.g., architecture, engineering, real estate) was responsible for its own projects. This concern for individual accountability was imperative to a multidisciplinary structure like DMJM's, and it was especially important as the firm acquired other firms. As one business leader described: "The issue with firms crawling with M and As [mergers and acquisitions] is how they are trading their shares internally, but also if the architects are ones that are comfortable and enjoy working at a growing corporation, rather than black cape guys who want to do their own thing. . . . They can't wait and be too dependent on others. . . . The architects and engineers have to go and get their own work . . . [and] make themselves visible."[9] Commenting on DMJM's position in a 1960 article in *Fortune* magazine, an anonymous California architect argued—citing "many architects" who regarded their work in terms of a *profession* rather than a *business*—that DMJM would have to make an economic sacrifice in order to achieve "first-rate architectural design."[10] Yet as a *business*, stripped of tacit professional standards and beliefs that ranked art over commerce, DMJM was not necessarily required to make a sacrifice; it merely had to hire architects who espoused the established capitalist logic and accepted the unwavering interest in profit by translating business procedure into architecture.

In 1964, DMJM hired young architects Cesar Pelli and Anthony Lumsden as design director and assistant, respectively. Both were associates at Eero Saarinen and Associates and its successor office Kevin Roche and John Dinkeloo and Associates. Saarinen and Pelli worked together on projects including the TWA Terminal at the Kennedy Airport in New York, and Lumsden, Roche, and Dinkeloo worked together on corporate headquarters and laboratories for companies such as IBM and Bell Telephone, a subsidiary of AT&T. Under Roche, Lumsden was the design manager for a new Bell Telephone Laboratories building in Holmdel, New Jersey, between 1957 and 1962.[11] Its now well-studied façade of reflective glass was cited as "The Biggest Mirror Ever" in *Architectural Forum* in 1967.[12] Less studied, however, was Lumsden's proposal to invert the structural mullions of the curtain wall to provide a continuously smooth surface to further conceal and smooth over the inner workings of the business. Despite the use of reflective mirror-glass and the distorted images of the environment that it captured on its surfaces, Roche ultimately rejected the proposal, because, in his modernist view, protruding vertical mullions were necessary to emphasize the standardization of business within.[13] This tension expressed the underlying shifts within the structure of businesses as they leaned into speculation more broadly and the underlying disagreements about how best to respond to these shifts architecturally.[14]

Once at DMJM, Pelli and Lumsden won design awards that helped elevate the perception of large architecture corporations in Los Angeles. In 1966, for instance, the Sunset International Petroleum Corporation commissioned DMJM to design a mountaintop housing community in Santa Monica, named Sunset Mountain Park, which was never built, though it received the First Design Award in 1966 from *Progressive Architecture* and was featured in a number of international architecture journals.[15]

DMJM also designed office buildings with mirror-glass façades throughout Los Angeles that challenged the uniformity of otherwise standardized, transparent, rectilinear, and low-cost corporate architecture. California architecture critic Esther McCoy argued that Pelli and Lumsden's projects pushed beyond the standard "kit of parts" typical of "the big office." "The big office," she suggested, "with its relentless flow of large-scale building, is often an agent through which change comes, even though the design comes out of the drawer. When the big offices pause to produce 'art' it is too often an essay into temple making, and the solution in the drawer might have been better for the city."[16] With the "tough mind" of Pelli in charge and Lumsden by his side, McCoy argued that DMJM was more sensitive than most to the tensions of the city, the city's economy, and its businesses. Together, they were compelled to "rethink design in terms of post-drawer needs. Commonsense architecture is lifted above dullness and it becomes the means through which the city is refreshed."[17] Not only did Pelli and Lumsden's projects help bolster DMJM's reputation as a preeminent design firm, they also helped establish a discourse about architecture in Los Angeles that was shaped by business.

Pelli and Lumsden were members of two prominent, though short-lived, Los Angeles design groups: the "Silvers," a group of architects known for the smooth, silver-like mirror-glass façades of their buildings; and the "LA Twelve," a group of twelve architects, in practice for twelve years or more, who exhibited twelve projects in 1976. Even though the practices of Pelli and Lumsden were underwritten by a firm that was growing by mergers and acquisitions, they were listed among the ranks of noted Southern California architects such as Craig Ellwood, Ray Kappe, John Lautner, and Frank Gehry.[18]

Growth

Pelli and Lumsden's theories of design were shaped by and helped produce corporate conglomerates—not only as DMJM was transforming into one before their eyes, but also as many of their clients were conglomerate enterprises acquiring companies in unrelated industries. One of Pelli and Lumsden's earliest projects at DMJM was a laboratory designed in 1966 for the microelectronics and semiconductor conglomerate Teledyne, a defense contractor during the Cold War whose growth during the 1960s characterized the proliferation of conglomerates in the US more broadly.[19]

Teledyne was established in 1960 by former Litton Industries executives Henry Singleton and George Kozmetsky when they acquired the stock of three existing microelectronics and control-systems companies and their two hundred employees.[20] (Litton Industries was a shrinking defense conglomerate in the business of communication, warfare, and navigation equipment; recall that it acquired the publishing house of *Progressive Architecture* in 1968—the magazine that had routinely featured the work of DMJM, granted its awards, and profiled its business.)[21] Fueled by the military and aerospace markets into which it lodged its systems technologies, Teledyne acquired seven companies in its first two years; by 1966, it was a Fortune 500 company with over five thousand employees.[22] By the end of the decade, the offerings of Teledyne's subsidiaries ranged from microelectronics to dental appliances and insurance, and Singleton described it as a "living plant." The individual subsidiaries within Teledyne represented different "branches"—each sprouting its own tertiary branches such that "no one business [was] too significant."[23] Singleton's decree of socioeconomic equivalency was a guiding tenant of corporate conglomeration: no one part could overshadow another. From this perspective, it was economically disadvantageous for any single person or business within the conglomerate to become *more* valuable than any other, which was an important and revealing caveat that, at DMJM, foreshadowed the abrupt end of Lumsden's tenure in 1993.

Singleton was an avid architectural philanthropist who commissioned Richard Neutra to design his own modernist glass house in Bel-Air in 1959 and Wallace Neff to design a second sprawling estate in Holmby Hills in 1973. Between these projects, he commissioned DMJM to design Teledyne Laboratories. Sited in a pastoral thirty-six-acre orange grove in Northridge, California, the manufacturing and research lab facility was completed in 1968. It included spaces for administration, engineering, and electronics assembly in compartmentalized rooms—rather than in a linear line of assembly (figure 17).

One of the biggest challenges in designing a building for a conglomerate business was reconciling the spatial demands of the present with the potentially divergent and far-flung subsidiaries of the future. Pelli argued that, like Singleton's "living plant" for

FIGURE 17. Rendering of Teledyne Laboratories, Northridge, California, 1968. © AECOM. Cesar Pelli Collection, Yale University Archives.

Teledyne as a whole, the labs building they were designing "could not be designed as a structure with a static future," since it would need to account for both flexibility and growth that could not yet be determined. In his descriptions of the project, Pelli asserted that "flexibility in architecture relates to the possibilities of change within a given area. Growth has to do with the addition of new areas and functions to existing ones."[24] He described the building as a dynamic "complex" comprising "several structures housing different functions" that was subject to expansion during any phase of its life.[25]

In Teledyne's site plan, dashed lines extended beyond the building's proposed walls to outline an expanded footprint, labeled "future expansion" (figure 18). These dashed lines were not unlike the dashed lines used in DMJM's own organization charts, which indicated the loose relationships between the firm's parts. In the Teledyne plan, the dashed spaces marked as "future" accounted for a new source of capital—speculation—that had an indirect and

Building: Enclosing Indeterminacy [117]

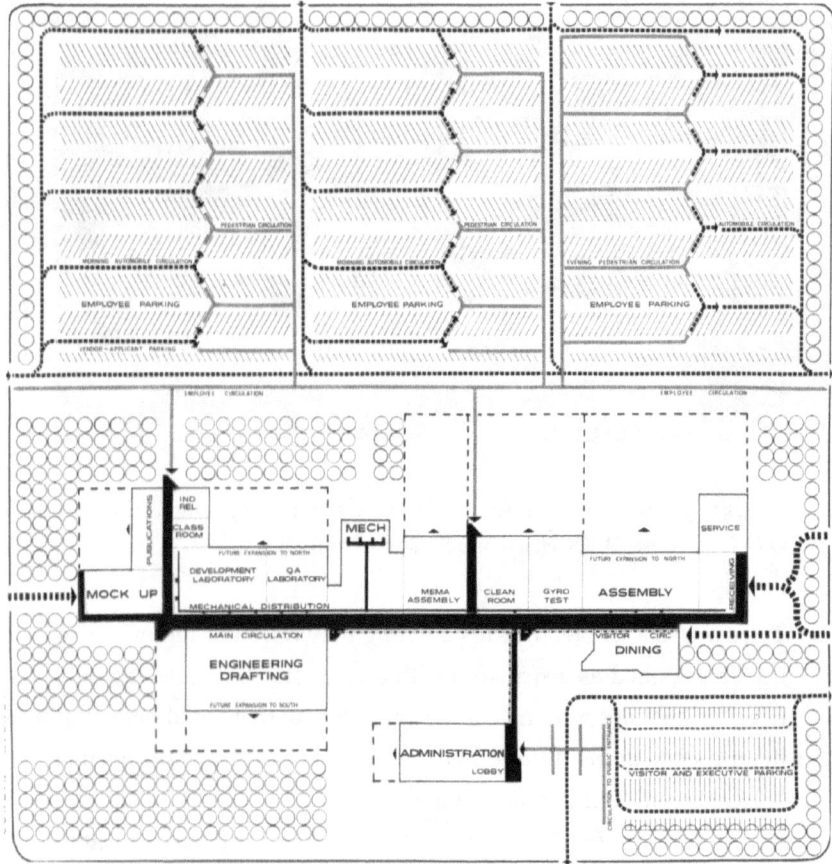

FIGURE 18. Site plan of Teledyne Laboratories, Northridge, California, 1968. Cesar Pelli Collection, Yale University Archives.

ambiguous relationship to the manual labor of microelectronics assembly. Even further, the administrative offices were pulled outward from the circulation core as a geographically transposed hierarchy based on north and south coordinates. The building quite literally took on the form of an organization chart transposed onto the ground, thereby maintaining the modernist relationship between form and function while also recognizing the difficulty of designing for a future business that did not yet exist.

Through the site plan, the conglomerate business was translated into spatial and geographic terms, and Pelli described the "complex" as perpetually incomplete and heterogeneous:

> One of the characteristics of growth or planning for growth is that it is different from what we thought it would be five years ago. To assume that you can add increments of the same thing five years later is unrealistic.... [Architects] prefer to think of something 'finished.' When they think of changes it is the changes inside a building.... By and large, architects are still designing temples. This is a static view of life, but today we recognize and welcome that life is change. Teledyne is not a building but a complex. Complexes are not homogenous; they are structures faced with problems of growth.... It is seldom possible to predetermine growth, and the problem is how to plan for undetermined growth without throwing the architecture away.[26]

Combining existing firms to create new "organisms" and building an image of rapid growth, architects were reappropriating the language of genetics in order to naturalize the terms of business. Geneticists, wrote architecture historian Sigfried Giedion, were interested in the possibility of crossbreeding organisms and plants to grow new ones, rather than merely reproducing the same ones. While the eighteenth century was responsible for mechanizing the process of genetic hybridization, he wrote, genetic alteration after the 1930s occurred at an unprecedented rate and a "gigantic" scale.[27] This 1960s interest in material "growth," therefore, indicated a shift away from the determinisms associated with standardization and mechanization.

Pelli described the Teledyne complex as a "living plant," much like an organism ripe for genetic manipulation. The multiple structures were organized around an eight-hundred-foot-long circulation "spine," including a mezzanine level for visitors, which was intended to support expansion and additions.[28] A concept later developed by Team X and, notably, the French trio Candilis-Josic-Woods who worked together from 1955 to 1968, the spine (and stem) was a concept that Pelli wrote about in his 1949 senior thesis at the University of Tucumán in Argentina, in which he compared it to a pedestrian-focused city street. As described by one critic in *Industry Week*, "the complex with a common spine is a system which accommodates widely dissimilar functions. . . . These considerations lead to a design in which a static kind of formal order is replaced by a dynamic order of forms in process."[29] Designed as an initial 165,000 square feet of space with an ability to expand to 400,000 square feet as Teledyne grew, only the circulation spine, mechanical spaces, cafeteria, and main lobby were fixed.[30] Three acute jogs, which Lumsden described as "fingers," protruded outward from the glass curtain wall and functioned on behalf of the corporate organism as joints for expansion (figure 19). In plan, the fingers provided the sprawling complex with a sense of directionality and forward thrust as they sat waiting to latch onto new companies.

The concept of a spine was refined in later projects by Pelli and Lumsden. These included a laboratory built in 1968–69 for the government-sponsored Communications Satellite Corporation (COMSAT) in Clarksburg, Maryland, where satellites were developed, tested, and manufactured. COMSAT was formed in 1962 in response to the federal government's inability to develop communication systems without relying intensely on private companies like Bell Labs. The governing board consisted of fifteen representatives from private companies as well as the federal government. Furthermore, COMSAT's shares were owned by a cross section of companies, including AT&T, RCA, Western Union International, and ITT.[31]

The circulation and service core of the COMSAT laboratory—designed, like that of Teledyne Labs, to expand in a clear and

FIGURE 19. Teledyne Laboratories, Northridge, California, 1968. Photo by Julius Shulman. © J. Paul Getty Trust. Getty Research Institute, Los Angeles (2004.R.10).

anticipated order, allowing for future expansion—was described as "Technological Imagery: Turnpike Version" in a 1970 article in *Progressive Architecture*.[32] Pelli defined and diagrammed "growth" in two ways for COMSAT—determinable and indeterminable—that positioned architecture as a mediating device, an infrastructure through which current and future companies could move in and out.

The mechanical and service distribution spaces, Pelli argued, could be physically extended by means of linear or standardized reproduction along a primary and secondary spine, which constituted "predetermined growth" (figure 20). However, due to the less predictable rate of company acquisitions, the spaces for business (the work) were described as "undetermined growth." From the inside

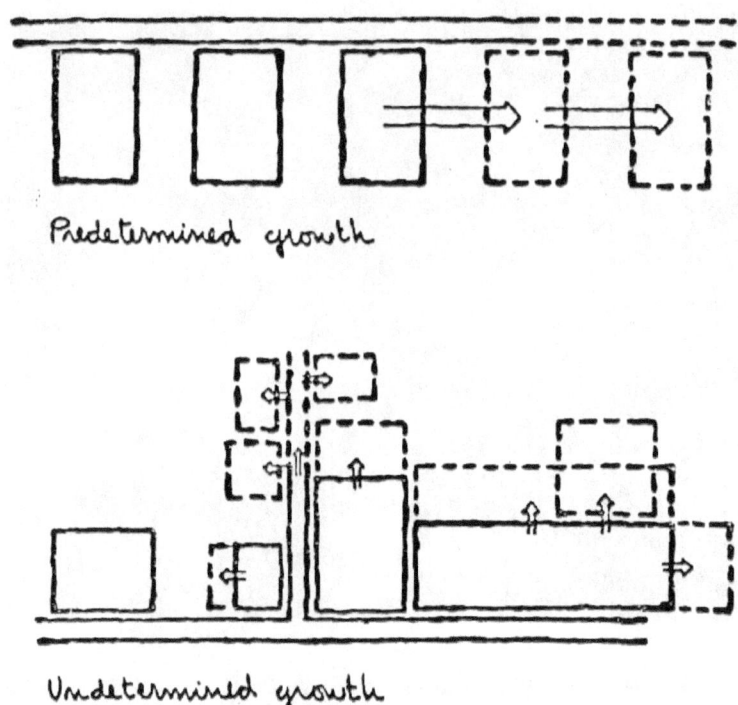

FIGURE 20. Diagram of COMSAT Laboratories, Clarksburg, Maryland, 1967. © AECOM. Cesar Pelli Collection, Yale University Archives.

out, the structure was described—much like DMJM—as "unfinished" and "open ended."

The concept of openness or indeterminacy was described by other architectural historians at the time, such as Umberto Eco, who argued that the concept was part of a broader categorical production of scientific "information" rather than "meaning," or of "informality" in art rather than modernist formality. In *The Open Work*, Eco wrote that "in the dialectics between work and openness, the very persistence of the work is itself a guarantee of both communication and aesthetic pleasure . . . [and] 'openness' . . . is the guarantee of a particularly rich kind of pleasure that our civilization pursues as one of its most precious values."[33] Yet in the client-driven work of architecture, as the designs for COMSAT and Teledyne suggest, openness and indeterminacy were explicitly seen as sources of economic capital, necessary for survival, rather than as sources of aesthetic pleasure.

Skin

Pelli and Lumsden argued that if they inverted a façade's mullions, glass could "wrap" around buildings in order to simultaneously conceal and emphasize the divergent parts of business. Lumsden referred to this new possibility of glass enclosure as a "membrane" akin to skin. To him, a membrane was a material response to conglomeration and the often disjointed operational units within it, which he defined as "non-directional" and as "a surface that modifies the transition from inside to outside. . . . Membrane means light weight [sic] non-gravitational enclosure. The functional, constructional and visual implication of this light weight enclosure indicates a radical departure for architecture. The analogy is to skin. . . . This notion is the opposite to the idea of a building as being 'all one thing.'"[34] In other words, membranes expressed the divergent programs or subsidiaries within a conglomerate, while still uniting them materially.[35] Thus, the COMSAT building was clad in an aluminum shell that rounded the otherwise sharp edges of the complex, a detail used on DMJM's own office building a few years later. The front of the Teledyne Labs complex was enclosed by a low-cost glass curtain wall of reflective, brown-tinted glass panels set within an aluminum mullion system, referred to as a "continuous mullion," to emphasize horizontality over repetitive verticality. The mullion system was stained black-brown to blend with the glass, which established a unifying system of aesthetic order through which additions to the company could be reconciled.

Lumsden argued that *any* material with an ability to simultaneously conceal and reveal the organizational structures beneath it could function as a membrane, thereby applying the infrastructural logic of business to decisions about materials that were otherwise considered unrelated. The membrane, no matter the material, was only one part of a broader system of organization. "Our fundamental interest," he suggested, "is not in glass walls nor their lightweight equivalent, although the notion of the skin is very significant in relation to the logic of production.... We are interested in developing a system that responds to reality, a design system that is not esoteric with respect to necessary data and sub-systems of the building."[36]

As architectural preservationist Daniel Paul has observed, Pelli and Lumsden pushed glass envelopes closer to a membrane condition with each project, including a six-story Federal Aviation Administration building in Hawthorne, California, designed concurrently with Teledyne Labs in 1966 and completed in 1973, for which they wrapped the volume in mirror-glass made smooth by inverting the vertical mullions and capping the tightly rounded corners with aluminum. In a Century City Medical Plaza tower and adjacent hospital, designed in 1967 and completed in 1969, the building—from top to bottom—was enclosed by a smooth, dark gray, monochromatic glass façade with similarly reversed mullions, protruding outward only three-eighths of an inch (nine millimeters), rather than the six or eight inches typical of modernist curtain walls.[37]

After Pelli left DMJM in 1968, Lumsden assumed the position of design director, and he continued to experiment with the curvilinear potentialities of glass in order to allow it to conform with greater malleability to the diverse programs within the buildings he designed. Among a series of mid-rise office buildings in Los Angeles, including DMJM's own office, he designed one office building for Century Bank, built in 1972, two unbuilt hotels of extruded cylindrical volumes—the Lugano Hotel and Convention Center in Switzerland

(1972) and the Beverly Hills Hotel (1973)—and the Manufacturers Bank Building in 1974, whose undulations represented a most advanced articulation of an undulating membrane condition (figure 21).

For Lumsden, the use of a membrane was not motivated by a material ability to produce images (except, perhaps, one of growth), nor was the concept applicable only to a particular material, such as glass. As an architectural response to the open-ended challenge of business *as* infrastructure, he argued that the concept of a membrane could apply to glass (as in the case of Teledyne Labs), aluminum (as in the case of the COMSAT building), or even water, which he referenced in his designs for wastewater treatment plants—here again, the "plant" was used to naturalize the process of urban and capital "growth."[38]

By the 1980s, the rhetoric of fragmentation that had characterized the corporate conglomerate was being used to characterize the contemporary city of Los Angeles as well—a city hooked on growth and disjointed by uncoordinated and private pursuits of land development.[39] However, a "growing" city presented the possibility of overloading the city's existing infrastructure, including its transportation systems and wastewater distribution facilities. During the 1970s, development briefly stalled as city government halted building permits due to dangerous overburdening of wastewater management and other infrastructure. Blackout zones barring all new construction and development were mapped onto large swaths of the city.[40]

Lumsden and the DMJM Design Division proposed a "machine within a garden" for the Sepulveda (later named the Donald C. Tillman) Water Reclamation Plant, borrowing the title of Leo Marx's 1964 book.[41] Nearly seven acres of Japanese gardens, designed by landscape architect Koichi Kawana and based on eighteenth-century wet strolling gardens, covered the site as a "buffer zone" to appease nearby residents.[42] Large pools of water and waterfalls swirled throughout the gardens, with fish and wildlife drinking and swimming in the water to demonstrate safe uses of reclaimed water.

FIGURE 21. Manufacturers Bank Building, Los Angeles, 1974. © Dale Lang, photographer.

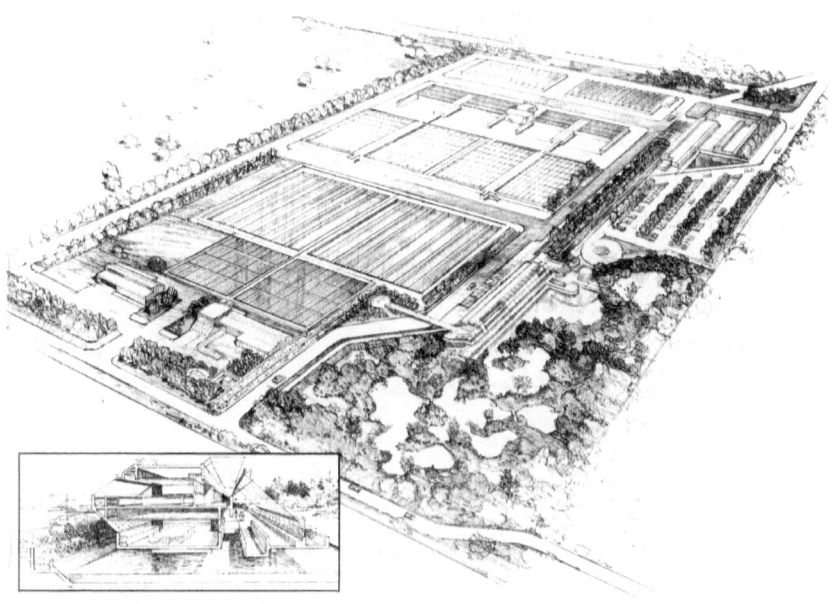

FIGURE 22. Aerial and section drawing of the Sepulveda (Tillman) Water Reclamation Plant, Los Angeles, 1973. From *DMJM Review*, Fall 1973. © AECOM.

Recalling the conglomerate rhetoric of Teledyne Labs, the design prioritized the building's section, anticipating the city's future expansion: "A major benefit of this aesthetic type is that it allows the front and sides of buildings to be different thus relatable to each façade's particular adjacencies and environment. This is essential in any multi-building complex such as a university campus or urban context."[43] Critic Esther McCoy described the Tillman plant by drawing attention to the membrane that held it together—not only the rolling glass or a metal skin, but the water flowing through, beneath, inside, and around it, which Lumsden described as calm, smooth, bubbling, swirling, splashing, tumbling, turbulent, and, like glass, reflecting colors of violet, green, gray, silver, and white. Indeed, Lumsden produced drawings and diagrams that distilled architecture to a stream of waterflow, from its input as sewage to its output as reclaimed water.

As the water rippled through the site, its reflective authority diverted both visitors' and critics' attention to the hues and images of the garden and sky reflected in the building's mirrors and water, concealing the economic processes of urban growth gurgling, churning, and filtering immediately behind it (figure 22). The architecture was *revealing* the process of wastewater reclamation to those who visited, as well as *concealing* the treatment processes—its smells and its swirls—required for an overpopulated city.[44]

Image

The representational power of the membranes designed by Pelli and Lumsden, as well as the images reflected in their mirrors, captured the attention of critics, theorists, and historians of postmodernism. Like the water at the Tillman Plant, the mirror-glass at Teledyne Labs was described as a screen of images, with critics highlighting the shimmering environment reflected in its surfaces—the hues of the blue daytime sky, the greens of the orange groves and lawns, the gold-pinks of the California sunset. The protruding "fingers" also reflected the building back onto itself in an endlessly self-reflecting feedback loop—a testament to the indeterminism of conglomeration.[45] Reyner Banham argued that the Teledyne Labs design appeared to revive the ostensible flash of a modernist California Case Study "style," suggesting that the mirror-glass curtain wall was appropriate to the needs of the business it enclosed, especially since the increasingly thin and inverted structural membranes boasted a "self-image" of high technology that characterized the microelectronics assembled within.[46] Again, though, to focus on the technologies and the surfaces that concealed them, as Banham did, was to overlook the economic rationales for the infrastructures demanded by businesses and cities.

Charles Jencks struggled to make sense of Lumsden's projects—he could not decide whether to classify them as late modern or postmodern. Focusing only on the façades, he described the buildings as "difficult cases" to classify, since their "slick" and "smooth" surfaces seemed to provoke symbolic meaning that was not clearly stated. While Jencks did not detail Lumsden's projects in *The Language of Post-Modern Architecture*, he included images of the undulating mirror-glass façades of Norman Foster's 1975 Willis Faber building and John Portman's 1976 Westin Bonaventure Hotel. Still searching for symbolic meaning in Lumsden's projects in later publications, he asked whether "the 'slick-tech' aesthetic of the smooth glass façade [was] intentional or a kind of inspired malapropism."[47] Was the undulating mirror-glass of Lumsden's Beverly Hills Hotel a testament to a "silver aesthetic" of Beverly Hills' capital power? Was his use of mirror-glass in a proposal for a 1976 bank branch tower, Bumi Daya, in Jakarta a reference to the "silver standard" of banking investment—with an "oil-slick" surface "suggesting a series of meanings without naming them, like the symbolic poetry of the nineteenth-century?"[48] Yet, as discussed earlier, Lumsden's projects did not *represent* but rather *produced* postmodernism in their engagement with language and their abstracted relationship to capital.

Similarly focused on representation, Jencks, Fredric Jameson, and, by extension, David Harvey argued that the smooth, mirror-glass surfaces came to represent the speculative nature of late capitalism and the high technologies of the post-1960s period.[49] Yet the architecture appeared to trap its observers in a fetishizing gaze. In *Utopia's Ghost*, architectural historian Reinhold Martin argued that the proliferation of mirror-glass during the 1960s and 1970s and its material ability to produce feedback loops of self-reflection and re-reflection not only represented late capitalism but belonged to it.[50] Martin suggested that most observers of the smooth, slick, and reflective buildings appeared to be lured into and trapped by the reflections of the mirror-glass surfaces—expecting to see a "global network" of capital behind the glass, they found only distorted illusory images of the environment and their own bodies projected onto the surfaces. He argued that it was only by looking *at* the mirror—the membrane—that one could peer "into the possible futures and possible pasts that may yet escape the entropy of reflection and re-reflection that is approached by postmodernity's self-reflexive feedback loops."[51] But, as we have seen, to look "at" the membrane is to risk falling into the same trap, since it holds open the apolitical jaws of materialism that are easily detached from the specific acts—and postindustrial business infrastructures—that made such membranes necessary. To look *at* the clean, reclaimed water at the Tillman plant, for example, was to accept without challenge how or why it was there in the first place.

Even Jameson's material history of the membrane trapped him within his own analyses of postmodern architecture, which risked an apolitical reading of material conditions. He argued that it was through the particular relationship between architecture and business that postmodernism was made visible: "Architecture is, however, of all the arts that closest constitutively to the economic, with which, in the form of commissions and land values, it has a virtually unmediated relationship: it will therefore not be surprising to find the extraordinary flowering of the new postmodern architecture grounded in the patronage of multinational business, whose expansion and development is strictly contemporaneous with it."[52] Yet Jameson, following Jencks's confusion about Lumsden's projects, also argued that the ability of architecture to mediate between finance and aesthetics was not through self-reference: "Jencks first allows us to see the way not to do this: that of thematic self-reference, as when Anthony Lumsden's Branch Bank project in Bumi Daya 'alludes to the silver standard and an area of investment where the bank's money is possibly headed.'"[53] Instead, Jameson argues, one should look to the smooth, increasingly thin glass skins—not for meaning, but to understand the relationship between multinational business and material culture. The skin, he argues, citing another of Jencks's own interpretations of Lumsden's projects, "decreases the mass and weight while enhancing the volume and contour—the difference between a brick and a balloon."[54] In other words, Jameson traps himself: do not look to the work of Lumsden, he argues, but instead look to the work of Lumsden.

However, Martin has argued that Jameson, like Jencks, appeared to be looking at the *images* projected on the Bonaventure's surfaces rather than at the surface itself, given that he described the mirror-glass as "distorted images of everything that surrounds it."[55] For Martin, the manifestations of finance capital were most obvious in the acute angles and façade protrusions of corporate headquarters, such as those designed by Phillip Johnson and John Burgee for the Investors Diversified Services Center (1974) in Minneapolis, their Pennzoil Place (1975) in Houston, or their Pittsburgh Plate Glass Place (1984) in Pittsburgh. The proliferation of mirror-glass allowed for a slick, oil-like mirroring surface to produce an especially appropriate aesthetic for Houston-based oil companies, such as Pennzoil, by concealing the underlying meanings of capital and privileging an illusion that helped produce the phantasm "oil"—itself a composite of objects, mechanisms, and embodied labor.[56] Martin argued that the mirror-glass surfaces did not *represent* oil, just as the membrane of Teledyne Labs did not *represent* microelectronics; instead, the glass surfaces produced each as a commodity fetish, as objects with "special powers," by simultaneously revealing—through extrusions, fingers, angled edges, or protrusions—and concealing (behind smooth reflective surfaces) the specific economic processes that lay beneath.[57]

Yet the history of conglomeration challenges us to push Martin's point further, since the membranes of conglomerate buildings—as intended and theorized by Pelli and Lumsden, for instance—produced conglomerate business as an end in itself: it was the infrastructure of conglomerate business, not just the ever-changing products or services that each company offered, that was rendered a commodity fetish by the façades. This was a fetishism that, as Laura Mulvey has described, risked turning the representational figure (the façade, for example) into a free-floating object that privileges vision and distances itself from any and all politics.[58]

We can scrutinize the businesses that Martin describes to illustrate this point. Investors Diversified Services Inc. was reconfigured after it was acquired by Alleghany Corporation (renamed American Express in 1984) and again after it acquired additional insurance companies during the 1980s. The Pittsburgh Plate Glass Company changed its name to PPG Industries Inc. in 1968 to represent the diversity of its offerings—from house paints to fiberglass and window screening. And the tenants of Pennzoil Place included not only Pennzoil, itself a conglomerate, but Zapata Petroleum, as well as the Pennzoil-owned United Gas Pipeline Company.

"Conglomerate"

The term *conglomerate* surfaced in several seemingly disparate corners of discourse about architectural form and composition during the late 1970s and 1980s—suggesting, to some, the arrival of postmodernism. Jencks centered, on the cover of his widely cited first and second editions of *The Language of Post-Modern Architecture* (first published in 1977 while he was a visiting professor of architecture at UCLA, where Lumsden was also teaching), a photograph of Minoru Takeyama's 1970 Ni-Ban-Kahn ("Building Number Two") in the Shinjuku ward of Tokyo. Jencks later referred to the building as a "conglomerate" (figure 23).[59] According to Jencks, the building's vivid rejection of homogeneity through interlocking geometries

FIGURE 23. Ni-Ban-Kahn, Tokyo, Japan, 1970. Cover, Charles Jencks, *The Language of Postmodernism*, 1977. © Rizzoli, New York.

celebrated its "functional differences," which were grouped around a narrow vertical circulation core. Like Teledyne Labs, however, the remaining volumes of Ni-Ban-Kahn were designed in only one month and under immense construction pressure—and thus were the result of functional indeterminacy and economic necessity. Consisting of independently owned commercial spaces, Ni-Ban-Kahn was intended to support eternal flux in tune with the demands of the rapidly changing urban economy immediately surrounding it. The building included a series of third-floor bars designed by Takeyama, a fourth-floor restaurant designed by the Kiso Design Office with a gambling den by Takeyama, fifth- and sixth-floor clubs designed by the Uchida Design Office, and finally a seventh-floor sauna designed by Takeyama.[60]

Despite the spatial, programmatic, and material contrasts between Teledyne Labs and Ni-Ban-Kahn, the two projects were united by the rhetoric of their enclosures and, more importantly, by the conglomerate businesses supporting them, where their geopolitical motivations were most visible. Like Lumsden, Takeyama used the term *membrane* to describe the relationship between the independent businesses and the whole. To Takeyama, the membrane was not the concrete wall of the building itself, but rather a thin layer of "plastic paint"—applied by hand and designed by artist Kiyoshi Awazu—of supergraphics, including a red and white bullseye, which suggested industrial code and caught Jencks's attention.[61] In discussing the membrane, Takeyama posed a guiding question: "How far am I justified in giving a relationship interpretation to forms, and how much indefiniteness may I allow to invade the nature of architectural expression?"[62] Takeyama argued that a building's membrane functioned as "an extremely visible boundary between interior and exterior and as a tangible object invisibly establishing relations with a perception of existence."[63] In other words, for Takeyama as for Lumsden, the membrane was responsible for both celebrating the ever-changing independent volumes and unifying them.

But looking at surface conditions can take us only so far. Only when we examine the infrastructures of the businesses that produced these buildings, including their histories, is the geopolitical significance of postmodern architecture made visible. The plan for Ni-Ban-Kahn, like those of Teledyne Labs and the COMSAT laboratory, was driven by geographic, political, and economic necessity: it was located in an area with a high volume of pedestrian traffic, and the fourteen individual bars were united with radically divergent leisure businesses in order to compete with the nearly twenty thousand bars and fifty thousand coffee shops and restaurants in the surrounding neighborhood.[64]

A widespread business practice during the 1960s that had faded by the mid-1980s, conglomeration challenged modernist business models that were driven by homogenization, reproducibility, and standardization. Even after architects departed firms such as DMJM, including Pelli in 1968, they continued describing projects as "conglomerates," demonstrating the posmodernizing effects of the businesses they were designing. Pelli designed a Ley Student Center expansion project at Rice University in Houston in 1986, for instance, as a series of interlocking geometries organized along a long circulation core. He argued that "all the shapes are, in a way, archetypal . . . cubes, prisms, pyramids—joined together in a dynamic conglomerate."[65]

The radical diversification of economic offerings was a political act, and businesses amassed power by acquiring economic entities on the margins of their primary means of production. Their rates and directions of growth were indeterminable *by design*. Despite the relative absence of discourse about conglomerate businesses in architecture, it is perhaps ironic that the term was applied by theorists and critics of postmodern architecture without interrogating the term's origins or its meanings—following, like the businessmen, the surface meaning of conglomerates without examining their inner workings. Yet this easy slip of terminology, from business into aesthetic, challenges a surface-based analysis of postmodern architecture. The all-out search for abstract meanings of surface aesthetics risked absolving architects of any sense of political or geographical consequence.

Individual Limits

The design rhetoric associated with conglomerates directly informed Lumsden's views about the role of architects at a moment when the discipline, profession, and public at large were questioning their value as individuals. And Lumsden's ability to make visible the economic value of design by identifying sites of material contingency enabled him to safeguard his role as but one member in the process of architectural production, especially as architects were being threatened by technology and mass production.[66] Akin to the membranes knitting together the volumes of Teledyne Labs or those proposed to envelop the Beverly Hills and Lugano hotels, Lumsden himself was often referred to as a spokesman of design—responsible for "disciplinary interfacing" between the multiple divisions of the office and for communicating the role and value of systems processes to other architects.[67] To the architects working with him, Lumsden adapted, insisting that DMJM was not compatible with a "star system" of architects—a system that, he argued, privileged a priori design decisions that promoted an attitude of withdrawal from the immediate processes and tools of architectural work, such as the economic, technological, or environmental underpinnings of a project.[68] Associating such a system with the kind of "plague" Albert Camus described in his 1947 novel—a 1940s plague in a French Algerian town that serves as an allegory of resistance to Nazi occupation—Lumsden asserted that "DMJM does not allow saints on the staff. Even if they are counting money instead of peas. Neither as an attitude for the profession nor in buildings as a product is withdrawal a possible position for a contributing design firm."[69]

Lumsden's history might be compared to other, more well-known architects within large firms, such as Gordon Bunshaft at SOM, who Nicholas Adams has shown relied more on technical expertise and management skills than previously known.[70] Lumsden argued that architects were stuck between two procrustean positions due to internalized yet polarized beliefs: that "architecture is art" and that "form follows function." While the first, he suggested, bypassed the functional and performance criteria of a project to impose a priori aesthetics, the second revealed a reductivist bias that reduced a building's function to hyperefficient "minimalist boxes."[71] Therefore, Lumsden was challenging architects to guard against historically constructed "preconceptions" so that buildings were not "controlled by biases that exclude important performance criteria."[72] Lumsden suggested that architects could employ an "analytical phase" to break down biases by testing their ideas against the "limits" of the present: construction costs, environmental determinants, and occupants' responses to a project.[73]

Lumsden's call to guard against preconceptions and predispositions was founded on a belief that it was possible for architects to be cognizant of their own biases—a position widely debated among social theorists during the 1970s and 1980s.[74] Lumsden was not suggesting that architects at DMJM should get rid of their preconceptions and subdue their dispositions altogether; rather, he challenged architects to prevent the rote translation of them into practice. In theories of practice emerging at the time, such as those of sociologist Pierre Bourdieu, history and culture were considered systems of acquired dispositions, functioning as "categories of perception and assessment," "classificatory principles," and the "organizing principles of action."[75] Bourdieu's important concept of "habitus" describes how these systems come "into the body" or "into the flesh." To guard against preconceptions as Lumsden suggested—and, thereby, to protect one's own habitus—was to form an impermeable barrier between the flesh of the body and the environment around it. Thus, the skin, as both a protective and deflective membrane of contingency and vulnerability between the flesh and the environment, united the architect and the conglomerate in terms of practice—each with skin capable of conforming to the variegated and heterogeneous distensions of flesh and its uneven layers of accumulated history, experience, and dispositions over time.

The identification of the skin as a layer of contingency helped to safeguard architects within the process of building production. In a brief section within his *Mechanization Takes Command*, Giedion described the skin as the material that posed the greatest resistance to mechanization during the nineteenth century. Unlike easily reproducible industrial materials, the skin was organically irreducible because of its environmental accumulations of dirt, hair, bristles, blood, and slime (his words), and its inherent fragility rendered it incapable of mechanical separation. This confrontation between organic matter and the machine, therefore, rendered the hand of the human operator within the slaughterhouse indispensable. In comparable terms, Lumsden insisted on the architect's ability to absorb—albeit only as deeply as the skin—the localized and environmental conditions of a project. This was directly correlated to the skin of conglomerate organisms, and the contingencies of both helped secure the architect's hand in the designing of buildings at DMJM, thus revealing the value of architects in late capitalism.[76]

By the time Ashland Oil acquired the firm in 1984, Lumsden's Design Division had established a substantial architectural name for DMJM. Among the projects and skills that Ashland deemed economically advantageous to its own portfolio of diversification, DMJM's *architectural* projects and design capabilities were cited most frequently in Ashland's annual report to shareholders, in which DMJM was described as a "consistently ranked leading design firm... with an international reputation for outstanding design, technological advances, strong project management, and strict cost and schedule control."[77] As Ashland withdrew from the architecture and engineering business in 1990, selling the firms it had acquired, Lumsden contributed one of the largest personal investments supporting an employee-led buyback, which resulted in AECOM.[78]

Yet Lumsden's power was called into question at AECOM during the early 1990s. His accumulated agency challenged the logic of the conglomerate, which, to recall the theories of Teledyne's Henry Singleton, was predicated on social and economic equivalency—the idea that no one part could be more significant than another. New leadership aimed to hire additional well-established architects in 1993 and 1994 at DMJM, which threatened Lumsden's agency. In 1994, DMJM, as one of five companies within AECOM, merged with Los Angeles architecture firm Keating Mann Jernigan Rottet (KMJR)—a group of architects who had joined together while working at Skidmore, Owings & Merrill's Houston office during the 1980s and who worked "as a team rather than follow[ing] established hierarchy models," an approach that "result[ed] from both experience and friendship."[79] In theory, these additions fit well with Lumsden's approach. However, the collaborative and team-based approaches were no longer valued by the company's executives or by the economy. Amid these impending changes, Lumsden was abruptly asked to leave in 1993, the moment he turned sixty-five—the maximum age of employment as established by DMJM's *Standard Practices Manual* in the 1960s. As one architect vividly recalled, he could see the "bean counters" worrying that Lumsden had accumulated too much power. Finally, members of the design department gathered in the conference room without Lumsden, and a new senior vice president argued that they were going to "change the design culture of this place." Rather than continue a collective and integrated practice, as had been celebrated for more than forty years, the firm adopted the language of the individual architect, falling back on long-outmoded tropes of a "gentleman's" profession: now they would form a *studio*.[80]

The structural shift from departments and divisions to a "studio" revealed a radical change in the structure and rationale of the business—an inevitable reset, a new beginning, or short-sighted regression. At minimum, it reflected how the economy no longer valued diversified conglomerate businesses with collective and collaborative workers, but instead favored businesses that were narrowly focused and had clear professional boundaries and a signature.[81] The establishment of a design "studio" carried with it an unavoidable genealogy of practice that imposed an inherent boundary upon architects and presented a contrasting image of them—as authorial individuals working alone, rather than as anonymous workers within a corporate bureaucracy.[82] The shift to a studio brought with it a history of practice that inherently limited the ability of architects to embrace positions and practices beyond the traditional domains of design, restricting their ability to define their work as socially and economically equivalent to that of a broader range of practitioners.

. . .

As business executives responded to the uncertainties of a postwar economy, the threat of Cold War catastrophe, and the pro-competition sanctions of the government, they began to "grow" their companies for their security by acquiring other firms, rather than by expanding from within. Business historians define these conglomerate mergers and acquisitions as extreme acts of explicitly modern, diversified business. However, architects, cultural theorists, and historians have described conglomerate headquarters and laboratories not as modern but as *postmodern*—a term defined largely by formal and material descriptions—by skirting the underlying processes, politics, and motivations that gave rise to them. Despite their attentiveness to the visible changes taking place within discourse and practice, these theorizations provide only a partial history of architecture and diminish the political and economic value of architectural work.

As architects and cultural critics borrowed the term *conglomerate* to introduce "postmodern architecture," they stripped buildings from their geography and politics to uphold a definition of architectural practice as reducible to enclosure, image, and aesthetics. Put another way, to focus on a conglomerate building's enclosure without caution was to ignore the capitalist rationale of (and for) architecture more broadly. As this history of DMJM and AECOM suggests, the acquiring of additional firms and lands represented the most advanced form of expansion possible within a conservative, deregulated, capitalist economy. Searching for abstract meanings of surface aesthetics and borrowing terms such as *conglomerate* by detaching them from their origins freed architects and historians alike from political and economic consequences. Tracing a fuller history of postmodernism, building on a political-economic line of thought initiated by scholars such as Mary McLeod, without falling into the traps set by capitalism's ebb and flow, requires a simultaneous examination of bottom-up and top-down economic forces in tune with their material effects.

4 *Contract*
Developing Architects

In 1961, DMJM architect Stanley Moe and project manager Bill Shope submitted a final report to Thailand's Ministry of Industry following a three-year "exploration" of groundwater on the Khorat Plateau in northeast Thailand. DMJM was responsible for drilling four hundred boreholes across sixty thousand square miles and assessing the viability of each for water. The report was part of a larger five-year development contract funded primarily by the US and facilitated by the International Cooperation Administration (ICA; later the United States Agency for International Development, USAID) for building water, electricity, and transportation infrastructure. The Thai and US governments described the gently populated plateau, long stewarded by the Isan people, as "undeveloped" and thus susceptible to the control of communist-backed "insurrectionists" who could subvert their authority.[1] Noting that underdevelopment was considered a "political problem," echoing many justifications of international development after World War II, Moe and Shope's report concluded that much of the plateau consisted of sandstone and conglomerate rock.[2]

Since the early Industrial Revolution, geologists had been classifying rock as conglomerate when widely disparate fragments were mixed, rounded, and united by rivers, glaciers, or wind. Cemented by sand or clay and hardened over time, conglomerate was considered an ideal aquifer because water quickly passed through its aggregate. Moe and Shope recommended areas with conglomerate rock because of this. "Conglomerate," they concluded. "Excellent possibilities for future development."[3] These conclusions in 1961 suggested that architects were legitimizing their expertise through the colonial and extractive economics of nation building as part of a larger project of American hegemony. More particular to the 1960s, they were considering conglomerates as material infrastructures for postwar development before they were considering them as infrastructures of postmodern businesses.

As has been well established, it was through projects in "developing" nations during the second half of the twentieth century that architecture and engineering firms in "developed" nations expanded, exported Western architectural expertise, and imparted the capitalist customs and terms of economic dependency that sustained a colonizing flow of capital, resources, and labor into the US.[4] As historian Jeffrey Cody has argued, architecture and engineering firms represented international development's "private hands" because they wore the "public gloves" of government funding.[5]

Often neglected within these histories of international development, and within histories of capitalist infrastructure more generally, is the way that economic development worked in tandem with military and political expansion—even after war. Rather than reconsidering the types of expertise or stylistic preferences that US architects exported abroad—and eclipsing the circumstances and conditions surrounding architectural procurement and production—or lumping such work into a vague complex of military-industrial complicity that risks trivializing architects' operations, this chapter considers why and how architects and engineers aligned themselves with the state in the postwar period, examining how the state's terms, tools, and techniques were incorporated as facts of architectural business before they were carried into the profession thereafter.

By the 1970s, architects not only had pressed their associations and regulatory institutions, including the American Institute of Architects and the National Council for Architectural Registration Boards, to adopt their expansionary lead through new codes of ethics, but had also encouraged them to adopt contract-based business models marketed as necessary for economic freedom and development: an eternal project with no foreseeable beginning or end.[6] Once the US government made visible the effectiveness of its tools for acquiring and managing its land possessions (and leases) abroad, architects and engineers saw how they could manage larger sets of business activity beyond the design of buildings.

Procurement

Throughout this book, I've discussed how young architects in the US were launching their professional careers after World War II by procuring local contracts for schools, housing, and urban infrastructure. When this demand waned during the early 1950s, architects partnered with engineers, as they had during the late nineteenth century, to increase their eligibility for a broader range of construction projects. Carrying the military-industrial alliances that had formed during World Wars I and II into the Cold War, the US government authorized significant funding for "architecture-engineering" services through the 1948 Marshall Plan for reconstruction in Europe and the 1949 and 1951 Mutual Defense Assistance/Security Acts for "containing" the spread of communism.[7] Additionally, the ICA, established in the mid-1950s, launched an "economic offensive" by funding infrastructure in developing countries as an alternative to the World Bank's loan programs.[8]

In DMJM's library was a well-used copy of a 1969 contracting primer, *Contracting with the Federal Government*, published in anticipation of the 1972 Brooks Act (the "Selection of Architects and Engineers" statute), which formalized the terms and restricted the methods of government procurement for architects and engineers.[9] The Brooks Act required the government to base its selection of contractors on competency, qualifications, and experience, rather than cost, proximity, and "who you knew."[10] Additionally, contracts were required to be publicly announced—a requirement that most government agencies fulfilled by publishing their notices in newsletters and magazines such as *Commerce Business Daily*, a federal magazine published by the US Department of Commerce beginning in 1962.

The requirement to demonstrate related "experience" reflected a fundamental concern of liberal economics at the time, described in 1945 by economist Friedrich Hayek, who argued that, unlike credentialed knowledge associated with reason or scientific experimentation, the knowledge of "particular circumstances of time and place"— of people, local conditions, and situations—constituted a firm's unique economic offerings.[11] Knowledge linked to experience was becoming distinct from modernist "innovation" and "experiment," as Raymond Williams later described.[12]

In many ways, the Brooks Act was seen as a reaction to claims of political corruption and biased procurement practices in the postwar period. Worried that contracts would be awarded "on the basis of political influence," Congress claimed that it needed to prohibit political contributions by architects. "Political influence has no place in the award of architect-engineer contracts inasmuch as such influence is both illegal and professionally unethical," a revised 1974 edition of the primer states.[13] Yet as discussed in chapter 1, such "influences" and campaign contributions in exchange for contracts continued, despite the Brooks Act, and they persist today.[14]

By the time the Brooks Act was signed into law, architecture and engineering firms had already been boosted by government contracts. As historian Robert Higgs has described, public-private contracts during the 1950s and 1960s were understood less as binding agreements or "firm deals" and more as "ongoing joint enterprises" among friends through which military officials and businessmen cooperated to suit their collective and individual interests.[15] One historian of the US Army, on whose work Higgs based his argument, wrote in 1959, the year Moe and Shope were finishing their Thailand report: "The relationship between the government and its contractors was gradually transformed from an arm's length relationship between two more or less equal parties in a business transaction into an undefined but intimate relationship . . . in which the financial, contractual, statutory, and other instruments and assumption of economic activity were reshaped to meet the ultimate requirements of victory in war."[16] With new terms of state patronage formalizing with each new contract, housing expert Charles Abrams similarly noted about development projects during the 1960s that "the fine line between the 'contact,' 'connection,' 'contract,' and 'fix' tends to grow fuzzy."[17] And instead of waiting for commissions to be published, air travel enabled architects and engineers to travel to meet and negotiate with federal officials or military commanders in person—sometimes without invitation. Abrams noted that contractors benefited from in-person visits as well as from the unclear and overlapping jurisdictions, organizational chaos, and corruption within agencies such as the ICA.[18]

Due to the urgency of development projects, firms were often required to complete their work with remarkable efficiency, often fronting their labor without immediate pay by taking on significant debt before contracts were signed. Costs, including labor, were typically paid as reimbursements; however, jurisdictional overlaps and bureaucratic disarray within the government often led to delays in payment. Therefore, development work was possible for firms like DMJM prior to the 1970s only because they employed a large number of people and because their diversified streams of revenue kept the firms afloat in instances of delayed or uncertain payment, if not national economic recessions.

Yet how, specifically, did firms such as DMJM procure their first government commissions? And on what "experience" did they base their initial eligibility? In 1951, with near-empty bank accounts, the DMJM partners forced their firm into debt: Phillip Daniel took out a Bank of America loan to print and send DMJM's first brochure, which "showed the availability of all 50 personnel," and he sent scattershot telegrams to command centers of the US Air Force and Navy.[19] The same year, Irv Mendenhall traveled to Washington, DC, to meet with the director of air force installations, who offered him a "courteous few minutes."[20] And at the suggestion of a Los Angeles taxi driver, Johnson traveled to London and Paris in 1952 to meet with an architect of the Joint Construction Agency.

"Phil [Daniel] had a gift for making contacts with interesting people about noteworthy projects," architect Stanley Moe wrote in his travel diary. Daniel's friendships with high-ranking government officials included Sir Frederick Snow, commander of the Order of the British Empire, as well as prominent aristocrats including Colin Tennant (portrayed by Pip Carter in the Netflix series *The Crown* in 2017).[21]

These inquiries caught the attention of the Strategic Air Command and Far East division of the air force, which led to the firm's first commissions designing, adapting, and expanding military bases—producing what anthropologist David Vine has described as a "base nation"—on land outside the US.[22] Adopting the language of the military, DMJM established a "branch" in Okinawa in 1953 where they worked within a Quonset hut from World War I, placing plywood sheets atop orange crates for use as chairs and tables.[23] From there, DMJM draftsmen worked to design the air force's Naha Airfield (and later a secret US Marines base at Henoko Bay) in Okinawa, as well as Andersen Air Force Base in Guam (figure 24). In addition, the firm opened branches in Tokyo where they designed US Air Force bases and missile facilities in Japan, US Army facilities in Korea, and US Navy facilities in Taiwan. Further, they opened branches in Rome,

FIGURE 24. Rendering of US Marine Corps Base at Henoko, Okinawa, Japan. From *A Presentation of the Work of Daniel, Mann, Johnson, & Mendenhall: Company General Brochure*, 1967. © AECOM. Stanley Moe Papers, Huntington Library, San Marino, California.

Paris, London, and Washington, DC, to design regional ballistic missile complexes in Europe.

However, when Defense Secretary Robert McNamara announced nearly a hundred base closures in 1954, government-supported architects and engineers were required to look for new clients and projects yet again. The US was claiming jurisdiction over more people living outside the contiguous states than within them, and international architecture and engineering firms such as DMJM employed more people abroad than in the US. DMJM employed nearly three hundred employees in Tokyo and London alone, more than in Los Angeles, and was listed among a group of eleven architecture firms operating internationally.[24]

To procure development projects in the 1960s, DMJM workers followed the same approach they had used in the 1950s for military work. By then, they could use their military design and drafting experience to demonstrate their readiness for development work. In one instance, in November 1967, DMJM vice president Barry Mountain traveled to the American Embassy in Jakarta with a representative of the steel manufacturing corporation Struthers Wells to meet with the US ambassador to Indonesia and with generals of Indonesia's new pro-Western president, Suharto—who had claimed the office in 1966 after leading the US-backed massacre of communists, women, and trade unionists and overthrowing the nationalist president Sukarno.[25] Indonesia was important to the Kennedy administration (and eventually the Johnson and Nixon administrations) because of its natural resources and strategic location for satellite communications. Economic aid to Indonesia from communist China, according to McNamara in 1960, would "deny the Free World countries the tremendous oil, tin, and rubber resources which the United States seeks to deny communists."[26]

Mountain's intentions were documented in a memo written by the US Embassy in Jakarta. The memo read: "On the basis of the contents of a draft 'letter of intent' which is said to be under consideration by the Indonesian Government but which, let it be clearly noted, has not been approved or signed, the prime mover of the group is DMJM which seeks to sell its and its associates['] 'engineering and industrial economic services'.... It appears to the reporting officer that DMJM hopes to take advantage of [US]AID's or [an]other financing agency's assistance in the forthcoming 'project' period of Indonesia's rehabilitation and development by being first in line."[27] Yet, given that this was before the time when contracts were required to be publicized, how would Mountain have learned about such possibilities? Architects such as Moe, who was based in Tokyo during the 1960s, scanned daily newspapers each morning, as Moe's travel diaries explain, looking for on-the-ground reports about grants or loans for international construction—especially as wars were about to break out or end. A *China Post* headline dated Friday, December 16, 1960, saved in Moe's personal archives, reads: "Indonesia, Red China Sign Dual Nationality Agreement."[28] In the article, Indonesia announced that it would honor the citizenship of Chinese Indonesians in return for development assistance from China. After reading an article like this, Moe would set it aside to show the partners of DMJM the next day, and they would follow up with their point-person at the ICA to see how the US government might be planning to counter with development aid of its own.

This approach paid off immensely for DMJM. On February 19, 1968, Moe read in the morning *Bangkok News*: "Foreign Capital Flows Back into Indonesia."[29] Moe marked a tall "!" next to a description of Suharto's call for international investments, which he was arguing was the best way to overcome Indonesia's $2.4 million debt. Moe circled contracts the article described as a "success." One was DMJM's: a $7 million contract with USAID to build a profit-sharing ground station for satellite communications with the US conglomerate ITT, heralded as the start of a "new era of closer contact and increased commerce between East and West."[30]

Project

As testament to the intimate relationships that were forming between architects and governing officials as defense and development work got underway, architects and engineers were exchanging letters with the directors, commanders, and city leaders with and for whom they were working—casually sharing memories and photographs of their time together, the physical settings serving as material records of their experiences. Thomas Naughten, director of the US Operations Missions to Thailand, frequently wrote to DMJM's

Barry Mountain and architect Bill Shope before and during their work in Thailand. "It was good to have been able to meet and talk with you while you were here, though I agree your visit was much too short," Naughten wrote to Shope and Mountain in October 1959 after they visited him in Washington, DC. "Bill Shope passed to me copies of pictures taken at my house. . . . They are good pictures and I am sure Mrs. Flegel will experience real nostalgia in looking at them."[31]

More than the drawings, infrastructures, or buildings they produced, these letters were seen as demonstrating the political success of individuals within an otherwise anonymous architecture and engineering firm in the postwar US—the letters served as evidence that architecture and engineering firms were helping defend and expand US sovereign power. Among the few types of documents architects archived and took with them when they retired, the letters, more comprehensively than other documents, reveal how capital was managed internally, including how fees from one project were used to offset the debt of another. Managing debt in this way was essential to the success of such firms, especially during an unstable era of postwar development. As scholars such as Maurizio Lazzarato and Denise Ferreira da Silva have shown, capital—and more particularly, debt—was historically used by the US and its contractors as a means of governance and control.[32] As these histories demonstrate, in the cases of development in particular, countries such as the US levied offers of assistance through infrastructural work as part of broader plans to "improve" or "modernize" in exchange for such things as land use.

To the surprise of members of the general public and even politicians, "aid" implied economic investments in US workers, equipment, and materials; the resulting structures were mere byproducts—the "magic hats" of modernism, Ijlal Muzaffar has called them, with architects and engineers as the magicians.[33] In a justification of foreign aid to the Foreign Relations Committee of the US

Senate in 1964, the director of USAID, David Bell, candidly explained to senators how aid funds circulated—moving not from the US to other countries, but instead from US taxpayers to the coffers of US companies:

> SENATOR MORSE [OREGON]: What percentage of the amount of money covered in this [Foreign Aid] bill, $224,600,000, is grant money and how much is loan money?
> MR. BELL [USAID]: These are grants, sir.
> SENATOR MORSE: This is complete grant money?
> MR. BELL: I believe without exception, Senator, yes.
> SENATOR MORSE: This is, in other words, money that we just turn over to these countries?
> MR. BELL: Most of it, Sir, is paid not to the countries themselves but to American institutions, universities, and so on, or to American technicians and advisors who work in the countries. The services, of course, are given to the countries.
> SENATOR MORSE: That is the conduit of the services and through that conduit the American taxpayer's money flows.
> MR. BELL: . . . The dollars stay in this country.[34]

However, despite the fact that the US paid contractors directly, government agencies still required countries to repay the exorbitant costs plus interest, resulting in economic and resource dependencies. One economist recalls in his controversial memoir how such projects were negotiated in Indonesia and elsewhere:

> Despite the fact that the money was returned almost immediately to the corporate members of the corporatocracy, the recipient country (the debtor) was required to pay it all back, principal plus interest. If . . . successful, the loans were so large that the debtor was forced to default on its payments after a few years. When this happened, we

... demanded our pound of flesh. This often included one or more of the following: control over United Nations votes, the installation of military bases, or access to precious resources such as oil. Of course, the debtor still owed us the money—and another country was added to our global empire.[35]

Yet debt management—managing cycles of boom and bust, development and defense—was precisely what architects and engineers at firms like DMJM were claiming as their expertise. For example, when DMJM first opened its Tokyo branch office in 1952 to work for the air force, there were twelve employees. Work began without a signed contract or cash advance, and salaries totaled $100,000—far exceeding the firm's Bank of America credit limit of $10,000.[36] How were these salaries paid? The archived letters show us. By that time, the revenues from the Los Angeles office included design fees from the Los Angeles Unified School District and the Culver City School District (when it marked its independence in 1947), as well as public works projects to help control flooding. These revenues were footing the labor costs of DMJM's international branches as they designed military bases abroad.[37] And the city was happy to provide a letter of support to the federal government stating so: "After thorough investigation of your qualifications," wrote Rear Admiral Cushing Phillips, president of the city's board of public works, on city letterhead in 1956, "you were selected by this Board for engineering contracts . . . from $1,068,600 to $6,493,300 [in construction costs]," in addition to new sewer facilities estimated to cost $40,700,000—the "largest [contract] ever awarded in this area."[38]

The "architectural projects" of Los Angeles, the partners argued, served as a "hedge against possible softening of the 'boom time' in architecture."[39] The hedging, however—coupled with the fact that more employees were working in DMJM branches abroad than in Los Angeles—brings us back to the production of post-Fordism and the slow separation between manual and intellectual labor, discussed in chapters 1 and 2. In tracing the flow of capital and the terms of labor with which it was associated, it is possible to see how the assumptions baked into the prefix *post* were misleading at best: manual labor had not necessarily ended; it was instead redistributed across vast geographies. The precarious and sometimes unpaid, temporary, and manual laborers—labor described as "hard costs"—were stationed abroad and listed like building materials.

Commercial invoices and packaging slips—bureaucratic requirements for reimbursement—offer vivid illustrations of the blurry categorizations of people, materials, and equipment. One invoice, for instance, dated April 15, 1960, lists various items required for the groundwater "exploration" project in Thailand, including eight Exide batteries, twelve volt, total $157.44; and six slips for American Iron Model, Double Bowl Overshot, total $345.90.[40] In another invoice, submitted a few months before, the requested items included three geologists for nine months, total $37,800; one senior typist, $10,200; two skilled laborers, $24,000; and two field assistants, $24,000.[41]

Continuing our forensic analysis of letters, it is also possible to determine how DMJM weathered the debts of development projects, such as those in Thailand and Indonesia, by using previous defense profits. In 1953, for example, a letter from Colonel Howard Reed of the air force noted his "feeling of appreciation" for the runways designed in Okinawa that cost in excess of $19.5 million.[42] In 1956, Captain C. W. Porter of the navy described the "very satisfactory close cooperation" in which DMJM and the navy worked, affirming DMJM's "expressed desire to be given an opportunity to continue work on any further development of the program."[43] In 1958, a year before the ICA contract with Thailand was formalized, Colonel William Leonhard, head of air force installations, wrote to Ken Johnson, who offered "appreciation for the high degree of interest and cooperation" in work for the air force's Ballistic Missile Division.[44] Also in 1958, the navy's officer in charge, K. D. Stickler, commended the firm for "excellent results" designing a navy store in Guam, which DMJM began working on in advance of the "actual letting of the contract," which resulted in "compliments" from the Bureau of Supplies and Accounts.[45] And the same year, J. H. Carter, director of a sentry weapon system (that fires at targets detected by sensors), expressed "gratitude for a job well done."[46]

While international architecture and engineering work came with significant risks, the debt management strategies of architecture and engineering firms were, when coupled with their new corporate status, quite lucrative. In one instance, DMJM completed a study on decentralizing the navy's resources, in preparation for a possible atomic attack, weeks ahead of schedule. "This lump sum job was so efficient," the firm's autobiography says, "that it resulted in excess profit which the firm, unsolicited, offered to refund the Navy, who refused. This reinforced our reputation as a firm with integrity, and led to other Department of Defense work."[47] In other words, profits amassed from designing military bases were paying for design labor on international infrastructure, just as revenues from designing schools in California had previously supported the military bases in Guam and Okinawa.

At the risk of overly emphasizing the military's influence, the social relationships with military personnel were described with affective and performative characteristics at DMJM, as akin to "ammunition." One architect shared in his oral history: "At first, they [Daniel and Johnson] thought they could survive on only school buildings, but Daniel and Johnson were actually more interested in foundational kinds of projects like the ones that the military had to offer. . . . [T]hey were friends with a whole bunch of military commanders that gave them some ammunition and put them on the map."[48] Supporting this point were books about guns in Stanley Moe's personal library, sandwiching DMJM's contracting primer. In one book, a bookmarked section drawing of a French Noel & Gueury pistol "system," patented in 1865, details how its rotating chamber was designed to fire multiple shots without reloading—illustrating the same concepts undergirding the multi-sector conglomerate that typified business by the late 1960s, the "urban systems" they were producing, and the systems of contracting that supported them.

A perhaps more important, yet far less considered, consequence of DMJM's military work was the material impact of design and construction labor on communities and their environments—in other words, the complicity of architects in the project of American hegemony. In Okinawa, for instance, the US offered rental payments to those willing to turn their land over to the US military; when landowners refused, the US forcibly seized the land by "bayonets and bulldozers," according to Okinawans, while offering infrastructure improvements to appease those who agreed to leases.[49] It was the bulldozer that, as Lucia Allais has described, had given the Allies an advantage during World War II—carving wide roads or transforming vast farmlands into orderly military bases.[50] As one member of the US Navy Construction Forces argued, "the bulldozer is—as construction men have always claimed—one of the mighty weapons of the war."[51]

DMJM proudly displayed bulldozers in its "company general brochure," prepared for potential clients, shown clearing roads that helped "speed basic development of new nations."[52] Beyond the violence of land seizures, however, war planes took off from the DMJM-constructed Andersen Air Force Base in Guam to drop ammunition during the Korean War; and, during the Vietnam War, B-52 bombers departed from there to attack the communist front in South Vietnam, at one point dropping bombs at a rate of eight thousand tons per month, killing more than one million people.[53]

Back in Los Angeles, DMJM was designing Titan I ballistic missile testing complexes in California and Colorado, Atlas and Mercury launch facilities at Cape Canaveral (called Cape Kennedy during 1963–73), and sonic testing facilities in Ohio following the Soviet Union's first successful intercontinental ballistic missile launch in 1950. Among companies active in Cold War military construction—including engineering firms Ralph M. Parsons Co. in Los Angeles and Giffels & Rosetti in Detroit—DMJM was described by an editor of *Engineering News-Record* as "the most successful firm of all in getting missile work" because of its "integrated" architecture and engineering services.[54] According to Department of Defense records, the number of the firm's military contracts dwarfed those of other architecture and engineering firms.[55] Between 1965 and 1988, DMJM worked on an average of thirty military contracts per year. By comparison, Leo A. Daly, based in Nebraska, averaged fourteen; Holmes and Narver in California, nine; Parsons in California, five; CRS in Texas, three; HOK in Missouri, two; SOM and Perkins & Will, one.[56]

In sum, the history of capital exchange through DMJM's individual commissions, which varied widely in geography, client, and scope, reveals how the "project" of urban development could not be defined as isolated buildings or infrastructures; instead, it was a system built over an extended period that was bolstered by continued war. It was this operating *system* of infrastructure and infrastructural space, as Keller Easterling has argued, that had become the "secret weapon of the most powerful people in the world."[57] By 1970, real estate, diversification, and land development constituted the "newest frontier in the business of architecture," but as discussed in chapter 1, architects and engineers at DMJM had learned these principles during the preceding "decade of development." As political activist Lyndon LaRouche described in 1960, this "project" of architecture-in-development could be seen as a sequential process that ultimately supported private capital. In the case of DMJM, the firm began with schools and defense architecture before working on highways, railways, and airports through which resources could be exchanged and redistributed. Private investment followed.⁵⁸

DMJM thus demonstrates in detail how, as Arturo Escobar has described, "the entire project of development, in which the industrialized countries were to aid poor countries to adopt strategies for 'modernization' and, eventually, join the ranks of the First World, was an immense design project."⁵⁹ Further, in thinking with Albena Yaneva and Bruno Latour, who have described how buildings-as-projects change in meaning and function long after their construction, DMJM's history of entangled contracts reveals how the "project" of government contracting firms such as DMJM or AECOM was redefined, between the 1950s and 1970s, as infrastructure that carried with it a promise of building in the future—setting in place an internalized and extractive *process* that could continue far after and beyond the scope of an architect's life.⁶⁰ As this history suggests, the "project" also began *before* design or drawing began—in the work of predesign—to take on an expanded scope that was seen as necessary in order to capture the full range of funding sources made possible by defense and development.

Terms

As they focused their attention on procuring contracts after World War II, architecture and engineering firms working for the government increasingly adopted the generalist term *contractor*—a designation historically associated with builders of public works and from which architects had worked hard to distance themselves during the second half of the nineteenth century.⁶¹ Yet this gradual disassociation from architecture was occurring just as the AIA was expanding the type and number of contract templates it offered for a fee: from contracts between architects, owners, and builders in the 1920s; to agreements with subcontractors, consultants, and interprofessional associates; to supplemental liability insurance contracts for each.[62]

A brief history of contracting within the construction industry reveals how this process unfolded. Most generally, the term *contractor* was used in the early eighteenth century to describe those who undertook the construction of public works, such as bridges. As historian Sara Wermiel writes, builders first subcontracted with tradesmen; once they could not manage or control the quality of subcontractors' work, or once it was no longer lucrative to subcontract the work to others, they began to hire other laborers directly.[63] This was the same kind of shift that occurred within architecture and engineering during the twentieth century: first, architects began working with "partners," before moving on to joint ventures and subcontracts with other firms. Eventually, they opted for outright acquisitions as they became conglomerates. Bound up with claims of freedom and liberal democracy, and unique to the US, as Wermiel argues, the term *contractor* was associated with individuals who, in their work for governments, "were not associated with any traditional trade."[64] And, to recall, the Department of Justice had claimed that professions such as architecture could no longer be considered "trades" by the 1970s—a designation that had historically protected it from antitrust sanctions—and thus freed it from restraint and oversight.

The firm of industrialist Frank Gilbreth—a disciple of Frederick Taylor's and known, with his wife Lilian, for time and motion studies—offers a clear example of how a single firm transitioned, during the late nineteenth century, from a trade specialist to a contracting generalist. In 1895, Gilbreth established a "general contracting" firm, Frank Gilbreth and Company, after earlier forays into machinery and quarrying had soured.[65] With this shift to contractor came an excessive proliferation of paperwork, theories about contracts, and publications about controlling costs and managing business—all part of an organizational system Gilbreth described as his "Field System."[66] Similarly, the architects and engineers who grew increasingly dependent on government projects after World War II, now defined by and through their federal contracts, were simultaneously shedding their associations with particular professions and embracing the generalist term *contractor*.

As we have seen, the government was friendly to corporations working on risky defense projects abroad, and the work was lucrative. While government contracts for architectural and engineering work capped fees for drawing and design at 6 percent during the 1960s, the fees for surveys, topographical work, soil borings, and other work "before design" were larger, and "experimental, developmental, or research work" could be allocated up to 15 percent of the cost of the work.[67] Although it was common in the private sector for architects to earn fixed fees or a percentage of the total construction cost, government work prohibited this practice in the public sector due to potential conflicts of interest or inefficiency.[68] Government contractors were paid using a cost-plus-fixed-fee method—a method described by Gilbreth in 1907 that became increasingly popular during and after World War II in an effort to encourage rapid production.[69] Gilbreth argued that a typical fixed contract ensured that the interests of building owners and the contractor were divergent, suggesting they were "a practical declaration of war" because contractors were forced to do their best in the shortest possible time; the cost-plus contract, by contrast, ensured that the contractor's and the client's motivations were the same.[70] Cost-plus contracts were particularly profitable for firms that were efficient with their time or overworked their employees (or both).

As an alternative to the standard percentage-based fee system, the AIA introduced its own "Fee-Plus-Cost System" for architects in 1915, published in the first *Handbook of Architectural Practice* in 1920.[71] The system was described along the lines laid out by Gilbreth, as uniting the interests of the owner and the architect, thereby yielding a "quasi-professional" relationship.⁷² Manual labor, such as drafting, and the overhead expenses required to support it (rent, heat, lighting, supplies, etc.) were expected to be charged as "costs," though the owner was expected to "trust" the architect to "expend economically and wisely, as well as honestly." Architects were, in other words, acting as financial advisors, and their professional advice had little effect on their remuneration.⁷³

Therefore, it was not only that the military was building businesses—bolstering military engineering-and-architecture firms, particularly in Southern California, while encouraging new concentrations of technology in Northern California (the beginnings of Silicon Valley); it was also that the contract terms themselves offered massive financial incentives. As historian Bill Leslie has shown, cost-plus contracts not only reduced risk and encouraged firms to open branches abroad or to expand operations from the East to the West Coast during the 1960s, but also enabled companies to charge the government for their own research and development.⁷⁴ With this additional capital, contractors were able to create new technologies, markets, and entire economic sectors outside their existing realms of production.

A detailed look at one specific contract of DMJM's reveals how capital and resources circulated in an architecture and engineering firm through cost-plus contracts, and how physical labor was negotiated and exploited as part of an effort to maximize profits toward creating new sectors. DMJM's 1958 contract for water exploration in Thailand, for instance, was cost-plus. Although written and issued by the ICA, the contract was between the Government of Thailand and DMJM. "The Government [of Thailand], through the ICA, has requested assistance from the United States of America," the contract reads, describing the work as part of a patriotic "tour of duty."⁷⁵

The financial terms of the contract stipulated that hard costs, such as drafting salaries, transportation, and equipment, would be reimbursed after the ICA controller received a voucher, supplier certificate, and two invoice copies. The contract included terms of employment as though DMJM were an employee of the state. Vacations? They could be granted at a rate of 1.5 workdays for each month of work, to be taken during or after the "tour of duty" or to be cashed in at the end. Sick leave? Thirteen days were allowed per year. Work-in-progress reports were due quarterly, and investing in other businesses, professions, or occupations in Thailand was strictly prohibited.[76] A fixed fee of $30,000 (or 9 percent of the total project ceiling of $335,000) was calculated at a rate of $156.00 per "man-month" for each worker, excluding secretaries, officers, and consultants, which was to be paid in monthly payments following the work.

However, there were flexibilities built into many parts of the contract. For instance, it was relatively easy to increase the "fixed" fee if additional man-months were needed, though overtime pay was permitted only for the laborers (the drillers). In other words, DMJM's drillers could earn additional pay if they worked overtime, but DMJM's "fixed" fee (and, thus, the firm's profit) would also increase per "man-hour" worked.

Indeed, most of the letters exchanged between DMJM and the ICA were about extensions of work and approvals for overworking. One, dated September 30, 1958, clarified that Thai workweeks were set at forty-eight hours, rather than forty. "Our recent work week," the letter from DMJM reads, "has been including four hours per day supervisory time for the sixteen hour day [80 hours per week]. . . . Overtime reported to August 31, 1958 has been approved at my request."[77] A year later, the payment ceiling for DMJM's work on the project increased to $637,000.

• • •

In this prehistory of business conglomeration, we have observed how capital, resources, and bodies were internationally distributed, exploited, and integrated as part of a larger project of American hegemony. As new relationships formed between the private sector and the state, the techniques and terms of the US military and government began to migrate to the businesses of architects and engineers. The remainder of this chapter will focus on examples of tools and initiatives, created by the US government for the purposes of war, that were acquired by architects for development, carried further into their businesses' subsidiary companies, and finally introduced to the profession as facts of architectural business.

Airplane

It was around a decommissioned World War II bomber, specifically a Douglas A-26 Invader (the same aircraft covertly used by the CIA in Indonesia to thwart Sukarno's regime), that DMJM organized its earliest subsidiary, DMJM Aerial and Associates, in 1964.[78] DMJM acquired the plane—built by Douglas Aircraft in Long Beach in the 1940s and considered versatile, since it was fast and could carry heavy bombs—for use in development work (figure 25). During the war, the planes had dropped thousands of bombs in Europe and Southeast Asia, including in the battle for control of the island of Biak, in present-day Indonesia, which the Allies hoped to capture in order to build military bases there.[79]

With the plane's long nose and engines on both sides of the cockpit, clear views of the ground were difficult; however, the airplane framed good views of the horizon. While the vertical views of land offered by most airplanes were touted as a "gift" of war by modernist architects such as Le Corbusier, the A-26 was well suited for professionals trained to divide and develop land planimetrically.[80] The plane included geodesic and photogrammetry equipment, which DMJM Aerial used in mapping, recording, and measuring the

FIGURE 25. DMJM's modified A-26 bomber. From US Department of Commerce, *International Commerce*, May 3, 1965, 5.

geophysical characteristics of land. A high-precision short-range navigation system (HIRAN) measured distances between points on the ground from the air—a technique used in combat during World War II.[81] As historian of science Theodore Porter writes, this quantification of distances—the turning of the distances into numbers for validity—was a political act.[82]

In war, high-frequency radio signals directed bombers to their targets by transmitting signals from planes to stations on the ground and back again. The total time it took the signal to travel and return indicated how far the bomber was from ground stations and therefore how close the target was. For the plane's use in surveying, radio stations were set up in the area to be mapped, and DMJM's bomber flew in repetitive lines; architects and engineers documented the land through photography, marked a precise network of points, and determined distances between them (figure 26). This practice was known as "trilateration."[83] The ultimate goal of trilateration was to control a place where the surveyors could not physically be, further internationalizing the practice of American architects, among other contractors, without a ground presence.[84]

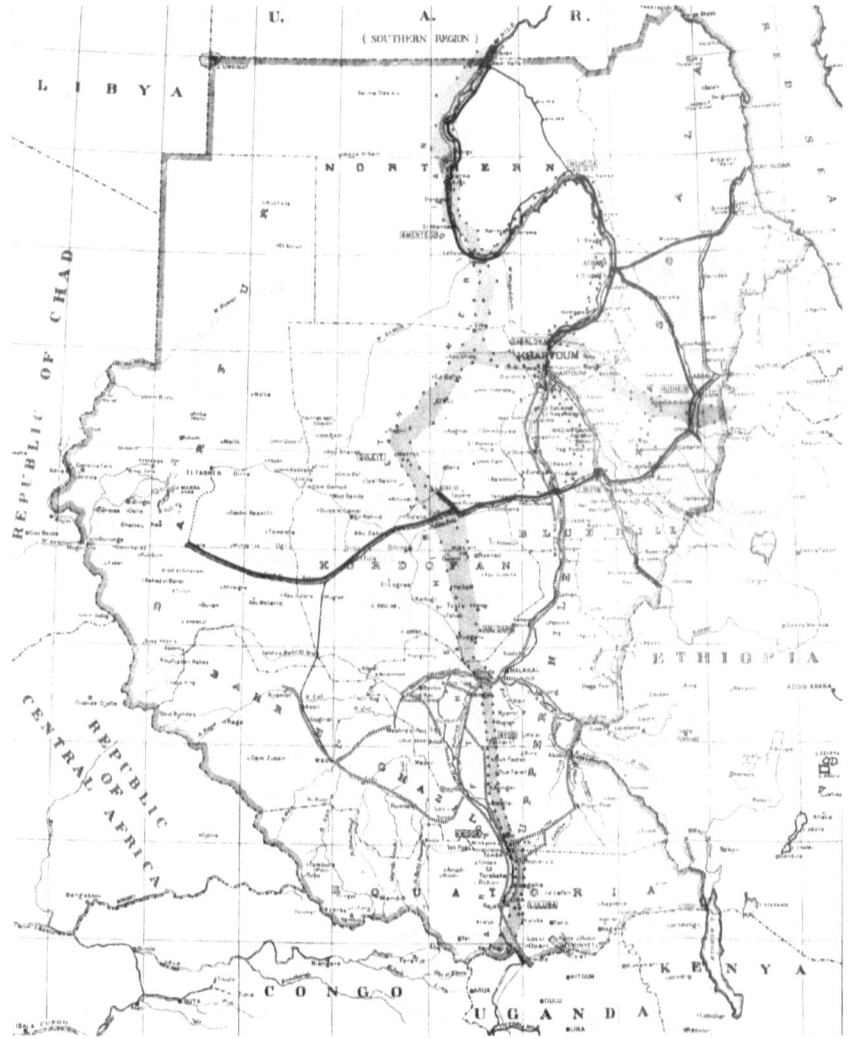

FIGURE 26. "Existing Survey Control," with hatched areas indicating first- and second-order trilateration for a Sudan highway. From DMJM, *Technical Report for the Post Sudan Highway*, prepared for the US Agency for International Development, 1962. Papers of Arthur Mann. Private collection. Courtesy of Karen Letterman.

Based in Beirut, DMJM's plane conducted land surveys in "developing" regions where American geodesists were racing to measure and record newly "liberated" countries. It was there where DMJM architects claimed to see "a future" in many developing nations. "It seems to me there's as much business in Africa as anyone wants," a senior engineer, Frank Collins, argued, "but US businessmen are not going after it intelligently."[85]

Survey and navigation instruments, such as a magnetometer, helped the architects identify petroleum and mineral deposits, while an aerial camera could record four thousand square miles without reloading. During the 1960s, DMJM was contracted to "search" for oil off the Ethiopian coast, document and determine the best land paths for a national desert highway in Sudan, study Nigeria's water supply, map and design a highway through Cameroon, study the economics of Lagos's water system, catalogue nearly forty-three thousand miles of "unmeasured land" in Liberia, and conduct "surveillance missions" in Central and South America.

These processes were applied to urban development projects in the US as well. Following their international development work, DMJM was hired to determine how the undeveloped land in some of the largest parcels in Southern California could return the greatest capital investment—by growing crops, drilling for oil, or subdividing for housing. These included planned communities during the mid-1960s such as Sunset Mountain Park, owned by the Sunset International Petroleum Company; Phillips Ranch, owned by Louis Lessner; and Westlake Village, owned by the American-Hawaiian Steamship Company.

Computer

It was around government-sponsored computers that DMJM formed a data processing subsidiary, Logicomp, and a spin-off business, Design Methods, at the end of the 1960s. DMJM was one of the earliest architecture and engineering firms in the US to acquire computers, including a Univac 9300 Data Communications System—a general-purpose business computer, used primarily for accounting and payroll. They also secured access to a Univac 1108, a powerful multiprocessor built for war. In 1967, DMJM hired Vahe Khachooni, a young Armenian-Iranian immigrant and architectural engineering graduate of Cal Poly San Luis Obispo and Penn State, who led the computer services division at DMJM before leading Logicomp with Phil Daniel and its offshoot, Design Methods, with Santa Barbara architect William Miller.[86]

Most useful to the firm's development work was the 3.5-ton Univac 1108 multiprocessor, first developed for missile guidance. Unlike the Univac 9300, which was an outgrowth of an early general-purpose business computer developed with funding from the US Census Bureau, the multiprocessing 1108 was an outgrowth of Univac's Athena, built to guide the nation's first underground intercontinental ballistic missile, the Titan I, which DMJM was designing during the late 1950s. Built by Sperry Rand, the Univac 1108 was the first commercially available multiprocessor designed to manage many functions simultaneously—many layers of defense—as a hallmark of Kennedy's "flexible response" defense strategy during the Cold War.[87]

In a request to Congress, one army colonel argued that a multiprocessing Univac computer was necessary to manage the unprecedented number of agencies, military groups, and multinational industries involved in defense work:

> The national mobilization effort can be broken down into 130 groups—industries, various government agencies and the like. Each has a part to play. Under each major part are sub parts. . . . [T]his is a tremendous calculating process. . . . [T]here are equations that cannot be solved by hand or by electrically operated computing machines because they involve millions of relationships that would take a lifetime to figure out. . . . [T]he hand system can't do the trick any

longer. . . . [B]ig operations are the same as mobilization—based on relationships of various groups. Get the relationships all lined up once, and the machine will give out with what can and can't be done.[88]

With up to three processing units, four memory banks, and two IOCs (controllers, each with sixteen channels, that connected to "peripherals" such as hard drives and keyboards), the Univac 1108 could be very busy indeed.

DMJM hired Logicomp and eventually Design Methods for its own projects, as did other municipalities and architecture firms, such as Charles Luckman Associates, Welton Becket and Associates, and William Pereira Associates, for "operations" research, among other things. According to a *Los Angeles Times* article, DMJM's computing subsidiaries signaled the "first time a Los Angeles architectural/engineering firm has gone so heavily into data processing," since computers with high processing power were too large and too expensive for most architects.[89]

For DMJM, computers helped architects resolve the "relational problems" of architecture—as they did for the military—including identifying how one building should or could relate to another or to the parts within them.[90] Using their own computer program, named MATRAN (Matrix Analysis), which Khachooni developed with Miller in 1969 on the Univac 1108, they turned the organization of work into a business, producing adjacency diagrams for architects' offices in the late 1960s and early 1970s. In one example for Welton Becket and Associates in Los Angeles (a firm eventually acquired by AECOM in 2009), they quantified distances, as they had in their development work, and relationships between various departments within the Becket office—from design to administration (figure 27).

A second use for the computer, related more to the extraction of resources than to defense or organizational analysis, was in master planning and land studies. DMJM used the 1108 to run a Harvard-

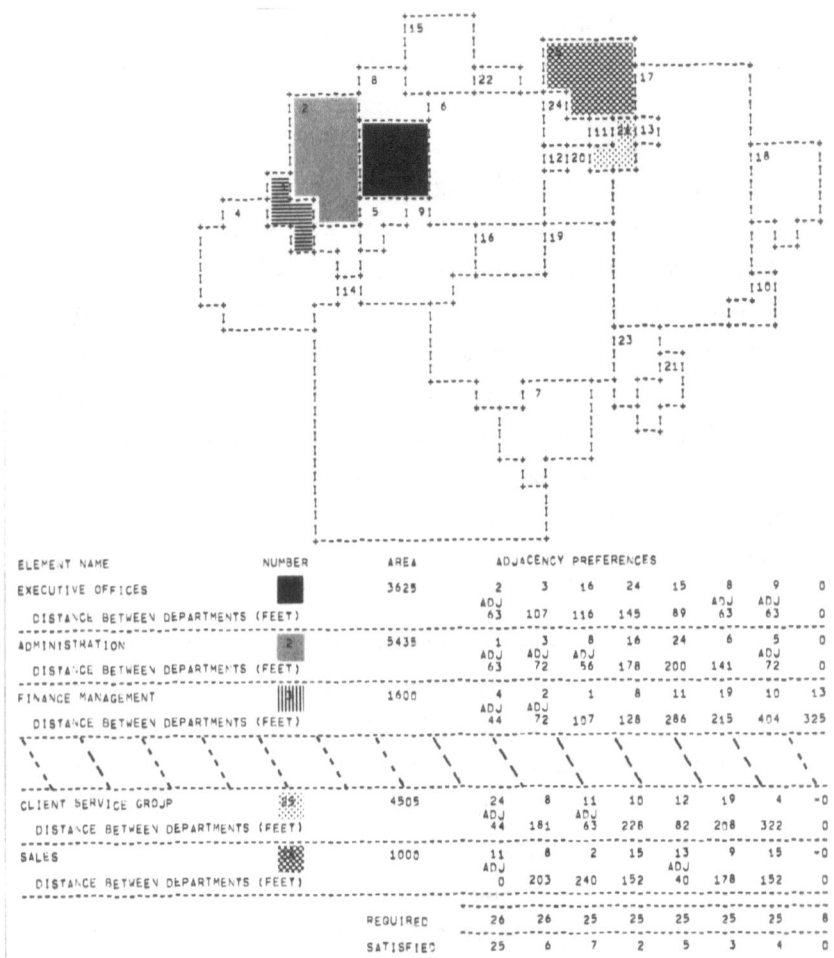

FIGURE 27. A computer-generated "space plan" for the office of Welton Becket and Associates. From *Datamation*, September 15, 1971. Courtesy of Vahe Khachooni.

developed program, SYMAP (Synagraphic Computer Mapping), to produce "proximal maps" that could assess the economic potentials of resources such as oil.

Beyond these practical uses, DMJM's computer programs—like many early computers used by architects—served to generate publicity, projecting an image of technological, if not developmentalist, expertise.[91] DMJM's computers were featured in Sperry Rand's quarterly magazine, *Input for Modern Management*, in 1969, and in publications of the Computer Sciences Corporation in the 1970s, as part of the company's marketing efforts.[92]

Meanwhile, Khachooni was sharing his knowledge not only with DMJM—where he gave three-hour after-work lectures on design-related computer programs—but also with the broader profession. Interest in "professional development" and post-college adult education was surging at the time, evident in new "professional development" initiatives within the AIA and in new for-profit institutions such as the University of Phoenix.[93] Khachooni shared his knowledge with national and local AIA chapters in California, Washington, Florida, and Michigan between 1968 and 1972, as well as at institutions such as UCLA Extension.[94]

Khachooni's lectures extended DMJM's earlier military-industrial-educational efforts, exemplified by its participation in the air force's 1960 "Education with Industry" program, where military officers took ten-month "tours of duty" at the firm to study management, mathematics, architecture, and construction.[95] One air force captain who trained at DMJM argued that the experience was comparable to a graduate program, reinforcing the resemblance of professional practice to the academy and highlighting how "development" connected education and capitalist growth.

In 1976, the AIA, the National Council of Architectural Registration Boards (NCARB), and the Association of Collegiate Schools of Architecture launched their own professional development program for systematizing the continuing education of architects, and a similar Intern-Architect Development Program (IDP) for recent graduates preparing for licensure.[96]

Yet these professional development programs were shaped by architects, like those at DMJM, whose careers were built on a twentieth-century defense-development economy. For example, Kansas architect Dwight Bonham, who cochaired the first IDP Coordinating Committee in 1977 on behalf of NCARB, began his career working as an architectural engineer for the Bureau of Reclamation at the Marcel Breuer–designed Grand Coulee Dam in Washington.[97] Built in 1942, the dam powered aluminum production in the Pacific Northwest to make planes and ships for the war, and later irrigated farmland to expand economic development and diversify crops in the Columbia River basin.[98]

Drawings

In 1960, DMJM caught the attention of *Fortune*'s editors. The magazine profiled the firm's architects and engineers not as designers of the "cultural world," but instead as political designers of "space": the space *between* people, cities, buildings, and industries. Similar framings were used by architects in other large firms at the time, including Nathaniel Owings of SOM, who titled his 1973 account of the firm *The Spaces in Between*.[99] The *Fortune* article claimed that "DMJM's main interests and passions lie outside the cultural world . . . and not only in the design of large spaces—which is how architects traditionally define their craft—but in space itself. DMJM's interest in the 'space business' is a natural outcome of its jobs in the missile field. . . . You name it, this company of architect-engineers has designed it: dams, schools, hydroelectric plants, apartment houses, air bases, 'hard' missile complexes. Next? Maybe lunar and space stations."[100] Within this space work, one such project—the Titan I intercontinental ballistic missile (ICBM)—reveals how the various tools of defense and development were built and exchanged through policy, contracts, and architecture itself.

In 1954, as military base construction slowed, the air force announced the Titan I as the nation's highest research priority and as an architecture of "deterrence" in the face of Soviet threat. As urban theorist Lawrence Vale has argued, the rationale for deterrence, unlike those for defense or nineteenth-century isolationism, was rooted in the ability to construct a credible perception of threat.[101] In the nation's first ICBM system, the Atlas (begun in 1946, the year DMJM formed), the missiles rested on "soft" aboveground structures with minimally protective architecture. The Titan, by contrast, was to be fully "hardened," with concealed underground silos from which missiles would rise to launch. It represented a pivotal shift in terms of computation technologies, architectural possibility, and the value and type of drawings produced by architects and engineers.[102]

The concurrent development of the Atlas and Titan programs was hotly debated, given their functional similarities, but in the end both programs were advanced, to ensure that national deterrence would not be overdependent on the yet-to-be-tested Atlas alone. And yet a single firm, DMJM, was designing both projects—including the air force's Atlas Launch Facilities in Cape Canaveral (1958) for launching military satellites and the Project Mercury launch pad (1957), from which John Glenn blasted into orbit in 1962.[103]

The air force selected DMJM's proposal, chosen from a group of submissions by twenty-seven firms, and founding architect Kenneth Johnson was chosen as project manager. This role was a fitting assignment for the former Hollywood actor, since the Titan was routinely described as a military performance with powerful deterrence effects akin to the entertaining effects of the culture industry.[104] Johnson organized an international joint venture with three other firms, named DMJM and Associates (DMJM&A). Held together by a single contract, thereby reducing risk, the joint venture included the Mason & Hanger–Silas Mason Company, a New York engineering and construction firm specializing in tunnel design, blasting, and radiation protection;[105] Leo A. Daly of Omaha, the architecture firm that had produced an underground headquarters for the air force's Strategic Air Command in 1954;[106] and the Pittsburgh-based chemical engineering firm Rust Engineering, which, prior to World War II, had designed an Atomic Energy Commission plant at Oak Ridge in Tennessee and a TNT plant in Paducah, Kentucky, in 1942.[107]

The design contract included three projects: a single-missile Titan prototype test facility, a three-missile training base facility at Vandenberg Air Force Base in California, and a fully operational complex at Lowry Air Force Base outside of Denver.[108] DMJM&A was hired to determine the wall thicknesses of silos and underground structures, identify the best way to load the propellant upon launch command, and, most importantly for the architects, determine the "spaces" between the missiles (the weapons) and the "control" and "power" facilities (the architecture).

In his own publications, DMJM's Phillip Daniel compared the process of drawing with and without computers (figure 28). The historical process of design, he argued, was often "dangerously" based on intuition and iteration rather than on calculated precision or "proof"; therefore, time and money were wasted.[109] Typically, wrote Daniel, an architect gathers criteria about a building's program and site before moving to a conceptual design stage, at which point

> a senior designer, along with others, produces 30, 50, or perhaps hundreds of sketches on flimsy paper until he intuitively recognizes one or more of the concepts to be sufficiently good to warrant concentrated additional development for final designs. At no time is there a formal testing of the validity of designs. . . . This is the common process used today. It has been used for the last 2,000 years! . . . There is no proof of 'what was done' or 'why it was done'. . . . This lack of proof is not only unfortunate, but dangerous.[110]

A computer, he argued, could help "validate" designs before drawings were even produced. In one illustrated example, published in *Aerospace Engineering* in 1961, Daniel described how the computer

FIGURE 28. Phillip Daniel with his analog computer and a model of the Apollo Lunar Module, ca. 1969. Courtesy of Vahe Khachooni.

was used to determine the distance between two interfering structures, such as between a hazardous reactor building and a laboratory. In his drawing, an Atlas missile stands ready to launch in the background (figure 29). To determine the optimal distance between the laboratory and the reactor building, he offered a calculus-based formula that considered the economic cost of material damage as a function of distance. In other words, the architect could use the computer to materially reconcile the political economy: the distance needed for safety.[111] Daniel's interest in mathematical "proof" revealed his desire to turn the collected experiences of the firm into power—to establish a theory that aimed to *manage* and *control* the world as it was, rather than produce new information about it.[112]

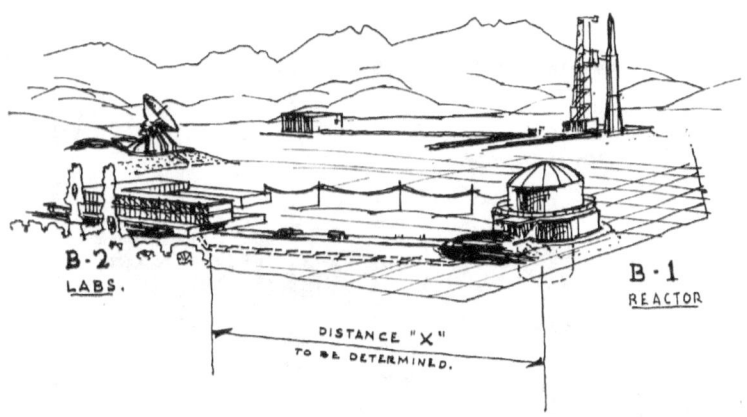

FIGURE 29. Phillip Daniel's diagram of a mathematical proof for calculating distances between buildings. From *Aerospace Engineering*, June 1961, 11.

The air force had proposed that the Titan squadrons be organized in concentrated clusters of nine missiles per site (nine-by-one configurations), such that the weapons would be close to the radio antenna and computer guiding them to their targets.[113] In 1958, though, after years of planning and negotiating, DMJM&A's drawings problematized that air force recommendation. As declassified meeting minutes from the Ballistic Missile Division show, Johnson explained to the air force that each nine-by-one complex would constitute a single target and thus subject an entire squadron to destruction with one strike. Following theories of dispersal and urban decentralization, DMJM&A proposed a configuration of nine distributed launchers arranged in three self-contained launch complexes with three missiles each, at three geographically dispersed sites located twelve to eighteen miles apart (figure 30).[114] Analogous to a recession striking a conglomerate, if one part of the complex was struck and could not return fire, there would be two others ready to fire back.

The DMJM&A design contract included both "hardened" facilities capable of surviving an atomic attack and "Hollywood-hard"

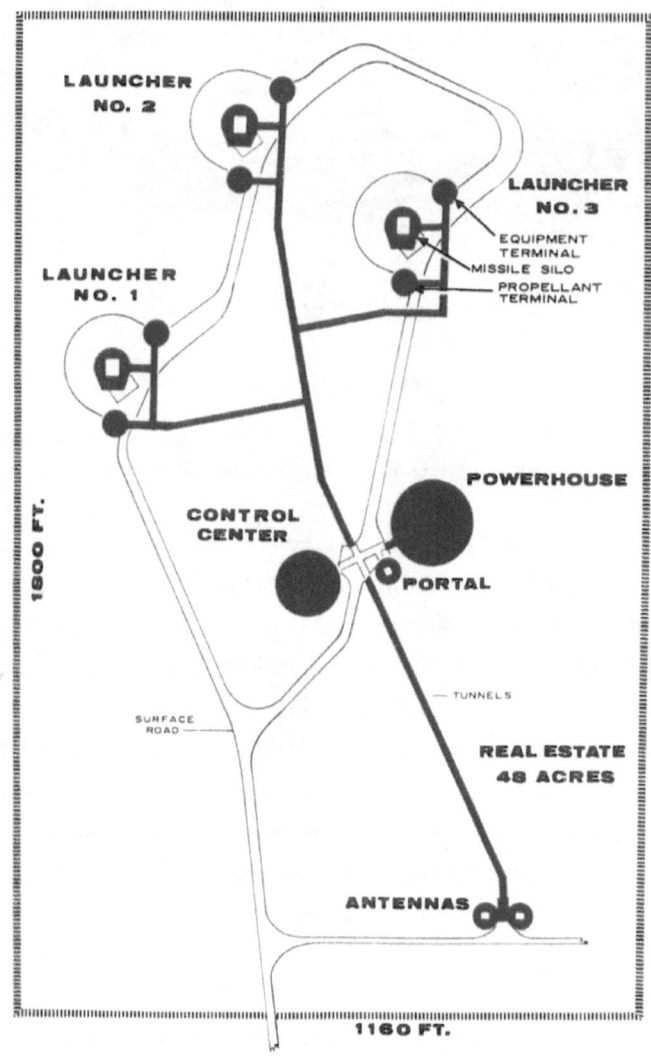

FIGURE 30. A typical launch complex of a Titan I ICBM. From *Aerospace Engineering*, June 1961, 10.

facilities that were fully operational but "hard" only in appearance, which reflected the separation between non-material and material economies as underscored by post-Fordism. Both Hollywood-hard and fully hardened complexes consisted of nearly identical components: a powerhouse, a control center, propellent terminals, and an interconnected set of fortified silos, as well as air ducts and miles of piping to fuel the missiles.[115]

Historian Tom Vanderbilt has argued that silos were "the ultimate incarnation of the modernist dictum that buildings were machines."[116] While the surfaces of the hard and Hollywood-hard silos were similar, the thickness of their cylinder walls differed underground.[117] Much thicker than the Hollywood-hard walls, the walls of the fully hardened silos were two feet thick at the bottom, expanding to nearly fourteen feet thick at the top (figure 31).[118]

The US military viewed the completed set of construction drawings as tools of significant value—of economic, political, and material value comparable to that of computers or warplanes. The contract for the Titan I ICBM was awarded as cost plus a 5.7 percent fixed fee, which totaled nearly $2.85 million—nearly the same price as a Univac 1108 computer. In total, the Titan I project required nearly nine hundred thousand hours of drawing, calculating, and negotiating, in response to twelve hundred continually changing criteria developed by the air force.[119] Beyond its economic value, the design labor was accounted for materially in that the drawings and specifications were measured like construction materials such as concrete and steel: the construction drawings for a single Titan I base weighed in at 3.5 tons—one whole ton more than a Univac 1108. "For the first time," a DMJM engineer argued, "this nation's retaliatory forces ... would be just as dependent on A-E [architecture-engineering] designed facilities as on the weapon itself."[120]

However, architects were not only producing computer drawings that exposed the material capabilities of the military and the

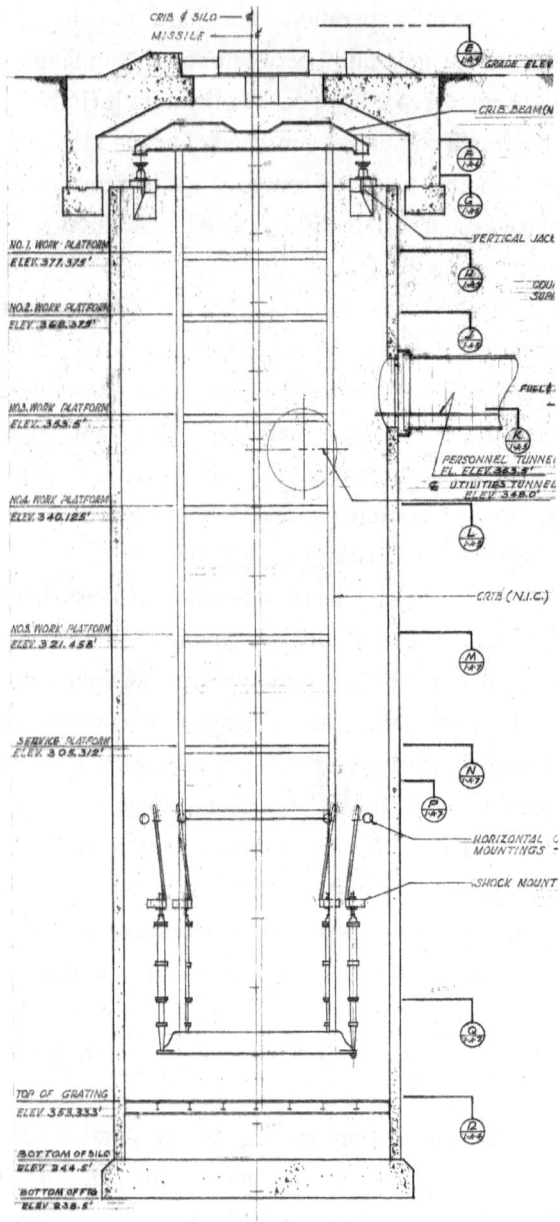

FIGURE 31. Section of "Hollywood-hard" Titan I ICBM silo, Operational Silo Test Facility, Vandenberg Air Force Base, California, 1959. Air Force Historical Research Division, Maxwell Air Force Base Archives, Alabama.

architects' material contributions. Part-time consulting architects, employed on a project-by-project basis, produced a second type of drawing, by hand: renderings. These renderings dramatized the missile's deterrence capacity while obscuring the differences between the hard and Hollywood-hard silos and their missiles. While the missile bases were described materially, akin to modern architecture, the missiles were described performatively, akin to stage sets, capable of lulling the everyday citizen into order and complacency.[121] Global war and technology thus depended on this newfound separation of material rhetoric from material truth. As Lucia Allais has described, architects were historically trained to connect their received experiences to the recovered experiences they then transposed—by rendering them—onto a drawing.[122] Yet by the 1960s, renderings within corporate practice were no longer used to *recover* historical loss but rather to *conceal* past experiences, making it impossible to discern what actually occurred—and, by extension, the material capabilities of a building, weapon, firm, or person.

Like the doors and topsoil that covered up the differences between hard and Hollywood-hard silos, the architectural renderings of the Titan I obscured their reality. In one striking rendering, a roaring Titan missile stands in launch position after emerging from its fortified lair (figure 32). The softly focused grayscale drawing was not made by a full-time architect or engineer at DMJM; rather, it was the work of an Oscar-winning Hollywood art director and University of Southern California architecture alumnus, Jack Martin Smith. A former classmate of Daniel and Johnson, he was known for his work as a lead artist and production designer on *The Wizard of Oz* (1939).[123] Hired as a consultant, rather than a bona fide DMJM employee, Martin Smith created a rendering that was reminiscent of his preproduction drawings of upturned test tubes clustered together for the Emerald City in *The Wizard of Oz*, in which a realistic stage set counterbalanced a dreamy

FIGURE 32. Rendering of a Titan I missile launcher by Jack Martin Smith. Papers of Stanley Moe. Private collection. Courtesy of Billie Moe Crouse.

FIGURE 33. Preproduction drawing by Jack Martin Smith of the Emerald City for *The Wizard of Oz*, ca. 1939. © Turner Entertainment Company. Production Design Drawing Collection, Margaret Herrick Library, Academy of Motion Picture Arts and Sciences, Beverly Hills, California.

backdrop to produce "theatrical realism" (figure 33).[124] The rendering of the missile, like the missile itself, served a new function as a form of both military deterrence and defense.

This description of material falsity in the renderings can be understood, on the one hand, as a manifestation of the "experience"-based Keynesian economics valued by the military, in which consumer optimism rested not on material fact but on a consumer's lack of access to fact.[125] On the other hand, it can be explained by a longer-standing practice and cycle of American imperialism embedded in the meaning of *corporate conglomerate*: expand and protect, defend and deter, destroy and develop. Architects upheld these purposeful distinctions by explicitly managing the distance between material fact and material rhetoric in order to maintain their sovereignty.[126]

. . .

Since the late nineteenth century, American architects had advocated sustained government patronage, but with limited success. It was not until the twentieth century, as part of a broader project of American hegemony, that infrastructural dependencies presented new political and economic dependencies between the US government and its contractors. Today, AECOM resembles a global empire more than an architecture and engineering firm. It describes itself, variously and interchangeably, as a "corporate conglomerate," a "defense contractor," and a "infrastructure consultant." A few of its services are familiar as architecture: in Los Angeles, for example, clients can hire AECOM to design buildings such as courthouses and police stations. Meanwhile, in Kabul, Afghanistan, AECOM workers maintain weapons and military vehicles and train local residents how to use them.[127] In Germantown, Maryland, workers support military logistics and missions of diplomacy.[128] In Las Vegas, government officials are shuttled by a discreet AECOM airline named "Janet" to the Nevada National Security Site.[129] In Springfield, Virginia, the firm monitors global security systems.[130] And the list goes on.

But the distinction established between material fact and economic value is made patently clear by legal sanctions against AECOM. In recent years, the company has been sued for knowingly fabricating its experiences and inflating its own value. "AECOM's public statements were *materially false* and misleading at all relevant times," a 2016 lawsuit stated, citing the company's practice of publicly trading stock at an "artificially inflated" price. In a separate case, in order to win contracts, the company was convicted of producing "falsified corporate records" and submitting "false statements to both federal and state government agencies."[131] Further, the company submitted false claims to the Federal Emergency Management Agency on behalf of its clients following Hurricane Katrina—earning a total of more than $300 million between 2005 and 2019 in total—and subsequently agreed to pay a settlement of $11.8 million.[132] Finally, during "maintenance and management" work for the US Army in Afghanistan, the firm was sued for allegedly falsifying timesheets by inflating "man-hour utilization" rates and billing for hours not worked. The case was largely dismissed, however, since the violations were not considered "material," or capable of influencing government decisions, by law. In other words, because the government was fully aware of the infractions, the company could not be held accountable.[133] At the same time that AECOM was allegedly falsifying its value, it was being celebrated by the mayor of Los Angeles, Eric Garcetti.[134] It had become the largest publicly traded revenue generator in Los Angeles, representing more gross domestic product than the countries it served.[135]

5 Portfolio
Valuing Practice

During the 1970s, as architects and engineers were restructuring their firms and acquiring others, they were debating the value of books to their "practice." By this I do not mean that they were considering, as in the past, the usefulness of books for publicly communicating their unique design methods or whether the books written about them aligned with their politics. Rather, they were concerned that standardized books, with fixed spines like the buildings they were designing, could no longer accurately contain or represent the full scope of their projects, services, and assets, since they were frequently changing. Finding new ways to represent the value of firms—and thus their price tags—was considered a critical task for survival in a late twentieth-century market economy throttled by mergers and acquisitions.

A case in point was engineer Richard Newman, whose interest in leaving the engineering firm Genge to work as deputy CEO for DMJM in 1977 was motivated, in large part, by his ability to purchase DMJM's shares at "book value."[1] In 1980, explaining investment jargon in simple terms to architects by linking it to survival, the management consultant Weld Coxe defined *book value* as "the working capital required to stay alive," reflecting "real worth rather than . . . assumptions about future return on investment."[2] In other words, book value—a concept stemming from the Great Depression that was waning as a primary measurement of work—was considered the worth of a firm's assets at a given moment, stated on a balance sheet, rather than its market value, or economic *potential* over time, conveyed by an income statement.[3] Therefore, "buying into" the firm by purchasing shares at book value could be lucrative for a firm with real estate and widely diversified projects, since the shares were likely to be worth more on the market in the future.

Most architects at the time valued their firms in this way. However, in an economy in which firms were frequently acquired, merged, or sold through stock transfers, architects were, by the 1960s, beginning to reappropriate a familiar book format—the portfolio—as a tool for considering time and managing future value. Once associated exclusively with artists and architects as cases for holding loose sheets of paper, portfolios had become useful for many purposes during the twentieth century. They were mandated by the War Department during World War II for holding temporary papers with critical details about troop positions and battle strategies; they inspired theories of investment and real estate purchases during the 1960s; and finally, by the 1970s, conglomerate firms themselves had become known as portfolios.

Yet this renewed interest in portfolios also reflected a broader interest in the ways in which architecture was described as a "practice." Prior to the 1960s, architects published succinctly organized "handbooks of practice" to standardize their office procedures, using glue-bound books to fix printed pages that together defined the relationships between architects and their individual constituents in order to promote economic growth and efficiency. By the 1960s, however, architects were transforming their handbooks into portfolios: binders with temporary and exchangeable leaflets—"circulars"—that were no longer exclusively dedicated to the managerial and transactional relationships between individuals, but also included those between the ever-changing businesses and associations, and their relationship with the public.

While the portfolio's prominence as a tool for the business of architecture was short lived, paralleling the rise and fall of conglomerates between the 1960s and 1980s, its use coincided not only with a newfound interest in income statements and quarterly or annual reports within offices, but also with another burst of books about architecture as a "practice": ethnographic, sociological, and historical studies produced by scholars who were examining and writing about architecture as a practice for the first time in decades. How, these scholarly books were asking, could architects boost their value and relevance to society through their work, rather than their products? Should they acquire new tools, add new services, or adopt new business procedures? Despite the urgent language of these texts, their questions were not entirely new. Indeed, the woes of the profession had served as prompts for authors writing about architecture as a practice every forty or so years since the 1850s, and they coincided with the occasional reformatting of architects' handbooks.

This chapter considers how the formats of books about "practice," and the perceived value of architecture described within them, changed in format and structure over the course of the twentieth century. By examining these two types of books—those produced by architects for business during economic booms, and those produced by scholars during the downturns that followed—it shows how the cyclical concerns of the profession fueled an economy of book-writing within the discipline. Taken together, it is possible to see how such books followed economic cycles, and that with each downturn, architecture was further abstracted and distanced from its origins in drawing. The concerns and theories within these texts about practice demonstrate how, despite their different audiences, architects and scholars alike shifted the sites of their perceived value, from the interactions between individuals during the 1920s to the interactions between businesses and professional associations during the 1960s, and finally to the interactions between professional associations and global political and economic systems by the 2010s, as texts became less about "practice" and more about "the practice of practice."

Practice Books

Architecture historians have long shown how the books that architects produce—from seventeenth-century treatises to nineteenth-century pattern books to twentieth-century professional handbooks—serve as "instruments" akin to their drawing tools (pencils, compasses, computers, etc.).[4] During the twentieth century, books not only helped architects establish and strengthen the standards of their profession, but also helped them establish the possibility of a "practice": once procedures were written, illustrated, read, and incorporated, they could then be set aside.[5] These books-as-instruments are, therefore, worthy of scholarly scrutiny, we are told, because they influence and are influenced by architectural work, and because they broaden architecture's disciplinary claims.[6] And while such books have often appeared as a flash in the pan due to the overwhelming inertia of capitalism's boom-and-bust cycles, it is worth recognizing not only how they help buildings outlive their physical forms, as Victor Hugo argued in 1831, but also how they help architects and scholars alike reproduce themselves (as architects, as professors), the organizations and institutions for which they work (firms, universities, governments), and the status quo that defines them.[7]

Before examining the changes within architects' handbooks and the scholarly books about them during the 1960s and 1970s, it is helpful to compare the moments when interest in architecture as a practice in the United States has been most pronounced—the 1920s–30s, 1960s–70s, and 2010s–20s—in order to see how and why such books were produced in the first place.

The first *Handbook of Architectural Practice* in the US, published by the American Institute of Architects in 1920, was conceptualized by Philadelphia architect and former AIA president Frank Miles Day of the firm Day & Klauder, known for designing college buildings and master plans. The handbook included advice, procedures, and contract templates that historian George Johnston has shown were useful in legitimizing the profession during the early twentieth century.[8]

Based on his own firm's "manual," Day's handbook was intended to help architects standardize their business operations, better direct their employees, and ensure greater consistency in the drawings they produced.[9] "If he relieve himself [sic] of the burden of business detail," the handbook's introduction reads, "the designer will be the freer to exert his creative and artistic talents."[10] The architect, the handbook continues, "by expressing his ideas in forms and words of exact contractual significance, by controlling machinery for their embodiment, by giving just decisions between conflicting interests, by breaking himself as worthy of his high calling, gives greater to his art the status of a profession. It is with that aspect of the Architect's work, professional practice and its servant, business administration, that this Handbook is concerned."[11] Without rehearsing Johnston's conclusions, suffice it to say that the 1920 handbook defined architecture's twentieth-century constituents—owners, architects, and builders—and their contractual relations through seven "parts," borrowing the material language from industrialization. It opened with details about "the architect and the owner" and ended with contracts and related "documents," listed for sale.[12]

When the handbook was published during the twenties, the US economy was growing at a staggering rate, and very few scholars were writing about the working conditions of architects. One exception, outside the US, was British historian Martin Briggs, whose 1927 *The Architect in History* offered a unique historical view into the traditions of European architects, rather than strictly the buildings or drawings they produced.[13] Published seven years after the first AIA handbook, Briggs's book was published on the eve of the Great Depression in Britain and the US. In the US, unemployment among architects quickly skyrocketed, reaching 90 percent by the early 1930s.[14] Nearly half of the country's architecture firms had closed, and a coalition of workers was rapidly organizing as the Federation of Architects, Engineers, Chemists, and Technicians, active between 1933 and 1946.[15] It was during the immediate postwar period that architects and scholars began to write more frequently about architecture as a "practice," debating and historicizing the value of architects to the general public. Historian Turpin Bannister examined the profession's demographics in forensic detail for the AIA in his 1954 *The Architect at Mid-Century*, and James Ackerman used the lens of "practice" that same year in his study of Italian architects' training and design processes during the High Renaissance.[16]

The AIA's handbook received only minor updates and revisions during the 1940s and 1950s. However, it was drastically revised as the postwar reconstruction work was cresting during the early 1960s, and as the heads of large corporate firms began directing the AIA. Edited by Washington-based architect Robert Piper, who became vice president and partner of Perkins & Will in Chicago soon after, the 1963 handbook featured a new title, format, and organization.[17] Retitled *The Architect's Handbook of Professional Practice*, the handbook now suggested that architects were engaged in a "professional practice" that was no longer confined to architecture.[18] Practice was no longer architectural, but rather professional.

Unlike the bound volume of the 1920s, the AIA's revised 1963 handbook was assembled as a loose binder of twenty leaflets, which were described as "Circulars of Information." And rather than focus on the standard relationships between the historical triad of individual architects, owners, and builders, the circulars focused instead on standardizing the role of the architect—still through contracts and procedures—in the public more broadly and in relation to industries and associations *outside* of the US. This emphasis on relationality bolstered the rationale for incorporating firms at the time, ultimately inspiring conglomeration and the anonymous, group-based and contract-based practices through which architectural firms were increasingly defined.

The first substantive chapter of the revised handbook, circular 2, "The Construction Industry," underscored the profound influence of construction on the profession and the national economy following post–World War II reconstruction. Circular 8, "The Architect and the Public," was dedicated to "development"—described as "all activities of the architect or his staff leading directly or indirectly to securing commissions."[19] Circular 20, "Comprehensive Services," urged architects to "modify the concept" of their "traditional role" in order to meet the demands of a rapidly evolving society.[20] And by including thirty-nine contract documents—far exceeding the six agreements offered in the previous 1950s edition—fifteen of which were dedicated to accounting and office management, the handbook was demonstrating how the AIA could increase its own revenue by expanding and diversifying its offerings.[21]

More than the printed words, perhaps, the change in the handbook's format most visibly paralleled and further encouraged structural changes within architecture firms. The circulars were hole-punched and held together by a single three-ring binder, mailed separately, so that each could be easily removed, updated, and reinserted—yet another infrastructure of incorporation that reflected and supported the increasing precarity and temporariness of work.[22] The handbook described its new format as "a recognition of the fact that in order for the Handbook to fulfill its purpose, it must be prepared to serve a fully informed and flexible profession, alert to the inevitable changes for improvement in a dynamic world."[23]

Three-ring binders, first patented in the US in 1857 by Henry Sisson, who later served as a US Army colonel in the Civil War, were not considered "books" with standardized pages, but rather "portfolios" for holding temporary and interchangeable sheets.[24] In these binders with metal hooks or teeth attached to spring-loaded "barrels," Sisson wrote in his patent application, "loose sheets" such as musical scores, newspapers, or engravings could be secured, preserved, and—importantly—easily detached, and "new ones added with the greatest facility."[25] Relevant to its origins and inspiration, Sisson was paymaster for the First Rhode Island Volunteer Infantry Regiment prior to his appointment as a colonel, responsible for managing payments from the state treasury to the military. And after commanding the "skirmishers," or vanguard soldiers, at the First Battle of Bull Run, he was promoted and made responsible for managing three military companies, which required frequent changes in strategy and troop positions while under significant fire, for which he was later widely celebrated.[26]

Sisson's history, both as a paymaster and as a colonel of multiple companies, shines a revealing light on the history of his patent, as well as the history of the portfolio in military use during the twentieth century. As noted earlier, the US War Department made portfolios mandatory during World War II.[27] Branches such as the air corps and army air force secured within them "circulars," typically produced in two copies—one for distributing and one for keeping—to communicate instructions or drawings of an "administrative" nature that were subject to "more or less frequent changes" and that, therefore, were not to be included as permanent manuals or policies.[28]

Portfolios, of course, have a much longer history within art and architecture. Villard de Honnecourt's thirteenth-century pigskin portfolio, for instance, encased drawings on parchment of animals and building details derived from elementary geometries. Renaissance examples include the folios of drawings kept by Leonardo da

Vinci and the treatises of architects, including Andrea Palladio and Sebastiano Serlio, whose illustrated plates included a wide range of building types, from public churches and amphitheaters to private villas.[29]

During the second half of the eighteenth century, as architectural academies and professions were forming, architects and students carried portfolios to showcase their work; some European artists and students carried them as if they were fashion pieces.[30] As the profession of architecture expanded to the US during the nineteenth century, historian Hyungmin Pai writes, portfolios were considered useful for publishing illustrations of past buildings and monuments in young professional journals, such as *Architectural Record*, to inspire architects in the future—a future value constructed by time passed.[31] Illustrated portfolios were not intended for those working within "practice" (synonymous with "business"), Pai suggests; they instead made academic discourse possible by linking the atelier and the library.[32] Rather than portfolios, architects in practice during the early twentieth century turned to manuals, catalogues, and handbooks to establish standards and procedures through writing, which linked the office to the construction site. Therefore, the transformation of the AIA's handbook into a portfolio during the 1960s—when firms themselves were coming to be known as "portfolios"—collapsed nineteenth-century distinctions between practice and academia or between the businesses of architecture, construction, and education. Indeed, as the AIA was assembling its new handbooks-as-portfolios, which helped it expand its business of contract documents, architecture firms such as DMJM were also assembling business portfolios during the 1960s in the same types of three-ring binders, which they updated each year.[33]

Furthermore, by the 1960s, architectural portfolios had taken on new meaning—meaning derived not from the history of architecture, but from economics. In fact, portfolios were directly informing corporate conglomeration. In 1952, Harry Markowitz, a young economist who had studied under Milton Friedman, devised a "modern portfolio theory" that would fundamentally alter the way businesses and individuals invested their resources and organized their businesses.[34] Markowitz's formula—a complex mathematical formula, like the one architects and engineers used to calculate optimal distances between missiles and buildings during the Cold War—helped businesses maximize capital returns for specific levels of risk. His theory encouraged diversification—the idea that offering different services or acquiring diverse firms could reduce a business's risk and boost its profit, even if only in short-term bursts. Following Markowitz's work, corporate conglomerates were known as "portfolio" firms throughout the 1960s and 1970s, as professional architectural associations and firms evolved and advanced a similar model of business.[35]

Reports and meeting minutes from national and state chapters of the AIA reveal that there, too, architects were carefully investing their funds. In New York's and California's AIA chapters, for instance, the revenue generated by their corporate membership, which was intended to be used for awards, fellowships, and operation costs, was carefully diversified and invested as bonds, preferred stocks, and common stocks.[36]

Book Practices

Following the 1963 revisions to the AIA's handbook, postwar economic growth peaked and then slowed. In 1966, the AIA hired management consultants—not unlike how firms such as DMJM and Perkins & Will had two decades earlier—to study the ways architects could streamline their contracting procedures and boost their revenues.[37] As discussed, back-to-back recessions struck the profession during the 1970s, deregulation efforts halted construction, the

Department of Justice was attacking the AIA for its anticompetitive ethical code, and firms were laying off workers and closing their doors. Some architects were filing petitions to unionize, as they had during the 1930s and 1940s, and outrage was surfacing about a profession that seemed oblivious to, and incapable of resolving, its long-standing inequities, low wages, and a growing sense of social irrelevance.[38] "Since the heady sixties," architectural historian Spiro Kostof wrote in 1977, "students of architecture . . . had been grappling with doubts about the relevance of their venerable calling."[39]

While architects were reorganizing their firms or acquiring others to keep their businesses afloat, university programs were also struggling to maintain their enrollments. Architecture schools were graduating more student-architects than there were jobs, and the profession was intensely oversaturated—there were 3.59 architects per ten thousand people in the US, which was the first time the number had surpassed 3.0 since the Depression.[40] Averting, rather than addressing, the structural problems of the profession and its sociopolitical and economic woes, including its long-standing inequities and contradictions, universities expanded their degree programs during the 1970s and 1980s by adding additional years and new PhD programs with distinct curricula.[41] Scholars produced by these PhD programs were writing new books about *practice*—a term that was popularized and heavily theorized within the social sciences at the time.[42] Practice was understood as a concept with which to describe people and their actions "on the ground," as well as the broader "structures" of the world that were embodied—incorporated—and then reproduced as actions, dispositions, or routines.[43]

Reflecting the schools of thought from which they emerged, the dissertations about practice during the 1970s and 1980s differed greatly in their methods. Some doctoral students in architecture focused their research on the craft, drawings, objects, and tools of the architect by studying them historically and extending the traditions of art historical research from which architecture had emerged as a "discipline," while others borrowed the methods of the social sciences and focused on the present.[44] Mary Woods, for example, who graduated from Columbia University in 1983, studied the historical role of professional journals in promoting the careers of prosperous nineteenth-century architects and their professional societies; this led to her 1999 book *From Craft to Profession*.[45] And Spiro Kostof produced an anthology with a group of doctoral students in 1977 about the history of the profession, including the guilds, associations, and corporations through which it was constituted.[46]

In other cases, architecture was studied ethnographically.[47] At Northwestern University, sociologist Judith Blau studied social systems, which influenced her 1977 book about the survival of architecture firms, their finances, and awards during economic downturns.[48] At UC Berkeley, sociologist Magali Sarfatti Larson wrote about professions, including architecture, in 1974, later published as a book in 1977.[49] Also at Berkeley, Dana Cuff's 1982 dissertation described the ways that architects across many medium-sized firms negotiated with their clients; this became her 1991 book *Architecture: The Story of Practice*.[50]

Echoing the architecture of a "portfolio," Cuff, among others, understood *practice* to mean "the embodiment, indeed, the expression, of a practitioner's everyday knowledge."[51] As accumulations of experience, *practice* in this definition closely resembled what sociologist Pierre Bourdieu had described as a person's "habitus" (discussed in chapter 3), a theoretical concept for understanding a person's embodied or "incorporated" experiences and cultures, which Bruno Latour later defined as a theory not unlike the multiprocessing computer or a corporate conglomerate, involving "circuitry through which plug-ins lend actors the supplementary tools—the supplementary souls—that are necessary to render a situation interpretable."[52]

Therefore, architectural "practice" came to have a history because it wrote one for itself. The intensity of this reflexivity coincided with the renewed attention to portfolios, conglomeration, and the rise of postmodernism, where it also manifested in buildings as mirrors (see chapter 3). While some scholars were holding up mirrors to the businesses of architecture in order to reproduce the discipline (the academy), others, inversely, were holding up mirrors to the discipline in order to reproduce the profession (firms). The texts-as-mirrors matched the mirrors-as-architecture, and together they provided evidence of late capitalism's indeterminacies.[53] In other words, when one mirror was held up to another, architects and the scholars studying them could see themselves—their reflections and re-reflections—while emboldening a system of self-value and self-regulation.

Finally, as scholars were writing about architecture as a practice, the AIA continued revising and expanding its handbook-as-portfolio. The 1973 handbook, edited by Steven Rosenfeld, then director of the AIA's Professional Practice Programs, was expanded to include twenty-one chapters within three binders, rather than one. And while the organization of material followed the 1960s edition without substantial revisions, even more attention was paid to construction: eight of the twenty-one chapters focused on construction processes, costs, contracts, and documents, again underscoring the financial influence of construction on the profession and economy.[54] The second and third binders included hundreds of contract forms and documents of practice—a trend of expansion that only continued: a decade later, in 1987, the eleventh edition of the handbook, edited by David Haviland, a professor of architecture at Rensselaer Polytechnic Institute, comprised *four* volumes. The first volume was dedicated to the "firm," underscoring the way in which firms, rather than individuals, were considered an irreducible unit of exchange (and acquisition) by the end of the twentieth century. The second volume was focused on the architectural "project," and volumes 3 and 4 were entirely dedicated to contract documents.[55]

By the middle of the 1990s, as the economy and the construction industry strengthened, the AIA's handbook returned to a single volume, and the ethnographies of the 1970s and 1980s reflected only an outdated past. Unemployment rates declined, deregulation subsided, and calls for "engagement" peppered articles by architects, theorists, and critics.

Speeding ahead: by 2010, on the heels of a severe economic recession, there was renewed interest, yet again, in studying architects' businesses and the conditions of their labor, as well as the values and inequities of the profession—architecture, again, as a "practice." Discourse about postmodernist representation was revived, and union drives and organizing campaigns resumed.[56] There were an unprecedented 8.67 architects per ten thousand people in the US by 2010, and architecture graduates were again unable to find jobs.[57]

By now, we can tell where this story is heading. There were fifty-one doctoral programs in architecture in the US by 2021, the majority of which had become pedagogically devoted to the study of architectural history, despite only a handful of full-time faculty positions open across the country.[58] Perhaps unsurprisingly, an overwhelming number of doctoral dissertations (including my own) focused on the history of large architecture firms, the tools that defined them, and the professions and political economies they influenced in the United States and around the world.[59] The geographical expansion of this work beyond Western traditions was new, as was the broader focus on influences on the professions, rather than the immediate work of firms or individual architects. However, the rhetoric of expansion that defined these texts was matched by professional associations, universities, and large firms similarly calling for "expansion" (often with no plans for structural change) to the definition and scope of who and what counts as an "architect" and as "architecture" in the present.[60] Driven by radically different motives, yet united by the rhetoric of practice, each text was begging the question whether their concerns would again fade away as the sense of economic precarity subsided.

Despite the methodological divide in scholarship by the 2010s, there was a growing emphasis on historiography among doctoral programs in the US (and elsewhere). With some exceptions, this meant that ethnographic texts about architects in practice were to be written from "outside" the discipline of architecture, often from outside the US altogether.[61] Notable ethnographic studies, including Albena Yaneva's 2009 study of the Dutch firm OMA, considered how architects and objects—like models and portfolios—operate within broader sociomaterial networks and have symmetrical forms of agency.[62] However, these studies often drew from science and technology studies and the actor-network theory (ANT), rather than the cultural studies of the 1970s and 1980s.

While ANT scholars such as Bruno Latour and Michel Callon have acknowledged the historicity of the subjects they study—as in Latour's recognition that some elements of society originate from other times and locations that are entwined with the present,[63] and Callon's acknowledgment that systems such as market economies are historical processes[64]—they have typically distanced themselves from historiography and downplayed the historicity of their subjects to afford a more intricate view of the present.[65] In their words, they leave the study of history to "professional" historians.[66]

However, by uniting historical and ethnographic scholarship—by bridging the academy and the profession, as the history of portfolios and texts about "practice" prompt us to do—it is possible see how broader economic cycles shape changes in architectural discourse and practice. The term *practice* itself provides clues for how to do this. When "practice theory" was first defined during the 1970s and 1980s, for instance, it was categorized as a theory of history: to study a practice was to study the ways that everyday actions were either producing or reproducing experiences, cultures, or actions of the past.⁶⁷ By combining historiographic and ethnographic methods, we can reveal not only the cyclical nature of architects' concerns, but also how those concerns were self-generating.

. . .

Together, these books about architecture reveal how the recurring and cyclical interests in "practice" shine a spotlight on the economic, political, and cultural conditions of architectural work, including its power dynamics and inequities. They also demonstrate how the profession, private firms, and academic institutions came to share an underlying capitalist logic by the 1970s. Today, it is more common for the term *practice* to obscure than to clarify. It is used as a stand-in for many things: a repeated act, a routine for learning, an office, a business, a building, or even a book itself. As a result, members of the profession and discipline, as well as architecture firms and universities, run free as self-serving agents, similarly instrumentalizing one another's woes through rhetorical calls to short-term action for their own survival.⁶⁸

Through a macrohistory of texts about architectural practice, charting how they change and transform from one historical period to the next, one can see how and why scholars turn the profession's capital into life for the survival of the discipline—just as architects turn the discipline's capital into life for the profession. To be sure, each new surge of publications about architecture-as-practice during the twentieth century carried with it a new burst of postrecession energy, organizing, anger, and strategy. The profession and the academy, albeit slowly, have opened themselves to a broader range of individuals, beyond the white men who have long defined architecture's Western history, including those at firms such as DMJM. Like the repeated mirrors of postmodernism, though, these expansions have been matched by an increased stronghold and redistribution of capital by a smaller percentage of (mostly) white men who remain at the top of firms and universities as board members, directors, and trustees. In tandem with careful examinations of architectural work, exposing the historical mechanisms of capitalist reproduction and its vicious cycles of life and death—including the structural relationships between institutions, such as firms, universities, and professional associations—may well help change the rate or timing of architecture's turn away from "practice." A theory of practice is, after all, a theory of history, and it need not be reproduced.

6 Vault

Keeping Secrets

When Leonard Lewin's satire *Report from Iron Mountain* hit the shelves in 1967, it caused panic within the government. "Cables have gone to US embassies," the magazine *U.S. News & World Report* wrote. "Play down public discussion of 'Iron Mountain'; emphasize that the book has no relation whatsoever to Government policy."[1] Inspired by a story that the stock market tumbled because of a "peace scare," the book follows a secret study group formed by the Kennedy administration, tasked with drafting a plan for the US to transition from a war-based to a peace-based economy. The group's conclusion? Perpetual war and division are essential to the country's good health; peace would only destroy it.[2] Written with the help of Harvard economist John Kenneth Galbraith, the story reads as nonfiction, following the group as it begins and ends its work inside a nuclear-bomb-resistant vault, known as Iron Mountain.

Formed in 1951 in New York's Hudson Valley, Iron Mountain, yet another Cold War corporation in the business of space and survival, was—and remains—a very real place. Dubbed the "vault against the atom," the company, originally Iron Mountain Atomic Storage Inc., was named for an actual mountain and its abandoned iron mine, which was sold and repurposed for storage.[3] According to its founder, Herman Knaust, a mushroom farmer turned records manager who formed the company after learning that many Jewish refugees had lost their identifying papers during World War II, Iron Mountain was the "safest spot in America." Located outside of the potential blast zone of New York City and armored with a retired bank vault door, Iron Mountain protected the paperwork of corporations when they could no longer be contained or efficiently managed within private offices: bank records, insurance policies, reference files, contracts. "Consider the continuity of government [for national survival]," one 1960 bulletin from the Office of Civil and Defense Mobilization read as the federal government admired Iron Mountain, taking notes for its own national archives. "Essential records, safely stored."[4] Today, like many multinational conglomerates, AECOM stores its records and retirement stocks in Iron Mountain.

. . .

When I was seven years into my research, by then mostly editing and rewriting, AECOM hired a new director of records management. After I had filled him in on my project, he shared a "report" from Iron Mountain: an Excel inventory of AECOM's boxes of paperwork, 4,638 of which contained DMJM's "legacy files."[5] "At Iron Mountain" read the last column for each box.

This was the closest I had been to seeing or touching the elusive records of DMJM. The boxes were listed by number and without a hint of what might be inside them. "It's literally all that we have to work with," the director explained.[6] Were the boxes in New York, where Iron Mountain was based? Would I be able to look at any of them? How many hours—years!—would it take to examine all 4,638? If only some, which and how would I choose? Despite the candidness of the new records director, I received a familiar response after asking for access: access could be granted only by the firm's legal counsel.

Amid a global pandemic, I waited another year and a half. By that point, I had spent enough hours asking "what if?" and sending follow-up emails to follow-up emails (1,046 emails, to be exact) that I had come to terms with the stories I had transcribed and the records I had collected. Nonetheless, AECOM's report from Iron Mountain confirmed the existence of DMJM's records, which suggested, as scholars Samia Henni and Ann Stoler argue in their histories of state archives, that the records may someday be accessible to the public, even if only to confirm what we already know.[7] As already discussed, much about the history of government contractors was explicitly left *off* official records, expressed instead through loose conversations, informal letters, or handwritten memos, despite the firms' constructed image of efficiency and organization. In a 1980 lawsuit against architecture firms in Massachusetts (the one mentioned earlier, in which architects were found guilty of quid pro quo), a court committee wrote that architects at DMJM had used "elaborate schemes to circumvent the laws limiting campaign contributions and requiring record-keeping and reporting, including the use of cashier's checks, false names, and the diversion of cash completely out of the reporting system."[8]

As Michael Osman has shown, architects' internal paperwork—schedules, contracts, budgets, and manuals—proliferated as architecture transformed into a big business during the early twentieth century.[9] By the 1960s, as the web of constituents outside the office with which architects were interfacing expanded, so too did the paperwork—letters, memos, contracts, notes, and reports. So much so, that new clerical workers, technologies, and storage space were needed to manage it. Compounded by concerns about information loss, which led to an "archive fever" and new duplication technologies, the protection of such paperwork within institutions and corporations, as historian Brett Spencer has argued about the US more broadly, was considered a primary way to ensure that the US could win a third world war; it would keep businesses, and thus the economy, alive.[10]

In 1951, the National Archives in Washington, DC, which now holds selected records of DMJM's international work, was preparing to install a fifty-five-ton "supervault" to protect the Charters of Freedom, while technology companies such as Xerox were unveiling their first machines for photocopying paper.[11] As DMJM's autobiography highlights, 1951 was also the year that Julius and Ethel Rosenberg were convicted of espionage after sharing "Top Secret" designs of nuclear missiles with the Soviet Union, and Senator Estes Kefauver of Tennessee was leading investigations into organized crime.[12] Kefauver, we should recall, had cosponsored the Celler-Kefauver "Anti-Merger" Act a year before in an effort to keep corporations from merging with or acquiring others, thus encouraging corporate diversification.[13]

Therefore, as DMJM's and Iron Mountain's histories reveal, the concerns about paper records and fragmenting corporations—separating, storing, and negotiating across multiple sites—were intimately tied together by a broader regime of Cold War secrecy. As Jacques Derrida notes in his 1994 lecture "Archive Fever," the word *secret* is derived from the Latin *secernere*, meaning "to separate."[14] For architectural practice, the demands for additional storage space and new records management technologies meant a new class of specialized workers—records managers and librarians, clearance officers and technologists—who would be responsible for separating and managing distinctions between original and duplicate, past and present, truth and rhetoric, life and death.

Rather than end this story about architects and their contributions to the political economy with speculation about the content of AECOM's stored records at Iron Mountain, exhausting ourselves within a recirculating vacuum that we now know how to avoid, this chapter considers how architects were contributing to this regime of secrecy through the production and management of paperwork, and how those contributions, in turn, bolstered the business of architecture. More importantly, this work led to the slow acceptance of long-marginalized workers in architecture, including women and people of color, who were hired at disproportionate rates within large government-contracting firms. With exceptions, many were hired to produce and maintain "secrets" before they were formally embraced by the profession as bona fide architects.

Despite the profession's calls for greater gender- and race-based equity across the profession of architecture during the 1960s and 1970s, it was, perhaps ironically, to firms such as DMJM that—despite persistent discrimination and exploitation—social movements could point for evidence of social change.

By weaving together stories of three workers at DMJM—a records manager, a computer technician, and a draftsman—this chapter shows how this new class of architectural worker was contributing to and maintaining not only the legacy of the firm, keeping well-organized personal papers open for public access long after retirement, but also that of the country itself.

Secrecy

By the 1950s, a new regime of secrecy was emerging in the United States—one born, primarily, of a scientific and technological concern about national security and sovereignty. As a bundle of discourses and practices, this regime was not only asserted through policy, but also transformed into physical reality.[15] Secrets were contributing to the escalation of a nuclear arms race, driving competition into the military-industrial-academic-scientific complexes, and undermining modernist norms of academic, scientific, and architectural transparency.[16] Secrecy took many forms—the government was guarding its military strategy, for example, and concealing its imperialist motives, while private enterprises were, for the same reasons or others, exercising their constitutional right to privacy.

Secrecy was not a new concept to architects. They had long withheld details about their tools and techniques as trade secrets—a form of professional "black-boxing." This secrecy spanned centuries, from the medieval guilds of Europe to the earliest professional architects in the US and beyond. Architects have often regarded their books and drawings as "personal secrets," hiding them like diaries from rivals—particularly at moments like the late 1960s, when competition for work was most fierce.[17]

Immediately following World War II, some architects began to deliberately *reveal* their secrets, relying not on guilds and oral traditions but on publishing houses, museums, and the state to legitimize their power through licenses, charters, and patents.[18] Modern architects have been defined in this way; they helped project the standards of private life onto the political world.[19] However, in the race to develop an atomic bomb and to construct military bases, satellites, and missile complexes, government-contracting architects were contractually obligated to embrace secrecy, eventually applying it to all terms of their work. It was this secrecy about work, some have argued, that enabled the profession of architecture to reemerge in the 1970s and 1980s as self-referential, self-regulated, self-valued, and thus "postmodern"—an effect of business materialized through the mirror-glass headquarters of corporate conglomerates.[20] Architecture had become, as Reyner Banham wrote in 1990, a "conspiracy of secrecy, immune from scrutiny, but perpetually open to the suspicion, among the general public, that there may be nothing at all inside the black box except a mystery for its own sake."[21]

A primary interest in secrecy, especially during the Cold War, stemmed from the government's concern about leaking military strategies and scientific or technological advancements. In the US, protocols for military secrets had existed in some form since the country's founding, including the 1789 federal "housekeeping privilege," which granted the president and state secretaries the authority to restrict information, such as troops' positions or attack plans.[22] By the middle of the twentieth century, protocols and procedures of secrecy were, as Peter Galison describes, "ratcheted up," penetrating all aspects of government and civic life.[23] While secrecy and record-keeping protocols were, at the start of the century, restricted to "prohibited places," such as those owned by the government, secrecy protocols expanded during the 1950s to include all places where government work and the discussions about it were taking place, including within the offices of government contractors.[24] As Cold War defense and deterrence strategies became dependent on scientific and technological research, including private-sector expertise and labor, there was a greater need to restrict "data": inventions, scientific progress, or architecture and engineering achievements wherever they were produced, discussed, or held.[25] Contracts with government agencies, such as the Atomic Energy Commission, stipulated that the government would own the rights to such work and that it must be guarded indefinitely.

In May 1962, amid speculation that the Soviet Union was installing nuclear-armed missiles in Cuba, DMJM draftsman Bill Coburn sat down at his drafting table in a small, undisclosed room one floor above DMJM's main office. He twisted the lock of a cold metal safe bolted to the floor next to his desk, pulled out a roll of drawings he had finished the evening before, and carefully erased the client's name—the CIA—as well as the building's name and its location. Only the lines, dimensions, and construction details remained. Once redacted, he rolled the drawings back up, tucked them under his arm, and flew by plane from Los Angeles to Washington, DC. There, he retreated to an isolated basement office, closed the door, and penciled on the same letters he had erased.

This was a standard routine for Coburn, who got his start at DMJM in 1956, drawing stationery sets and business cards for the

FIGURE 34. Business cards of DMJM architect William Coburn, 1956–1995. Courtesy of William Coburn.

firm. The business cards proved useful to him in organizing his various identities as a worker, moving across and within various DMJM subsidiaries and joint ventures—some simultaneously—throughout his career (figure 34).

By removing the building's location, Coburn was severing the building from the ground. By removing the client's name, he was obscuring any association between DMJM and the CIA. And by removing his office from the drafting rooms at DMJM, he was isolating his work from the primary work of architects and engineers. In a missile-based war, after all, those able to calculate distances between buildings or cities held the most power.[26]

The drawings in this particular case were for the renovation of a blocky, six-story concrete building at the Washington Navy Yard in DC, anonymized as "Building 213," into which the nation's top photo surveillance program—the CIA's National Photographic Interpretation Center (NPIC)—planned to move the following year. The CIA had outgrown its existing office space in the Steuart Motor Company Building in DC, requiring "large areas" to accommodate overwhelming volumes of paper records and reference material, as well as for new computers and equipment.[27] The project was classified by the government as Top Secret, which meant that the planning details, funding amounts, and construction details of Building 213 were not to be disclosed to anyone in the DMJM office, let alone the public.[28]

Coburn describes arriving with Phil Daniel at the Steuart Motor Company Building (figure 35) in Washington, DC, where the NPIC (then the Photographic Intelligence Center, or PIC) was discretely located on the top floor, noting humorous contradictions in the government's practices:

> Walking in, you'd see glass windows with soap on them—nothing really to help identify anything in there. We would walk in through the door and walk down to the elevator. That's where the guard sat. We would check in, and then someone would come down to get us when they were ready. Here we were, designing a new facility for them, but we had to wait while they took blankets and covered over all of the equipment they were using so that we couldn't see it—the same equipment that we had to accommodate in the new building. Talk about overkill![29]

The irony in Coburn's story is further emphasized by another fact. The photo interpreters of the PIC were examining aerial photographs, measuring buildings and the distances between them, by comparing them with architectural drawings—those produced by

FIGURE 35. Steuart Motor Company, Washington, DC, 1967. Emil A. Press Collection, DC History Center.

Coburn and others at DMJM for the air force—to identify missile bases and confirm whether the Soviets were constructing them (figure 36).[30] Moreover, DMJM's Phillip Daniel had written many of the reference texts shelved in the CIA library, including the procedures for identifying ballistic missile complexes from spy planes above.[31] Invoking the long history of projective drawings in architecture, a classified report from 1961, authored by DMJM's "Special Projects Division," recommends using "high contrast" images to identify buildings by analyzing their shadows on the ground—representations of built forms, like drawings—to identify with precision the types of structures that cast them.[32]

The CIA, today, claims to have no drawings associated with the design and construction of Building 213. Material evidence of DMJM's design work is conveyed instead through oral histories, not unlike the lore of the medieval guilds, as well as declassified

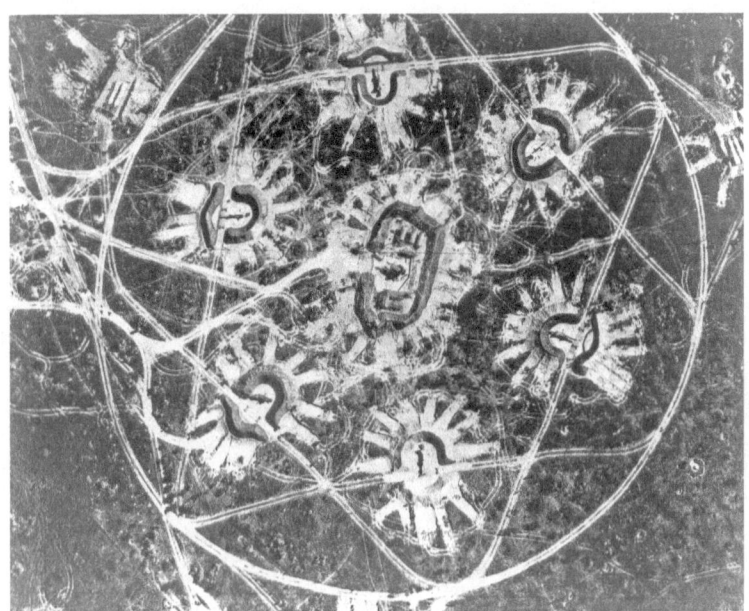

FIGURE 36. Aerial photograph of a completed Soviet surface-to-air missile site, 1962. Dino Brugioni Collection, NASM.2012.0004, National Air and Space Museum, Smithsonian Institution.

memoranda and letters of exchange between DMJM architects. The latter materials are traceable to DMJM by architects' initials or descriptions of their firm, even though their full names, budgets, and equipment were redacted, leaving a paper infrastructure akin to the physical infrastructures of cities through which people, resources, and capital circulated. In one such memo, the DMJM architects discuss the appearance of the lobby and material cost savings.[33] In others, they outline discrepancies between drawings and construction, including the fabrication of cabinets and oversized racks without authorization, which was driving up costs and delaying the project (figure 37).[34] In yet another, they describe the sequence of spaces through which the CIA director, John McCone, and his wife should tour the

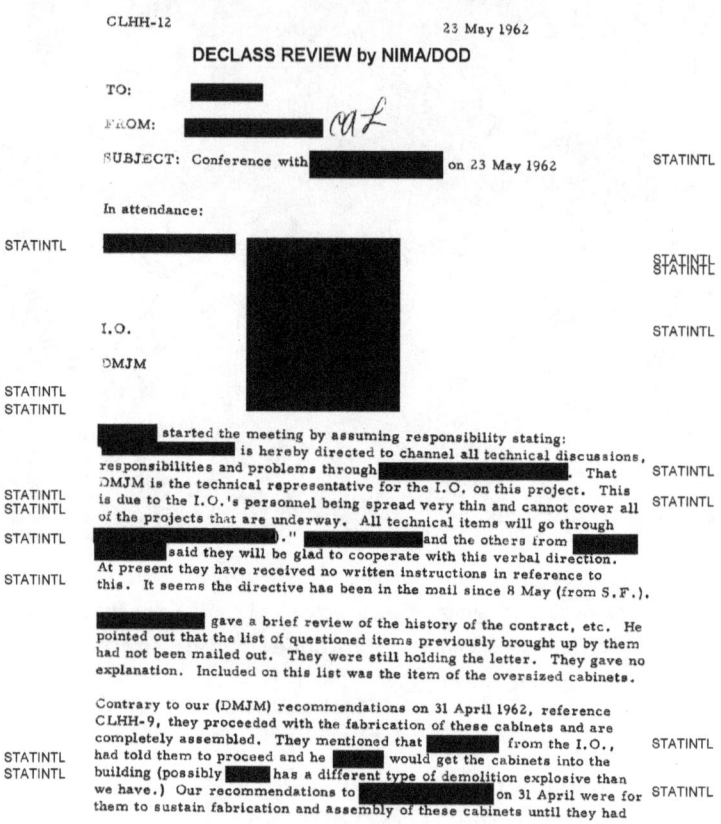

FIGURE 37. Redacted CIA records of a May 23, 1962, conference regarding the National Photographic Interpretation Center. CIA Special Collections.

completed Building 213 for the first time. "In the opinion of architects," the anonymous architect wrote, they should begin in the cafeteria, since its walls were covered in California redwood paneling and this would be of "personal interest" to the McCones with their California roots.[35]

Before directing the CIA, McCone had served as a government advisor and as chairman of the Atomic Energy Commission—and before that, he was a mechanical engineer at the California engineering and construction firm Bechtel.[36] Recall this book's opening vignette: Stanley Smith, vice president of DMJM, socializing with colleagues from Bechtel and McCone himself at Bohemian Grove in 1982, on a gentlemen's retreat under towering redwoods—like the redwoods that had been cut and planed into panels for interior use in Building 213.

The tour, outlined floor by floor and conveyed by text, rather than drawings or photographs, highlighted the HVAC systems and control panels and the "tank farm" on the third floor of [redacted] chemicals, which were thought to be of interest to McCone. In the scripted tour, however, the vault was prioritized: it marked a shift away from a prior dependency on small individual safes like the one in which Coburn stored his drawings. Now there were large vaulted areas in which work could be left out, where classified work would not need to be covered.[37]

Hiding

More general than concerns about military strategy, Cold War concepts of secrecy were traceable to *arcana imperii*, the political ethos in Roman law associated with the construction of empire, whereby a ruler claiming absolute power could exclude or withhold information in order to assert authority or make tyranny appear to be free government.[38] Historian Daniel Immerwahr has described how this ethos came into play after World War II, when the US government downplayed its control of territories outside the contiguous US, from Guam to Puerto Rico and the US Virgin Islands, omitting their names and histories from maps, paperwork, and public speeches to "hide" evidence of an "empire" state of mind.[39]

The changing connotations of the word *conglomerate* can be traced in regard to these patterns of secrecy, hiding, and imperialism. During the early twentieth century, historians and political leaders used the term to describe empires "with no racial, geographic, or linguistic reasons for their association" beyond power, from ancient Rome to China to Russia to the United States.[40] During World War I, for example, when the US Senate debated the meaning and threat of empires-as-conglomerates, "greedy conglomerates" were contrasted with the perceived innocence of a unified body, a "nation." A senator from Mississippi argued that the government could mask its thirst for geographic and material power by investing in infrastructures and technologies for *other* countries as development or war aid, thereby putting an "end forever to the infamous lie that the American people are not a nation but are nothing but a conglomerate association of dollar hunters and of dollar makers."[41]

Not until after World War II did the US begin to satisfy that senator's call for a veil of national unity, by directing attention toward international development while downplaying the status of previously conquered territories that formed the "Greater" United States. While the terms, tools, and techniques of conglomeration migrated from the government to private enterprises, so too did cultures and expectations about hiding or masking relationships with an imperial state. For instance, it was common for those working within government-adjacent organizations, as Max Weber described in his classic analysis of bureaucracy, to withhold information or keep secrets in order to maintain what they believed to be the democratic character of the state.[42] By hiding their knowledge and actions from criticism, they defended themselves against political cultures they saw as competitive, paranoid, and insecure.[43] Architecture and engineering firms in the 1960s joined in this subterfuge by masking or removing the parts of their companies that represented direct links with the state—as with Coburn's secondary office for drawing. As DMJM's history

FIGURE 38. Vahe Khachooni (left) and Jean-Pierre Denis discuss their computing responsibilities with a Univac 9300. From Sperry Rand, *Input for Modern Management* (1969), 14. Courtesy of Vahe Khachooni.

reveals, one means of keeping technologies secret—especially those acquired through government contracts, such as computers—was to form a subsidiary around them.

Phillip Daniel, who read mathematics books for fun and tinkered with an analog computer in his office to "relax," was bursting with excitement after hiring Vahe Khachooni, a young Armenian-Iranian immigrant who was quickly appointed head of computer services at DMJM, in 1967 (figure 38). However, the use of computers was hotly contested within the office, in part because they represented a dependency on government-backed technologies, and in part because they challenged expectations about what work should be done manually. Aside from Daniel, the DMJM partners were vehemently opposed to spending money on computers. "Mendenhall didn't think computers were the way forward . . . [he thought] that they were a fad of some kind," Khachooni tells me. "They didn't want to approve any more expenditures, and Phil Daniel was having a hard time convincing them that computers were the future. They [the engineers] said, 'Oh no, we can do it faster by hand.'"[44]

Rather than fully embrace computers in the office, Khachooni and Daniel formed a data processing subsidiary, Logicomp—and later, at the end of the 1960s, Khachooni formed a spin-off business, Design Methods, with architect William Miller, while still working at DMJM.

Despite the lack of support for computers, Daniel and Khachooni created a method for discussing and using them in business. Khachooni recalls: "Daniel would say 'my stupid partners, if you ask them, they would have never even invented matches. . . . And you're wasting your time here.' He told me 'I want you to quit DMJM, go outside, and start a new company [Design Methods]. It has to be confidential and you can't tell anyone. . . . DMJM cannot know about this, ok? You go and do it, and I will support you. My name will never come up because they can sue me. If you need more money, just tell me.' And we took off."[45]

Even conversations about the *procedures* of secrecy—about the steps required to form a corporate subsidiary around an expensive computer that had been designed for a missile-based war, for example—were written down on loose notes and memos and physically separated from the office. As discussions about forming Design Methods were beginning, Khachooni explains, "Daniel would call me up, I would go to their floor, close the door, and he would tell the secretary not to take any calls. And we would discuss it [forming a computer subsidiary]. . . . Every time I would go to his office, the secretary knew the rules. We closed the door and would lock it from the inside. And start talking about everything else. And, we started getting bigger and bigger contracts."[46]

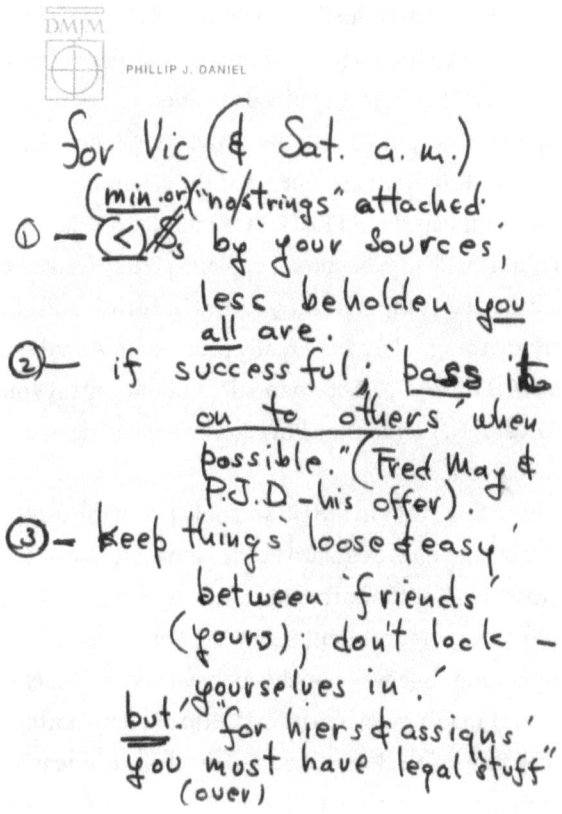

FIGURE 39. Memo from Phillip Daniel to Vahe Khachooni. Courtesy of Vahe Khachooni.

In one private note Daniel wrote for Khachooni on DMJM stationery (figure 39), he offers tips for starting Design Methods: "(1) Min[imum] or 'no strings' attached. [The less money] by 'your sources', less beholden you all are. (2) If successful, 'pass it on to others' when possible.... (3) Keep things 'loose & easy' between 'friends' (yours); don't lock yourselves in! *But!* 'for hiers [*sic*] & assigns,' you must have legal 'stuff.'"

DMJM had purchased its first computer, a Univac 9200, in 1965 (followed by an upgraded 9300) for accounting, payroll, and budget expense analysis, but Khachooni was trained to operate far larger computing machines, including the Univac 1108, developed in the 1950s by Sperry Rand, which supported the scientific and engineering computer language FORTRAN (FORmula TRANslator).[47] "When I got there [at DMJM]," Khachooni explains, "they walked over and showed me the new computer [the 9200]. Tape drives and all that. . . . I didn't say anything. They were really proud of it. And the next day, I said, 'where is the FORTRAN manual?' and the guy says oh, it can't handle FORTRAN. I said, 'then how do you expect me to use it?' The 9200 was not workable."[48]

There were few 1108s in the US and only two at the time in Southern California: one in El Segundo at the University Computing Corporation, to which Khachooni connected by telephone cable, and one at the Jacobi Computation Center in West Los Angeles, to which he drove. Computing time was not cheap, however, so Khachooni routinely visited at 1:00 a.m., when it cost $600 per hour, rather than the daily hourly rate of $1,800–2,000.[49] His clearance was built into DMJM's defense contracts, stipulating that he would need Top Secret government clearance so that he could access these computers.

Khachooni and Miller programmed the 1108 not only to calculate distances between places, but also to hide information about the world. At Design Methods, Khachooni and Miller hired two mathematics researchers to develop one of many graphics programs: a secondary program that mathematically "hid" lines of buildings located behind others so that computer drawings could render structures as the eye would see them—as opaque objects, rather than a transparent system of lines. Computer scientist Lawrence Roberts of MIT offered a limited solution to that "hidden-line problem" in 1963, and Ruth Weiss of Bell Labs provided another in 1965, but it was not until the mid-1980s that computer algorithms were able to address all types of line and edge conditions.⁵⁰ By 1970, DMJM's subprogram could remove lines behind others in order to create a sense of depth, and this helped clients visualize the impacts a new design might have on the city around it, such as which views or buildings might be blocked. While examples of DMJM's hidden-line projects were published, the steps for hiding the lines or otherwise operating the computer program were not described. Khachooni claims to have deliberately omitted details about the way DMJM used its computer in public lectures, thus black-boxing a proprietary concept of business for a competitive advantage. In a 1971 article in *Datamation*, Miller describes Design Methods and a project of theirs in San Francisco. It is featured on the issue's cover: a computer-generated skyline of the city, including a dizzying overlay of all possible lines. This cover image is contrasted with a "clean" view of the city within the article, with the obstructed lines removed. However, even in this computer-industry magazine, there was no description of these drawings in the article, and no mention of the proprietary tools, the people, or the process that had been used to produce them.

Similarly, in regard to the secrecy around drawings that DMJM produced for the CIA, it was not the material facts of the tools, bombs, or buildings that the government was most worried about DMJM revealing. As Alex Wellerstein argues, antinuclear activists and journalists pieced together bits of information and circulated drawings of bombs and missiles in magazines and newspapers, and the government did not react to their disclosures.⁵¹ Coburn's and Khachooni's experiences suggest that it was rather the *sequence of events*—the steps necessary to design, build, or launch a bomb, building, or country—that was being hidden. Whether a matter of trade secrets or defense strategy, the secrecy was predicated on separation—keeping "one frame separated from another"—such that no one could connect the "before" setup to the "after."⁵² In other words, despite the overwhelming emphasis on the science, materials, and technologies of bombs and missiles (and buildings), control over the narrative sequence of the past was viewed as most politically and economically significant to sovereignty and, thus, to political and economic power.

Records

By the 1970s, new measures of government oversight were established through laws aimed not only at safeguarding US interests, but also at protecting citizens from the state and holding it accountable. On the one hand, legislation such as the Freedom of Information Acts of 1966 and 1977 and the Privacy Act of 1974 granted citizens the right to access government records while also limiting the government's use of personal information. On the other hand, as committees such as the Watergate, Church, and Pike Committees began investigating government conduct and government contractors, they produced unprecedented volumes of paperwork that became increasingly unmanageable—both in government and in business.

As part of these many investigations, DMJM was scrutinized by the CIA and by the Senate Watergate Committee. One Senate report states that former DMJM vice president Barry Mountain, who was the administrative chair of the Republican National Committee (RNC) supporting Nixon, was investigated because he had appointed former CIA officer James McCord as head of security for the RNC during the time of the Watergate scandal. McCord was one of the first to be indicted for burglary, conspiracy, and wiretapping.[53]

But this report was only a tiny part of a massive investigative effort: more than ten thousand records were created as part of the Watergate scandal alone, and additional workers and computers were required to process and manage this incredible and unprecedented volume of records.[54] Within architecture firms, a new managerial class of laborers was similarly responsible for this growing area of work. Although initially these new workers were hired along stereotypically gendered lines, an increasing number of women were hired—first as secretaries, librarians, and data processors.[55] Eventually, once they had fractured the rigid patriarchal barriers to entry by working as secretaries and records managers, women began to normalize their place within architecture—including as architects—more broadly.

As mentioned earlier, the act of designating a record of the past a "secret" was supported in law by "housekeeping privilege," a 1789 federal statute—created when the legislative and executive branches of government were competing to establish procedural control over defense, diplomacy, and security information—that has long been interpreted as granting certain government "executives" and "secretaries" the authority to release or withhold records about the country's past. The law was reaffirmed in 1958.[56] However, this frequently cited yet often misunderstood "privilege" was originally established not to encourage practices of exclusion or concealment but instead to encourage the production, storing, and management of records—to "help General Washington get his administration underway by spelling out the authority for executive officials to set up offices and file Government documents."[57]

While preparing documents more for private storage than for a public archive, the "housekeepers" at DMJM held Top Secret clearance. One such bearer of "housekeeping privilege" was Carol Ann Bakeman, who eventually became the firm's chief librarian and records manager. Bakeman was a self-taught librarian who, prior to DMJM, had worked at the Hughes Aircraft Company.[58] In 1969, DMJM's Economics Division hired her as a part-time librarian to catalogue and make accessible the firm's library and records of past projects (figure 40). If easily accessible, the DMJM directors believed, records could yield time savings and lead to bigger projects, since they demonstrated "experience" and ensured historical

FIGURE 40. Carol Ann Bakeman, DMJM. Papers of Carol Ann Bakeman. Private collection. Courtesy of Laurie Bakeman.

continuity. In other words, in the organization of the firm's records of the past was economic potential for the future.

Journal articles and newspapers celebrated Bakeman's "housework"—the kind of work historically associated with women's unwaged "labor of love"—by comparing it explicitly to the domestic sphere, highlighting its prominence within the "man's world" of waged work.[59] During her long career, Bakeman was appointed corporate librarian in 1971, manager of information and office services in 1979, and senior vice president of AECOM in the early 2000s. The scope of her work increased throughout her career along a gendered line of "housekeeping" and without a pay increase. In addition, she managed the firm's telecommunications, travel arrangements, fleet of cars, executive dining room, and all "house" furniture and "space plans."[60]

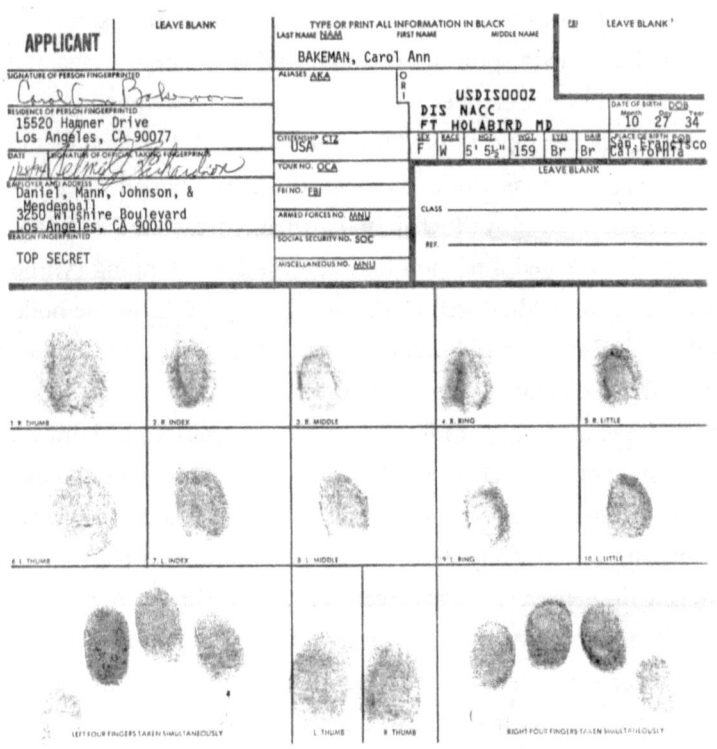

FIGURE 41. Bakeman's application, with fingerprints, to the FBI for Top Secret clearance. Papers of Carol Ann Bakeman. Private collection. Courtesy of Laurie Bakeman.

Importantly, Bakeman also held Top Secret clearance. First granted in 1961 and renewed in the early 1990s, the clearance enabled her to work as DMJM's facility security officer—a position requiring strict government review, including fingerprinting and background checks (figure 41).[61] The officer status made her one of DMJM's official "housekeepers": not only was she maintaining and reproducing the firm's history, she was maintaining and reproducing the history of the US.

In 1978, as part of a housekeeping assignment, Bakeman surveyed the archiving procedures and records management technologies in use by large architecture firms. She stated prominently, on the first page of her report, that "the future of DMJM is dependent on knowledge of its past work."[62] Despite the size of these firms, and the collective practices by which they were defined, their record-keeping protocols revealed a tension between the long-standing symbolic value of an individual architect's hand drawings and the methods of mechanical reproduction. In the case of The Architects Collaborative (TAC), Bakeman notes that "they don't trust scale on bringing back drawings from 35 mm. . . . They check their original drawings against all others." This was also the case at other firms, including CRS in Houston and William Pereira & Associates in Los Angeles. At many firms, especially those with state contracts, architects were "trying to keep everything forever," in one form or another. At Pereira's firm, she writes, they tried microfilming but "didn't like reproduced copies[,] tried reducing drawings but still didn't like copies[, and] bringing back to accurate scale was a problem."[63]

In keeping records of "everything," the corporate firms were unlike many noted modernist architects who often resorted to extreme acts of destruction—obsessively selecting and deleting stages of the work—in order to appear self-designed.[64] The architect Peter Eisenman, by contrast, claims to have kept everything, akin to an art collector: "As a collector, I keep scraps of paper, letters, and other materials."[65] According to him, "We do not do any selection. When it overwhelms us, we just put everything into storage."[66] However, as Sylvia Lavin has described, the primary archives of Eisenman's work held at the Canadian Centre for Architecture (CCA) reveal a different story. The archival record for his House I, for example, includes mostly drawings and very few documents.[67] Many of Eisenman's drawings were produced by hand and autographed as they were archived (at the request of the institutions, he has claimed), which exposes his desire to appear self-designed rather than designed by others (such as a state or bureaucracy).[68] This is not unlike the archival violence described by Adolf Loos, who notably destroyed all of the documents in his studio and argued that "the gentleman is a man who only carries out work with the help of destruction."[69]

In any case, these archival and record-keeping efforts and practices raise important questions about the roles that storage companies and cultural institutions alike play in deciding which legacies are safeguarded and why. In addition to storage companies such as Iron Mountain, many private archives were established during the postwar period through family trusts, for the same purposes as the archives of corporate architecture conglomerates.[70] The CCA, for instance, was founded by Phyllis Bronfman Lambert in 1979, just as her father's corporate conglomerate, Bronfman Distillers Corporation, was radically diversifying from whiskey to oil, entertainment, and chemicals.[71] As with DMJM or storage companies such as Iron Mountain, the ability to reproduce a family's legacy and extend its lifeline depended on a business as materially diverse and as carefully maintained as its members, and it was economically fueled by access to self-crafted legacies of (mostly) men about men.

The trajectory of Bakeman's career, from the Hughes Aircraft Company to DMJM, characterizes a broader trajectory of women working within postwar corporate architecture firms, in part to curate those legacies. As with Bakeman, it was common for women to enter corporate architecture firms after first working within government or government-contractor offices. The earliest women architects hired at DMJM, such as Zelma Wilson in 1949, held drafting positions in city planning offices or departments of parks and recreation before they were considered to be "prepared" for private practice with their white male contemporaries. The same was true for the first African American architects within large firms, such as Robert Kennard and Rolland Cooper at DMJM, hired in 1952.[72]

Women architects reported higher rates of employment in government jobs than men during the 1960s. Given that many large architecture firms were closely aligned with the government, women's relatively large numbers in those firms was unsurprising. By the middle of the 1970s, architecture firms of fifty or more employees employed disproportionately more women than smaller firms, despite representing less than 4 percent of architects across the US at the time.[73] Norma Sklarek, the first African American woman licensed to practice architecture in the US, was unable to find work after graduating from Columbia University in 1950. After being rejected by a dozen firms in New York, she was hired by the New York Department of Public Works in 1950 and by SOM in 1955.[74] Zelma Wilson was hired by DMJM only after working for the Los Angeles City Planning Department, yet she was fired during the Red Scare. According to one of Wilson's acquaintances, "she was told to pack up her belongings and be out of the office by 5 p.m. When she asked why, she was told that she had selected 'the wrong colors of paint on her last project.'"[75]

In surveys conducted by the AIA in 1975, women described never-ending discriminatory "mental blocks" in the minds of male supervisors, architects, and business leaders who prevented them from entering firms as designers or as business leaders.[76] Even as architects, women described their work as "secret" so as not to rattle the "gentlemen's" profession. As Wilson told a *Los Angeles Times* reporter, "In those days, women architects were rare. And when there was a woman architect, it was kept a deep dark secret. Julia Morgan did her drawings in the basement. And she designed 800 other buildings including several on the Stanford campus, but she died unknown, alone and penniless.... For a female to say she wanted to be an architect was like saying 'I want to walk on the moon,' especially at Santa Rosa High School. Yes, I'm a Ventura County girl."[77]

By the 1970s, photographs of women peppered public-facing annual reports at DMJM and company brochures, including in a page of

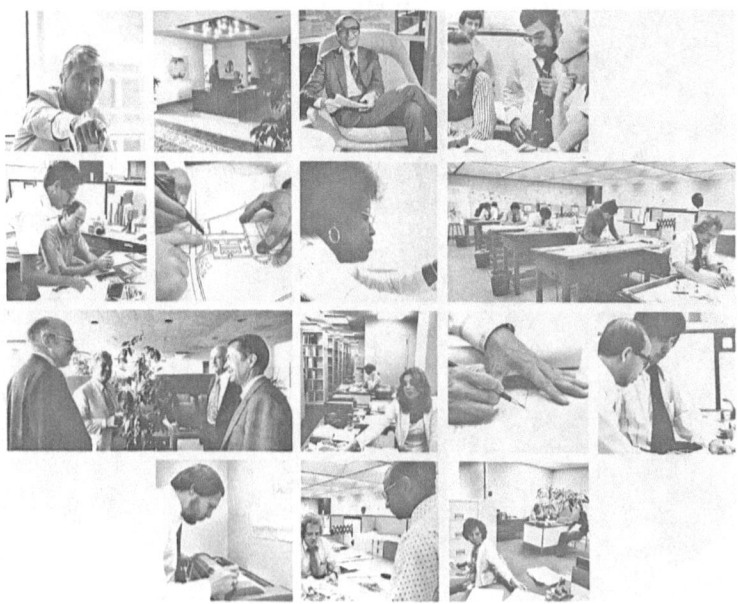

FIGURE 42. "Personnel," from DMJM, *New Towns*, ca. 1975. Papers of Arthur Mann. Private collection. Courtesy of Karen Letterman.

photos of different people, from different moments, ordered and separated by a grid of white space (figure 42). However, very few made their way into the ranks of administration, as is evident in photographs of the (mostly) white group of executives who gathered annually for corporate retreats (figure 43). As business historian Louis Hyman has argued, a woman's work was considered a "luxury" by 1970s standards; her labor was viewed as "temporary," her income "supplemental."[78]

DMJM architect Ellen Wright describes how deeply ingrained gendered labor conventions were when she was hired in the 1980s:

> The first day I was there, someone literally asked me to make coffee. I said, 'No, I'm sorry, I didn't get a graduate degree in architecture for

FIGURE 43. DMJM Professional Council retreat, Vail, Colorado, June 21, 1975. Papers of Arthur Mann. Private collection. Courtesy of Karen Letterman.

you to ask me to make coffee. You'll need to ask someone else'. . . . And I remember, when I was about one or two years in, looking around at the sea of white male engineers and thinking 'wow, I'll never fit in.' But it was absolutely freeing, because I didn't even have to try. And I kind of feel like, for most of the women who worked there, there was no attempt to be anything other than who they were. And so I guess it was almost a reaction to the culture, rather than the culture being nurturing.[79]

A decade earlier, an AIA subcommittee on "women and minorities in architecture" had prepared a survey about women in the profession and academia to help inform new affirmative action policies. Within it, one respondent noted that "continuous repetition of the masculine gender and the word 'men' in reference to architects, employers, technical employees and AIA members, and the use of the feminine gender and the word 'women' in reference to secretaries and spouses tends to reinforce traditional ideas of the roles of women and men in the profession."[80] Yet these gendered divisions of labor had begun to break down, if only marginally, not because of social pressures, but because of big business.

When DMJM's board of directors was conducting a search in 1981 for a new member, founding partner Art Mann proposed nominating a woman. In a handwritten note for his colleagues, titled "DMJM Board," he wrote: "How about a top woman businesswoman. I don't have a name in mind, but a little research could turn up a lot of names. The DMJM Board needs a feminine touch. I got tired of the beady eyed business men. How about a beady eyed woman? The [illegible] plus aside from some astute thinking would be the *P.R. effect*. She need not be in the design or construction fields, just so long as she has business experience."[81] Mann's proposal, ultimately rejected by the other directors, underscored the perceived role that women played within conglomerate architecture firms: "public relations." This was made visible by the "executive dining room" in the firm's Los Angeles office, which was managed by Bakeman. It was there that the firm hosted private lunches and drinking events with public guests, such as directors of various city departments. Wright, who began her career at DMJM in 1985, recalls: "I remember the first time there was a woman [guest]—a woman who was very high up in the city—and she was invited in for lunch and it was hilarious to me because I got an invite to the corporate dining room. But I was normally just the third drafter to the left, and now they pretended I was way more special than that because they had a woman guest."[82]

Wright argues that the striking homogeneity of white men and the prominence of women secretaries during the 1970s helped produce "exceptional women architects"—those whom Gwendolyn Wright has described as historically anonymous, tolerant of discrimination, and less recognized.⁸³ It was common for women at DMJM to react to that striking homogeneity and form their own firms after some time—after leaving or being forced out—or lead nationally recognized design organizations. Zelma Wilson, recognized as a pioneering architect, launched her own firm in 1967 and was named an AIA Fellow in 1983. Kim Day, hired at DMJM during the 1970s and the first woman architect to become a vice president there, left to become executive director of Los Angeles World Airports in 2003 and CEO of Denver International Airport in 2008. And Ellen Wright, following her career at DMJM, was director of terminal design at Los Angeles World Airports.⁸⁴

. . .

Today, most of DMJM's records are stored at Iron Mountain alongside those of real estate enterprises, government agencies, and insurance companies like CBRE, IBM, and MetLife. Iron Mountain now offers companies both physical protection and economic protection, promising money for life after work, assuming that workers live long enough to retire. AECOM stores ten thousand shares of employee retirement funds in Iron Mountain as public stock.⁸⁵ AECOM and Iron Mountain are united in a mutual business that manages and exploits the cycles of life—from life above ground to death below ground, not omitting the movement from one world to another. The relationship between the two companies could be described architecturally. To invoke terms used by Matthew Soules in his architectural analysis of twentieth-century finance, they have worked together to produce empty zombies of architectural speculation above ground and the cavernous icebergs of storage below ground to protect themselves, their legacies, and the status quo.⁸⁶

Beyond Iron Mountain, the private house emerges as a site for storing AECOM's records and, thus, those of the government.

Daughters, sons, and other relatives of former DMJM workers have proudly stored and maintained boxes, binders, folders, and company drawings in their closets, attics, and garages—spaces in between the office and the vault where ephemeral letters and notes were carefully guarded. Together, these sites *are* the firm's archives and unofficial archives of the state. Thanks to them, the firm's past can be made accessible to the public—or at least to historians and ethnographers as intermediaries between private archives and the public—and hence the possibility of historical transformation is kept alive.

Conclusion

The 1946 partnership founded by architects Phillip Daniel, S. Kenneth Johnson, and Arthur Mann was hardly recognizable by 1990. As part of a corporate conglomerate named AECOM, spanning seventy-one international offices, the architects and engineers working there were contributing to a deeply political enterprise. While DMJM was only one component of AECOM's multinational and multisectoral practice, it had crafted a corporate script informed by the tools and techniques of American imperialism—one that both AECOM and the profession of architecture could follow.

Despite their prominence and impact, DMJM's and AECOM's stories should not be considered isolated tales nor exceptional cases within the history of architecture. Instead, they illustrate broader social patterns: architects forming friendships and alliances with the government, consolidating capital, and taking hold of professional and academic institutions—the very institutions that now determine who can be considered an architect, what knowledge and skills they need to learn, and the terms and conditions of their labor.

Today, it is far more common for accounts of US dependency on private-sector companies to focus on technology, finance, or oil giants. Meanwhile, architects continue to be mythologized for their creative genius in both public and professional spheres, while large architecture and engineering firms remain unchecked—wielding their political and economic influence over the material aspects of everyday life and designing the very codes and infrastructures of dependency that sustain public-private relationships. Contrary to most perceptions of architects and architecture, it is, as we have seen, in the making of the most physically *unremarkable* buildings—the plants, airports, highways, and offices—where we have found the profession's most politically remarkable acts. For these reasons, it is now common for the US government, as well as increasingly prominent private equity companies—companies investing in all sectors of the economy by acquiring businesses—to consider architecture and engineering companies as models, recognizing them for their ability to retain employees, build careful and personal relationships, and demonstrate public value.

When I first began studying AECOM, I anticipated encountering a complex world of collaborative work: anonymous workers increasingly spread across time zones, redundant departments, and vast geographies. Although my expectations were somewhat naive, I did not foresee uncovering deeply entrenched practices of cronyism and corruption that, as it turns out, lie at the heart of the profession. As we consider what to make of histories such as this, one immediate response may be to amplify the contemporary calls within architecture for *deprofessionalization*. After all, even the US government has questioned architecture's "elite" status. While these critiques have emerged as talking points of academic discourse every thirty or forty years, coinciding with union drives and calls for independent institutions, the inertia and complexity of multinational firms can make change feel insurmountable. However, within these discussions are many suggested alternatives: some suggest unionization, as in the film industry, while others propose certification systems, as in aviation, pharmacy, or finance, or democratic cooperatives inspired by countries with socialist or communist histories. What remains too often overlooked or poorly understood within these discussions, however, is the vulnerabilities inherent in corporate capitalism itself—its pressure points, contradictions, and, consequently, its levers of disruption. My hope is that histories of architects' political and economic maneuvers, such as AECOM's, may help expose some of these levers and reveal how they operate. Indeed, as labor scholars like the late Jane McAlevey have argued, it is in the history of corporate organization, political corruption, and insider games that organizers can learn their most useful lessons.[1]

Despite long-standing arguments and contemporary lamentations that architectural practice and architectural education are radically disjointed—that the "business-oriented" profession is unlike the "ideologically focused" discipline—it became increasingly clear to me in finishing this research that schools of architecture and architecture corporations were, to the contrary, quite similar. Not only are they deeply interconnected, with the conditions of one fueling the other, but their differentiated rhetoric is, too, sharply contradicted by similar practices.

In 1992, sociologist Robert Gutman argued that "the language of the attorney about corporation law, of the accountant about plowed-back earnings, or of the marketing strategist about positioning is inevitably assimilated into the discourse of architects, just as it is standard now in the thinking of their clients."[2] And not in academia, he argued, but only in practice could architects learn these new languages. Along similar lines, Dana Cuff explained that by isolating design from theories of capital accumulation or capitalist critique, "schools highlight the importance of pure design by removing from its study key aspects of professional practice: the client or patron, the coordinated group process of design, and economic and power relations. . . . Architects are thus not trained to be alert to significant relations of authority, economics, power, group decision-making processes, management, and so on."[3]

A parallel history of the accrediting and regulatory bodies of architecture schools, including their corporate sponsors, might reveal how the rhetorical disagreements between academia and practice that Cuff and Gutman describe were also being undermined by the practices of universities themselves. A look at their profit-motivated criteria, fundraising "foundations," expanding degree programs, boards of trustees, and survival mechanisms reveals the cautionary tale of another slow hollowing over the past three decades: expectations about public service, cultural production, and history—concepts once at the heart of the profession—have been removed from curricula, replaced with regulation, technology, and business.[4] Meanwhile, architecture and engineering firms (including AECOM, Gensler, and Albert Kahn) now train architects through corporate universities, such as "AECOM University," while universities-as-corporations have similarly lost their focus on cultural production.[5] However, in recent years—as during the late 1960s, when new schools of architecture and academic associations were forming outside of universities—activist organizations such as The Architecture Lobby or Dark Matter University have formed summer schools, night schools, free schools, and weekend schools to teach these missing lessons, just as nonprofits have taken up services once central to architects' business. Yet these *are* the schools of a *deprofessionalized* architecture—a roadmap for practitioners to follow.

The blurry personal boundaries and loose political relationships on which architects built their postwar careers, as documented throughout this book, complicate the ways in which architects and urban practitioners can (or should) be studied by scholars within disciplines such as art and architecture, which are based in material traditions. Today, architecture firms, architectural labor, and architectural practices have piqued the interest of many scholars and scholar-activists—who, however, tend to approach their subjects with the same framing and methods that have long enabled firms such as DMJM to go unnoticed. On the one hand, to focus on contemporary conditions alone risks failing to see how such conditions may be cyclical or part of deeper, historical traditions. On the other hand, to focus too narrowly on a specific moment of the past or on the history of architecture's material conditions risks "thingifying" the subject, to borrow Aimé Césaire's expression—that is, the embodied (colonial) tendency to turn everything into an object (drawings, buildings, computers, etc.). Rather than choosing one or the other, to combine the two approaches—focusing on historical actions, relationships, cultures, beliefs, and associations *in tandem with* their material and contemporary consequences—may help keep both the discipline and the business of architecture in check while offering clues about how to *transform* the world, rather than merely reproduce it.

Histories of architects and architecture firms often end by describing how firms collapsed, dispersed, or went bankrupt—such as Caudill Rowlett Scott (CRS) in Texas, which was fractured in 1994, or The Architects Collaborative (TAC) in Massachusetts, which went bankrupt in 1995. But historians and architects alike would do well to consider the broader political and economic connections of architectural work by tracing how practices and cultures continue long after (or before) the existence of any single firm, building, architect, or drawing. To study a firm such as TAC might mean to consider the various successor firms that broke off as independent—as an "ecology," borrowing Isabelle Stenger's theory of practice—and that continued to operate after the firm's bankruptcy, including the Cambridge Seven Associates, formed in 1962, or Architectural Resources Cambridge, formed in 1969.[6] To describe the history of CRS as a practice might mean to describe the ways in which the firm's culture persisted after its so-called demise, carried forth by its architecture group after it was sold to Missouri-based Helmuth, Obata + Kassabaum (HOK) in 1994; by its engineering and construction groups when they were sold to California-based Jacobs Engineering; and by its cogeneration group, CRSS Capital, when it was sold to the engineering firm Tractebel.

This perpetual fracturing and recombining of firms serves as a reminder that AECOM, too, represents only one particular version of architectural practice along a continuum of capitalist development. Thus, to view AECOM—or any multinational corporate conglomerate—as a final version of architectural practice would be to disregard the imminent efforts by architects to adapt to economic systems and shifting means of production in the future.

Today, critics and historians describe AECOM as an all-powerful, fire-breathing, multiheaded "Leviathan"—the biblical sea dragon, a source of chaos. It is a familiar metaphor used by business historians Alfred D. Chandler Jr. and Bruce Mazlish to describe multinational corporations more generally, and most famously by Thomas Hobbes to characterize the state or commonwealth in the sixteenth century.[7] Returning to the words of a senior vice president of AECOM, introduced at the beginning of the book, it is evident that the firm achieves its Leviathan status through its work, rather than its built products: "We are AECOM, we can do anything."[8]

While the stories and projects we have examined illustrate in detail not just *why* but *how* multinational corporations like AECOM operate as Leviathans within the world, it is worth recalling the biblical account of Leviathan, in which the Hebrew God, Yahweh, tears it apart. Yahweh crushes Leviathan's many heads, feeds them to the Hebrews in the wilderness, and, in doing so, settles the chaos of the sea—a vivid allegory for dismantling consolidated systems of corporate power. This metaphor resonates with the history of architecture as a decidedly turbulent urban profession with multi-headed corporations at its helm. To extend it: while multinational architecture conglomerates constitute a seemingly all-powerful form of capitalist practice and reproduction, emboldened by the state and epitomized by firms like AECOM, we must not forget the possibility, ever looming, that the invisible hand of capitalism or the many visible hands of regulation could fragment or destroy Leviathan at any moment. To the Yahwehs of the world: unite!

Appendix

TABLE A1. Distribution (%) of Architectural Firms by Number of Employees, 1972–2017

Size (employees)	1972	1977	1982	1987	1992	1997	2002	2007	2012	2017
Small (<20)	93.3	94.8	93.1	92.0	93.2	92.0	90.7	90.9	91.6	90.8
Medium (20–99)	6.2	4.7	5.1	7.3	6.3	7.3	8.3	8.0	7.4	8.3
Large (100+)	0.5	0.5	0.7	0.8	0.6	0.7	1.0	1.1	1.0	0.9

Sources: US Department of Commerce, Bureau of the Census, *Census of Selected Services, 1972,* Subject Statistics, vol. 1, tbl4; ———, *Census of Service Industries, 1977,* Subject Series, vol. 1, tbl4; ———, *Census of Service Industries, 1982,* Industry Series, Establishments and Firm Size, tblsa; ———, *Census of Service Industries, 1987,* Industry Series, Establishments and Firm Size, tblsa; ———, *Census of Service Industries, 1992,* Subject Series: Establishments and Firm Size, tblsa; ———, *Economic Census, 1992,* Subject Series: Professional, Scientific, and Technical Services, Establishments and Firm Size, tblsa; ———, *Economic Census, 1997,* Subject Series: Professional, Scientific, and Technical Services, Establishments and Firm Size, tbls; ———, *Economic Census, 2002,* Subject Series: Professional, Scientific, and Technical Services, Establishments and Firm Size, tbls; ———, *Economic Census, 2012,* Subject Series: Professional, Scientific, and Technical Services, Establishments and Firm Size, tbls; ———, *Economic Census, 2017,* Subject Series: Professional, Scientific, and Technical Services, Establishments and Firm Size, tbls.

Note: Economic census data are reported on years ending in 2 and 7. These data include only firms operating for the entire year.

TABLE A2. Distribution (%) of Architectural Employees by Firm Size, 1972–2017

Size (employees)	1972	1977	1982	1987	1992	1997	2002	2007	2012	2017
Small (<20)	54.7	59.0	50.9	50.6	50.6	49.1	44.7	42.7	43.6	43.7
Medium (20–99)	30.1	25.5	28.0	29.8	28.7	30.9	31.6	30.7	30.5	36.8
Large (100+)	15.2	15.5	21.1	19.6	18.4	20.0	23.7	26.6	25.9	19.5

Sources: US Department of Commerce, Bureau of the Census, *Census of Selected Services*, 1972, Subject Statistics, vol. 1, tbl4; ———, *Census of Service Industries*, 1977, Subject Series, vol. 1, tbl4; ———, *Census of Service Industries*, 1982, Industry Series: Establishments and Firm Size, tbl5a; ———, *Census of Service Industries*, 1987, Industry Series: Establishments and Firm Size, tbl5a; ———, *Census of Service Industries*, 1992, Subject Series: Establishments and Firm Size, tbl5a; ———, *Economic Census*, 1992, Subject Series: Professional, Scientific, and Technical Services, Establishments and Firm Size, tbl5a; ———, *Economic Census*, 1997, Subject Series: Professional, Scientific, and Technical Services, Establishments and Firm Size, tbl5a; ———, *Economic Census*, 2002, Subject Series: Professional, Scientific, and Technical Services, Establishments and Firm Size, tbl5; ———, *Economic Census*, 2012, Subject Series: Professional, Scientific, and Technical Services, Establishments and Firm Size, tbl5; ———, *Economic Census*, 2017, Subject Series: Professional, Scientific, and Technical Services, Establishments and Firm Size, tbl5.

TABLE A3. Receipts (%) of Architectural Firms by Firm Size, 1972–2017

Size (employees)	1972	1977	1982	1987	1992	1997	2002	2007	2012	2017
Small (<20)	58.5	58.4	48.3	46.7	46.0	45.4	39.5	36.6	38.8	38.8
Medium (20–99)	27.8	24.7	28.3	31.3	32.7	29.5	32.9	31.4	30.1	39.9
Large (100+)	13.7	16.9	23.2	22.0	21.0	38.4	27.6	32.4	31.1	21.3

Sources: US Department of Commerce, Bureau of the Census, *Census of Selected Services, 1972, Subject Statistics,* vol. 1, tbl4; ———, *Census of Service Industries,* 1977, Subject Series, vol. 1, tbl4; ———, *Census of Service Industries, 1982, Industry Series: Establishments and Firm Size,* tbl5a; ———, *Census of Service Industries, 1987, Industry Series: Establishments and Firm Size,* tbl5a; ———, *Census of Service Industries, 1992, Subject Series: Establishments and Firm Size,* tbl5a; ———, *Economic Census, 1992, Subject Series: Professional, Scientific, and technical Services, Establishments and Firm Size,* tbl5a; ———, *Economic Census, 1997, Subject Series: Professional, Scientific, and Technical Services, Establishments and Firm Size,* tbl5a; ———, *Economic Census, 2002, Subject Series: Professional, Scientific, and Technical Services, Establishments and Firm Size,* tbl5; ———, *Economic Census, 2012, Subject Series: Professional, Scientific, and Technical Services, Establishments and Firm Size,* tbl5; ———, *Economic Census, 2017, Subject Series: Professional, Scientific, and Technical Services, Establishments and Firm Size,* tbl5.

TABLE A4. US Architecture Firms (%) by Legal Type, 1967–2012

Type	1972	1977	1982	1987	1992	1997	2002	2007	2012	2017
Individual proprietorship	33.0	40.3	28.1	29.0	27.6	24.0	19.1	15.8	11.4	10.3
Partnership	22.1	17.4	11.7	9.6	7.6	7.2	8.6	9.7	8.8	8.4
Corporation	21.4	31.4	60.0	61.3	64.6	68.6	72.3	74.5	79.8	81.3
Other	23.7	10.9	0.2	0.1	0.2	0.2	0.01	0.03	0.01	0.02

Sources: US Department of Commerce, Bureau of the Census, *Census of Selected Services*, 1972, Subject Statistics, vol 1, tbl4; ———, *Census of Service Industries*, 1977, Subject Series, vol. 1, tbl4; ———, *Census of Service Industries*, 1982, Industry Series: Miscellaneous Subjects, tbl7; ———, *Census of Service Industries*, 1987, Industry Series: Miscellaneous Subjects, tbl7; ———, *Census of Service Industries*, 1992, Subject Series: Establishments and Firm Size, tbl7; ———, *Economic Census*, 1997, Subject Series: Professional, Scientific, and Technical Services, Establishments and Firm Size, tbl7; ———, *Economic Census*, 2002, Subject Series: Professional, Scientific, and technical Services, Establishments and Firm Size; ———, *Economic Census*, 2007, Subject Series: Professional, Scientific, and Technical Services, Establishments and Firm Size; ———, *Economic Census*, 2012, Subject Series: Professional, Scientific, and Technical Services, Establishments and Firm Size; ———, *Economic Census*, 2017, Subject Series: Professional, Scientific, and Technical Services, Establishments and Firm Size.

Note: Data for corporations in 1972 include corporate form and corporate form "unknown." "Corporations" includes all forms of corporations. "Other" includes other companies and professional service organizations.

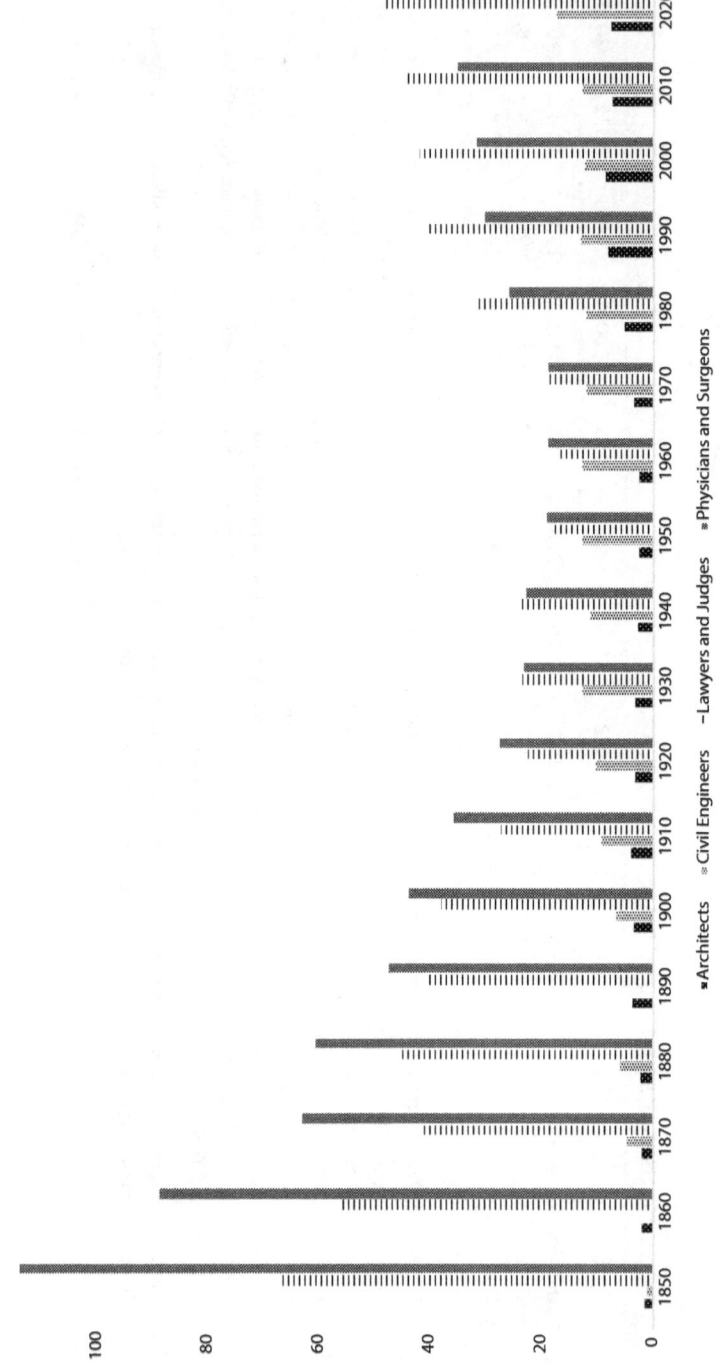

FIGURE A1. Professionals per urban population (ratio per 10,000 people). Sources: (1850–1970) Gutman, *Architectural Practice: A Critical View*, 121; (1980–2020) US Bureau of the Census, *Census of Population: Detailed Occupation and Other Characteristics*.

Notes

Introduction

1. This opening vignette is based on a photo of Deaver and Smith at the Sahara camp, which Smith mailed to Deaver in late September 1982. The photograph is now part of Deaver's archives. See Records of the White House Office of the Deputy Chief of Staff (Reagan Administration), Michael K. Deaver's Correspondence Files, Ronald Reagan Library, Simi Valley, CA.

2. The Bohemian Club was founded in San Francisco in 1872, and members continue to meet each summer to this day. The primary clubhouse at Bohemian Grove was designed by architect Bernard Maybeck in 1903. See Baxter, "Maybeck's Bohemian Clubhouse," 8–15. For a general history of the Bohemian Club and its influences, see Domhoff, *The Bohemian Grove and Other Retreats: A Study in Ruling-Class Cohesiveness*; Sutton, *America's Secret Establishment: An Introduction to the Order of Skull & Bones*; Rothkopf, *Superclass: The Global Power Elite and the World They Are Making*.

3. Letter from Michael Deaver to Stanley Smith, October 12, 1982, Records of the White House Office of the Deputy Chief of Staff (Reagan Administration), Michael K. Deaver's Correspondence Files, Ronald Reagan Library, Simi Valley, CA.

4. Matthews, "Chancellor Schmidt on Busman's Holiday in Bohemian Grove."

5. Until a "money-social element" led to the "death" of artistic "genius" ten years after its founding, as one artist wrote, artists and musicians were primary members of the early Bohemian Club. Cited in Domhoff, *The Bohemian Grove and Other Retreats*, 55.

6. AECOM, "Imagine It. Delivered. 2017 Annual Report," January 18, 2018. On population, see United Nations Population Fund, "World Population Dashboard." On gross domestic product, see The World Bank, "World Development Indicators."

7. Cuff, *Architecture: The Story of Practice*; Gutman, *Architectural Practice: A Critical View*; Blau, *Architects and Firms: A Sociological Perspective on Architectural Practice*; Woods, *From Craft to Profession: The Practice of Architecture in Nineteenth-Century America*.

8. Rand, *The Fountainhead*.

9. Vaillancourt, "The Quiet Giant: With a Massive Roster of Projects, AECOM, and Its 920 Local Employees, Are Poised to Shape the Future of Downtown."

10. Leach, "The (Ac)credit(ation) Card," 228.

11. On the compensation of AECOM's executives, see AECOM, US Securities and Exchange Commission, Schedule 14A, 2018, p. 70, https://www.sec.gov/Archives/edgar/data/868857/000104746919000207/a2237463zdef14a.htm (accessed October 3, 2018).

12. Seward, "Making It Big."

13. On change in business history, see Lamoreaux, Raff, and Temin, "Beyond Markets and Hierarchies: Toward a New Synthesis of American Business History."

14. As testament to recent historical interest in large firms or revisionist histories of small ones, see, among others, Franch i Gilabert et al., *OfficeUS: Atlas*; Ciccarelli, Lombardi, and Mingardi, *Largest Architectural Firms*.

15. See Cuff, "The Ethos and Circumstance of Design"; Larson, *The Rise of Professionalism: A Sociological Analysis*; Deamer, "Work."

16. Rybczynski, "Economic Downturns and the Architectural Profession."

17. For a recent analysis of architecture during a recession, see Carnevale, Cheah, and Strohl, "Hard Times: College Majors, Unemployment, and Earnings."

18. Woods, *From Craft to Profession*, 83.

19. Harder, "Architectural Practice—an Art and a Business."

20. See Landau, *George B. Post, Architect: Picturesque Designer and Determined Realist*; Balmori, "George B. Post: The Process of Design and the New American Architectural Office (1868–1913)"; Weisman, "The Commerical Architecture of George B. Post."

21. Woods, *From Craft to Profession*, 119.

22. Bannister, *The Architect at Mid-Century*, 63.

23. Bannister, *The Architect at Mid-Century*.

24. On the studio, see Jones, "The Romance of the Studio and the Abstract Expressionist Sublime"; Jacobson, *In the Studio: Visual Creation and Its Material Environments*.

25. Hitchcock, "The Architecture of Bureaucracy and the Architecture of Genius."

26. This point was made, though rarely, during the 1980s and has been reiterated more recently in regard to the same period. See Blau, *Architects and Firms*; Lavin, *Architecture Itself and Other Postmodernization Effects*.

27. Albert Kahn Associates, "Albert Kahn Associates"; also see Zimmerman, "Building the World Capitalist System: The 'Invisible Architecture' of Albert Kahn Associates of Detroit, 1900-1961"; Zimmerman, *Albert Kahn Inc.: Architecture, Industry, and Labor, 1905-1961*.

28. Perkins & Will, "Firm Profile"; also see Litke, "Perkins & Will: The First 50 Years."

29. As of 2020, Gehry Partners included six corporate subsidiaries and affiliate organizations registered in the State of California alone: Frank O. Gehry Associates Incorporated (est. 1967); Frank O. Gehry Associates, II, Incorporated (est. 2006); Gehry International, Incorporated (est. 2002); Gehry Design, Limited Liability Corporation (est. 2002); and Gehry Materials, Incorporated (est. 2010). In addition, Gehry Technologies, LLC, operated from 2002 to 2018, until a partnership was announced between Trimble Consulting and Gehry Partners in 2014, in which Trimble purchased Gehry Technologies, including its modeling software and consulting rights, even though the name changes and rights transfer did not occur until 2018. Five Gehry entities continued to operate as subsidiaries of Trimble Consulting: Gehry Technologies Consultoria e Software Ltda. (Brazil); Gehry Americas Services S de RL de CV (Mexico); Gehry Technologies Americas S de RL de CV (Mexico); Gehry Technologies Netherlands BV (Netherlands); and Gehry Technologies Middle East, LLC (Qatar).

30. As of 2022, SHoP's subsidiaries include SHoP Architects, P.C. (2001); Shopw25participant, LLC (2007); Shopw25thirdfloor, LLC (2007); Shopw-25fourthfloor, LLC (2007); Shopapplications, LLC (2008); SHoP Architects, LLP (2014); Shop Africa, LLC (2014); Shop Aust, LLC (2014); Shppf Dm, LLC (2020); SHoP Architects, Inc. (Delaware) (2021); 2435 Fdb DM, LLC (2021); 729 Second Ave Dm LLC (2021); Doublegadvisor, LLC (2021); Timing Chain, LLC (2021); 30littleramisland, LLC (2021); Lenape471, LLC (2021); Downstate914, LLC (2021); 729 Second Ave Dm, LLC (2021); Tailed Apprentice, LLC (2021); Envelope City, Inc. (2021). Cayer, "Architecture University, Incorporated"; Roche, "Organizing Shop: Follow the Sweat Equity."

31. For these data and their sources, see the appendix.

32. By 1992, 0.6 percent of firms were larger than one hundred people and 93.2 percent were smaller than twenty. Revenue data about 1972 were obtained and analyzed from US Department of Commerce, Bureau of the Census, *Census of Business, 1972*, Subject Statistics, vol. 1, tbl4. Data about 1992 were obtained and analyzed from US Department of Commerce, Bureau of the Census, *Economic Census, 1992*, Subject Series: Establishments and Firm Size, tbl5a. Data about 1997 were obtained and analyzed from US Department of Commerce, Bureau of the Census, *Economic Census 1997*, Subject Series: Professional, Scientific, and Technical Services, Establishments and Firm Size, tbl5a.

33. Executive of AECOM in email exchange with the author, February 19, 2016.

34. For data specific to architecture, see Building Design, "The World's Largest Architecture Practices," 14. For data specific to the firm as a whole, see AECOM, *Imagine It. Delivered. 2017 Annual Report*.

35. *Management Methods*, "Profile of a New Kind of Manager: How to Pack Pleasure and Profit into a Partnership," 28.

36. This definition appeared in amendments made to the 1890 Sherman Antitrust Act, the landmark statute that prohibited monopolies. The first amendment, passed by the Clayton Antitrust Act of 1914, specifically prohibited price discrimination as well as mergers and acquisitions (under section 7) if they were to lead to decreased competition. A second was the Celler-Kefauver Act in 1950, often referred to as the "Anti-Merger Act," which included provisions against acquisitions even by acquiring assets, and it prohibited vertical and conglomerate mergers if they were to result in reduced competition. In draft reports by the Federal Trade Commission in 1948, conglomerates were initially defined very specifically as "those in which there is little or no discernible relation between the business of the purchasing and the acquired firm," before concluding with a much broader application in the final 1950 amendment. US Federal Trade Commission, "Report of the Federal Trade Commission on the Merger Movement: A Summary Report," 59. See "Celler Kefauver Act," Public Law ch. 1183–1184, December 29, 1950, 1125–28, http://legisworks.org/congress/81/publaw-899.pdf (accessed November 12, 2017).

37. Chandler, *The Visible Hand: The Managerial Revolution in American Business*, 480–81; also see Lamoreaux, Raff, and Temin, "Beyond Markets and Hierarchies."

38. Lamoreaux, *The Great Merger Movement in American Business, 1895–1904*.

39. Trailblazing industrial organizations such as DuPont and General Electric set a precedent for diversified conglomerates as early as the 1920s, when DuPont diversified its manufacturing from gunpowder to paint, and General Electric from electricity to radio and television broadcasting. It was not until the 1960s that a "merger mania" of conglomerates grew to enormous proportion. See Chandler and Mazlish, *Leviathans: Multinational Corporations and the New Global History*; Editors of *Fortune*, *The Conglomerate Commotion*; Fligstein, "The Structural Transformation of American Industry: An Institutional Account of the Causes of Diversification in the Largest Firms, 1919-1979," 311-36; Lamoreaux, *The Great Merger Movement in American Business, 1895-1904*, 422.

40. King and Langdon, *The CRS Team and the Business of Architecture*, 209.

41. Cohen, "The Economic Aspects of Conglomerates," 49.

42. Arendt, *The Origins of Totalitarianism*, 124-35.

43. On the Roman Empire as conglomerate, see Southern and Dixon, *The Late Roman Army*, 11. On the relationship between modern conglomerate empires and war, see Barzilai, *Golem: Modern Wars and Their Monsters*, 107.

44. US Government Printing Office, *Congressional Record—Senate*, October 3, 1963, 18741.

45. On the conglomerate's history, see Chandler, *The Visible Hand*, 481-82; Jacoby, "The Conglomerate Corporation"; Editors of *Fortune*, *The Conglomerate Commotion*; Fligstein, "The Structural Transformation of American Industry"; Lamoreaux, Raff, and Temin, "Beyond Markets and Hierarchies."

46. Schatz, "The Studio System and Conglomerate Hollywood." On the Hollywood studio system, also see Long, *Playing the Percentages: How Film Distribution Made the Hollywood Studio System*.

47. Sinykin, *Big Fiction: How Conglomeration Changed the Publishing Industry and American Literature*.

48. On wartime and postwar publishing, see Shanken, *194X: Architecture, Planning, and Consumer Culture on the American Home Front*.

49. Good Jobs First, "Violation Tracker."

50. Klein, *The Shock Doctrine: The Rise of Disaster Capitalism*.

51. Wellerstein, *Restricted Data: The History of Nuclear Secrecy in the United States*, 8.

52. Stoler, *Along the Archival Grain: Epistemic Anxieties and Colonial Common Sense*; Des Chene, "Locating the Past"; Henni, *Colonial Toxicity: Rehearsing French Nuclear Architecture and Landscape in the Sahara*; Dudley, *Building Antebellum New Orleans: Free People of Color and Their Influence*.

53. Scott, *Seeing Like a State: How Certain Schemes to Improve the Human Condition Have Failed*; Césaire, *Discourse on Colonialism*.

54. White, "A Practical Past," 14; also see Clifford and Marcus, *Writing Culture: The Poetics and Politics of Ethnography*; White, *The Content of the Form: Narrative Discourse and Historical Representation*; White, *Metahistory: The Historical Imagination in Nineteenth-Century Europe*.

55. Comaroff and Comaroff, *Ethnography and the Historical Imagination*, 10.

56. On classic structural analysis and ethnography, see Lévi-Strauss, *Structural Anthropology*.

57. Traverso, *Singular Pasts: The "I" in Historiography*, 28.

58. Traverso, 35.

59. Traverso in Blackwood, "First-Person Histories Reframe the Past."

Chapter One

1. Chandler, *The Visible Hand: Architecture and Regulation in America*; also see Fligstein, "The Spread of the Multi-divisional Form among Large Firms, 1919–1979."

2. For these data and their sources, see the appendix.

3. Gutman, "Architecture: The Entrepreneurial Profession," 39–40.

4. Arendt, *The Origins of Totalitarianism*, 124–35; Lenin, "Imperialism, the Highest Stage of Capitalism."

5. On the limits of economic growth within professions in capitalist societies and surpassing "traditional society," see, among others, Rostow, *The Stages of Economic Growth: A Non-Communist Manifesto*, 4.

6. Breckenfeld, "The Architects Want a Voice in Redesigning America."

7. Architecture in the US was never fully able to control a market for services. See Larson, "Emblem and Exception: The Historical Definition of the Architect's Professional Role." On the 1909 Canon of Ethics, see *The American Architect*, "Forty-Third Annual Convention: American Institute of Architects."

8. On the architect as gentleman, see Saint, *The Image of the Architect: The History and Theory of Professional Practice*, 96–114; Dixon, "A White Gentlemen's Profession?" On the architect as businessman, see Woods, *From Craft to Profession: The Practice of Architecture in Nineteenth-Century America*; Saint, *The Image of the Architect*, 72–95; Johnston, *Assembling the Architect: The History and Theory of Professional Practice*. On architects and their clients, see Jenkins, *Architect and Patron*; Ellis and Cuff, *Architects' People*.

9. Parsons, "The Professions and Social Structure," 458.

10. For a top-down argument, see Wickersham, "From Disinterested Expert to Marketplace Competitor: How Anti-monopoly Law Transformed the Ethics and Economics of American Architecture in the 1970s." For a bottom-up argument, see Deamer, *Architecture and Labor*, 71-88.

11. Davis, "Has Globalism Made Architecture's Professional Ethics Obsolete?"

12. Levinson, *An Extraordinary Time: The End of the Postwar Boom and the Return of the Ordinary Economy*. On gross domestic product, see Coyle, *GDP: A Brief but Affectionate History*.

13. For a most influential example, see Smith, *The Wealth of Nations*.

14. Harvey, *A Brief History of Neoliberalism*, 12-13.

15. Woods, *From Craft to Profession*, 32.

16. Woods, 36-41. During the antebellum period, the early associations favored "architectural science" as a means to gaining legitimacy. By the 1870s, this was criticized by the leaders of the AIA as too "practical," and thus a "professional" was linked more to artistry.

17. New York was the first state to pass a license law, but it was vetoed by the governor, who argued that it was a means for organizing a professional trade union and therefore was considered class legislation. See Ricker, "Results of License Law for Architects in Illinois," 28.

18. This ruling was established in the case of medical practitioners in *FTC v. Raladim Co.* in 1931. See Deamer, "The Sherman Antitrust Act and the Profession of Architecture," 9. For a general theory of these sanctions against professions, see Friedman, *Capitalism and Freedom*, 137-60.

19. *United States v. The American Institute of Architects*, at 3.

20. Bork, *The Antitrust Paradox: A Policy at War with Itself*.

21. See Gutman, *Architectural Practice: A Critical View*, 46-49; Wickersham, "From Disinterested Expert to Marketplace Competitor: How Anti-monopoly Law Transformed the Ethics and Economics of American Architecture in the 1970s."

22. There were 53,670 architects in 1970. US Census Bureau, *Census of Service Industries, Subject Series*, 1970, vols. 1, tbl.1.

23. Whitehouse, "Architect Fits Snugly into Owner's Role."

24. See, among others, Lapidus, *Architecture: A Profession and a Business*.

25. Woods, *From Craft to Profession*, 83, 168-69.

26. US Government Printing Office, "Statement of Robert F. Hastings, President, American Institute of Architects; Accompanied by William L. Slayton, Executive Vice President, and Michael Barker, Director, Urban Programs," 1202.

27. Holleman and Gallagher, *Smith, Hinchman & Grylls: 125 Years of Architecture and Engineering, 1853-1978*.

28. For a recent study that makes this argument, see The Temple Hoyne Buell Center, *The A&E System: Public Works and Private Interest in Architectural and Engineering Services, 2000-2020*.

29. Klein, *The Shock Doctrine: The Rise of Disaster Capitalism*.

30. At the state level, California's state architect, Fred Hummel (1968-73), who served under then governor Ronald Reagan, was named vice president of DMJM in 1984, when his firm, Hummel/Giles, was acquired, and, like a political figure, he "represented the organization [DMJM] throughout the state." *Los Angeles Times*, "Hummel New DMJM Officer." DMJM vice president Samuel B. Nelson also served as the California state director of public works under Ronald Reagan in the late 1960s, though he worked at DMJM before and returned in 1971. See *Los Angeles Times*, "S. B. Nelson Returns to DMJM Post."

31. Mountain rejoined DMJM after serving the RNC in 1973. See Letter from Barry F. Mountain to S. Kenneth Johnson, "Administration-Honors, Commissions, and Appointments," August 11, 1970, Stanley Moe family papers, private collection.

32. DMJM was awarded a $2 million contract for the design of the Holyoke Community College in Massachusetts in 1968 in exchange for over $30,000 in cash payments by the firm to the Republican Party, which were delivered in person by DMJM's Barry Mountain. Special Commission for the Commonwealth of Massachusetts, "Final Report to the General Court of the Special Commission Concerning State and County Buildings," 164-65.

33. *Los Angeles Times*, "AIA Announces '76 Design Awards"; Nairn, "Building Types Study 509: College Buildings."

34. Dean, "Honor Awards: New Buildings, Recyclings, and Mies."

35. Special Commission for the Commonwealth of Massachusetts, "Final Report to the General Court of the Special Commission Concerning State and County Buildings," 37.

36. Special Commission for the Commonwealth of Massachusetts, 1.

37. Thomas, "Prejudice and Pragmatism: The Commercial Architect in the Development of Postwar London"; Xue and Ding, *A History of Design Institutes in China from Mao to Market*; López, "The Technical State: Programs, Positioning, and the Integration of Architects in Political Society in Mexico, 1945-1955."

38. Friedman, "The Business Community's Suicidal Impulse," 6.

39. Congress did not pass the proposal until 1972 under Nixon, and Owings resigned from the commission in 1982, by which time it was renamed the Pennsylvania Avenue Development Corporation. Owings also helped place SOM's David Childs on the National Capitol Planning Commission, which protected the

federal government's interests in all design and planning efforts in the DC region, including coordinating the budgets for publicly funded projects. For an inside perspective, see Mitchell, *The Crisis of the African American Architect: Conflicting Cultures of Architecture and (Black) Power*, 150–51. For more on SOM, see Adams, *Skidmore, Owings & Merrill: SOM since 1936*.

40. Schwarzer, "The Sources of Architectural Nationalism."

41. Owings, *The Spaces in Between: An Architect's Journey*, 244.

42. Yaneva, *Crafting History: Archiving and the Quest for Architectural Legacy*.

43. Stevens, *Developing Expertise: Architecture and Real Estate in Metropolitan America*, 8.

44. Charles Luckman quoted in Koehler, "Luckman Tells All about Ogden." On control and neoliberal ideology in architecture, see Spencer, *The Architecture of Neoliberalism: How Contemporary Architecture Became an Instrument of Control and Compliance*.

45. *The Desert Sun*, "Luckman Announces Change"; also see *Chicago Tribune*, "Politics a Hindrance: Luckman."

46. See, among others, Young, "Keynote Address to 1968 AIA National Convention, Portland, OR."

47. Franklin, "Mutual Benefits."

48. King and Langdon, *The CRS Team and the Business of Architecture*, 164–65.

49. Whitehouse, "Architect Fits Snugly into Owner's Role." On Gwathmey, see *The Washington Post*, "Cabell Gwathmey: Director of DC Agency."

50. Perkins, "Mergers and Acquisitions: An Outline: Marriage Manual for Architectural Firms."

51. Real estate and construction management were common first steps for diversifying architecture firms, including CRS in Houston, which developed construction management practices, and John Portman in Atlanta, whose development efforts grew notoriety. The union between CLA and Ogden resulted in the formation of the real estate development company Ogden Development Corporation, which lasted until 1973. Ogden was named a "big operative" in a special feature about American conglomerates in *Time* in 1969 that was presented to Congress. For a synopsis of architects in the development process during the 1970s, see Krum, "Architects in the Development Process: Emerging Professional Roles"; Hastings, "Extension of Remarks: Conglomerates, Tuesday, March 11, 1969."

52. On sociological studies of architecture at the time, see Gutman, "Architecture: The Entrepreneurial Profession"; Larson, "Emblem and Exception: The Historical Definition of the Architect's Professional Role"; Blau, *Architects and*

Firms: A Sociological Perspective on Architectural Practice; Brain, "Practical Knowledge and Social Control: The Professionalization of Architecture in the United States"; Freidson, *The Professions and Their Prospects*; Gans, "Toward a Human Architecture: A Sociologist's View of the Profession"; Cullen, "Structural Aspects of the Architectural Profession"; Cuff, *Architecture: The Story of Practice*.

53. Larson, *The Rise of Professionalism: A Sociological Analysis*.

54. Larson, 136–58.

55. Larson, "Emblem and Exception"; Cullen, "Structural Aspects of the Architectural Profession."

56. For a map of the urban concentration of architects in the US, see US Bureau of Labor Statistics, "Occupational Employment and Wage Statistics."

57. For a comparison of urban professionals since the nineteenth century, see the appendix.

58. Freidson, "The Changing Nature of Professional Control."

59. On the deprofessionalization thesis from the 1970s, see Haug, "Deprofessionalization: An Alternative Hypothesis for the Future"; and a similar, more recent argument in Deamer, "Deprofessionalization and Architecture." On the proletarianization thesis, see Esland, "Professions and Professionalism"; Braverman, *Labor and Monopoly Capital: The Degradation of Work in the Twentieth Century*.

60. For the census data on which I base these summaries, see tables A1–A3.

61. See tables A2 and A3

62. For the census data on which I base these summaries, see the appendix.

63. For data including and prior to 1970, see Gutman, *Architectural Practice*, 122. For 2020 data, US Bureau of Labor Statistics, "Current Population Survey: Employed Persons by Detailed Occupation."

64. For more recent analyses of this shift within professions, see Brint, *In an Age of Experts: The Changing Role of Professionals in Politics and Public Life*; Larson, "Professions Today: Self-Criticism and Reflections for the Future."

65. Tafuri and Hays, "Toward a Critique of Architectural Ideology." For a more recent analysis, see D'Aprile and Spencer, "Notes on Tafuri, Militancy, and Unionization."

66. Larson, *The Rise of Professionalism*.

67. See Larson, "Professions Today: Self-Criticism and Reflections for the Future," 27–42; Larson, "Notes on Technocracy: Some Problems of Theory, Ideology, and Power."

68. The phrase "late capitalism" was used during the 1980s and 1990s to describe the shift from corporate capitalism to finance capitalism, and it described

both the positive and negative impacts of the political economy. In the past two decades, these shifts have been described as "neoliberalism," which is characterized by the same underlying political-economic shifts, but often associated with a darker narrative of power, greed, and crusade that DMJM's history does not embody. For an overview of this distinction, see Ortner, "On Neoliberalism." On the early theories of late capitalism, see Mandel, *Late Capitalism*. For one way in which architecture and neoliberalism have been intertwined more generally, see Spencer, *The Architecture of Neoliberalism*.

69. On the history of drafting, see Johnston, *Drafting Culture: A Social History of Architectural Graphic Standards*.

70. See, among others, Gramsci, *Selections from the Prison Notebooks of Antonio Gramsci*, 278–318; Jessop, "Fordism and Post-Fordism: A Critical Reformulation."

71. See *Architectural Record*, "Producer of Production Lines"; *Architectural Forum*, "Industrial Buildings: Albert Kahn Inc." For a more critical overview, see Zimmerman, *Albert Kahn Inc.: Architecture, Industry, and Labor, 1905-1961*.

72. Owings, *The Spaces in Between: An Architect's Journey*, 66. Despite resisting incorporation to remain a partnership, SOM remained a top-ranked firm by measures of size, though DMJM surpassed SOM in 1990. See *Engineering News-Record*, "The Top 500 Design Firms," April 1991.

73. Allen, *Flowcharting: From Abstractionism to Algorithmics in Art and Architecture*, 111–34. On the history of the organization chart, see Chandler, "Origins of the Organization Chart."

74. On SOM, see Giedion, "The Experiment of S.O.M." On Kahn, see Hitchcock, "The Architecture of Bureaucracy and the Architecture of Genius"; *Architectural Record*, "Producer of Production Lines"; Zimmerman, "The Labor of Albert Kahn."

75. For excellent business histories that outline the shifts from twentieth- to twenty-first-century firm structures, see Hughes, "From Firm to Networked Systems"; Powell, "The Capitalist Firm in the 21st Century."

76. Lazzarato, "Immaterial Labor," 133. See Harvey, *The Condition of Postmodernity: An Enquiry into the Origins of Cultural Change*, 141–72; Antonio and Bonanno, "A New Global Capitalism? From 'Americanism and Fordism' to 'Americanization-Globalization'"; Hughes, *American Genesis: A Century of Invention and Technological Enthusiasm, 1870-1970*.

77. Drucker, *Concept of the Corporation*, xvi.

78. Drucker, xvi.

79. Boyle, "Architectural Practice in America, 1865–1965—Ideal and Reality."

80. Chandler, *Strategy and Structure: Chapters in the History of the Industrial Enterprise.*

81. Chandler, 48.

82. Cover, *Engineering News-Record* (May 1961).

83. Stinson, "The Money-Makers (and Some Losers): What the Reports Show."

84. See, e.g., *Engineering News-Record*, "The Top 500 Design Firms," May 1982.

85. *Canadian Builder*, "The Parkin Organization." On Parkin, see Fraser, McMordie, and Simmins, *John C. Parkin, Archives and Photography: Reflections on the Practice and Presentation of Modern Architecture.*

86. For a critical overview of these theories, see Harvey, *Spaces of Capital: Towards a Critical Geography*; Lenin, "Imperialism, the Highest Stage of Capitalism."

87. See Wallerstein, *The Modern World-System.*

88. Roy Ash, cited in Celler, "Remarks before the Senate."

89. Saint, *Architect and Engineer: A Study in Sibling Rivalry.*

90. Albert Dorman in discussion with the author, February 8, 2016.

91. Harvey, *The Condition of Postmodernity*, 141–72.

92. Hyman, *Temp: How American Work, American Business, and the American Dream Became Temporary.*

93. Harvey, *The Condition of Postmodernity*, 147–52.

94. Soja, *Postmodern Geographies: The Reassertion of Space in Critical Social Theory*, 185.

95. Toffler, *Future Shock.*

96. Atkinson, "Emerging UK Work Patterns."

97. Evans and Bell, "Emerging Themes in Flexible Work Patterns"; Harvey, *The Condition of Postmodernity*, 151.

98. Latour, "Where Are the Missing Masses? The Sociology of a Few Mundane Artifacts," 246. Also see Bourdieu, *The Field of Cultural Production: Essays on Art and Literature*; Ortner, *Anthropology and Social Theory: Culture, Power, and the Acting Subject.* For this argument in architecture, see Yaneva, *The Making of a Building: A Pragmatist Approach to Architecture*; Cuff, *Architecture: The Story of Practice.*

99. See, especially, Berle, *The Modern Corporation and Private Property*; Drucker, *Concept of the Corporation*; Chandler, *The Visible Hand.* For a cultural history of the corporation in architecture, see Kubo, "Architecture Incorporated: Authorship, Anonymity, and Collaboration in Postwar Modernism."

100. Enion, "Practical Means to Higher Profits"; also see American Institute of Architects, "The Architect's Office."

101. Bruegmann, *The Architects and the City: Holabird & Roche of Chicago, 1880–1918*, 116. On the status of the profession by 1950, see Bannister, *The Architect at Mid-Century*.

102. On the anxieties associated with anonymity and the corporation, see Kubo, "The Anxiety of Anonymity: On the Historiographic Problem of Walter Gropius and The Architects Collaborative."

103. Enion, "Practical Means to Higher Profits," 51; Sapers, "The Case for Licensing Law Reforms."

104. Allied Architects Association included architects Octavius Morgan, Reginald Davis Johnson, George Edwin Bergstrom, David Allison, Myron Hunt, Elmer Grey, Sumner Hunt, and Sumner Spaulding. On the court case and ruling, see *People v. Allied Architects Association of Los Angeles*. In 1968, California ratified the Moscone-Knox Professional Corporations act with specific provisions for professionals, including architects. See California Law, "California Corporations Code: Professional Corporations."

105. In 1972, there were 1,203 incorporated architecture firms, 3,361 sole proprietorships, and 2,252 partnerships in the US. By 1977, there were 2,276 corporations, 4,409 sole proprietorships, and 1,908 partnerships. A decade later, in 1987, there were 10,571 corporations, 5,001 individual proprietorships, and 1,652 partnerships. From US Bureau of the Census, *Census of Service Industries*, tbl4; US Bureau of the Census, *Census of Service Industries, Subject Series*, tbl7.

106. Hardt and Negri, *Empire*, 221.

107. Perkins & Will, "Firm Profile"; also see Litke, "Perkins & Will: The First 50 Years."

108. Shair, *Out of the Middle East: The Emergence of an Arab Global Business*, 184.

109. Shair, 185.

110. Shair, 193. In 1990, the Dar Group acquired the independent pipeline and sub-sea engineering consultancy Penspen; in 1998, the Paris-based interior design firm Pierre-Yves Rochon; in 2004, the South African railway engineering consulting firm R&H Railway Consultants; and the firm has since expanded into China and India. By 2005, the Dar Group's annual income was half a billion dollars, with over 40 percent of the firm's revenue from the Americas, 25 percent from the Middle East, and its remaining income from Europe, Africa, and Asia.

111. For a parallel argument about AECOM, see Cuff, "Architecture's Undisciplined Urban Desire."

112. Shair, *Out of the Middle East*, 197.

113. This discussion follows Marx's and Lenin's theories of capitalist exploitation and imperialism. Harvey, *Spaces of Capital*.

114. On Dar Al-Handasah's work at the mosque, see Touba, "Conservation in an Islamic Context: A Case Study of Makkah." On the conceptual connections to speculative development, see Saliba, *Urban Design in the Arab World: Reconceptualizing Boundaries*, 189.

115. Makarem, "The Bottom-Up Mobilization of Lebanese Society against Neoliberal Institutions: The Case of Opposition against Solidere's Reconstruction of Downtown Beirut," 510.

116. King and Langdon, *The CRS Team and the Business of Architecture*, 2002, 209.

117. Former CRS architect and president in discussion with the author, May 15, 2015.

118. At the time of the split, CRS had acquired the engineering firm J.E. Sirrine and was named Caudill Rowlett Scott Sirrine (CRSS). Tombesi, "Capital Gains and Architectural Losses: The Transformative Journey of Caudill Rowlett Scott (1948–1994)."

119. On TAC's history, see Kubo, "The Anxiety of Anonymity."

120. Vernon, "Multinational Enterprise and National Sovereignty"; also see Magdoff and Sweezy, "Notes on the Multinational Corporation."

121. Jones, "Multinational from the 1930s to the 1980s," 84.

122. Cody, *Exporting American Architecture, 1870–2000*.

123. Smith, *The Wealth of Nations Book V*, ch. 1, pt. 3, articles 1 and 2.

124. Jacoby, "The Conglomerate Corporation"; also see US Government Printing Office, "The Role of Giant Corporations in the American and World Economies: Automobile Industry."

125. Cuneo et al., *Contracting with the Federal Government: A Primer for Architects and Engineers*. For a more comprehensive history of legislation about fees, wages, and competition in architecture, see Deamer, "The Sherman Antitrust Act and the Profession of Architecture."

126. As cited in Polenberg, *War and Society: The United States, 1941–1945*, 12; also see Lichtenstein, *Labor's War at Home: The CIO in World War II*.

127. Davis and Diekmann, "The Decline and Fall of the Conglomerate Firm in the 1980s: The Desinstitutionalization of an Organizational Form."

128. Coase, "The Nature of the Firm."

129. Williamson, "The Modern Corporation: Origins, Evolution, Attributes," 1539; he later refined his theory of governance in Williamson, "The Theory of the Firm as Governance Structure: From Choice to Contract."

130. Harvey, *The Urban Experience*, 22; also see Harvey, "From Managerialism to Entrepreneurialism: The Transformation in Urban Governance in Late Capitalism"; Harvey, *The Urbanization of Capital*.

131. Harvey, *The Urban Experience*, 54.

132. See *Engineering News-Record*, "The Top 500 Design Firms," April 1991; *Engineering News-Record*, "The Top 500 Design Firms," May 1971.

133. Membership director of American Institute of Architects–Los Angeles in email exchange with the author, February 19, 2021.

134. Storper and Christopherson, "Flexible Specialization and Regional Industrial Agglomerations: The Case of the US Motion Picture Industry."

135. Scott, *Technopolis: High-Technology Industry and Regional Development in Southern California*.

136. Scott and Soja, "Los Angeles: Capital of the Late Twentieth Century"; see, among others, Scott and Soja, *The City: Los Angeles and Urban Theory at the End of the Twentieth Century*; Dear, "Los Angeles and the Chicago School: Invitation to a Debate."

137. Jencks, *Heteropolis: Los Angeles, the Riots and the Strange Beauty of Hetero-Architecture*.

138. Cited in Wrenn, "The Tenth Decade: 1957–1966."

139. Pfeifer and Kirkham, "Merger of AECOM and URS to Create Giant LA Construction Firm"; DMJM, "Mayor Bradley Tours LA Office," 1.

Chapter Two

1. Albert Dorman in discussion with the author, February 8, 2016.

2. This transitional process is described by Hannah Arendt, who argues that "expansion for expansion's sake" was a motivating principle for imperialists during the last third of the nineteenth century, who met national limitations to capitalist production and turned to policy in order to enter world politics. While politics, she argues, is the central idea of imperialism, its origins were business speculation and the expansion of industrial production. Arendt, *The Origins of Totalitarianism*. On the shift from firms to systems, see Hughes, "From Firm to Networked Systems."

3. DMJM, *1946-1955 Daniel, Mann, Johnson, & Mendenhall*.

4. Hitchcock, "The Architecture of Bureaucracy and the Architecture of Genius."

5. These included donations from a Protestant nurseryman, an Irish Catholic former governor, and a German Jewish banker. See Servín and Engstran, *Southern California and Its University: A History of USC, 1880-1964*.

6. Norwood, "The Architect's Knowledge: Imagining the Profession's Historical Body, 1797–1883," 11. On this argument outside of architecture, see Abercrombie, *Aims and Techniques of Group Teaching*.

7. Gibbs, *Outside In: The Architecture of Smith and Williams*, 16. Despite the rhetoric of moving beyond a Beaux Arts model, historians have noted that many early architects working within the film industry were still most regarded for their ability to accurately reproduce historical styles. Many of the historical preferences of the architects were later translated into "studio styles." MGM was known for an affinity for the clean lines of modernism, while the Warner Brothers productions reflected European expressionists. Heisner, *Hollywood Art: Art Direction in the Days of the Great Studios*, 38–39.

8. Weatherhead, "Note on Education in Architecture"; also see Howell-Ardila, "The USC Connection: Origins and Context in the Work of Whitney R. Smith," 91. For a comprehensive history of the USC program, see Howell-Ardila, "'Writing Our Own Program': The USC Experiment in Modern Architectural Pedagogy, 1930 to 1960."

9. Weatherhead, "Architecture and Life," K12.

10. On Santa Maria's population, see Beaumont Library District, "Historical US Census Populations of Places, Towns, and Cities in California, 1850–1990." On Crawford, see Contreras, "Crawford Had Designs on Central Coast."

11. Johnson and his siblings, known in the industry as the "Johnson Kids," starred in *Our Gang* serials and other films. Johnson was later a stand-in for actor Gary Cooper, and he worked in the art department at MGM while studying at USC. DMJM, *1946–1955 Daniel, Mann, Johnson, & Mendenhall*, 4.

12. In a survey conducted of 123 USC graduates in architecture in 1939, 13 percent of the former students worked in the film industry, two-thirds as practicing architects, and the remainder worked as contractors, interior designers, or government officials. Howell-Ardila, "'Writing Our Own Program,'" 39, 42.

13. The many other USC-trained film designers included William Horning (1934 graduate) for *The Wizard of Oz* (1939), *Gigi* (1958), and *Ben-Hur* (1959); Edward Carfagno (1933 grad) for *The Bad and the Beautiful* (1952), *Julius Caesar* (1953), and *Ben-Hur* (1959); and Boris Leven (1932 grad) for *Alexander's Ragtime Band* (1938) and *West Side Story* (1961). The overlap between architecture and film production has persisted, though less prolifically. Numerous production designers, including Dean Tavoularis for *The Godfather* (1972) and *Apocalypse Now* (1972), and Dante Ferretti for *Shutter Island* (2010) and *Gangs of New York* (2002), were trained as architects. There has been relatively little scholarly attention to the relationship between film practice and architecture practice. For an excellent

theoretical and historical overview, see Drapkin Dercle, "Cinema and Architecture: Towards Understanding the Cinematic Sense of Place and Its Relationships to the Built Environment."

14. Daniel was also in a relationship with Mendenhall's sister, Faye Mendenhall, and both couples were married in the early 1940s. See DMJM, *1946-1955 Daniel, Mann, Johnson, & Mendenhall*, 4. The tendency of architectural partnerships to begin as family businesses was not uncommon. During the nineteenth century, for instance, Richard Upjohn's New York office epitomized a familial structure. See Woods, *From Craft to Profession: The Practice of Architecture in Nineteenth-Century America*, 116.

15. "Experience Record of Arthur E. Mann," family papers of Arthur Mann, private collection, courtesy of Karen Letterman. Most were brief stints of one or two months as a draftsman, the longest of which was with Gordon B. Kaufmann, best known for his work on the Hoover Dam. He worked as a draftsman and job captain for Kaufmann, as well as for architect Adrian Wilson.

16. Gabler, *Walt Disney: The Triumph of the American Imagination*, 591-92. On the culture industry, see Horkheimer and Adorno, "The Culture Industry: Enlightenment as Mass Deception."

17. On this theory of liberation, see hooks, *Teaching to Transgress: Education as the Practice of Freedom*, 59-76.

18. Mann, "Letter to Bill Shope," n.d., 1.

19. "In Memorium: Obituary of Phillip Daniel," 1974, family papers of Stanley Moe, private collection.

20. DMJM, *1946-1955 Daniel, Mann, Johnson, & Mendenhall*, 6.

21. Charles Moore argued that the Granada Buildings "reek of panache among Southern California's architecture and design community." See Moore, Becker, and Campbell, *The City Observed: Los Angeles: A Guide to Its Architecture and Landscapes*, 146. On the initial details of the construction of the Granada Buildings, see *Los Angeles Times*, "Trio of Major Units to Rise: Three Projects Announced to Cost $1,000,000 Each; Unique Structure Goes Up at Lafayette Park Place; Temple and Store Addition Figure in Activity," E1.

22. The development was a financial risk for Harper, who lost ownership of the building only five years later during the Depression. The complex was listed on the National Register of Historic Places in 1986. Gualtieri, "Granada Shoppes and Studios."

23. This was common among corporations forming at the time; see Langlois, *The Corporation and the Twentieth Century: The History of American Business Enterprise*, 315-402.

24. DMJM, *1946–1955 Daniel, Mann, Johnson, & Mendenhall*, 6.

25. Freedgood, "'Dimjim': Architects for the Space Age," 124. This sentiment was also shared by architects such as Art Gensler, who repeatedly explained in self-publications that he began his company in 1956 with only $200 to his name. See Gensler and Lindenmayer, *Art's Principles: 50 Years of Hard-Learned Lessons in Building a World-Class Professional Services Firm*, xvi, 276; Gensler and Meeker, *Art Gensler: Building a Global Architecture and Design Firm (Oral History)*, 162.

26. Cited in Moe, *Right Place, Right Time!*, 285.

27. *Management Methods*, "Profile of a New Kind of Manager: How to Pack Pleasure and Profit into a Partnership," 27.

28. *Management Methods*, "Profile of a New Kind of Manager," 27–30.

29. *Southwest Builder and Contractor*, "Daniel, Mann, Johnson & Mendenhall: How Teamwork Has Built a Thriving Architect-Engineer Firm," n.p.

30. Lubatkin, "Mergers and the Performance of the Acquiring Firm." On McKinsey, see McDonald, *The Firm: The Story of McKinsey and Its Secret Influence on American Business*. On publishing, see Sinykin, *Big Fiction: How Conglomeration Changed the Publishing Industry and American Literature*.

31. *Management Methods*, "Profile of a New Kind of Manager," 28. BAH only provided written advice to Perkins & Will. Most change at Perkins & Will came from a subsequent manager between 1946 and 1980, when John Goodall, who was both a lawyer and real estate executive for Marshall Field, became partner. Goodall set up the firm's first accounting system, established limits to the amount of money each partner could glean from profit (like at DMJM) to build up a substantial cushion, and wrote the firm's manual of organization. See Fogarty, "Architecture at a Profit."

32. *Management Methods*, "Profile of a New Kind of Manager," 27–28. After an initial six-week survey, Russell signed a twelve-month contract as a business manager, with a stipulation that he would have complete control of finances and organization, and he demanded partner salary in addition to 40 percent of total profits. Since this deal still promised more than they had made in the past, he was hired.

33. *Business Week*, "Six Partners with Six Personalities," 184.

34. Mann, "Letter to Bill Shope," n.d., 5.

35. Unlike DMJM, which owed its organizational structure to management and accounting experts, SOM claimed that its long-term survival was due to its legal counsel, Marshal Grosscup Sampsell, who negotiated their contracts and extended lines of credit as the firm began. Nat Owings described him, in contrast to Skidmore or Owings, as "orderly," "calm," and "cautious." Though he was an essential part of the organization since 1936, he remained detached from it. Owings

noted that the partnership documents by which SOM operated were always changing and hardly written down: Sampsell himself epitomized the law and operating agreements. See Owings, *The Spaces in Between: An Architect's Journey*, 70.

36. For an overview of this history, from medieval guilds to the Bauhaus to SOM, see Boyle, "Architectural Practice in America, 1865–1965—Ideal and Reality."

37. Albert Dorman in discussion with the author, February 8, 2016.

38. Albert Dorman in discussion with the author, February 8, 2016.

39. See Drucker, *Concept of the Corporation*; also see Tarrant, *Drucker, the Man Who Invented the Corporate Society*.

40. Langlois, *The Corporation and the Twentieth Century*, 324.

41. Schulman, *From Cotton Belt to Sunbelt: Federal Policy, Economic Development, and the Transformation of the South, 1938–1980*, 141–42.

42. Smith, *The Wealth of Nations Books Book V*, ch. 1, pt. 3.

43. *Architectural Record*, "Organization for Efficient Practice: Daniel, Mann, Johnson, & Mendenhall, Architects & Engineers," 192.

44. On these histories, see Shanken, *194X: Architecture, Planning, and Consumer Culture on the American Home Front*.

45. The Detroit architecture and engineering firm Giffels & Rossetti was ranked as the "biggest." Between 1957 and 1958, Perkins & Will dropped from the ninth spot to the thirty-fourth; SOM dropped from second to eleventh; and Albert Kahn dropped from seventh to twelfth. SOM, however, did not report data in 1958, so the numbers for SOM in 1958 were based on 1957 revenue data. These positions changed quite readily over the next several decades, as SOM and DMJM often traded positions. Editors of *Architectural Forum*, *The 1959 FORUM Directory of the 100 Biggest Architects, Contractors, Clients*; Editors of *Architectural Forum*, *The 1958 FORUM Directory of the 100 Biggest Architectural Firms, Building Customers, Building Contractors*.

46. Douglas Russell received an award from the LA City Council on behalf of DMJM for the firm's contributions to the city's business growth in 1958. For a photo of the award reception, see the Valley Times Collection, Los Angeles Public Library.

47. For a wide range of excerpts from manuals in architecture practice since the turn of the twentieth century, see Franch i Gilabert et al., *OfficeUS: Manual*.

48. Emphasis added. "Intra-company Relationships," in DMJM, *Standard Practices Manual*, December 15, 1965, Stanley Moe Papers, Huntington Library, San Marino, CA.

49. *Architectural Record*, "Organization for Efficient Practice," 193.

50. DMJM, "Articles of Incorporation of Daniel, Mann, Johnson, & Mendenhall," February 1, 1960, Secretary of State, California.

51. See "Age Limits," "Employment of Friends and Relatives," and "Maternity Terminations," in DMJM, *Standard Practices Manual*, December 15, 1965, Stanley Moe Papers, Huntington Library, San Marino, CA.

52. DMJM, "Corporate Objectives," *Standard Practices Manual*, January 7, 1974, 2, Stanley Moe Papers, Huntington Library, San Marino, CA.

53. The construction recession was most severe between 1973 and 1975, after which annual rates of recovery slowly and unsteadily improved until 1982. By 1983, annual growth surged. Larson, *Behind the Postmodern Facade: Architectural Change in Late Twentieth-Century America*, 257; Blau, *Architects and Firms: A Sociological Perspective on Architectural Practice*, 114–19.

54. John Morris Dixon in email exchange with the author, May 5, 2024.

55. *Progressive Architecture*, "Profile: Daniel, Mann, Johnson and Mendenhall: A Summation of Parts," 74.

56. *Engineering News-Record*, "The Top 500 Design Firms," July 1966. By 1968, DMJM was the highest-ranked firm in which architecture was included, and SOM was ranked sixth. The top firms by revenue were predominantly engineering firms, with Howard, Needles, Tammen & Bergendoff ranked first; DeLeuw, Cather & Co. ranked second; and Sargent & Lundy Engineers ranked third. *Engineering News-Record*, "The Top 500 Design Firms," May 1968.

57. DMJM was ranked thirteenth by revenue in 1982 among all architecture, engineering, and planning firms. The top firms were "Engineering-Architecture" firms, respectively listed as The Resource Sciences Corp., Sargent & Lundy, and Biggs & Hill Inc. DMJM was the largest "Architecture-Engineering" firm, followed by the CRS Group Inc. *Engineering News-Record*, "The Top 500 Design Firms," May 1982.

58. The growth plan for the firm defined a goal of increasing firm revenue and employee size by 15–20 percent per year. "DMJM Basic Organization," *Standard Practices Manual*, September 1, 1969, 1–2, Stanley Moe Papers, Huntington Library, San Marino, CA.

59. "DMJM Basic Organization," 1–2.

60. Harvey, *The Condition of Postmodernity: An Enquiry into the Origins of Cultural Change*, 151.

61. DMJM, *New Towns*, n.d., 2, family papers of Arthur Mann, private collection.

62. These master plans included Taif New Town, Al Kharj New Town, Sports City, and a Satellite New Town, in Riyad, Saudi Arabia, for the Corps of Engineers

Italy, as well as Al Hasa, Safaniya, and North Dhahran communities in Saudi Arabia for ARAMCO.

63. The prominent accounting firm Arthur Young & Company, for example, credited DMJM for having a superior management structure compared to many large industrial organizations. Many leading law offices in Los Angeles also began to replicate the management structure of DMJM as a model for engaging with similar practitioner-types that were historically individualistic. Albert Dorman in discussion with the author, April 27, 2016.

64. Smith, "DMJM in Architecture."

65. In a special volume published by *Fortune* in 1967 dedicated to the rise of conglomerates, a pervasive resistance to the term itself by business leaders was correlated to the lack of form and pejorative connotations associated with antitrust evasion and monopolistic practices. Editors of *Fortune, The Conglomerate Commotion*, 3. Those resisting the term at DMJM frequently argued that it was not until DMJM's successor firm, AECOM, ventured into financial services in the 2010s that the firm became a bona fide conglomerate.

66. Albert Dorman in discussion with the author, February 8, 2016.

67. Leading up to a Celler-Kefauver Amendment in 1950 to the Sherman Antitrust Act (1890), which included provisions against a broader definition of acquisitions and mergers, FTC reports in 1948 initially defined "conglomerate acquisitions" very specifically as "those in which there is little or no discernible relation between the business of the purchasing and the acquired firm," before concluding with a much broader application in 1950. US Federal Trade Commission, "Report of the Federal Trade Commission on The Merger Movement: A Summary Report," 59.

68. *Engineering News-Record*, "Genge Unites 20 Subsidiaries into a National Design Network."

69. Former architect in discussion with the author, February 17, 2016.

70. *Los Angeles Times*, "Data Processing Firm Acquired."

71. Konkel, "Getting in Step with CAEDS."

72. DMJM's listed subsidiaries in 1982 included American Science & Engineering Co.; Arctic Slope Technical Services Inc.; Associated Design Planning & Art Inc.; DMJM International; DMJM/Thomson Ltd.; Development and Technology Consultants Inc., Philippines; Logicomp Corp.; Real Estate Resources; Technical Management Services Inc.; TMSI Arabia Ltd., Saudi Arabia; TMSI Contractors Inc.; and Wilhamp Inc. *Engineering News-Record*, "The Top 500 Design Firms," May 1982, 95.

73. *Progressive Architecture*, "Profile: Daniel, Mann, Johnson and Mendenhall," 74.

74. Pastier, "What's Brown—Brown All Over?"

75. Klingmann, *Brandscapes: Architecture in the Experience Economy*, 71.

76. *Los Angeles Times*, "High Rise Features Rare Wood."

77. DMJM, "One Park Plaza," 1.

78. See *Los Angeles Times*, "One Park Plaza Gets Eight New Tenants"; *Los Angeles Times*, "Underground Computers: Univac Leases Area for Marketing Office."

79. Cayer, "Architecture University, Incorporated"; Roche, "Organizing Shop: Follow the Sweat Equity."

80. *Progressive Architecture*, "Profile: Daniel, Mann, Johnson and Mendenhall," 78.

81. Albert Dorman in discussion with the author, February 8, 2016.

82. For a parallel history about the diversification of firms in tune with urban economies, see Gensler and Meeker, *Art Gensler*, 209.

83. This proposal was one of many "experimental cities" by DMJM. This example is from a joint proposal for a "Minnesota Experimental City," by DMJM and ABT Associates, a social science research and consulting firm located in Cambridge, Massachusetts.

84. DMJM, *Company General Brochure: A Presentation of the Work of Daniel, Mann, Johnson, & Mendenhall*.

85. Emphasis added. *The New York Times*, "Company News: Ashland's Future May Not Be in Oil: Competitive Edge Sought in Diversity," D4.

86. Ashland Oil Company, *Annual Report*, 29–30.

87. DMJM maintained semiautonomy as a subsidiary within AECOM until 2007, when AECOM was publicly listed on the New York Stock Exchange, though it merged with and was reconfigured numerous times. In 2000, for example the firms Frederic R. Harris and DMJM merged to create "DMJM Harris," to focus on "infrastructure and transportation business segments"; and Holmes and Narver Inc. merged with DMJM to form "DMJM H&N" to focus on "facilities business segments." In 2003, DMJM H&N was reorganized again into DMJM Design, DMJM Management, and DMJM Technology. Rodengen, *AECOM: 20 Years and Counting*, 38–40.

88. The six outlined corporate objectives were Technical and Professional Activities, Personnel and Career Development, Growth in Services, Geographical Expansion, Expanded Activities, and Ownership.

89. AECOM, "Annual Professional Report," 3.

90. AECOM, 1.

91. Albert Dorman in discussion with the author, February 8, 2016.

92. Cited in Seward, "Making It Big."

93. By the 2000s, the firm's global headquarters was separated and located in the SunAmerica Center on the Avenue of the Stars, designed by Johnson Fain and built in 1990, while the former DMJM office, which included the design, engineering, and planning services, moved from DMJM's former One Park Plaza offices to Downtown's City National Plaza in 2001, and again in 2015 to Downtown's One California Plaza. See Berton, "Architect Firm DMJM to Move Its Headquarters Downtown"; Miet, "AECOM to Lease at One California Plaza."

94. See, for example, an overview of AECOM's urban projects: Cuff, "Architecture's Undisciplined Urban Desire," 94.

Chapter Three

1. Editors of *Architectural Forum*, *The 1959 FORUM Directory of the 100 Biggest Architects, Contractors, Clients.*

2. An abbreviated version of this text was first published in the journal *Architectural Histories*. See Cayer, "Aesthetics of Indeterminacy: The Architecture of Conglomerates."

3. Louise A. Mozingo, *Pastoral Capitalism: A History of Suburban Corporate Landscapes.*

4. For those who favored the representation argument, see Jameson, "Postmodernism, or the Cultural Logic of Late Capitalism"; Jencks, *The Language of Post-Modern Architecture*; Harvey, *The Condition of Postmodernity: An Enquiry into the Origins of Cultural Change*. For those more recently part of the "belonged to" argument, see Martin, *Utopia's Ghost: Architecture and Postmodernism, Again.*

5. Chandler, *The Visible Hand: The Managerial Revolution in American Business*, 480–82; also see Fligstein, "The Spread of the Multi-Divisional Form among Large Firms, 1919–1979."

6. Lavin, *Architecture Itself and Other Postmodernization Effects.*

7. For Pelli, see *Architectural Digest*, "Cesar Pelli," 179. On Jencks, see Jencks, *The Story of Post-Modernism*, 54. It is also worth noting that Alison and Peter Smithson developed a theory of "Conglomerate Order," which they frequently explained through La Grancia di Cuna in Siena, Italy. While the Smithsons' practices were radically different from DMJM's, in their observation of conglomerate order they position the farmer as a capitalist: "At its simplest, it [Conglomerate Ordering] can be explained through a farm. On a farm, a stone wall between fields pens in but also shelters the sheep in the snow time. Each part of a structure

needs to perform and encompass many tasks. In our time, we thought this way of building should be developed. It is nonformal and does not use classic geometry. . . . That's what conglomerate ordering is: to build it like a farmer when he's making a decision—'Well, if I have to do all that work, I also want it to do that and that and that.' Everything should have multiple uses." Peter Smithson cited in Spellman and Unglaub, *Peter Smithson: Conversations with Students: A Space for Our Generation*, 48. For their extended theory, see Smithson and Smithson, *Italian Thoughts*.

    8. Freedgood, "'Dimjim': Architects for the Space Age," 180.

    9. Former business executive in discussion with the author, September 2, 2015.

    10. Freedgood, "'Dimjim': Architects for the Space Age," 183.

    11. Martin, *The Organizational Complex: Architecture, Media, and Corporate Space*.

    12. *Architectural Forum*, "The Biggest Mirror Ever."

    13. Paul, "The Aesthetics of Efficiency: Contexts and the Early Development of Late-Modern Glass Skin Architecture."

    14. Martin, *The Organizational Complex*. As design manager of the Bell Labs project, Lumsden proposed an inverted structural mullion to provide a continuously smooth surface. However, Roche rejected the proposal, primarily due to his interest in the ability of vertical mullions to produce surface shadows to reinforce the standardizing effects of the mullions. See Paul, "The Aesthetics of Efficiency."

    15. Lyndon, "Problem: Landscaping the Santa Monica Mountains."

    16. McCoy, "Planned for Change," 106.

    17. McCoy, 106.

    18. The "Silvers" emerged as a response to the debate between the neomodernist "Whites" and the postmodernist "Grays," and they were named for the slick silver aesthetic of many of their projects, as highlighted by two conferences at UCLA in 1974 and 1976, respectively titled "Four Days in May" and "Four Days in April." The Silvers included DMJM architects Lumsden and Pelli, Frank Dimster of William Pereira's office, Paul Kennon of CRS, Tim Vreeland of AC Martin (and former assistant to Louis Kahn), Eugene Kupper, and Craig Hodgetts. The "Los Angeles 12" was an exhibition in 1976 at the Cesar Pelli–designed Pacific Design Center, which formed out of a 1974 project by Charles Slert (later an architect at DMJM) and his professor Bernard Zimmerman at Cal Poly Pomona in 1974. The group known as the LA Twelve consisted of Roland Cote, Daniel Dworsky, Craig Ellwood, Frank Gehry, Ray Kappe, John Lautner, Jerrold Lomax, Anthony Lumsden, Leroy Milly, Cesar Pelli, James Pulliam, and Bernard Zimmerman.

19. See Holland, *When the Machine Stopped: A Cautionary Tale from Industrial America*; Lamoreaux, Raff, and Temin, "Beyond Markets and Hierarchies: Toward a New Synthesis of American Business History."

20. Roberts and McVicker, *Distant Force: A Memoir of the Teledyne Corporation and the Man Who Created It, with an Introduction to Teledyne Technologies*, 18. Perhaps ironically, Teledyne was acquired by Litton Industries in 1994, and then later by Northrop Grumman in 2001.

21. On Litton Industries, see O'Green, *Putting Technology to Work: The Story of Litton Industries*.

22. O'Green, *Putting Technology to Work*.

23. Cited in Roberts and McVicker, *Distant Force*, 22.

24. DMJM, "Manufacturing and Research Facility for Teledyne Systems Company."

25. These concerns about growth and flexibility paralleled other critically influential discussions within architecture, from Yona Friedman's superstructures to Archigram's designs to Habraken's "scaffolding." However, for the purposes of this article, I focus on the close relationship between business practice and architecture. Beyond this, the morphologies epitomized by Teledyne were similarly referenced and folded into new modes of spatial and architectural organization. These included the early work of Christopher Alexander, as well as the parallel interest in "growth" of the Japanese Metabolists.

26. Cesar Pelli, quoted in McCoy, "Planned for Change," 103, 105.

27. Giedion, *Mechanization Takes Command: A Contribution to Anonymous History*, 247–48.

28. For more on the history of Pelli's attention to the "spine," see Paul, "The Aesthetics of Efficiency," 26. For more on the connection of the spine to the street, see DMJM, "Manufacturing and Research Facility for Teledyne Systems Company," 8.

29. *Industry Week*, "Plant Design Allows for Change," 91.

30. DMJM, "Manufacturing and Research Facility for Teledyne Systems Company," 1.

31. Kepos and Derdak, *International Directory of Company Histories*, vol. 11. For more on ITT's history, see Burns, *Tales of ITT: An Insider's Report*; Sampson, *The Sovereign State: The Secret History of ITT*.

32. *Progressive Architecture*, "Technological Imagery: Turnpike Version"; also see Slotten, "Satellite Communications, Globalization, and the Cold War."

33. Eco, *The Open Work*, 104.

34. Anthony Lumsden, quoted in Inaba and Zellner, *Whatever Happened to LA? Architectural and Urban Experiments, 1970–1990*, 29.

35. Ross, "The Development of an Esthetic System at DMJM," 111.

36. Morton, "Anti-gravitational Mass," 66.

37. Paul, "The Aesthetics of Efficiency," 34.

38. For more on the history of the "plant" as it relates to this project, see Lavin, "Reclaiming Plant Architecture."

39. Fogelson, *The Fragmented Metropolis: Los Angeles, 1850–1930*. While Fogelson's focus was on early twentieth-century Los Angeles, geographers and historians have noted that fragmentation reached a new intensity during the late twentieth century. See Fishman, "Foreword."

40. Letter from The Industrial Association of the San Fernando Valley to Senator Alan Cranston, October 18, 1977, California State University Northridge Special Collections, Northridge, CA.

41. Marx, *The Machine in the Garden: Technology and the Pastoral Ideal in America*.

42. Kawana's Japanese gardens include the botanical gardens at the Los Angeles County Museum of Art and at San Diego's Balboa Park.

43. *Engineering News-Record*, "Design Frills Dominate L.A. Sewage Plant: Effluent Eyed for Irrigation Use," 11.

44. Whiteson, "Innovative Designs Can Enliven Even Those Difficult Buildings." For an overview of the opposition, see Smith, "Regional Water Authority Collides with Growth of Metropolitan Area," WS14.

45. Pastier, *Cesar Pelli*, 26–29.

46. Banham, *Los Angeles: The Architecture of Four Ecologies*, 214–15.

47. Jencks, *Architecture Today*, 67.

48. Jencks, *Late-Modern Architecture and Other Essays*, 72.

49. For Harvey, the "mirror" held an ability to produce images, imagery, and imaginary money to deflect attention from contradictory truths. Harvey, *The Condition of Postmodernity*, 329–35.

50. Martin, *Utopia's Ghost*, 114.

51. Martin, 114.

52. Jameson, "Postmodernism, or the Cultural Logic of Late Capitalism," 53–92.

53. For Jencks's original description, see Jencks, *The New Moderns: From Late to Neo-Modernism*, 85; also see Jameson, "The Brick and the Balloon: Architecture, Idealism and Land Speculation," 44.

54. Jameson, "The Brick and the Balloon," 44.

55. Jencks, *Late-Modern Architecture and Other Essays*, 66.

56. Martin, *Utopia's Ghost*, 99.

57. Martin, 97.

58. Mulvey, "Visual Pleasure and Narrative Cinema," 581–90.

59. Ni-Ban-Kahn was built near its sister, Ichi-Ban-Kahn (Building Number One), which was commissioned by the same client, though unlike Ni-Ban-Kahn, the latter was entirely rented rather than divvied up among owners and varying functions. For at least one use of the "conglomerate," see Jencks, *The Story of Post-Modernism: Five Decades of the Ironic, Iconic and Critical in Architecture.*

60. Takeyama, "Omni-Rental-Stores: Ni-Ban-Kahn," 65.

61. Jencks, *The Language of Post-Modern Architecture*, 54.

62. Takeyama, "The Reinstatement of the Film Membrane," 70.

63. Takeyama, 70.

64. *Design Journal*, "High Rise Fun Palaces," 59–63.

65. Pelli, cited in Editors of *Architectural Digest*, "Cesar Pelli" 179.

66. Even with Lumsden at the helm, many architects left soon after they were hired, due to inherent cultural incompatibilities associated with the demands of a commercially motivated practice. In 1978, for example, DMJM acquired New Orleans architecture and engineering firm Curtis and Davis. Davis assumed a position as senior vice president of DMJM and remained based in New Orleans at a newly named DMJM Curtis & Davis. Yet Davis left after ten years, arguing: "It was a very pleasant but not terribly challenging experience for me. For ten years with DMJM I quite candidly was paid handsomely for a minimum amount of productive work, and as soon as I reached the ten-year period which permitted me to be tenured, I resigned from the firm and received the funds which I had earned through their very generous retirement plan." Davis, *It Happened by Design: The Life and Work of Arthur Q. Davis*, 56.

67. *Progressive Architecture*, "Profile: Daniel, Mann, Johnson and Mendenhall: A Summation of Parts," 76.

68. *Progressive Architecture*, 76.

69. *Progressive Architecture*, 76.

70. Adams, *Gordon Bunshaft and SOM: Building Corporate Modernism.*

71. Lumsden, "Preconception Analysis," 10. The concern of "preconception" in architecture is by no means new. Historically, the concern of preconception has been linked to "style," when, at the turn of the twentieth century, for example, Louis Sullivan argued that a "man's preconception always governs unless he possesses genuine culture.... For his knowledge, such as it is, is ready-made, precisely as he believes architecture to be ready-made." Sullivan, "On the Historic Styles."

72. Lumsden, "Preconception Analysis," 6. These ideas were initially developed by Lumsden during the 1970s, as cited in public lectures and in interviews

in *Progressive Architecture* (1972). Lumsden pointed to the underlying patterns of voids in the façades of buildings, such as those surrounding the Piazza San Marco in Venice, Italy, including the twelfth-century Byzantine Basilica, the fourteenth-century Gothic Doge's Palace, and the sixteenth-century Renaissance Library. He suggested that each of the buildings' organizational systems, as revealed by the rhythm of voids in their façades, were similar despite their drastically dissimilar construction dates and motives.

73. Ross, "The Development of an Esthetic System at DMJM," 112.

74. Cultural sociologist Anthony Giddens argued that subjects were at least "partially knowing" and could reflect on their own circumstances, while other social theorists, such as Pierre Bourdieu, Michel Foucault, and Michel de Certeau, argued that subjects were largely unaware of the deeply internalized dispositions structuring their actions. See Giddens, *Central Problems in Social Theory: Action, Structure, and Contradiction in Social Analysis*. For a concise historical overview of these varying positions, see Ortner, *Anthropology and Social Theory: Culture, Power, and the Acting Subject*, 1–18.

75. Bourdieu, *In Other Words: Essays Towards a Reflexive Sociology*, 13.

76. This sentiment was also shared by architects working at other diversified architectural corporations in which architects were tasked to reveal the inherent economic value of their work after the 1960s. In Texas, for example, at Caudill Rowlett Scott (CRS), then president and CEO Paul Kennon, who was formerly a colleague of Lumden's and Pelli's at Saarinen's and then in Roche and Dinkeloo's office before joining CRS in 1964, argued: "First, a designer has to be able to free the intuition and bring basic intellectual capacities to bear on that freed-up, innate and instinctive knowledge. . . . Second, a designer must be committed to the design realities of the situation—context, time, money, program. . . . The ability to suspend judgement while searching for cause and effect relationships in seeking a design direction will allow the key influences to emerge and the design intentions to be given form." Paul Kennon, quoted in *Space Design*, "CRS: Design in a Process-Oriented Firm."

77. Ashland Oil Company, *Annual Report*, 1984, 28.

78. Ashland Oil Company, *Annual Report*, 1990, 4.

79. KMJR was established by Richard Keating, Michael Mann, Robert Jernigan, and Lauren Rottet after an attempt to establish a Los Angeles SOM office failed to take hold. See Riddle, "Building on Change."

80. Former architect in discussion with the author, Los Angeles, September 2, 2015.

81. LeBaron and Speidell, "Why Are the Parts Worth More Than the Sum? 'Chop Shop,' a Corporate Valuation Model"; Morck, Shleifer, and Vishney, "Do Managerial Objectives Drive Bad Acquisitions?," 31–48.

82. See, among others, Palmer, *Architecture at Work: DMJM Design Los Angeles*; Rodengen, *AECOM: 20 Years and Counting*.

Chapter Four

1. Keyes, *Isan: Regionalism in Northeastern Thailand*. For histories of development in Thailand during this period, see Jacobs, *Modernization without Development: Thailand as an Asian Case Study*; Riggs, *Thailand: The Modernization of a Bureaucratic Polity*.

2. Watson and Dirlam, "The Impact of Underdevelopment on Economic Planning." On the politics of archaeology in Thailand, see Peleggi, "Excavating Southeast Asia's Prehistory in the Cold War," 98.

3. Daniel, Mann, Johnson & Mendenhall, International, "Final Report: Ground Water Exploration of the Khorat Plateau," 24.

4. On dependency, see Shvartzberg Carrio, "Infrastructures of Dependency: US Steel's Architectural Assemblages on Indigenous Lands"; Bodenheimer, "Dependency and Imperialism: The Roots of Latin American Underdevelopment." On architects and development, see Stanek, "Architects from Socialist Countries in Ghana (1957–67): Modern Architecture and Mondialisation"; Levin, *Architecture and Development: Israeli Construction in Sub-Saharan Africa and the Settler Colonial Imagination, 1958–1973*; Aggregate [Group], *Architecture in Development: Systems and the Emergence of the Global South*.

5. Cody, *Exporting American Architecture, 1870–2000*. On the globalization of architecture firms, see Ren, *Building Globalization: Transnational Architecture Production in Urban China*.

6. On the history of this process as it pertains to corporations, see Jacoby, "The Conglomerate Corporation"; also see Statement of Neil H. Jacoby, Professor of Business Economics and Policy, UCLA, before Congress, in US Government Printing Office, "The Role of Giant Corporations in the American and World Economies: Automobile Industry."

7. Pierpaoli, *Truman and Korea: The Political Culture of the Early Cold War*.

8. On the report written by an advisory board led by Nelson Rockefeller and submitted to President Truman, on which he based his plans for the ICA, see International Development Advisory Board, "Partners in Progress," March 1951,

https://www.trumanlibrary.gov/library/research-files/summary-partners-progress-report-president-international-development?documentid=NA&pagenumber=1. On Rockefeller, including his work positioning Venezuela and its oil as a pilot project to expand capitalism in the Global South, see Fabiana López-Durán, "Food Capital: Fantasies of Abundance and Nelson Rockefeller's Architectures of Development in Venezuela, 1940s-1960s," in Aggregate [Group], *Architecture in Development*, 303-22.

9. DMJM's library is now partially shelved at the Huntington Library in California within the Stanley Moe collection. The first edition of the contracting primer was written by three contract attorneys and a former director of governmental affairs for the AIA, and it was published by the Committee on Federal Procurement of Architect-Engineer Services in association with several professional societies.

10. The first edition of *Contracting with the Federal Government: A Primer for Architects & Engineers* (1969) was an important and routinely referenced book in the DMJM library. The Brooks Act led to an amendment to the Federal Property and Administrative Services Act of 1949, Title IX, "Selection of Architects and Engineers," requiring the Federal Government to select firms on the basis of competency, qualifications, and experience, rather than price. See Cuneo et al., *Contracting with the Federal Government: A Primer for Architects and Engineers*, 1969.

11. Hayek, "The Use of Knowledge in Society." For a brief overview of these parallels in architecture as they pertain to the history of neoliberalism, see Easterling, "Coda: Liberal"; Cupers, Mattsson, and Gabrielsson, *Neoliberalism on the Ground*.

12. Williams, "Experience," 126-29. The production and consumption of "experiences," management consultants later clarified, were central to the consumer economy by the end of twentieth century. See Pine and Gilmore, *The Experience Economy: Work Is Theatre & Every Business a Stage*.

13. Cuneo et al., *Contracting with the Federal Government: A Primer for Architects and Engineers*, 1974, 9.

14. For an analysis of contemporary architects and engineers contributing to political campaigns, see The Temple Hoyne Buell Center, *The A&E System: Public Works and Private Interest in Architectural and Engineering Services, 2000-2020*.

15. Higgs, *Depression, War, and Cold War: Studies in Political Economy*, 54; also see Adams, *The Politics of Defense Contracting: The Iron Triangle*; Beaumont, "Quantum Increase: The MIC in the Second World War"; *The Wall Street Journal*, "Defense Contracts Yield Higher Profits Than Private Work, Navy Study Says."

16. Smith, *The Army and Economic Mobilization*, 312.

17. Abrams, *Man's Struggle for Shelter in an Urbanizing World*, 79.

18. Abrams, 100. For a further analysis of this disorder, see Aggregate [Group], *Architecture in Development*, 1–22.

19. *Southwest Builder and Contractor*, "Daniel, Mann, Johnson & Mendenhall: How Teamwork Has Built a Thriving Architect-Engineer Firm."

20. DMJM, *1946–1955 Daniel, Mann, Johnson, & Mendenhall*, 9.

21. Moe, *Right Place, Right Time!*, 277–78.

22. Vine, *Base Nation: How U.S. Military Bases Abroad Harm America and the World*.

23. After years of production during World War II, Quonset huts were also available for experimental repurposing into domestic and religious structures by architects. See Cohen, *Architecture in Uniform: Designing and Building for the Second World War*, 383–423.

24. On the number of architects working abroad, see Angel, *Directory of American Firms Operating in Foreign Countries*. For an analysis of these figures and the globalization of architecture more broadly, see Cody, *Exporting American Architecture, 1870–2000*, 123–55; Knox and Taylor, "Toward a Geography of the Globalization of Architecture Office Networks"; Ren, *Building Globalization: Transnational Architecture Production in Urban China*. On the expansion of American empire abroad during this period, see Immerwahr, *How to Hide an Empire: A History of the Greater United States*.

25. Kim, "US Covert Action in Indonesia in the 1960s: Assessing the Motives and Consequences"; also see Bevins, *The Jakarta Method: Washington's Anticommunist Crusade & the Mass Murder Program That Shaped Our World*.

26. Cited in Kim, "US Covert Action in Indonesia in the 1960s: Assessing the Motives and Consequences," 64; also see McMahon, *Colonialism and Cold War: The United States and the Struggle for Indonesian Independence, 1945–1949*, 76.

27. Department of State, US Embassy Djakarta, "Business Proposal of Struthers Research & Development Corporation, Daniel, Mann, Johnson & Mendenhall, and Stanford Research Institute," 4.

28. *China Post*, "Indonesia, Red China Sign Dual Nationality Agreement," 1.

29. Job, "Foreign Capital Flows Back into Indonesia," 15.

30. ITT World Communications, "Indonesia Enters Space Age with Earth Satellite Station."

31. Naughten, "Letter to Barry F Mountain, DMJM," October 5, 1959.

32. Lazzarato, *Governing by Debt*; Ferreira da Silva, *Unpayable Debt*.

33. Muzaffar, *Modernism's Magic Hat: Architecture and the Illusion of Development without Capital*.

34. US Congress, Senate, Committee, *Foreign Assistance 1964*, 162.

35. Perkins, *The New Confessions of an Economic Hit Man*, 13–14.

36. DMJM, *1946–1955 Daniel, Mann, Johnson, & Mendenhall*, 13.

37. When Culver City broke from Los Angeles as its own city, DMJM was awarded several new school commissions, including sixteen projects in one board meeting. DMJM, *1946–1955 Daniel, Mann, Johnson, & Mendenhall*, 9. On the school projects and Culver City's history, see Anger, "The History of the Culver City Unified School District—Culver City, California."

38. Phillips, "Letter to DMJM," May 4, 1956.

39. *Southwest Builder and Contractor*, "Daniel, Mann, Johnson & Mendenhall: How Teamwork Has Built a Thriving Architect-Engineer Firm."

40. "Invoice No. 132," April 18, 1960, in Doris Talbert, "Letter to Director, USOM," April 18, 1960, US National Archives.

41. "Request for Release of Counterpart Funds," January 13, 1960, in Nai Apilas Ostananda, Memorandum to Mr. Gill, February 29, 1960, US National Archives.

42. Reed, "Letter to Jack Lipmann," May 28, 1953.

43. Porter, "Letter to Daniel, Mann, Johnson & Mendenhall," July 6, 1956.

44. Leonhard, "Letter to S. K. Johnson," March 14, 1958.

45. Stickler, "Letter to DMJM," July 22, 1958.

46. Carter, "Letter to DMJM," September 16, 1958.

47. DMJM, *1946–1955 Daniel, Mann, Johnson, & Mendenhall*.

48. William Coburn in discussion with the author, July 28, 2016.

49. Rabson, "Henko and the US Military: A History of Dependence and Resistance"; also see Yoshida, *Democracy Betrayed: Okinawa under US Occupation*, 58–75.

50. Allais, *Designs of Destruction: The Making of Monuments in the Twentieth Century*, 139.

51. Cited in Cave, *We Build, We Fight!*, 69.

52. DMJM, *Company General Brochure: A Presentation of the Work of Daniel, Mann, Johnson, & Mendenhall*, n.p.; cited in Cave, *We Build, We Fight!*, 69.

53. Guenter, *America in Vietnam*, 442–53.

54. *Engineering-News Record*, "The Top 500 Design Firms," May 1971.

55. Freedgood, "'Dimjim': Architects for the Space Age," 121. For analyses of the military-industrial complex and SOM, see Martin, *The Organizational Complex: Architecture, Media, and Corporate Space*.

56. US Records of Prime Contracts Awarded by the Military Services and Agencies: Series 1965-1975; 1975-2006, https://aad.archives.gov/aad/series-description.jsp?s=492&cat=GS29&bc=,sl (accessed February 12, 2017).

57. Easterling, *Extrastatecraft: The Power of Infrastructure Space*, 15.

58. Larouche, "The Third Stage of Imperialism," 90; also see Aggregate [Group], *Architecture in Development*.

59. Escobar, *Designs for the Pluriverse*, 59.

60. Latour and Yaneva, "Give Me a Gun and I Will Make All Buildings Move: An ANT's View of Architecture."

61. On the history of contracting, see Johnston, *Assembling the Architect: The History and Theory of Professional Practice*; Wermiel, "Norcross, Fuller, and the Rise of the General Contractor in the United States in the Nineteenth Century"; Spencer, "The Contract, the Contractor, and the Capitalization of American Building, 1873–1930."

62. Most additions to the types and conditions of the AIA's contracts occurred between 1951 and 1963. See American Institute of Architects, *The Handbook of Architectural Practice*, 1951; American Institute of Architects, *The Handbook of Architectural Practice*, 1963.

63. Wermiel, "Norcross, Fuller, and the Rise of the General Contractor in the United States in the Nineteenth Century."

64. Wermiel, 3298.

65. Wood and Wood, *Frank and Lillian Gilbreth*; also see Martin, *The Organizational Complex*, 92.

66. Gilbreth, *Field System*; Martin, *The Organizational Complex*, 92.

67. Cooper, "Government Contracts in Public Administration: The Role and Environment of the Contracting Officer."

68. US Government Printing Office, "Government Procurement and Contracting."

69. Gilbreth, "The 'Cost-Plus-a-Fixed-Sum' Contract."

70. See Danhof, *Government Contracting and Technological Change*.

71. Johnston, *Assembling the Architect*, 121.

72. American Institute of Architects, *A Handbook of Architectural Practice*, 1920, 50.

73. American Institute of Architects, 135–36.

74. Leslie, "The Biggest 'Angel' of Them All: The Military and the Making of Silicon Valley," 50; also see Kenney and Florida, "Venture Capital in Silicon Valley: Fueling New Firm Formation."

75. US Foreign Assistance Agencies, "Contract between the Government of Thailand and Daniel, Mann, Johnson and Mendenhall, Inc," 1.

76. US Foreign Assistance Agencies, "Contract."

77. Peterson, "Memorandum to 'All Drillers' Re: Overtime."

78. Cooper and Koelich, "Clandestine US Operations: Indonesia 1958, Operation 'Haik.'"

79. Mesko, *A-26 Invader in Action*; O'Leary, "Database: Douglas Invader," 42; also see Thompson, *Douglas A-26 and B-26 Invader*.

80. See Le Corbusier's references to "gift" in Le Corbusier, *Aircraft*, 8–9.

81. Rourke, "Wings over West Africa," 5.

82. Porter, *Trust in Numbers: The Pursuit of Objectivity in Science and Public Life*, xxi.

83. Dille, "The Missile-Era Race to Chart the Earth," 124.

84. US Department of the Army, *Surveying Computer's Manual: Department of the Army's Technical Manual TM 5-237*, 236.

85. Frank Collins, quoted in Rourke, "Wings over West Africa," 4.

86. At Penn State, Khachooni studied under Gifford Albright, the head of the Architectural Engineering Department, who was an early and leading advocate of computers in architecture. Albright was a longtime friend of Phillip Daniel. Before his career in academia, Albright worked as a research director for the US Navy Civil Engineer Corps and as a projects officer supervising the navy's structural tests at the Nevada Test Site. He developed computer-generated building integration systems, such as a computing program named Project Man-Machine System for the Optimum Design and Construction of Buildings (Project MOD-CON). Albright studied civil and sanitary engineering and building engineering construction at MIT, after which he developed systems for the chief of engineers of the US Army. See *Navy Civil Engineer*, "Need for Blast Shelters Sparks Careers of Two Reserve CECs," 34; Albright, *Planning Atomic Shelters: Guidebook for Architects and Engineers*.

87. The first central logic and control computers, developed by Sperry Rand, were delivered to the White Sands Missile Range in New Mexico, Bell Telephone Laboratories, and Kwajalein Atoll in the Pacific Ocean test range in 1965. See Gray and Smith, "Sperry Rand's Third-Generation Computers 1964-1980," 3-16. On Flexible Response, see Stromseth, *The Origins of Flexible Response: NATO'S Debate over Strategy in the 1960s*; Zagore and Kilgour, "Assessing Competing Defense Postures: The Strategic Implications of 'Flexible Response'"; Gavin, "The Myth of Flexible Response: United States Strategy in Europe during the 1960s."

88. *Corpus Christi Times*, "Army Asks Congress for Electronic Calculator."

89. *Los Angeles Times*, "Data Processing Firm Acquired." According to William Miller, computer manufacturers were slow to develop programs for the architecture industry because of its relatively small market size and because many computer developers had a limited understanding about what architects

actually did. Miller, "From Academe to Commercial Use in Ten Years: Computers in Architecture," 1.

90. Miller, Khachooni, and Olsten, "Matrix Method for Grouping an Interrelated Set of Elements," 304; also see Miller, "Computer-Aided Space Planning," 28–34.

91. For a history of the image of computational expertise, see McMahon, "Predictive Machines: Data, Computer Maps, and Simulation." For a history of computation and corporate management in architecture, see Tobey, "Drawing Management: Corporate Organization, International Practice, and the Making of Computer Aided Design."

92. Henehan, "Shapers of the Future."

93. One prominent example was the California-based "Institute for Professional Development" (rebranded in Arizona as the University of Phoenix in 1976). Its founder John Sperling, a self-proclaimed socialist interested in class bias, became interested in adult education following the faculty and student strikes of 1968. See his memoir, Sperling, *Rebel with a Cause: The Entrepreneur Who Created the University of Phoenix and the For-Profit Revolution in Higher Education*; also see Hanford, "The Story of the University of Phoenix."

94. Karousatos, "Letter to Vahe Khachooni," March 23, 1972; Alam, "Letter to Vahe Khachooni," May 9, 1972; Khachooni, "Letter to Stu Rose," March 27, 1972; Slayton, "Letter to Victor Khachooni," October 15, 1971; American Institute of Architects, "Brochure: Computerized Project Management"; University Extension, UCLA, "Course Catalog: Lifelong Learning," September 23, 1969; University Extension, UCLA, "Course Catalog: Lifelong Learning," September 21, 1970; University Extension, UCLA, "Course Catalog: Lifelong Learning," March 30, 1970.

95. Among a collection of more than thirty-five industries active in the early 1960s, DMJM was the only architecture and engineering firm in the military training program. *Los Angeles Times*, "Architectural Firm Joins in New Program," M22; also see DMJM, "DMJM Sponsors USAF Intern."

96. Osman, "The Intern Program: A Progress Report," 47, 63.

97. Bonham also became the NCARB president in 1981. See NCARB, "Dwight M. Bonham, FAIA."

98. Simonds, *The Columbia Basin Project*.

99. Owings, *The Spaces in Between: An Architect's Journey*.

100. Freedgood, "'Dimjim': Architects for the Space Age," 121; also see Carlson, "Buildings for the Space Age."

101. Vale, *The Limits of Civil Defence in the USA, Switzerland, Britain, and the Soviet Union: The Evolution of Policies since 1945*, 41–42.

102. The Atlas prototype was designed by architecture and engineering firm Holmes & Narver of Orange, California, with missiles manufactured by the Consolidated Vultee Aircraft Corporation (Convair) outside of San Diego in a modernist manufacturing plant designed by Charles Luckman and William Pereira, also of Los Angeles. For a useful overview of these different defense strategies, see Lonnquest and Winkler, *To Defend and Deter: The Legacy of the United States Cold War Missile Program*, 70.

103. DMJM, *1956–1965 Daniel, Mann, Johnson, & Mendenhall*. On this history, see Nesbit, *Ground Control: A Design History of Technical Lands and NASA's Space Complex*. Also see Stumpf, *Titan II: A History of a Cold War Missile Program*, 14.

104. Horkheimer and Adorno, "The Culture Industry: Enlightenment as Mass Deception."

105. Two important precedents in the portfolio of Mason & Hanger–Silas Mason were the Lincoln tunnels, constructed for the New York Port Authority in 1954, and Silas Mason's engineering of the Nevada Test Site for the US Atomic Energy Commission, established in 1951, where materials, shelters, and entire buildings were tested in controlled conditions against the blast effects of nuclear weapons. The test site, which included towers, bunkers, instrument stations, and complexes, was surveyed and outlined by the architecture-engineering firm Holmes and Narver, which would later become part of AECOM and merged with DMJM.

106. Prior to the design of the new underground facility, the Strategic Air Command was located in the former World War II complex built for the Martin Bomber Company, designed by Albert Kahn Associates.

107. Carlson, "Buildings for the Space Age," 178.

108. The single-missile facility was intended to be used to test the weapon system, after which it was to be used for training. However, in December 1960, after a series of tests, a missile fell too quickly back into the silo, rupturing the fuel tanks and destroying the facility beyond repair. Greene, *The Development of the SM-68 Titan*, 98. Both Vandenberg and Lowry were selected from two hundred possible locations, due to their strategic location and proximity to manufacturers of missiles and their components. In 1957, the decision to reserve Lowry for the first Titan squadron was made through a process of elimination, in which each possible site was evaluated for its target coverage, reaction potential, and maximum survival (adequate warning time, dispersal, and concealment). In addition, Lowry was near the Martin Company's manufacturing center, which was concurrently developing and manufacturing the missile. Air Force Ballistic Missiles Committee, "Minutes of the Eighth Meeting."

109. Daniel, "Application of Operations Research for Site Planning Facilities Support."

110. Daniel, 26.

111. Daniel, 83–84.

112. I borrow this definition of *proof* from Popper, *The Open Society and Its Enemies*, 263–64.

113. The subsequent Titan system, the Titan II, was all-inertial rather than all-radiational, and it therefore no longer needed to be clustered in groups of three.

114. On urban dispersal and organizational defense, see Martin, *The Organizational Complex*, 7; also see Monteyne, *Fallout Shelter: Designing for Civil Defense in the Cold War*, 10. According to DMJM records, DMJM submitted preliminary drawings to the Ballistic Missile Division on July 10, 1958, indicating a three-by-three configuration rather than an undispersed nine-by-one; according to the Ballistic Missile Division's records, it approved this change on July 18. Squadrons 1 and 2, in Colorado, were slightly closer. Rosenberg, "USAF Ballistic Missiles 1958–1959." At Lowry, the dispersal distance between the complexes was only six miles, while the air force insisted that eighteen miles was optimal. The explanation first provided by the air force was that the distance was reduced due to the difficulty of acquiring additional land, but other accounts suggest that the reduced distance was because construction began after the eighteen-mile standard was set. See *Missiles and Rockets*, "First Hard Site for Titan I Takes Form."

115. Kudroff, "The First Titan Hardened Facilities," 11. For a comprehensive overview of the construction components, as well as the launch processes, see Gies, "Hell Hole: Launching the Titan Missile," 191–200.

116. Vanderbilt, *Survival City: Adventures among the Ruins of Atomic America*, 161.

117. Alexander and Ressegieu, "$550 Million for ICBM Facilities."

118. For additional construction details, see *Western Construction*, "Missile Base Construction"; *Engineering News-Record*, "Now—Millions for Missile Bases."

119. Kudroff, "The First Titan Hardened Facilities," 46.

120. Kudroff, 46.

121. Horkheimer and Adorno, "The Culture Industry."

122. Allais, "Rendering: On Experience and Experiments."

123. Martin Smith was later known for his work as art director on *Cleopatra* (1963), *Fantastic Voyage* (1966), and *Hello, Dolly!* (1969). Set design was part of the architecture curriculum at USC, where many noted production designers were educated during the 1930s alongside Daniel and Johnson. These included architecture fraternity-mate Hilyard Brown (1937 grad), known for his work on *Citizen Kane* (1941) and later *Cleopatra* (1963); Henry Bumstead (1937 grad), known for

To Kill a Mockingbird (1962) and *The Sting* (1973); William Horning (1934 grad), known for *The Wizard of Oz* (1939), *Gigi* (1958), and *Ben-Hur* (1959); Edward Carfagno (1933 grad), known for *The Bad and the Beautiful* (1952), *Julius Caesar* (1953), and *Ben-Hur* (1959); and Boris Leven (1932 grad), known for *Alexander's Ragtime Band* (1938) and *West Side Story* (1961). On USC during this period, see Howell-Ardila, "'Writing Our Own Program': The USC Experiment in Modern Architectural Pedagogy, 1930 to 1960."

124. Rickey, "Art Directors: Theatrical Realism"; Beguiristain, *The Actors Studio and Hollywood in the 1950s: A History of Theatrical Realism*. Jack Martin Smith argued that the concept of Emerald City was based on a small photograph of a sketch of pre–World War I Germany, which he said looked like test tubes upside down. Harmetz, *The Making of* The Wizard of Oz, 215.

125. On the relationship between Keynes and architecture firms, see two analyses of Arup: Dutta, "Marginality and Metaengineering: Keynes and Arup"; Ross, "Creative Uncertainty: Arup Associates, Fire Safety, and the Metaengineering of Government."

126. US Department of Justice, Office of Public Affairs, "United States Joins Lawsuit against AECOM Alleging False Claims in Connection with Hurricane Disaster Relief."

127. AECOM Technology Corporation, "AECOM Joint Venture Awarded U.S. Army Contract Worth Up to US $181.9 Million to Support Afghanistan National Army's Technical Equipment Maintenance Program."

128. AECOM, "AECOM Wins Contract with U.S. Department of State to Provide Diplomatic Platform Support Services."

129. *Flightaware.com*, "N5177C Aircraft Registration"; also see Warnica, "Janet, the Mysterious Airline That Serves Area 51, Is Hiring."

130. AECOM Technology Corporation, "AECOM Completes Acquisition of McNeil Technologies."

131. Powers, "US Court Disputes $1.8B AECOM Damage Award in 'Remarkable Fraud' Suit."

132. US Department of Justice, Office of Public Affairs, "AECOM to Pay 11.8 Million to Resolve False Claims Act Allegations in Connection with Hurricane Disaster Relief."

133. Seiden, "AECOM Whistleblower to Argue War Needs Trumped Afghanistan Fraud."

134. Seiden, "AECOM Whistleblower."

135. AECOM's 2019 revenue was $20.2 billion—more than that of ninety-seven nations. United Nations Statistics Division, "National Accounts."

Chapter Five

1. Richard Newman in discussion with the author, March 1, 2016.

2. Coxe, *Managing Architectural and Engineering Practice*, 133. For another explanation by an SOM partner, see Eyerman, "Methods of Establishing a Firm's Value."

3. The first descriptions of book value were by Benjamin Graham and David Dodd. See Graham and Dodd, *Security Analysis*, 485. Contemporary investors argue that "book value" became irreverent during the end of the twentieth century, when companies became increasingly focused on acquiring more and more cash without "retaining" it.

4. On the history of pattern books, see Upton, "Pattern Books and Professionalism: Aspects of the Transformation of Domestic Architecture in America, 1800–1860"; Di Valmarana, *Building by the Book*; Smeins, *Building an American Identity: Pattern Book Homes and Communities*. On architects' business handbooks, see Johnston, *Assembling the Architect: The History and Theory of Professional Practice*.

5. Cuff, *Architecture: The Story of Practice*.

6. The argument about studies of practice as they relate to the discipline is offered by Alexander and May, *Design Technics: Archaeologies of Architectural Practice*. The argument about studies of practice as they relate to the profession is offered by Johnston, *Assembling the Architect*. On the crafting of architects' legacies, see Yaneva, *Crafting History: Archiving and the Quest for Architectural Legacy*.

7. Hugo, *The Hunchback of Notre Dame*. On books and eighteenth-century print culture in architecture, see Wittman, *Architecture, Print Culture, and the Public Sphere in Eighteenth-Century France*.

8. Johnston, *Assembling the Architect*, 20–26.

9. Johnston, 20.

10. American Institute of Architects, *A Handbook of Architectural Practice*, 11.

11. American Institute of Architects, 11.

12. American Institute of Architects, 8–10.

13. Briggs, *The Architect in History*.

14. Bacon, "The Federation of Architects, Engineers, Chemists and Technicians (FAECT): The Politics and Social Practice of Labor," 454; Hamlin, "The Architect and the Depression," 152.

15. Schuman, "Professionalization and the Social Goals of Architects: A History of the Federation of Architects, Engineers, Chemists, and Technicians"; also see Bacon, "The Federation of Architects, Engineers, Chemists and Technicians

(FAECT): The Politics and Social Practice of Labor"; ABI Collective, "Our Best Organizer!"

16. Bannister, *The Architect at Mid-Century*; Ackerman, "Architectural Practice in the Italian Renaissance."

17. On Piper, see Kates, "Robert Johnston Piper, 1926–2010." The handbook's formatting of the information within remained largely unchanged in subsequent editions over the next decades. Minor revisions reflected an incremental layering of new regulations, as well as an increasing concern about preserving records for use in the future. By 1943, the handbook's editors adopted a more definitive title: *The Handbook*, instead of *A Handbook*, opening with an overview of "Registration of Architects," which included an overview of the National Council of Architectural Registration Boards. American Institute of Architects, *The Handbook of Architectural Practice*, 1943.

18. For a review of these changes, see Gutman, "The Architect's Handbook of Professional Practice."

19. American Institute of Architects, *The Architect's Handbook of Professional Practice*, 1963, 1 (ch. 8).

20. American Institute of Architects, 1 (ch. 20).

21. American Institute of Architects, *The Handbook of Architectural Practice*, 1951. In the 1960s editions of the handbook, the contract series included the A-series (Owner-Contractor), B-series (Owner-Architect), C-Series (Architect-Consultant), D-Series Documents (Architect-Industry), E-Series (Architect-Producer), G-Series (Architect's Accounting Forms), and J-Series (Standards).

22. On the history of twentieth-century "temporary" work, see Hyman, *Temp: How American Work, American Business, and the American Dream Became Temporary*.

23. American Institute of Architects, *The Architect's Handbook of Professional Practice*, 1963, 1.

24. Sisson, "Temporary Binder." While one of the earliest portfolio patents in the US, there were earlier precedents in Europe, including a patent by German inventor Friedrich Soennecken.

25. Sisson, 1.

26. Sisson was commemorated in 1919 by then governor of Massachusetts Calvin Coolidge, and he was appointed as Republican lieutenant governor of Rhode Island in 1874. National Park Service, "Henry T. Sisson."

27. US War Department, *Technical Manual: Maintenance Policies, Publications, and Forms*, 24.

28. Halley and James, *Preliminary Inventory of the Records of the War Production Board*.

29. On Honnecourt, see Barnes, *The Portfolio of Villard de Honnecourt: A New Edition and Color Facsimile*. On Renaissance portfolios, see Pai, *The Portfolio and the Diagram: Architecture, Discourse, and Modernity in America*. For a broad historical overview of the portfolio since the Renaissance, see Farrell, "From Portafoglio to Eportfolio: The Evolution of Portfolio in Higher Education."

30. Farrell, "From Portafoglio to Eportfolio."

31. Pai, *The Portfolio and the Diagram*.

32. Pai, 37.

33. On the AIA's contracts, see Deamer, "Contracts of Relation." For a broad survey of manuals within architecture firms, see Franch i Gilabert et al., *OfficeUS: Manual*.

34. Markowitz, "Portfolio Selection"; also see Lintner, "The Valuation of Risk Assets and the Selection of Risky Investments in Stock Portfolios and Capital Budgets."

35. On the firm-as-portfolio, see Davis, Diekmann, and Tinsley, "The Decline and Fall of the Conglomerate Firm in the 1980s"; Williamson, *Markets and Hierarchies: Analysis and Antitrust Implications*; Fligstein and Dauber, "Structural Change in Corporate Organization."

36. Schwartzman, "Finance"; Polledri, "Architectural Services from a Developer's Point of View."

37. Case and Company, *The Economics of Architectural Practice*, 1968.

38. Blau, *Architects and Firms: A Sociological Perspective on Architectural Practice*; Gutman, "Architecture: The Entrepreneurial Profession." On one unsuccessful union drive at SOM, see US National Labor Relations Board, "Decisions of National Labor Relations Board: Skidmore, Owings & Merrill." On the DOJ sanctions, see Wickersham, "From Disinterested Expert to Marketplace Competitor: How Anti-monopoly Law Transformed the Ethics and Economics of American Architecture in the 1970s"; Deamer, *Architecture and Labor*, 89–96.

39. Kostof, *The Architect: Chapters in the History of the Profession*, xvii.

40. Gutman, *Architectural Practice: A Critical View*, 120–21.

41. These additions came not long after some professional programs converted to a four-plus-two degree model of education that ended with a master's of architecture, rather than a five-year bachelor's. Williamson, "Degree Nomenclature."

42. Gutman, "Emerging Problems of Practice."

43. Bourdieu, *Outline of a Theory of Practice*; Giddens, *Central Problems in Social Theory: Action, Structure, and Contradiction in Social Analysis*; Sahlins,

Historical Metaphors and Mythical Realities: Structure in the Early History of the Sandwich Islands Kingdom.

44. McLeod, "The End of Innocence: From Political Activism to Postmodernism," 196.

45. Woods, "The American Architect and Building News 1876-1907"; Woods, *From Craft to Profession: The Practice of Architecture in Nineteenth-Century America.*

46. Kostof, *The Architect.*

47. Dana Cuff, "Foreword," in Kostof, *The Architect*, x.

48. Blau, "The Structure of Science"; Blau, *Architects and Firms.*

49. Larson, "The Development of Modern Professions: Monopolies of Competence and Bourgeois Ideology"; Larson, *The Rise of Professionalism: A Sociological Analysis.*

50. Cuff, "Negotiating Architecture: A Study of Architects and Clients in Design Practice"; Cuff, *Architecture.*

51. Cuff, *Architecture*, 4.

52. Latour, *Reassembling the Social: An Introduction to Actor-Network-Theory*, 209. Bourdieu, *In Other Words: Essays towards a Reflexive Sociology*; also see Oakeshott, *On History and Other Essays*, 1-48. Several sociologists have since used Bourdieu's framework to analyze architecture. See, most notably, Jones, *The Sociology of Architecture: Constructing Identities.* For a critique of this framework, see Larson, "Practice and Education in 21st Century Architecture: A Sociologist's View."

53. Martin, *Utopia's Ghost: Architecture and Postmodernism, Again*, 93-112; also see Cayer, "Aesthetics of Indeterminacy: The Architecture of Conglomerates."

54. *The Architect's Handbook of Professional Practice*, 1973.

55. *The Architect's Handbook of Professional Practice*, 1987.

56. See, among others, The Architecture Lobby, "The Architecture Lobby Unionization Working Group"; Roche, "Organizing Shop: Follow the Sweat Equity"; Ling, "Inside the Historic Union Drive at SHoP Architects"; Roche, "Union at Bernheimer Architecture Ratifies Collective Bargaining Agreement."

57. US Census Bureau, "Special EEO 2000 Tabulation, Detailed Occupations."

58. ACSA, "ACSA Institutional Data Report."

59. A sample of recent dissertations focusing on architecture practice includes Sachs, "Environmental Design and the Expansion of Architectural Practice, 1937-1973"; Lange, "Tower Typewriter and Trademark: Architects, Designers and the Corporate Utopia, 1956-1964"; Jung, "Organization and Abstraction: The Architec-

ture of Skidmore, Owings & Merrill from 1936 to 1956"; Kubo, "Architecture Incorporated: Authorship, Anonymity, and Collaboration in Postwar Modernism"; Norwood, "The Architect's Knowledge: Imagining the Profession's Historical Body, 1797–1883"; Gupta, "The Architecture of Dispossession: Migrant Sarifa Settlements and State-Building in Iraq." Selected books include Wang, *The Architectural Profession of Modern China: Emerging from the Past*; Hua, *Shanghai Urban Planning Design and Research Institute/Shanghai Xiandai Architectural Design Group*; Jones, *The Sociology of Architecture*; Johnston, *Assembling the Architect*; Alexander and May, *Design Technics*; Ciccarelli, Lombardi, and Mingardi, *Largest Architectural Firms*.

60. Among other examples, see Bell and Wakeford, *Expanding Architecture: Design as Activism*; Yoon and Howeler, *Expanded Practice: Howeler and Yoon Architecture*; Roberts, "Expanding Modes of Practice"; ACSA, "Expanding the View."

61. For recent exceptions, see Morris, "An Ethnography of Three Michigan Architecture Firms: The Effect of Organizational Culture on Workplace Client Engagement"; Dharia, *The Industrial Ephemeral: Labor and Love in Indian Architecture and Construction*.

62. See Yaneva, *The Making of a Building: A Pragmatist Approach to Architecture*; Houdart and Minato, *Kuma Kengo: une monographie décalée*; Loukissas, *Co-Designers: Cultures of Computer Simulation in Architecture*. On the actor-network theory in architecture, see Latour and Yaneva, "Give Me a Gun and I Will Make All Buildings Move: An ANT's View of Architecture."

63. Latour, "On Recalling Ant."

64. Callon, "Actor-Network Theory—The Market Test."

65. Yaneva, *Crafting History*.

66. Latour and Woolgar, *Laboratory Life: The Construction of Scientific Facts*.

67. Ortner, *High Religion: A Cultural and Political History of Sherpa Buddhism*, 199. The anthropological studies that defined practice through history include Wolf, *Europe and the People without History*; Geertz, *Negara: The Theatre State in Nineteenth-Century Bali*; Cohn, "History and Anthropology: The State of Play"; Cohn, *Colonialism and Its Forms of Knowledge: The British in India*. For an overview, see Ortner, *Anthropology and Social Theory*.

68. Cayer, "Architecture University, Incorporated," 251.

Chapter Six

1. *U.S. News & World Report*, "Hoax of Horror? A Book That Shook White House"; also see Leo, "'Report' on Peace Gets Mixed Views"; Navasky, "Conspiracy Theory Is a Hoax Gone Wrong."

2. Lewin, *Report from Iron Mountain: On the Possibility & Desirability of Peace*. For a similar analysis of war and peace in Western modernity, see Latour, *War of the Worlds: What about Peace?*

3. *Los Angeles Times*, "Work Rushed on Atom War Proof Vaults: Caves in New York Will Be Used to Store Treasures," 15; also see Halbrook, "Offering Life after 'The Bomb,' and Safe Storage of Documents," 1; Lowry, "Old Iron Mountain Now Atom-Proof Storage Vault," B7; *The New York Times*, "Upstate Iron Mine Atom-Proof Vault," 11; Smith, "Changes Salted at Storage Area," F9; Bechtold, "Records Stored Underground," 8.

4. Office of Civil and Defense Mobilization, "Text of Director Hoegh's Address to a Symposium on Records Preservation."

5. DMJM's records were moved when AECOM moved offices in 2001. The AECOM global headquarters was located in the Sun America Center on the Avenue of the Stars, designed by Johnson Fain and built in 1990, while the former DMJM office, which offered the design, engineering, and planning services, moved from DMJM's former One Park Plaza offices to Downtown's City National Plaza in 2001, and again in 2015 to Downtown's One California Plaza. See Berton, "Architect Firm DMJM to Move Its Headquarters Downtown"; Miet, "AECOM to Lease at One California Plaza."

6. AECOM director of records management in email exchange with the author, October 22, 2020.

7. Stoler, *Along the Archival Grain: Epistemic Anxieties and Colonial Common Sense*; Henni, *Colonial Toxicity: Rehearsing French Nuclear Architecture and Landscape in the Sahara*.

8. Special Commission for the Commonwealth of Massachusetts, "Final Report to the General Court of the Special Commission Concerning State and County Buildings," 64.

9. On the management of architectural paperwork during the early twentieth century, see Osman, *Modernism's Visible Hand: Architecture and Regulation in America*, 165–84.

10. Spencer, "Rise of the Shadow Libraries: America's Quest to Save Its Information and Culture from Nuclear Destruction during the Cold War."

11. On Xerox, see Hiltzik, *Dealer of Lightning: Xerox PARC and the Dawn of the Computer Age*; Smith and Alexander, *Fumbling the Future: How Xerox Invented, Then Ignored, the First Personal Computer*. On the National Archives, see Lindee, *Rational Fog: Science and Technology in Modern War*.

12. DMJM, *1946–1955 Daniel, Mann, Johnson, & Mendenhall*, 7.

13. Celler-Kefauver Act of 1950, H. R. 2734, 81st Cong., 2d Sess. 5,6, ch. 1184, pp. 1125–26.

14. Derrida, *Archive Fever: A Freudian Impression*.

15. On the definition and analysis of nuclear secrecy as a "regime," see Wellerstein, *Restricted Data: The History of Nuclear Secrecy in the United States*.

16. See Wellerstein, *Restricted Data*; also see Brodie, "Learning Secrecy in the Early Cold War: The RAND Corporation."

17. Woods, *From Craft to Profession: The Practice of Architecture in Nineteenth-Century America*, 66; Carpo, *Architecture in the Age of Printing: Orality, Writing, Typography, and Printed Images in the History of Architectural Theory*, 23–41.

18. Krause, *Death of the Guilds: Professions, States, and the Advance of Capitalism, 1930 to the Present*.

19. Colomina, *Privacy and Publicity: Modern Architecture as Mass Media*.

20. On this argument of re-referentiality, see Cuff, *Architecture: The Story of Practice*, 36; Larson, *Behind the Postmodern Facade: Architectural Change in Late Twentieth-Century America*.

21. Banham, "A Black Box: The Secret Profession of Architecture," 25.

22. In the US, members of the First Continental Congress kept meeting proceedings secret; during the Revolutionary War, the Continental Army was prohibited from communicating with "the enemy," and presidents, such as George Washington, used their implied constitutional authority to control the dissemination of information. Richardson, *A Compilation of Messages and Papers of the Presidents, 1789-1897, vol. 1*, 71. There are earlier artifacts of secrecy within nation-states, especially those associated with military efforts and planning, including Sun Tzu's *The Art of War*, published in the fifth century BC.

23. Galison, "Secrecy in Three Acts"; Quill, *Secrets and Democracy: From Arcana Imperii to WikiLeaks*.

24. Newman, "Control of Information Relating to Atomic Energy."

25. In the early twentieth century, as Galison lays out, the Espionage Act of 1917 was aimed at preventing people from stealing and revealing information about national defense that might injure the country. These expanded restrictions were part of the Atomic Energy Act in 1946, ratified the year DMJM was born, and its revisions in 1954. For government work, such as design work for the Atomic Energy Commission, contracts with private-sector firms specified that the government would own the rights to their work. Galison, "Secrecy in Three Acts," 952–53.

26. See, for example, Dille, "The Missile-Era Race to Chart the Earth," 129.

27. White, "Memorandum for Deputy Director of Central Intelligence Re: Case History on Buildings 213 and 213A."

28. The relocation to Building 213 was due to a growing number of committees and staff that required a larger briefing room for meetings than was offered by the Steuart Building. The scope of the work included the remodeling and conversion of a "warehouse-type space" to "office and laboratory space." See "Memo for the Record: Remodeling of Building No. 213." For an overview of NPIC's history, including the spaces they occupied, see O'Connor, *NPIC: Seeing the Secrets and Growing the Leaders: A Cultural History of the National Photographic Interpretation Center*.

29. William Coburn in discussion with the author, July 28, 2016.

30. O'Connor, *NPIC*.

31. On the history of architect-involved aerial identification during war, see Allais, *Designs of Destruction: The Making of Monuments in the Twentieth Century*.

32. DMJM, "Staff Study Critique on Minimum Image Interpretation"; DMJM, "Familiarization of Photo Interpretation by Minimum Image Interpretation"; DMJM, "Automatic Handling Systems Requirement for the PIC"; DMJM, "Photo Interpretation by Mirror Image Quality Concept"; DMJM, "Past-Present-Future of Intelligence Acquisition." On the history of shadows as an origin for architectural drawing, see, among others, Evans, *Translations from Drawing to Building and Other Essays*.

33. CIA, "Memorandum for Deputy Director Re: Appearance of the Lobby and Sixth Floor of Building 213."

34. DMJM, "Letter to [Redacted] Re: Conference with [Redacted]"; CIA, "Memorandum for Chief, Production Services Division: Re: DMJM Report on Tank Farm."

35. CIA, "Memorandum from [Redacted] to C.F.C. and E.H. Re: Suggestions Regarding Future Inspection Tour by the Director CIA, of the New Facility"; also see O'Connor, *NPIC*.

36. Holding similar anticommunist sentiments, Steve Bechtel and McCone maintained a transactional relationship that has been documented within recent declassified documents and scholarship. Sally Denton describes this history in Denton, *The Profiteers*. One writer has argued that Bechtel was considered "the most secret corporation" to engineer the world—a business whose operations "mimicked those of the CIA," with an ability to gather "intelligence" much like the CIA. McCartney, *Friends in High Places: The Bechtel Story: The Most Secret Corporation and How It Engineered the World*, 460.

37. CIA, "Memorandum from [Redacted] to Deputy Assistant Director, Production Re: Report of Inspection, NPIC."

38. Gajda and Woodman, "Tacitus and Political Thought in Early Modern Europe, c. 1530–c. 1640"; Quill, *Secrets and Democracy*; also see Hannah Arendt's writings on secrecy and imperialism in Arendt, *The Origins of Totalitarianism*, 207–21; Arendt, *Crises of the Republic*, 419–37.

39. Immerwahr, *How to Hide an Empire: A History of the Greater United States*.

40. On the Roman empire as conglomerate, see Southern and Dixon, *The Late Roman Army*, 11. On the US versus Russia, see congressional discourse in 1963, when Senator William Bray stated that "this Russian empire, held together by force, is the last conglomerate empire." US Government Printing Office, *Congressional Record—Senate*, October 3, 1963, 18741. On the relationship between conglomerate empire and war, see Barzilai, *Golem: Modern Wars and Their Monsters*, 107; on China, see Smith, "The Transformation of Tientsin," 176.

41. US Government Printing Office, *Congressional Record—Senate*, April 23, 1917, 947.

42. Weber, *From Max Weber: Essays in Sociology*.

43. Weber, 233.

44. Vahe Khachooni in discussion with the author, November 12, 2021.

45. Vahe Khachooni in discussion with the author, November 24, 2021.

46. Vahe Khachooni in discussion with the author, November 12, 2021.

47. Henehan, "Shapers of the Future," 12–15.

48. Vahe Khachooni in discussion with the author, November 24, 2021.

49. Vahe Khachooni in discussion with the author, March 17, 2022.

50. Weiss, "Be Vision, a Package of IBM 7090 FORTRAN Programs to Draw Orthographic Views of Combinations of Plane and Quadric Surfaces."

51. Wellerstein, *Restricted Data*, 347.

52. Wellerstein, 344.

53. US Government Printing Office, "Presidential Campaign Activities of 1972, Senate Resolution 60: Watergate and Related Activities, Phase I," 231–71.

54. On the processing labor of the Senate Watergate Committee, see Spencer, "The Word Processing of Watergate and the Metaphysics of Information."

55. On women in early computation groups within large architecture firms, see Doyle and Senske, "SOM's Computer Group: Narratives of Women in Early Architectural Computing."

56. Lebovic, *Free Speech and Unfree News: The Paradox of Press Freedom in America*, 184; Richardson, *A Compilation of Messages and Papers of the Presidents, 1789-1897*.

57. Cited in Russell, "A Convenient Blanket of Secrecy: The Oft-Cited but Nonexisting Housekeeping Privilege," 746.

58. When Bakeman was first hired at the Hughes Aircraft Company, she could neither write shorthand notes nor type; while there, she enrolled in a local typing program. She was eventually appointed head of research. See *Wilshire Press*, "More Reports from Women Successful in Man's World."

59. *Wilshire Press*, "More Reports from Women Successful in Man's World." On unwaged housework, see Federici, *Wages against Housework*.

60. In 1988, Bakeman filed a complaint for a salary "adjustment," not a raise, arguing that she was severely underpaid compared to her counterparts in other companies, whose comparable salaries topped $75,000 ($164,980.35 in 2021 USD). She requested $52,000 ($114,386 in 2021 USD). Bakeman, "Memorandum to Jim Ebright," July 15, 1988.

61. Bakeman was not the only facility officer; she worked alongside Richard Ratia, DMJM's government contact compliance and facility security officer.

62. Bakeman, *A Study of the Management and Preservation of Records for Daniel, Mann, Johnson & Mendenhall*.

63. Bakeman, n.p.

64. On this history, see Lavin, "History for an Empty Future."

65. Yaneva, *Crafting History: Archiving and the Quest for Architectural Legacy*, 47.

66. Yaneva, 43.

67. Lavin, "History for an Empty Future."

68. Eisenman argued: "People were telling me, 'Why aren't you signing your drawings?' Some collecting institutions would not take my drawings unless I signed them. So, I signed them after the fact, but I never signed drawings at the start. I was not conscious." Cited in Yaneva, *Crafting History*, 46.

69. Colomina, *Privacy and Publicity*, 10.

70. Other important collections and museums that opened or expanded during this period were the Menil Collection in Houston, Texas (1982), the Wexner Center for the Arts in Columbus, Ohio (1983), the Museum of Modern Art's expansion (1984), and the Allen Art Museum in Oberlin, Ohio (1977).

71. Curtis, "The Bronfman Family."

72. On Robert Kennard, see Kennard and Henderson, *African-American Architects of Los Angeles: Robert A. Kennard*. On Wilson, see Laskey, *Rebel and Architect Oral History Transcript, 1988–1989: Zelma Wilson*.

73. While the majority of men reported their titles as "project architect," "principal," or "partner," the majority of women reported their titles as "em-

ployee" or "draftperson" and received significantly lower salaries, fewer ownership opportunities, and reduced benefits. See American Institute of Architects Task Force on Women in Architecture, "Affirmative Action Plan." For an early history of women in corporate architecture firms, see Stevens, "Struggle for Place: Women in Architecture: 1920–1960."

74. See Sklarek and Henderson, *African-American Architects of Los Angeles: Norma Merrick Sklarek*.

75. Barzman, "Small Town Girl."

76. The 1970 US Census reported that 3.7 percent of architects were women; 1.2 percent were registered; and 0.9 percent were members of the profession. The average firm sizes reported by men and women were 8.5 and 15.5, respectively. Edelman, *Status of Women in the Architectural Profession*.

77. Barzman, "Small Town Girl."

78. Hyman, *Temp: How American Work, American Business, and the American Dream Became Temporary*, 51.

79. Ellen Wright in discussion with the author, December 19, 2019.

80. American Institute of Architects Task Force on Women in Architecture, "Affirmative Action Plan," 31.

81. Emphasis added. Mann, "DMJM Board," May 15, 1981.

82. Ellen Wright in discussion with the author, December 19, 2019.

83. Wright, "On the Fringe of the Profession: Women in American Architecture."

84. The first woman vice president at DMJM was Debra Lambeck, named in 1988, who was a corporate attorney, not an architect.

85. AECOM, "Annual Report," 19. Other prominent companies that AECOM owned shares of included pharmaceutical company Pfizer, financial institutions such as JPMorgan Chase and Wells Fargo, and technology companies including Microsoft, Cisco Systems, and Danaher Corp.

86. Soules, *Icebergs, Zombies, and the Ultra Thin*.

Conclusion

1. McAlevey, *No Shortcuts: Organizing for Power in the New Gilded Age*.
2. Gutman, "Emerging Problems of Practice," 198.
3. Cuff, *Architecture: The Story of Practice*, 45.
4. As an example of this, see National Architectural Accrediting Board, *Conditions for Accreditation*, 1–3.
5. Cayer, "Architecture University, Incorporated."

6. Stengers, "Introductory Notes on an Ecology of Practices."

7. Kubo, "Architecture Incorporated: Authorship, Anonymity, and Collaboration in Postwar Modernism," 301; Chandler and Mazlish, *Leviathans: Multinational Corporations and the New Global History*; also see Hobbes, *Leviathan, or The Matter, Forme and Power of a Common Wealth Ecclesiasticall and Civil*.

8. Seward, "Making It Big."

Bibliography

Abercrombie, Jane. *Aims and Techniques of Group Teaching*. London: Society for Research on Higher Education, 1970.
ABI Collective. "Our Best Organizer!" *Avery Review* 66 (2024). https://averyreview.com/issues/66/our-best-organizer.
Abrams, Charles. *Man's Struggle for Shelter in an Urbanizing World*. Cambridge, MA: MIT Press, 1966.
Ackerman, James S. "Architectural Practice in the Italian Renaissance." *Journal of the Society of Architectural Historians* 13, no. 3 (October 1954): 3–11.
ACSA. "ACSA Institutional Data Report," June 2021. https://www.acsa-arch.org/wp-content/uploads/2021/06/2021_ACSA_IDR_0720.pdf.
———. "Expanding the View," 2021. https://www.acsa-arch.org/proceeding/109th-acsa-annual-meeting-proceedings-expanding-the-view/.
Adams, Gordon. *The Politics of Defense Contracting: The Iron Triangle*. New Brunswick, ON: Transaction Books, 1982.
Adams, Nicholas. *Gordon Bunshaft and SOM: Building Corporate Modernism*. New Haven, CT: Yale University Press, 2019.
———. *Skidmore, Owings & Merrill: SOM since 1936*. London: Phaidon Press, 2007.
AECOM. "AECOM Completes Acquisition of McNeil Technologies." News release, August 27, 2010. https://investors.aecom.com/node/10311/pdf.
———. "AECOM Joint Venture Awarded U.S. Army Contract Worth up to US $181.9 Million to Support Afghanistan National Army's Technical Equipment Maintenance Program." News release, January 10, 2011. https://investors.aecom.com/news-releases/news-release-details/aecom-joint-venture-awarded-us-army-contract-worth-us1819.

———. "AECOM Wins Contract with U.S. Department of State to Provide Diplomatic Platform Support Services." Press release, June 26, 2019. https://aecom.com/sa/press-releases/aecom-wins-contract-with-u-s-department-of-state-to-provide-diplomatic-platform-support-services/.

———. "Annual Professional Report." Los Angeles: AECOM Technology Corporation, 1990.

———. "Annual Report." Form 11-K. Security and Exchange Commission, June 29, 2015.

———. *Imagine It. Delivered. 2017 Annual Report.* Los Angeles: AECOM, 2018.

Aggregate [Group], ed. *Architecture in Development: Systems and the Emergence of the Global South.* New York: Routledge, 2022.

Air Force Ballistic Missiles Committee. "Minutes of the Eighth Meeting," February 7, 1957. Air Force Historical Research Division, Maxwell Air Force Base Archives, Alabama.

Alam, Dale V. "Letter to Vahe Khachooni," May 9, 1972. Papers of Vahe Khachooni. Private collection.

Albert Kahn Associates. "Albert Kahn Associates." March 14, 2018. http://www.albertkahn.com/what.php.

Alexander, Charles B., and Fred E. Ressegieu. "$550 Million for ICBM Facilities." *Missiles and Rockets*, September 21, 1959.

Alexander, Zeynep Çelik, and John May, eds. *Design Technics: Archaeologies of Architectural Practice.* Minneapolis: University of Minnesota Press, 2020.

Allais, Lucia. *Designs of Destruction: The Making of Monuments in the Twentieth Century.* Chicago: University of Chicago Press, 2018.

———. "Rendering: On Experience and Experiments." In *Archaeologies of Architectural Practice*, 1–44. Minneapolis: University of Minnesota Press, 2020.

Allen, Matthew. *Flowcharting: From Abstractionism to Algorithmics in Art and Architecture.* Zurich, Switzerland: gta, 2023.

The American Architect. "Forty-Third Annual Convention: American Institute of Architects." Vol. 96, no. 1774 (1909): 277–89.

American Institute of Architects. "The Architect's Office." In *Architect's Handbook of Professional Practice*, 3–6. Washington, DC: AIA, 1971.

———. "Computerized Project Management." AIA Continuing Education, March 18, 1972. Papers of Vahe Khachooni. Private collection.

———. *A Handbook of Architectural Practice.* Washington, DC: Press of the American Institute of Architects, 1920.

———. *The Handbook of Architectural Practice.* Washington, DC: AIA, 1943.

———. *The Handbook of Architectural Practice.* Washington, DC: AIA, 1951.

———. *The Architect's Handbook of Professional Practice*. Washington, DC: AIA, 1963.
———. *The Architect's Handbook of Professional Practice*. Washington, DC: AIA, 1973.
———. *The Architect's Handbook of Professional Practice*. Washington, DC: AIA, 1987.
American Institute of Architects Task Force on Women in Architecture. "Affirmative Action Plan for the Integration of Women in the Architectural Profession and the American Institute of Architects." Washington, DC: AIA, 1975.
Angel, Juvenal L. *Directory of American Firms Operating in Foreign Countries*. New York: World Academy Press, 1966.
Anger, Walter E. "The History of the Culver City Unified School District—Culver City, California." Master's thesis, University of Southern California, 1967.
Antonio, Robert J., and Alessandro Bonanno. "A New Global Capitalism? From 'Americanism and Fordism' to 'Americanization-Globalization.'" *American Studies*, 2000.
Architectural Forum. "The Biggest Mirror Ever." April 1967.
———. "Industrial Buildings: Albert Kahn Inc." August 1938.
Architectural Record. "Organization for Efficient Practice: Daniel, Mann, Johnson, & Mendenhall, Architects & Engineers." June 1960, 189–93.
———. "Producer of Production Lines." June 1942, 39–42.
The Architecture Lobby. "The Architecture Lobby Unionization Working Group," n.d. https://architecture-lobby.org/working-groups/unionization.
Arendt, Hannah. *Crises of the Republic*. New York: Harcourt Brace Jovanovich, 1972.
———. *The Origins of Totalitarianism*. San Diego, CA: Harcourt Brace & Co., 1973.
Ashland Oil Company. *Annual Report*. Ashland, KY: Ashland Oil Company, 1984.
———. *Annual Report*. Ashland, KY: Ashland Oil Company, 1986.
———. *Annual Report*. Ashland, KY: Ashland Oil Company, 1990.
Atkinson, John. "Emerging UK Work Patterns." In *Flexible Manning—the Way Ahead*, 1–12. Brighton, UK: Institute of Manpower Studies and Manpower, 1984.
Bacon, Mardges. "The Federation of Architects, Engineers, Chemists and Technicians (FAECT): The Politics and Social Practice of Labor." *Journal of the Society of Architectural Historians* 76, no. 4 (2017): 454–63.
Bakeman, Carol Ann. "Memorandum to Jim Ebright," July 15, 1988. Bakeman family papers. Private collection.
———. *A Study of the Management and Preservation of Records for Daniel, Mann, Johnson & Mendenhall*. Los Angeles: DMJM, 1978.

Balmori, Diana. "George B. Post: The Process of Design and the New American Architectural Office (1868–1913)." *Journal of the Society of Architectural Historians* 46, no. 4 (December 1987): 342–55.

Banham, Reyner. "A Black Box: The Secret Profession of Architecture." *New Statesman and Society*, October 12, 1990, 22–25.

———. *Los Angeles: The Architecture of Four Ecologies*. Berkeley: University of California Press, 2009.

Bannister, Turpin C. *The Architect at Mid-Century*. New York: Reinhold, 1954.

Barnes, Carl Franklin. *The Portfolio of Villard de Honnecourt: A New Edition and Color Facsimile*. Farnham, UK: Ashgate, 2009.

Barzilai, Maya. *Golem: Modern Wars and Their Monsters*. New York: New York University Press, 2020.

Barzman, Norma. "Small Town Girl: At 70-Something, Ojai Architect Has Too Much Experience and Is Having Too Much Fun to Retire." *Los Angeles Times*, April 26, 1990.

Baxter, Alfred W. "Maybeck's Bohemian Clubhouse." *Bohemian Club Library Notes*, Summer 1985.

Beaumont Library District. "Historical US Census Populations of Places, Towns, and Cities in California, 1850–1990," March 11, 2007. https://web.archive.org/web/20070311132131/http:/bld.lib.ca.us/virtualreference/calif_historical_census_population.htm.

Beaumont, Roger A. "Quantum Increase: The MIC in the Second World War." In *War, Business and American Society: Historical Perspectives on the Military Industrial Complex*, edited by Benjamin Franklin Cooling. Port Washington, NY: Kennikat Press, 1977.

Bechtold, Henry J. "Records Stored Underground." *Morgantown Post*, May 8, 1961.

Beguiristain, Mario Eugenio. *The Actors Studio and Hollywood in the 1950s: A History of Theatrical Realism*. Lewiston, NY: Edwin Mellen Press, 2006.

Bell, Bryan, and Katie Wakeford. *Expanding Architecture: Design as Activism*. New York: Metropolis Books, 2008.

Bello, Walden F., David Kinley, and Elaine Elinson. *Development Debacle: The World Bank in the Philippines*. San Francisco and Oakland, CA: Institute for Food and Development Policy and Philippine Solidarity Network, 1982.

Berle, Adolf A. *The Modern Corporation and Private Property*. New Brunswick, NJ: Transaction, 1991 [1932].

Berton, Brad. "Architect Firm DMJM to Move Its Headquarters Downtown." *Los Angeles Times*, June 26, 2001. https://www.latimes.com/archives/la-xpm-2001-jun-26-fi-14770-story.html.

Bevins, Vincent. *The Jakarta Method: Washington's Anticommunist Crusade & the Mass Murder Program That Shaped Our World*. New York: Public Affairs, 2021.

Blackwood, Kate. "First-person histories reframe the past." *Cornell Chronicle*, February 3, 2023. https://news.cornell.edu/stories/2023/02/first-person-histories-reframe-past. Accessed September 14, 2024.

Blau, Judith R. *Architects and Firms: A Sociological Perspective on Architectural Practice*. Cambridge, MA: MIT Press, 1984.

———. "The Structure of Science." PhD diss., Northwestern University, 1972.

Bodenheimer, Susanne. "Dependency and Imperialism: The Roots of Latin American Underdevelopment." In *Readings in U.S. Imperialism*, edited by K. T. Fann and Donald C. Hodges. Boston: Porter Sargent, 1971.

Bork, Robert H. *The Antitrust Paradox: A Policy at War with Itself*. New York: Free Press, 1993.

Bourdieu, Pierre. *The Field of Cultural Production: Essays on Art and Literature*. New York: Columbia University Press, 1993.

———. *In Other Words: Essays towards a Reflexive Sociology*. Stanford, CA: Stanford University Press, 1990.

———. *Outline of a Theory of Practice*. Translated by Richard Nice. Cambridge: Cambridge University Press, 1977.

Boyle, Bernard Michael. "Architectural Practice in America, 1865-1965—Ideal and Reality." In *The Architect: Chapters in the History of the Profession*, edited by Spiro Kostof, 309-44. Berkeley: University of California Press, 2000.

Brain, David. "Practical Knowledge and Social Control: The Professionalization of Architecture in the United States." *Sociological Forum* 6 (1991): 239-68.

Braverman, Harry. *Labor and Monopoly Capital: The Degradation of Work in the Twentieth Century*. New York: Monthly Review, 1974.

Breckenfeld, Gurney. "The Architects Want a Voice in Redesigning America." *Fortune* 84, no. 5 (1971): 144-47, 198-99, 203-4, 206.

Briggs, Martin. *The Architect in History*. Oxford: Clarendon Press, 1927.

Brint, Steven G. *In an Age of Experts: The Changing Role of Professionals in Politics and Public Life*. Princeton, NJ: Princeton University Press, 1996.

Brodie, Janet. "Learning Secrecy in the Early Cold War: The RAND Corporation." *Learning in the Early Cold War: The RAND Corporation* 35, no. 4 (2011): 643-70.

Bruegmann, Robert. *The Architects and the City: Holabird & Roche of Chicago, 1880-1918*. Chicago Architecture and Urbanism. Chicago: University of Chicago Press, 1997.

Building Design. "The World's Largest Architecture Practices." *Building Design Magazine*, January 2017.

Burns, Thomas S. *Tales of ITT: An Insider's Report*. Boston: Houghton Mifflin, 1974.

Business Week. "Six Partners with Six Personalities." January 19, 1957, 176-82.

California Law. "California Corporations Code: Professional Corporations," 1968. https://leginfo.legislature.ca.gov/faces/codes_displayText.xhtml?lawCode=CORP&division=3.&title=1.&part=4.&chapter=&article=.

Callon, Michel. "Actor-Network Theory—The Market Test." In *Actor Network Theory and After*, edited by John Law and John Hassard, 181-95. Oxford: Blackwell, 1999.

Candilis, George. *Planning and Design for Leisure*. Stuttgart, Germany: Karl Kramer, 1972.

Carlson, David B. "Buildings for the Space Age." *Architectural Forum*, September 1960.

Canadian Builder. "The Parkin Organization." April 1961, 32.

Carnevale, Anthony P., Ban Cheah, and Jeff Strohl. "Hard Times: College Majors, Unemployment, and Earnings." Washington, DC: Georgetown University Center on Education and the Workforce, January 2012.

Carpo, Mario. *Architecture in the Age of Printing: Orality, Writing, Typography, and Printed Images in the History of Architectural Theory*. Cambridge, MA: MIT Press, 2001.

Carter, J. H. "Letter to DMJM," September 16, 1958. Stanley Moe Papers. Huntington Library, San Marino, CA.

Case and Company. *The Economics of Architectural Practice*. Washington, DC: American Institute of Architects, 1968.

Cave, Hugh B. *We Build, We Fight!* New York: Harper & Brothers, 1944.

Cayer, Aaron. "Aesthetics of Indeterminacy: The Architecture of Conglomerates." *Architectural Histories* 1, no. 1 (2023). https://journal.eahn.org/article/id/8305/.

———. "Architecture University, Incorporated." *Ardeth* 10, no. 11 (2023): 251-71.

Cayer, Aaron, and Dana Cuff. "UNFIT: Los Angeles and the Empty Glass Box." *Thresholds*, no. 44 (2016): 43-58.

Celler, Emanuel. "Remarks before the Senate." *Congressional Record*, April 17, 1967, 9873-8975.

Césaire, Aimé. *Discourse on Colonialism*. New York: Monthly Review Press, 2000.

Chandler, Alfred D., Jr. "Origins of the Organization Chart." *Harvard Business Review* 66, no. 2 (1988).

———. *Strategy and Structure: Chapters in the History of the Industrial Enterprise*. Cambridge, MA: MIT Press, 1966 [1962].

———. *The Visible Hand: The Managerial Revolution in American Business*. Cambridge, MA: Belknap Press of Harvard University Press, 2002.

Chandler, Alfred D., Jr., and Bruce Mazlish, eds. *Leviathans: Multinational Corporations and the New Global History*. Cambridge: Cambridge University Press, 2005.

Chicago Tribune. "Politics a Hindrance: Luckman." March 8, 1970.

China Post. "Indonesia, Red China Sign Dual Nationality Agreement." December 16, 1960.

CIA. "Memo for the Record: Remodeling of Building No. 213," March 9, 1961. FOIA Release CIA-RDP78-04608A000400070028-7. CIA Special Collections. https://www.cia.gov/readingroom/docs/CIA-RDP78-04608A000400070028-7.pdf.

———. "Memorandum for Chief, Production Services Division: Re: DMJM Report on Tank Farm," December 12, 1962. FOIA Release CIA-RDP78B047A001800070013-2. CIA Special Collections.

———. "Memorandum for Deputy Director Re: Appearance of the Lobby and Sixth Floor of Building 213," January 23, 1963. FOIA Release CIA-RDP78-040608A000400070008-9. CIA Special Collections.

———. "Memorandum from [Redacted] to C.F.C. and E.H. Re: Suggestions Regarding Future Inspection Tour by the Director CIA, of the New Facility," January 8, 1963. CIA Archives.

———. "Memorandum from [Redacted] to Deputy Assistant Director, Production Re: Report of Inspection, NPIC," October 11, 1963. CIA Archives.

Ciccarelli, Lorenzo, Sara Lombardi, and Lorenzo Mingardi, eds. *Largest Architectural Firms*. Firenze: Edifir, 2021.

Clifford, James, and George E. Marcus. *Writing Culture: The Poetics and Politics of Ethnography*. Berkeley: University of California Press, 2010.

Coase, Ronald. "The Nature of the Firm." *Economica* 4 (November 1937): 386–405.

Cody, Jeffrey W. *Exporting American Architecture, 1870–2000*. New York: Routledge, 2003.

Cohen, Jean-Louis. *Architecture in Uniform: Designing and Building for the Second World War*. Montréal and New Haven, CT: Canadian Centre for Architecture and Yale University Press, 2011.

Cohen, Jerome B. "The Economic Aspects of Conglomerates." *St. John's Law Review* 44 (1970): 49–60.

Cohn, Bernard S. *Colonialism and Its Forms of Knowledge: The British in India*. Princeton, NJ: Princeton University Press, 1996.

———. "History and Anthropology: The State of Play." *Comparative Studies in Society and History* 22, no. 2 (April 1980): 198–221.

Colomina, Beatriz. *Privacy and Publicity: Modern Architecture as Mass Media*. Cambridge, MA: MIT Press, 2000.

Comaroff, John L., and Jean Comaroff. *Ethnography and the Historical Imagination*. Boulder, CO: Westview Press, 1992.

Contreras, Shirley. "Crawford Had Designs on Central Coast." *Santa Maria Times*, November 18, 2017. https://santamariatimes.com/lifestyles/columnist/shirley_contreras/shirley-contreras-crawford-had-designs-on-central-coast/article_056b51a3-d969-5a01-9536-74d03c47ebae.html.

Cooper, Phillip J. "Government Contracts in Public Administration: The Role and Environment of the Contracting Officer." *Public Administration Review* 40, no. 5 (1980): 459–68.

Cooper, Tom, and Marc Koelich. "Clandestine US Operations: Indonesia 1958, Operation 'Haik.'" *Publication of Air Combat Information Group*, September 1, 2003. https://www.acig.org/artman/publish/article_175.shtml.

Corpus Christi Times. "Army Asks Congress for Electronic Calculator." September 27, 1951.

Coxe, Weld. *Managing Architectural and Engineering Practice*. New York: Wiley, 1980.

Coyle, Diane. *GDP: A Brief but Affectionate History*. Princeton, NJ: Princeton University Press, 2014.

Cuff, Dana. *Architecture: The Story of Practice*. Cambridge, MA: MIT Press, 1991.

———. "Architecture's Undisciplined Urban Desire." *Architectural Theory Review* 19, no. 1 (2014): 92–97.

———. "The Ethos and Circumstance of Design." *Journal of Architectural and Planning Research* 6, no. 4 (1989): 305–20.

———. "Negotiating Architecture: A Study of Architects and Clients in Design Practice." PhD diss., University of California, Berkeley, 1982.

Cullen, John. "Structural Aspects of the Architectural Profession." In *Professions of Urban Form*, edited by Judith R. Blau, Mark La Gory, and John Pipkin. Albany: State University of New York Press, 1983.

Cuneo, Gilbert A., Harold F. Blasky, Eldon H. Cromwell, and Philip A. Hutchinson Jr., eds. *Contracting with the Federal Government: A Primer for Architects and Engineers*. Silver Spring, MD: Committee of Federal Procurement of Architect-Engineer Services, 1969.

———. *Contracting with the Federal Government: A Primer for Architects and Engineers.* Silver Spring, MD: Committee of Federal Procurement of Architect-Engineer Services, 1974.

Cupers, Kenny, Helena Mattsson, and Catharina Gabrielsson, eds. *Neoliberalism on the Ground: Architecture & Transformation from the 1960s to the Present.* Culture, Politics, and the Built Environment. Pittsburgh, PA: University of Pittsburgh Press, 2020.

Curtis, Christopher G. "The Bronfman Family." *The Canadian Encyclopedia*, October 2013.

D'Aprile, Marianela, and Douglas Spencer. "Notes on Tafuri, Militancy, and Unionization." *The Avery Review* 56 (April 2022). https://averyreview.com/issues/56/notes-on-tafuri.

Danhof, Clarence H. *Government Contracting and Technological Change.* Washington, DC: The Brookings Institution, 1968.

Daniel, Mann, Johnson & Mendenhall, International. "Final Report: Ground Water Exploration of the Khorat Plateau." Bangkok, July 1961.

Daniel, Phillip J. "Application of Operations Research for Site Planning Facilities Support." *Aerospace Engineering*, June 1961, 26–27, 81–84.

Davis, Arthur Q. *It Happened by Design: The Life and Work of Arthur Q. Davis.* Jackson: University of Mississippi Press, 2009.

Davis, Gerald F., and Kristina A. Diekmann. "The Decline and Fall of the Conglomerate Firm in the 1980s: The Desinstitutionalization of an Organizational Form." In *The New Economic Sociology*, edited by Frank Dobbins, 188–233. Princeton, NJ: Princeton University Press, 2004.

Davis, Gerald F., Kristina A. Diekmann, and Catherine H. Tinsley. "The Decline and Fall of the Conglomerate Firm in the 1980s: The Deinstitutionalization of an Organizational Form." *American Sociological Review* 59, no. 4 (August 1994): 547.

Davis, Michael. "Has Globalism Made Architecture's Professional Ethics Obsolete?" In *Architecture, Ethics, and Globalization*, edited by Graham Owen, 121–32. New York: Routledge, 2009.

Deamer, Peggy. *Architecture and Labor.* New York: Routledge, 2020.

———. "Contracts of Relation." e-flux, November 2017. https://www.e-flux.com/architecture/representation/159198/contracts-of-relation/.

———. "Deprofessionalization and Architecture." *Graz Architecture Magazine* 19 (2022).

———. "The Sherman Antitrust Act and the Profession of Architecture." In *Architecture and Labor*, 71–88. New York: Routledge, 2020.

———. "Work." *Perspecta* 47 (2014): 27–39.

Dean, Andrea O. "Honor Awards: New Buildings, Recyclings, and Mies." *AIA Journal*, April 1976, 36–56.

Dear, Michael. "Los Angeles and the Chicago School: Invitation to a Debate." *City & Community* 1, no. 1 (March 2002): 5–32.

Denton, Sally. *The Profiteers: Bechtel and the Men Who Built the World*. New York: Simon & Schuster, 2016.

Department of State, US Embassy Djakarta. "Business Proposal of Struthers Research & Development Corporation, Daniel, Mann, Johnson & Mendenhall, and Stanford Research Institute," November 1, 1967. US National Archives, US Foreign Assistance Agencies.

Derrida, Jacques. *Archive Fever: A Freudian Impression*. Chicago: University of Chicago Press, 1996.

Des Chene, Mary. "Locating the Past." In *Anthropological Locations: Boundaries and Grounds of a Field Science*, edited by Akhil Gupta and James Ferguson, 68–85. Berkeley: University of California Press, 1997.

The Desert Sun. "Luckman Announces Change." June 27, 1977.

Design Journal. "High Rise Fun Palaces." 1986, 59–63.

Dharia, Namita. *The Industrial Ephemeral: Labor and Love in Indian Architecture and Construction*. Oakland: University of California Press, 2022.

Di Valmarana, Mario, ed. *Building by the Book, vol. 1*. Charlottesville: Center for Palladian Studies in America and University Press of Virginia, 1984.

Dille, John. "The Missile-Era Race to Chart the Earth," May 12, 1958.

Dixon, John M. "A White Gentlemen's Profession?" *Progressive Architecture* 75, no. 11 (November 1994): 55–61.

DMJM. *1946-1955 Daniel, Mann, Johnson, & Mendenhall*. Los Angeles, 2008.

———. *1956-1965 Daniel, Mann, Johnson, & Mendenhall*. Los Angeles, 2008.

———. "Automatic Handling Systems Requirement for the PIC," April 26, 1961. FOIA Release CIA-RDP78B04770A002500060002-8. CIA Special Collections. https://www.cia.gov/readingroom/docs/CIA-RDP78B04770A002500060002-8.pdf.

———. *Company General Brochure: A Presentation of the Work of Daniel, Mann, Johnson, & Mendenhall*, 1967.

———. "DMJM Sponsors USAF Intern." *DMJM News*, Winter 1981, 7.

———. "Familiarization of Photo Interpretation by Minimum Image Interpretation," April 28, 1961. FOIA Release CIA-RDP78B04770A002500060002-8.

CIA Special Collections. https://www.cia.gov/readingroom/docs/CIA-RDP78B04770A002500060002-8.pdf.
———. "Letter to [Redacted] Re: Conference with [Redacted]," May 23, 1962. FOIA Release CIA-RDP78B04747A001800070017-8. CIA Special Collections.
———. "Manufacturing and Research Facility for Teledyne Systems Company," May 7, 1969. Pelli Clarke Pelli Architects, Series II Collection, Yale University Library Manuscripts and Archives, New Haven, CT.
———. "Mayor Bradley Tours LA Office." *DMJM News*, 1980, 1.
———. "One Park Plaza." *DMJM Review*, Spring 1973.
———. "Past-Present-Future of Intelligence Acquisition," April 28, 1961. FOIA Release CIA-RDP78B04770A002500060002-8. CIA Special Collections. https://www.cia.gov/readingroom/docs/CIA-RDP78B04770A002500060002-8.pdf.
———. "Photo Interpretation by Mirror Image Quality Concept," April 26, 1961. FOIA Release CIA-RDP78B04770A002500060002-8. CIA Special Collections. https://www.cia.gov/readingroom/docs/CIA-RDP78B04770A002500060002-8.pdf.
———. "Staff Study Critique on Minimum Image Interpretation," July 17, 1961. FOIA Release CIA-RDP78B04770A002500060002-8. CIA Special Collections. https://www.cia.gov/readingroom/docs/CIA-RDP78B04770A002500060002-8.pdf.
Domhoff, G. William. *The Bohemian Grove and Other Retreats: A Study in Ruling-Class Cohesiveness*. New York: Harper & Row, 1974.
Doyle, Shelby, and Nick S. Senske. "SOM's Computer Group: Narratives of Women in Early Architectural Computing." *International Journal of Architectural Computing* 19, no. 3 (2020): 213–25.
Drapkin Dercle, Julie. "Cinema and Architecture: Towards Understanding the Cinematic Sense of Place and Its Relationships to the Built Environment." PhD diss., University of California, Berkeley, 1992.
Drucker, Peter F. *Concept of the Corporation*. New York: John Day, 1972.
Dudley, Tara A. *Building Antebellum New Orleans: Free People of Color and Their Influence*. Austin: University of Texas Press, 2021.
Dutta, Arindam. *The Bureaucracy of Beauty: Design in the Age of Its Global Reproducibility*. New York: Routledge, 2007.
———. "Marginality and Metaengineering: Keynes and Arup." In *Governing by Design: Architecture, Economy, and Politics in the Twentieth Century*, edited by Aggregate [Group], 237–68. Pittsburgh, PA: University of Pittsburgh Press, 2012.

Easterling, Keller. "Coda: Liberal." In *Architecture and Capitalism: 1825 to the Present*, 202–16. New York: Routledge, 2014.

———. *Extrastatecraft: The Power of Infrastructure Space*. New York: Verso, 2014.

Eco, Umberto. *The Open Work*. Translated by Anna Cancogni. Cambridge, MA: Harvard University Press, 1989 [1962].

Edelman, Judith, ed. *Status of Women in the Architectural Profession*. Washington DC: American Institute of Architects, 1975.

Editors of *Architectural Digest*. "Cesar Pelli." *Architectural Digest: The AD 100 Architects*, August 15, 1991, 178–79.

Editors of *Architectural Forum*. *The 1958 FORUM Directory of the 100 Biggest Architectural Firms, Building Customers, Building Contractors*. New York: Time Inc., 1958.

———. *The 1959 FORUM Directory of the 100 Biggest Architects, Contractors, Clients*. New York: Time Inc., 1959.

Editors of *Fortune*. *The Conglomerate Commotion*. New York: The Viking Press, 1970.

Ellis, William Russell, and Dana Cuff, eds. *Architects' People*. New York: Oxford University Press, 1989.

Engineering News-Record. "Design Frills Dominate L.A. Sewage Plant: Effluent Eyed for Irrigation Use." June 14, 1984, 26–27.

———. "Genge Unites 20 Subsidiaries into a National Design Network." December 1973, 23–24.

———. "Now—Millions for Missile Bases." February 27, 1958, 21–23.

———. "The Top 500 Design Firms." May 1971, 45–67.

———. "The Top 500 Design Firms." May 1982, 62–95.

———. "The Top 500 Design Firms." April 1991.

Enion, Richard A. "Practical Means to Higher Profits." *AIA Journal*, November 1969, 47–51.

Escobar, Arturo. *Designs for the Pluriverse: Racial Interdependence, Autonomy, and the Making of Worlds*. Durham, NC: Duke University Press, 2018.

Esland, Geoff. "Professions and Professionalism." In *Politics of Work and Occupations*, edited by Geoff Esland and Graeme Salaman, 213–50. Toronto: University of Toronto Press, 1980.

Evans, Alastair, and Jenny Bell. "Emerging Themes in Flexible Work Patterns." In *Flexible Patterns of Work*, edited by Chris Curson, 1–25. London: Institute of Personnel Management, 1986.

Evans, Robin. *Translations from Drawing to Building and Other Essays*. London: AA Publications, 2023.

Eyerman, Thomas J. "Methods of Establishing a Firm's Value." *AIA Journal*, August 1974, 55.
Farrell, Orna. "From Portafoglio to Eportfolio: The Evolution of Portfolio in Higher Education." *Journal of Interactive Media in Education* 2020, no. 1 (2020).
Federici, Silvia. *Wages against Housework*. Bristol, UK: Falling Wall Press, 1975.
Ferreira da Silva, Denise. *Unpayable Debt*. London: Sternberg Press, 2022.
Fishman, Robert. "Foreword." In Robert M. Fogelson, *The Fragmented Metropolis: Los Angeles, 1850-1930*, 2nd. ed. Berkeley: University of California Press, 1993.
Flightaware.com. "N5177C Aircraft Registration." June 2, 2006. https://flightaware.com/resources/registration/N5177C.
Fligstein, Neil. "The Spread of the Multi-divisional Form among Large Firms, 1919-1979." *American Sociological Review* 50 (1985): 377-91.
———. "Structural Change in Corporate Organization." *Annual Review of Sociology* 15 (1989): 73-96.
———. "The Structural Transformation of American Industry: An Institutional Account of the Causes of Diversification in the Largest Firms, 1919-1979." In *The New Institutionalism in Organizational Analysis*, edited by Walter W. Powell and Paul DiMaggio, 311-36. Chicago: University of Chicago Press, 1991.
Fogarty, Frank. "Architecture at a Profit." *Architectural Forum*, September 1957, 128-31, 214.
Fogelson, Robert M. *The Fragmented Metropolis: Los Angeles, 1850-1930*. Cambridge, MA: Harvard University Press, 1967.
Franch i Gilabert, Eva, Ana Miljački, Carlos Minguez Carrasco, Jacob Reidel, and Ashley Schafer, eds. *OfficeUS: Manual*. Zurich, Switzerland: Lars Müller, 2017.
Franch i Gilabert, Eva, Ana Miljački, Ashley Schafer, and Michael Kubo, eds. *OfficeUS: Atlas*. Zurich, Switzerland: Lars Müller, 2015.
Franklin, James R. "Mutual Benefits." *Architecture*, October 1990, 97-98.
Fraser, Linda M., Michael McMordie, and Geoffrey Simmins. *John C. Parkin, Archives and Photography: Reflections on the Practice and Presentation of Modern Architecture*. Calgary, AB: University of Calgary Press, 2013.
Freedgood, Seymour. "'Dimjim': Architects for the Space Age." *Fortune*, August 1960, 121-25, 177-78, 180.
Freidson, Eliot. "The Changing Nature of Professional Control." *Annual Review of Sociology* 10, no. 1-20 (1984).
———. *The Professions and Their Prospects*. Beverly Hills, CA: Sage, 1973.

Friedman, Milton. "The Business Community's Suicidal Impulse." *Cato Policy Report* 21, no. 2 (April 1999), 6–7.

———. *Capitalism and Freedom*. Chicago: University of Chicago Press, 1982 [1962].

Gabler, Neal. *Walt Disney: The Triumph of the American Imagination*. New York: Vintage Books, 2006.

Gajda, Alexandra, and A. J. Woodman. "Tacitus and Political Thought in Early Modern Europe, c. 1530–c. 1640." In *The Cambridge Companion to Tacitus*, 253–68. Cambridge: Cambridge University Press, 2009.

Galison, Peter. "Secrecy in Three Acts." *Social Research* 77, no. 3 (2010): 941–74.

Gans, Herbert. "Toward a Human Architecture: A Sociologist's View of the Profession." *Journal of Architectural and Planning Research* 31, no. 2 (1977): 258–68.

Gavin, Francis J. "The Myth of Flexible Response: United States Strategy in Europe during the 1960s." *The International History Review* 23, no. 4 (2001): 847–75.

Geertz, Clifford. *Negara: The Theatre State in Nineteenth-Century Bali*. Princeton, NJ: Princeton University Press, 1980.

Gensler, Arthur, and Michael Lindenmayer. *Art's Principles: 50 Years of Hard-Learned Lessons in Building a World-Class Professional Services Firm*. San Bernardino, CA: Wilson Lafferty, 2015.

Gensler, Arthur, and Martin Meeker. *Art Gensler: Building a Global Architecture and Design Firm (Oral History)*. Oakland: University of California, 2015.

Gibbs, Jocelyn Dian. *Outside In: The Architecture of Smith and Williams*. Santa Barbara, CA: Art, Design & Architecture Museum, University of California, Santa Barbara in Association with Getty Publications, 2014.

Giddens, Anthony. *Central Problems in Social Theory: Action, Structure, and Contradiction in Social Analysis*. Berkeley: University of California Press, 1979.

Giedion, Sigfried. "The Experiment of S.O.M." *Bauen Und Wohnen* 11, no. 4 (1957): 109–14.

———. *Mechanization Takes Command: A Contribution to Anonymous History*. New York: Oxford University Press, 1948.

Gies, Joseph. "Hell Hole: Launching the Titan Missile." In *Wonders of the Modern World: Thirteen Great Achievements of Modern Engineering*. New York: Thomas Y. Crowell, 1966.

Gilbreth, Frank B. "The 'Cost-Plus-a-Fixed-Sum' Contract." *Industrial Magazine* 6 (1907): 31–37.

———. *Field System*. New York: Myron C. Clark, 1908.
Good Jobs First. "Violation Tracker." https://www.goodjobsfirst.org/violation-tracker. Accessed November 12, 2023.
Graham, Benjamin, and David L. Dodd. *Security Analysis*. London: McGraw Hill, 1996.
Gramsci, Antonio. *Selections from the Prison Notebooks of Antonio Gramsci*. Edited by Quintin Hoare and Geoffrey Nowell Smith. London: Lawrence and Wishart, 1971.
Gray, George T., and Ronald Q. Smith. "Sperry Rand's Third-Generation Computers 1964-1980." *IEEE Annals of the History of Computing*, March 2001.
Greene, Warren E. *The Development of the SM-68 Titan*. US Air Force, Strategic Air Command Historical Publications Series 62-63-1, August 1962.
Gualtieri, Kathryn. "Granada Shoppes and Studios." National Register of Historic Places Inventory Nomination Form, US Department of the Interior, November 20, 1986.
Guenter, Lewy. *America in Vietnam*. New York: Oxford University Press, 1978.
Gupta, Huma. "The Architecture of Dispossession: Migrant Sarifa Settlements and State-Building in Iraq." PhD diss., Massachusetts Institute of Technology, 2020.
Gutman, Robert. *Architectural Practice: A Critical View*. New York: Princeton Architectural Press, 1988.
———. "Architecture: The Entrepreneurial Profession." *Progressive Architecture*, May 1977, 55–58.
———. "The Architect's Handbook of Professional Practice." *Journal of Architectural Education* 45, no. 2 (1992): 122–24.
———. "Emerging Problems of Practice." *Journal of Architectural Education* 45, no. 4 (July 1992): 198–202.
Halbrook, Sherry. "Offering Life after 'The Bomb,' and Safe Storage of Documents." *Capital District Business Review* 13, no. 49 (1987).
Halley, Fred G., and Josef C. James, eds. *Preliminary Inventory of the Records of the War Production Board*. Washington, DC: The National Archives, 1948.
Hamlin, Talbot Faulner. "The Architect and the Depression." *The Nation* 137 (August 23, 1933): 152–53.
Hanford, Emily. "The Story of the University of Phoenix." American Public Media, n.d. http://americanradioworks.publicradio.org/features/tomorrows-college/phoenix/story-of-university-of-phoenix.html. Accessed March 4, 2023.

Harder, Julius F. "Architectural Practice—an Art and a Business." *The Brickbuilder* 11, no. 4 (April 1902): 74–77.

Hardt, Michael, and Antonio Negri. *Empire*. Cambridge, MA: Harvard University Press, 2003.

Harmetz, Aljean. *The Making of* The Wizard of Oz. Chicago: Chicago Review Press, 2013 [1977].

Harvey, David. *A Brief History of Neoliberalism*. Oxford: Oxford University Press, 2005.

———. *The Condition of Postmodernity: An Enquiry into the Origins of Cultural Change*. Oxford: Blackwell, 1989.

———. "From Managerialism to Entrepreneurialism: The Transformation in Urban Governance in Late Capitalism." *Geografiska Annaler B: Human Geography* 71, no. 1 (1989): 3–17.

———. *Spaces of Capital: Towards a Critical Geography*. New York: Routledge, 2001.

———. *The Urban Experience*. Baltimore: Johns Hopkins University Press, 1989.

———. *The Urbanization of Capital: Studies in the History and Theory of Capitalist Urbanization*. Baltimore: Johns Hopkins University Press, 1985.

Hastings, Keith. "Extension of Remarks: Conglomerates, Tuesday, March 11, 1969." In *Congressional Record: Proceedings and Debates of the 91st Congress*, 115: 6029–32. Washington, DC: US Government, 1969.

Haug, Marie R. "Deprofessionalization: An Alternate Hypothesis for the Future." *The Sociological Review Monograph Series* 20, no. S1 (1973): 195–211.

Hayek, Friedrich A. "The Use of Knowledge in Society." *American Economic Review*, no. 35 (September 1945): 519–30.

Heisner, Beverly. *Hollywood Art: Art Direction in the Days of the Great Studios*. Jefferson, MO: McFarland, 1990.

Henehan, Mark. "Shapers of the Future." *Input for Modern Management* 5, no. 1 (1969): 12–15.

Henni, Samia. *Colonial Toxicity: Rehearsing French Nuclear Architecture and Landscape in the Sahara*. Amsterdam: Framer Framed, 2024.

Higgs, Robert. *Depression, War, and Cold War: Studies in Political Economy*. Oakland, CA: Independent Institute, 2006.

Hiltzik, Michael A. *Dealer of Lightning: Xerox PARC and the Dawn of the Computer Age*. New York: HarperCollins, 1999.

Hitchcock, Henry-Russell. "The Architecture of Bureaucracy and the Architecture of Genius." *Architectural Review*, no. 101 (1947): 3–6.

Hobbes, Thomas. *Leviathan, or The Matter, Forme and Power of a Common Wealth Ecclesiasticall and Civil*. New York: Cosimo, 2009 [1651].
Holland, Max. *When the Machine Stopped: A Cautionary Tale from Industrial America*. Boston: Harvard Business School Press, 1989.
Holleman, Thomas J., and James P. Gallagher. *Smith, Hinchman & Grylls: 125 Years of Architecture and Engineering, 1853-1978*. Detroit, MI: Wayne State University Press, 1978.
hooks, bell. *Teaching to Transgress: Education as the Practice of Freedom*. New York: Routledge, 1994.
Horkheimer, Max, and Theodor Adorno. "The Culture Industry: Enlightenment as Mass Deception [1944]." In *Dialectic of Enlightenment*, edited by Gunzelin S. Noerr. Stanford, CA: Stanford University Press, 2002.
Houdart, Sophie, and Chihiro Minato. *Kuma Kengo: une monographie décalée*. Paris: Ed. Donner Lieu, 2009.
Howell-Ardila, Deborah. "The USC Connection: Origins and Context in the Work of Whitney R. Smith." In *Outside In: The Architecture of Smith and Williams*, 89-105. Los Angeles: Art, Design & Architecture Museum, University of California, Santa Barbara in Association with Getty Publications, 2014.
———. "'Writing Our Own Program': The USC Experiment in Modern Architectural Pedagogy, 1930 to 1960." Master's thesis, University of Southern California, 2010.
Hua, Xiahong. *Shanghai Urban Planning Design and Research Institute/Shanghai Xiandai Architectural Design Group*. Shanghai: Tongji University Press, 2014.
Hughes, Thomas P. *American Genesis: A Century of Invention and Technological Enthusiasm, 1870-1970*, 2nd ed. Chicago: University of Chicago Press, 2004.
———. "From Firm to Networked Systems." *The Business History Review* 7, no. 3 (2005): 587-93.
Hugo, Victor. *The Hunchback of Notre Dame*. New York: Hyperion, 1996 [1831].
Hyman, Louis. *Temp: How American Work, American Business, and the American Dream Became Temporary*. New York: Viking, 2018.
Immerwahr, Daniel. *How to Hide an Empire: A History of the Greater United States*. New York: Farrar, Straus and Giroux, 2020.
Inaba, Jeffrey, and Peter Zellner. *Whatever Happened to LA? Architectural and Urban Experiments, 1970-1990*. Los Angeles: SCI-Arc, 2005.
Industry Week. "Plant Design Allows for Change." March 25, 1974, 83-91.
ITT World Communications. "Indonesia Enters Space Age with Earth Satellite Station." Press release, September 29, 1969. https://d3s05znv45ku4h

.cloudfront.net/Box+021/011_Telecommunications+Meetings+ITT,+1969 .pdf (accessed November 4, 2022).

Jacobs, Norman. *Modernization without Development: Thailand as an Asian Case Study*. New York: Praeger, 1971.

Jacobson, Brian R., ed. *In the Studio: Visual Creation and Its Material Environments*. Oakland: University of California Press, 2020.

Jacoby, Neil H. "The Conglomerate Corporation." *Financial Analysts Journal* 26, no. 3 (June 1970): 35–38, 40–42, 44–48.

Jameson, Fredric. "The Brick and the Balloon: Architecture, Idealism, and Land Speculation." *New Left Review*, March–April 1998.

———. "Postmodernism, or the Cultural Logic of Late Capitalism." *New Left Review*, no. 146 (August 1984).

Jencks, Charles. *Architecture Today*. New York: H. N. Abrams, 1988.

———. *Heteropolis: Los Angeles, the Riots and the Strange Beauty of Hetero-Architecture*. New York: St. Martin's Press, 1993.

———. *The Language of Post-Modern Architecture*. New York: Rizzoli, 1977.

———. *Late-Modern Architecture and Other Essays*. New York: Rizzoli, 1980.

———. *The New Moderns: From Late to Neo-Modernism*. New York: Rizzoli, 1990.

———. *The Story of Post-Modernism: Five Decades of the Ironic, Iconic and Critical in Architecture*. Chichester, UK: Wiley, 2011.

Jenkins, Frank. *Architect and Patron*. London: Oxford, 1960.

Jessop, Bob. "Fordism and Post-Fordism: A Critical Reformulation." In *Pathways to Industrialization and Regional Development*, edited by Michael Storper and Allen J. Scott, 42–62. London: Routledge, 1992.

Job, Peter. "Foreign Capital Flows Back into Indonesia." *Bangkok World*, February 19, 1968.

Johnston, George Barnett. *Assembling the Architect: The History and Theory of Professional Practice*. London: Bloomsbury Visual Arts, 2020.

———. *Drafting Culture: A Social History of Architectural Graphic Standards*. Cambridge, MA: MIT Press, 2008.

Jones, Caroline. "The Romance of the Studio and the Abstract Expressionist Sublime." In *Machine in the Studio: Constructing the Postwar American Artist*, 1–59. Chicago: University of Chicago Press, 1998.

Jones, Geoffrey. "Multinational from the 1930s to the 1980s." In *Leviathans: Multinational Corporations and the New Global History*, edited by Alfred D. Chandler Jr. and Bruce Mazlish, 81–104. Cambridge: Cambridge University Press, 2005.

Jones, Paul. *The Sociology of Architecture: Constructing Identities.* Liverpool, UK: Liverpool University Press, 2011.

Jung, Hyun-Tae. "Organization and Abstraction: The Architecture of Skidmore, Owings & Merrill from 1936 to 1956." PhD diss., Columbia University, 2011.

Karousatos, Fotis N. "Letter to Vahe Khachooni," March 23, 1972. Papers of Vahe Khachooni. Private collection.

Kates, Joan Giangrasse. "Robert Johnston Piper, 1926–2010." *Chicago Tribune*, November 16, 2010. https://www.chicagotribune.com/2010/11/16/robert-johnston-piper-1926-2010-2/.

Kennard, Robert A, and Wesley H Henderson. *African-American Architects of Los Angeles: Robert A. Kennard.* Los Angeles: Oral History Program, UCLA, 1995.

Kenney, Martin, and Richard Florida. "Venture Capital in Silicon Valley: Fueling New Firm Formation." In *Understanding Silicon Valley: The Anatomy of an Entrepreneurial Region*, edited by Martin Kenney, 71–97. Stanford, CA: Stanford University Press, 2003.

Kepos, Paula, and Thomas Derdak, eds. *International Directory of Company Histories, vol. 11.* Chicago: St. James Press, 1995.

Keyes, Charles F. *Isan: Regionalism in Northeastern Thailand.* Ithaca, NY: Cornell University, 1967.

Khachooni, Vahe. "Letter to Stu Rose," March 27, 1972. Papers of Vahe Khachooni. Private collection.

Kim, Jaechun. "US Covert Action in Indonesia in the 1960s: Assessing the Motives and Consequences." *Journal of International and Area Studies* 9, no. 2 (2002): 63–85.

King, Jonathan, and Philip Langdon, eds. *The CRS Team and the Business of Architecture.* College Station: Texas A&M University Press, 2002.

Klein, Naomi. *The Shock Doctrine: The Rise of Disaster Capitalism.* London: Penguin Books, 2008.

Klingmann, Anna. *Brandscapes: Architecture in the Experience Economy.* Cambridge, MA: MIT Press, 2007.

Knox, Paul L., and Peter J. Taylor. "Toward a Geography of the Globalization of Architecture Office Networks." *Journal of Architectural Education* 58, no. 3 (February 2005): 23–32.

Koehler, Robert E. "Luckman Tells All About Ogden." *AIA Journal*, June 1970, 52–55.

Konkel, Paul. "Getting in Step with CAEDS." *DMJM Review*, 1978.

Kostof, Spiro. *The Architect: Chapters in the History of the Profession.* Berkeley: University of California Press, 1977.

Krause, Elliott A. *Death of the Guilds: Professions, States, and the Advance of Capitalism, 1930 to the Present.* New Haven, CT: Yale University Press, 1999.

Krum, Wendy G. "Architects in the Development Process: Emerging Professional Roles." Master's thesis, Massachusetts Institute of Technology, 1981.

Kubo, Michael. "The Anxiety of Anonymity: On the Historiographic Problem of Walter Gropius and The Architects Collaborative." In *Terms of Appropriation: Modern Architecture and Global Exchange*, edited by Amanda Reeser Lawrence and Ana Miljački. New York: Routledge, 2017.

———. "Architecture Incorporated: Authorship, Anonymity, and Collaboration in Postwar Modernism." PhD diss., Massachusetts Institute of Technology, 2017.

Kudroff, Marvin J. "The First Titan Hardened Facilities." *Aerospace Engineering*, June 1961, 10–11, 41–46.

Lamoreaux, Naomi R. *The Great Merger Movement in American Business, 1895–1904.* Cambridge: Cambridge University Press, 1988.

Lamoreaux, Naomi R., Daniel M. G. Raff, and Peter Temin. "Beyond Markets and Hierarchies: Toward a New Synthesis of American Business History." *The American Historical Review* 109, no. 2 (2003): 404–33.

Landau, Sarah Bradford. *George B. Post, Architect: Picturesque Designer and Determined Realist.* New York: Monacelli Press, 1998.

Lange, Alexandra. "Tower Typewriter and Trademark: Architects, Designers and the Corporate Utopia, 1956–1964." PhD diss., New York University, 2005.

Langlois, Richard N. *The Corporation and the Twentieth Century: The History of American Business Enterprise.* Princeton, NJ: Princeton University Press, 2023.

Lapidus, Morris. *Architecture: A Profession and a Business.* New York: Reinhold, 1967.

Larouche, Lyndon Marcus. "The Third Stage of Imperialism." In *Readings in U.S. Imperialism*, edited by K. T. Fann and Donald C. Hodges. Boston: Porter Sargent, 1971.

Larson, Magali Sarfatti. *Behind the Postmodern Facade: Architectural Change in Late Twentieth-Century America.* Berkeley: University of California Press, 1995.

———. "The Development of Modern Professions: Monopolies of Competence and Bourgeois Ideology." PhD diss., University of California, Berkeley, 1974.

———. "Emblem and Exception: The Historical Definition of the Architect's Professional Role." In *Professionals and Urban Form*, edited by Judith Blau, Mark La Gory, and John S. Pipkin, 49–86. Albany, NY: SUNY Press, 1983.

———. "Notes on Technocracy: Some Problems of Theory, Ideology, and Power." *Berkeley Journal of Sociology* 17, no. 5 (1972), 7.
———. "Practice and Education in 21st Century Architecture: A Sociologist's View." In *Quid Novi? Dilemas do ensino de arquitetura no seculo 21*, edited by Fernando Lara and Sonia Marques. Austin, TX: nhamericapress, 2015.
———. "Professions Today: Self-Criticism and Reflections for the Future." *Sociologia: Problemas e Praticas* 88 (2018): 27-42.
———. *The Rise of Professionalism: A Sociological Analysis*. Berkeley: University of California Press, 1977.
Laskey, Marlene L., ed. *Rebel and Architect Oral History Transcript, 1988-1989: Zelma Wilson*. Los Angeles: Oral History Program, UCLA, 1994.
Latour, Bruno. "On Recalling Ant." *The Sociological Review* 47, no. 1 (May 1999): 15-25.
———. *Reassembling the Social: An Introduction to Actor-Network-Theory*. Oxford: Oxford University Press, 2005.
———. *War of the Worlds: What about Peace?* Edited by John Tresch. Translated by Charlotte Bigg. Chicago: Prickly Paradigm Press, 2002.
———. "Where Are the Missing Masses? The Sociology of a Few Mundane Artifacts." In *Shaping Technology/Building Society: Studies in Sociotechnical Change*, edited by Wiebe E. Bijker and John Law, 225-58. Cambridge, MA: MIT Press, 1992.
Latour, Bruno, and Steve Woolgar. *Laboratory Life: The Construction of Scientific Facts*. Princeton, NJ: Princeton University Press, 1986 [1979].
Latour, Bruno, and Albena Yaneva. "Give Me a Gun and I Will Make All Buildings Move: An ANT's View of Architecture." In *Explorations in Architecture: Teaching, Design, Research*, edited by Geiser Reto, 80-89. Basel, Switzerland: Birkhauser, 2008.
Lavin, Sylvia. *Architecture Itself and Other Postmodernization Effects*. Montreal: Canadian Center for Architecture and Spector Books, 2020.
———. "History for an Empty Future." *E-Flux*, October 2016. https://www.e-flux.com/architecture/superhumanity/68713/history-for-an-empty-future/.
———. "Reclaiming Plant Architecture." *Eflux*, August 2019. https://www.e-flux.com/architecture/positions/280202/reclaiming-plant-architecture/.
Lazzarato, Maurizio. *Governing by Debt*. Semiotext(e) Intervention Series 17. South Pasadena, CA: Semiotext(e), 2015.
———. "Immaterial Labor." In *Radical Thought in Italy: A Potential Politics*, edited by Paolo Virno and Michael Hardt, 132-47. Minneapolis: University of Minnesota Press, 1996.

Le Corbusier. *Aircraft*. London: Trefoil, 1935.

Leach, Neil. "The (Ac)credit(ation) Card." In *The Architect as Worker: Immaterial Labor the Creative Class, and the Politics of Design*, edited by Peggy Deamer, 228–40. London: Bloomsbury Academic, 2016.

LeBaron, Dean, and Lawrence S. Speidell. "Why Are the Parts Worth More Than the Sum? 'Chop Shop,' a Corporate Valuation Model." In *The Merger Boom*, edited by L. E. Browne and E. S. Rosengren. Boston: Federal Reserve Bank of Boston, 1987.

Lebovic, Sam. *Free Speech and Unfree News: The Paradox of Press Freedom in America*. Cambridge, MA: Harvard University Press, 2016.

Lenin, Vladimir. "Imperialism, the Highest Stage of Capitalism." In *Lenin: Selected Works, vol. 1*, 715–19. Moscow: Progress, 1963.

Leo, John. "'Report' on Peace Gets Mixed Views." *The New York Times*, November 5, 1967.

Leonhard, William E. "Letter to S. K. Johnson," March 14, 1958. Stanley Moe Papers. Huntington Library, San Marino, CA.

Leslie, Stuart W. "The Biggest 'Angel' of Them All: The Military and the Making of Silicon Valley." In *Understanding Silicon Valley: The Anatomy of an Entrepreneurial Region*, edited by Martin Kenney, 48–70. Stanford, CA: Stanford University Press, 2003.

Lévi-Strauss, Claude. *Structural Anthropology*. New York: Basic Books, 1963.

Levin, Ayala. *Architecture and Development: Israeli Construction in Sub-Saharan Africa and the Settler Colonial Imagination, 1958–1973*. Durham, NC: Duke University Press, 2022.

Levinson, Marc. *An Extraordinary Time: The End of the Postwar Boom and the Return of the Ordinary Economy*. New York: Basic Books, 2016.

Lewin, Leonard C. *Report from Iron Mountain: On the Possibility & Desirability of Peace*. New York: Dial Press, 1967.

Lichtenstein, Nelson. *Labor's War at Home: The CIO in World War II*. Philadelphia: Temple University Press, 2010.

Lindee, M. Susan. *Rational Fog: Science and Technology in Modern War*. Cambridge, MA: Harvard University Press, 2020.

Ling, Isabel. "Inside the Historic Union Drive at SHoP Architects." *Curbed*, February 4, 2022. https://www.curbed.com/2022/02/shop-architects-union-drive-shuts-down.html.

Lintner, John. "The Valuation of Risk Assets and the Selection of Risky Investments in Stock Portfolios and Capital Budgets." *The Review of Economics and Statistics* 47, no. 1 (February 1965): 13.

Litke, Ronald. "Perkins & Will: The First 50 Years." *Inland Architect*, October 1985, 11–15.
Long, Derek. *Playing the Percentages: How Film Distribution Made the Hollywood Studio System*. Austin: University of Texas Press, 2024.
Lonnquest, John C., and David F. Winkler. *To Defend and Deter: The Legacy of the United States Cold War Missile Program*. Washington, DC: US Department of Defense, 1996.
López, Albert José-Antonio. "The Technical State: Programs, Positioning, and the Integration of Architects in Political Society in Mexico, 1945–1955." In *Architecture in Development: Systems and the Emergence of the Global South*, edited by Aggregate [Group], 161–78. New York: Routledge, 2022.
Los Angeles Times. "AIA Announces '76 Design Awards." October 31, 1976.
———. "Architectural Firm Joins in New Program." October 7, 1962, M22.
———. "Data Processing Firm Acquired." September 21, 1975.
———. "High Rise Features Rare Wood." May 21, 1972.
———. "Hummel New DMJM Officer." July 8, 1984.
———. "One Park Plaza Gets Eight New Tenants." April 23, 1972.
———. "S. B. Nelson Returns to DMJM Post." January 10, 1971.
———. "Trio of Major Units to Rise: Three Projects Announced to Cost $1,000,000 Each; Unique Structure Goes Up at Lafayette Park Place; Temple and Store Addition Figure in Activity." October 2, 1929.
———. "Underground Computers: Univac Leases Area for Marketing Office." October 22, 1972, D17.
———. "Work Rushed on Atom War Proof Vaults: Caves in New York Will Be Used to Store Treasures." May 13, 1951.
Loukissas, Yanni. *Co-Designers: Cultures of Computer Simulation in Architecture*. New York: Routledge, 2012.
Lowry, Cynthia. "Old Iron Mountain Now Atom-Proof Storage Vault." *The Washington Post*, June 15, 1952.
Lubatkin, Michael. "Mergers and the Performance of the Acquiring Firm." *The Academy of Management Review*, April 1983.
Lumsden, Anthony J. "Preconception Analysis." *Space Design*, no. 9311 (November 1993): 6–11.
Lyndon, Joyce Earley. "Problem: Landscaping the Santa Monica Mountains." *Arts and Architecture*, 1966, 38.
Magdoff, Harry, and Paul M. Sweezy. "Notes on the Multinational Corporation." In *Readings in U.S. Imperialism*, edited by K. T. Fann and Donald C. Hodges. Boston: Porter Sargent, 1971.

Makarem, Hadi. "The Bottom-Up Mobilization of Lebanese Society against Neoliberal Institutions: The Case of Opposition against Solidere's Reconstruction of Downtown Beirut." In *Contentious Politics in the Middle East: Popular Resistance and Marginalized*, edited by Fawaz A. Gerges, 501–22. New York: Palgrave Macmillan, 2015.

Management Methods. "Profile of a New Kind of Manager: How to Pack Pleasure and Profit into a Partnership." September 1957, 26–31, 88–95.

Mandel, Ernest. *Late Capitalism*. London: New Left Books, 1975.

Mann, Arthur. "DMJM Board," May 15, 1981. Family papers of Arthur Mann. Private collection.

———. "Letter to Bill Shope," n.d. Family papers of Arthur Mann. Private collection.

Markowitz, Harry. "Portfolio Selection." *The Journal of Finance* 7, no. 1 (March 1952): 77.

Martin, Reinhold. *The Organizational Complex: Architecture, Media, and Corporate Space*. Cambridge, MA: MIT Press, 2003.

———. *Utopia's Ghost: Architecture and Postmodernism, Again*. Minneapolis: University of Minnesota Press, 2010.

Marx, Leo. *The Machine in the Garden: Technology and the Pastoral Ideal in America*. Oxford: Oxford University Press, 1979.

Matthews, Jay. "Chancellor Schmidt on Busman's Holiday in Bohemian Grove." *The Washington Post*, July 24, 1982. https://www.washingtonpost.com/archive/politics/1982/07/24/chancellor-schmidt-on-busmans-holiday-in-bohemian-grove/2a2806ee-4322-470f-8cad-1675d016ffb0/.

McAlevey, Jane. *No Shortcuts: Organizing for Power in the New Gilded Age*. New York: Oxford University Press, 2016.

McCartney, Laton. *Friends in High Places: The Bechtel Story: The Most Secret Corporation and How It Engineered the World*, revised ed. New York: Ballantine Books, 1989.

McCoy, Esther. "Planned for Change." *Architectural Forum*, August 1968, 102–7.

McDonald, Duff. *The Firm: The Story of McKinsey and Its Secret Influence on American Business*. New York: Simon & Schuster, 2013.

McLeod, Mary. "The End of Innocence: From Political Activism to Postmodernism." In *Architecture School: Three Centuries of Educating Architects in North America*, edited by Joan Ockman, 162–201. Cambridge, MA: MIT Press, 2012.

McMahon, Catherine F. "Predictive Machines: Data, Computer Maps, and Simulation." In *A Second Modernism: MIT, Architecture, and the "Techni-*

Social" Moment, edited by Arindam Dutta, 436–73. Cambridge, MA: MIT Press, 2013.

McMahon, Robert J. *Colonialism and Cold War: The United States and the Struggle for Indonesian Independence, 1945–1949*. Ithaca, NY: Cornell University Press, 1981.

Mesko, Jim. *A-26 Invader in Action*. Carrollton, TX: Squadron/Signal, 1980.

Miet, Hannah. "AECOM to Lease at One California Plaza." *Los Angeles Business Journal*, June 3, 2015. https://labusinessjournal.com/real-estate/aecom-lease-one-california-plaza/.

Miller, William R. "Computer-Aided Space Planning." *Proceedings of the 7th Design Automation Workshop*, 1970.

———. "From Academe to Commercial Use in Ten Years: Computers in Architecture." *Datamation*, September 15, 1971.

Miller, William R., Vahe Khachooni, and James Olsten. "Matrix Method for Grouping an Interrelated Set of Elements." *Proceedings of the 1st Annual Environmental Design Research Association Conference*, 1970.

Missiles and Rockets. "First Hard Site for Titan I Takes Form." September 5, 1960, 32–33.

Mitchell, Melvin L. *The Crisis of the African American Architect: Conflicting Cultures of Architecture and (Black) Power*. Lincoln, NE: Writers Advantage, 2003.

Moe, Stanley Allen. *Right Place, Right Time! The Inspiring Adventures of Stanley A. Moe, Trailblazer, World Traveler, Architect, Storyteller; Making the Most of Life's Possibilities*. Edited by Billie Moe Crouse and Susan Baldwin Stroh. Sandia, NM: Billie Moe Crouse, 2020.

Monteyne, David. *Fallout Shelter: Designing for Civil Defense in the Cold War*. Minneapolis: University of Minnesota Press, 2011.

Moore, Charles, Peter Becker, and Regula Campbell, eds. *The City Observed: Los Angeles: A Guide to Its Architecture and Landscapes*. New York: Vintage Books, 1984.

Morck, Randall, Andrei Shleifer, and Robert W. Vishney. "Do Managerial Objectives Drive Bad Acquisitions?" *Journal of Finance* 45 (1990).

Morris, Jennifer. "An Ethnography of Three Michigan Architecture Firms: The Effect of Organizational Culture on Workplace Client Engagement." PhD diss., University of Michigan, 2019.

Morton, David. "Anti-gravitational Mass." *Progressive Architecture*, July 1976, 66–69.

Mozingo, Louise A. *Pastoral Capitalism: A History of Suburban Corporate Landscapes*. Cambridge, MA: MIT Press, 2011.

Mulvey, Laura. "Visual Pleasure and Narrative Cinema." In *The Bloomsbury Anthology of Aesthetics*, n.d.

Muzaffar, Ijlal. *Modernism's Magic Hat: Architecture and the Illusion of Development without Capital*. Austin: University of Texas Press, 2024.

Nairn, Janet. "Building Types Study 509: College Buildings." *Architectural Record* 162, no. 7 (1977): 109–24.

National Architectural Accrediting Board. *Conditions for Accreditation*. Washington, DC: NAAB, 2020.

National Park Service. "Henry T. Sisson." Civil War Soldiers and Sailors System, July 11, 2011. http://www.civilwar.nps.gov/cwss/soldiers.cfm.

Naughten, Thomas E. "Letter to Barry F Mountain, DMJM," October 5, 1959. Record Group 469, Series Central Subject Files. US National Archives.

Navasky, Victor. "Conspiracy Theory Is a Hoax Gone Wrong." *New York Magazine*, November 15, 2013. https://nymag.com/news/features/conspiracy-theories/iron-mountain-hoax/.

Navy Civil Engineer. "Need for Blast Shelters Sparks Careers of Two Reserve CECs." Vol. 1 (1960).

NCARB. "Dwight M. Bonham, FAIA." https://www.ncarb.org/about/history-ncarb/past-presidents/dwight-bonham. Accessed June 12, 2023.

Nesbit, Jeffrey S. *Ground Control: A Design History of Technical Lands and NASA's Space Complex*. New York: Routledge, 2024.

The New York Times. "Company News: Ashland's Future May Not Be in Oil: Competitive Edge Sought in Diversity." December 1, 1980, D4.

———. "Upstate Iron Mine Atom-Proof Vault." September 30, 1962.

Newman, James R. "Control of Information Relating to Atomic Energy." *Yale Law Journal* 56 (47 1946): 769–802.

Norwood, Bryan. "The Architect's Knowledge: Imagining the Profession's Historical Body, 1797–1883." PhD diss., Harvard University, 2018.

Oakeshott, Michael. *On History and Other Essays*. Indianapolis, IN: Liberty Fund, 1999.

O'Connor, Jack. *NPIC: Seeing the Secrets and Growing the Leaders: A Cultural History of the National Photographic Interpretation Center*. Alexandria, VA: Acumensa Solutions, 2015.

Office of Civil and Defense Mobilization. "Text of Director Hoegh's Address to a Symposium on Records Preservation." *Information Bulletin*, no. 172 (March 7, 1960). https://www.cia.gov/readingroom/docs/CIA-RDP70-00211 R001000200001-9.pdf.

O'Green, Fred W. *Putting Technology to Work: The Story of Litton Industries*. New York: Newcomen Society of the United States, 1988.

O'Leary, Michael. "Database: Douglas Invader." *Aeroplane* 30, no. 5 (May 2002): 37–58.

Ortner, Sherry B. *Anthropology and Social Theory: Culture, Power, and the Acting Subject*. Durham, NC: Duke University Press, 2006.

———. *High Religion: A Cultural and Political History of Sherpa Buddhism*. Princeton, NJ: Princeton University Press, 1989.

———. "On Neoliberalism." *Anthropology of This Century*, no. 1 (May 2011).

Osman, Mary E. "The Intern Program: A Progress Report." *AIA Journal*, December 1979, 47, 63, 71.

Osman, Michael. *Modernism's Visible Hand: Architecture and Regulation in America*. Minneapolis: University of Minnesota Press, 2018.

Owings, Nathaniel. *The Spaces in Between: An Architect's Journey*. Wilmington, MA: Houghton Mifflin, 1973.

Pai, Hyungmin. *The Portfolio and the Diagram: Architecture, Discourse, and Modernity in America*. Cambridge, MA: MIT Press, 2002.

Palmer, Sarah, ed. *Architecture at Work: DMJM Design Los Angeles*. New York: Edizioni Press, 2004.

Parsons, Talcott. "The Professions and Social Structure." *Social Forces* 17, no. 4 (May 1939): 457–67.

Pastier, John. *Cesar Pelli*. Monographs in Contemporary Architecture. New York: Whitney Library of Design, 1980.

———. "What's Brown—Brown All Over?" *Los Angeles Times*, October 28, 1974.

Paul, Daniel D. "The Aesthetics of Efficiency: Contexts and the Early Development of Late-Modern Glass Skin Architecture." Master's thesis, California State University, Northridge, 2004.

Peleggi, Maurizio. "Excavating Southeast Asia's Prehistory in the Cold War: American Archaeology in Neocolonial Thailand." *Journal of Social Archaeology* 16, no. 1 (2016): 94–111.

People v. Allied Architects Association of Los Angeles. No. LA 9482. Supreme Court of California, June 20, 1927.

Perkins, Bradford. "Mergers and Acquisitions: An Outline: Marriage Manual for Architectural Firms." *AIA Journal*, 1976, 46.

Perkins, John. *The New Confessions of an Economic Hit Man*. London: Ebury Press UK, 2018.

Perkins & Will. "Firm Profile." https://perkinswill.com. Accessed December 12, 2017.

Peterson, York. "Memorandum to 'All Drillers' Re: Overtime," September 30, 1958. US National Archives, US Foreign Assistance Agencies.

Pfeifer, Stuart, and Chris Kirkham. "Merger of AECOM and URS to Create Giant LA Construction Firm." *Los Angeles Times*, July 13, 2014. https://www.latimes.com/business/la-fi-aecom-merger-20140714-story.html.

Phillips, Cushing. "Letter to DMJM," May 4, 1956. Stanley Moe Papers. Huntington Library, San Marino, CA.

Pierpaoli, Paul G., Jr. *Truman and Korea: The Political Culture of the Early Cold War*. Columbia, MO: University of Missouri, 1999.

Pine, B. Joseph, and James H. Gilmore. *The Experience Economy: Work Is Theatre & Every Business a Stage*. Boston: Harvard Business School Press, 1999.

Polenberg, Richard. *War and Society: The United States, 1941–1945*. New York: Lippincott Williams & Wilkins, 1972.

Polledri, Sharon Lee. "Architectural Services from a Developer's Point of View." *Architecture California* 13, no. 3 (December 1991): 50–52.

Popper, Karl. *The Open Society and Its Enemies*. London: Routledge, 2002.

Porter, C. W. "Letter to Daniel, Mann, Johnson & Mendenhall," July 6, 1956. Stanley Moe Papers. Huntington Library, San Marino, CA.

Porter, Theodore M. *Trust in Numbers: The Pursuit of Objectivity in Science and Public Life*. Princeton, NJ: Princeton University Press, 1995.

Powell, Walter W. "The Capitalist Firm in the 21st Century." In *The Twenty-First-Century Firm*, edited by Paul DiMaggio, 33–68. Princeton, NJ: Princeton University Press, 2001.

Powers, Mary B. "US Court Disputes $1.8B AECOM Damage Award in 'Remarkable Fraud' Suit." *Engineering News-Record*, March 28, 2021.

Progressive Architecture. "Profile: Daniel, Mann, Johnson and Mendenhall: A Summation of Parts." June 1972, 72–83.

———. "Technological Imagery: Turnpike Version." August 1970, 70–75.

Quill, Lawrence. *Secrets and Democracy: From Arcana Imperii to WikiLeaks*. Houndmills, Basingstoke, UK: Palgrave Macmillan, 2014.

Rabson, Steve. "Henko and the US Military: A History of Dependence and Resistance." *Asia-Pacific Journal* 10, no. 2 (2012). https://apjjf.org/2012/10/4/steve-rabson/3680/article.

Rand, Ayn. *The Fountainhead*. New York: Bobbs-Merrill, 1943.

Reed, Howard H. "Letter to Jack Lipmann," May 28, 1953. Stanley Moe Papers. Huntington Library, San Marino, CA.

Ren, Xuefei. *Building Globalization: Transnational Architecture Production in Urban China*. Chicago: University of Chicago Press, 2011.

Richardson, J. D. *A Compilation of Messages and Papers of the Presidents, 1789–1897*, vol. 1. Washington, DC: US Government Printing Office, 1896.

Ricker, N. Clifford. "Results of License Law for Architects in Illinois." *The Brickbuilder* 10 (February 1901): 28–31.

Rickey, Carrie. "Art Directors: Theatrical Realism." *Film Comment* 18, no. 1 (1982): 32–33.

Riddle, Danette. "Building on Change." In *Architecture at Work: DMJM Design Los Angeles*, 14–21. New York: Edizioni Press, 2004.

Riggs, Fred W. *Thailand: The Modernization of a Bureaucratic Polity*. Honolulu: East-West Center Press, 1966.

Roberts, Bryony, ed. "Expanding Modes of Practice." *Log* 38 (2020).

Roberts, G. A., and Robert J. McVicker. *Distant Force: A Memoir of the Teledyne Corporation and the Man Who Created It, with an Introduction to Teledyne Technologies*. Self-published by George A. Roberts, 2007.

Roche, Daniel. "Organizing Shop: Follow the Sweat Equity." *New York Review of Architecture*, February 17, 2022. https://newyork.substack.com/p/organizing-shop.

———. "Union at Bernheimer Architecture Ratifies Collective Bargaining Agreement." *The Architect's Newspaper*, July 25, 2024. https://www.archpaper.com/2024/07/union-bernheimer-architecture-ratifies-collective-bargaining-agreement.

Rodengen, Jeffrey L., ed. *AECOM: 20 Years and Counting*. Fort Lauderdale, FL: Write Stuff Enterprises, 2010.

Rosenberg, Max. "USAF Ballistic Missiles 1958–1959." USAF Historical Division Liaison Office, July 1960. National Security Archive, George Washington University, Washington, DC.

Ross, Liam. "Creative Uncertainty: Arup Associates, Fire Safety, and the Metaengineering of Government." In *Neoliberalism on the Ground*, edited by Kenny Cupers, Helena Mattson, and Catharina Gabrielsson, 270–93. Pittsburgh, PA: University of Pittsburgh Press, 2020.

Ross, Michael Franklin. "The Development of an Esthetic System at DMJM." *Architectural Record*, May 1975, 111–20.

Rostow, Walt. *The Stages of Economic Growth: A Non-Communist Manifesto*. Cambridge: Cambridge University Press, 1960.

Rothkopf, David J. *Superclass: The Global Power Elite and the World They Are Making*. New York: Farrar, Straus and Giroux, 2009.

Rourke, James. "Wings over West Africa." *International Commerce*, 1965.

Russell, William Bradley, Jr. "A Convenient Blanket of Secrecy: The Oft-Cited but Nonexisting Housekeeping Privilege." *William & Mary Bill of Rights Journal* 14, no. 2 (June 2005): 745-73.

Rybczynski, Witold. "Economic Downturns and the Architectural Profession." *Review: Zell & Lurie Real Estate Center*, 2009, 85-92.

Sachs, Avigail. "Environmental Design and the Expansion of Architectural Practice, 1937-1973." PhD diss., University of California, Berkeley, 2009.

Sahlins, Marshall. *Historical Metaphors and Mythical Realities: Structure in the Early History of the Sandwich Islands Kingdom*. Ann Arbor: University of Michigan Press, 1981.

Saint, Andrew. *Architect and Engineer: A Study in Sibling Rivalry*. New Haven, CT: Yale University Press, 2007.

———. *The Image of the Architect*. New Haven, CT: Yale University Press, 1983.

Saliba, Robert. *Urban Design in the Arab World: Reconceptualizing Boundaries*. New York: Routledge, 2015.

Sampson, Anthony. *The Sovereign State: The Secret History of ITT*. London: Hodder and Stoughton, 1973.

Sapers, Carl M. "The Case for Licensing Law Reforms." *AIA Journal*, November 1969, 52-56.

Schatz, Tom. "The Studio System and Conglomerate Hollywood." In *The Contemporary Hollywood Film Industry*, edited by Paul McDonald and Janet Wasko, 13-39. Oxford: Blackwell, 2008.

Schulman, Bruce J. *From Cotton Belt to Sunbelt: Federal Policy, Economic Development, and the Transformation of the South, 1938-1980*. Durham, NC: Duke University Press, 1994.

Schuman, Tony. "Professionalization and the Social Goals of Architects: A History of the Federation of Architects, Engineers, Chemists, and Technicians." In *The Design Professions and the Built Environment*, edited by Paul L. Knox, 12-41. New York: Nichols, 1988.

Schwartzman, Daniel. "Finance." *Oculus*, August 1964, 9.

Schwarzer, Mitchell. "The Sources of Architectural Nationalism." In *Nationalism and Architecture*, edited by Raymond Quek, Darren Deane, and Sarah Butler, 19-38. Farnham, UK: Ashgate, 2012.

Scott, Allen J. *Technopolis: High-Technology Industry and Regional Development in Southern California*. Berkeley: University of California Press, 1993.

Scott, Allen J., and Edward W. Soja. "Los Angeles: Capital of the Late Twentieth Century." *Society and Space*, no. 4 (1986): 249-54.

———, eds. *The City: Los Angeles and Urban Theory at the End of the Twentieth Century*. Berkeley: University of California Press, 2005.

Scott, James C. *Seeing Like a State: How Certain Schemes to Improve the Human Condition Have Failed*. New Haven, CT: Yale University Press, 1999.

Seiden, Daniel. "AECOM Whistleblower to Argue War Needs Trumped Afghanistan Fraud." *Bloomberg Law*, May 20, 2021. https://news.bloomberglaw.com/federal-contracting/aecom-whistleblower-to-argue-war-needs-trumped-afghanistan-fraud.

Servín, Manuel P., and Iris Wilson Engstran. *Southern California and Its University: A History of USC, 1880–1964*. Pasadena, CA: Ward Ritchie Press, 1969.

Seward, Aaron. "Making It Big." *Architects Newspaper*, June 16, 2010. https://archpaper.com/2010/06/making-it-big/.

Shair, Kamal A. *Out of the Middle East: The Emergence of an Arab Global Business*. London: I. B. Tauris, 2006.

Shanken, Andrew Michael. *194X: Architecture, Planning, and Consumer Culture on the American Home Front*. Minneapolis: University of Minnesota Press, 2009.

Shvartzberg Carrió, Manuel. "Infrastructures of Dependency: US Steel's Architectural Assemblages on Indigenous Lands." In *Architecture in Development: Systems and the Emergence of the Global South*, edited by Aggregate [Group], 217–36. New York: Routledge, 2022.

Simonds, W. J. *The Columbia Basin Project*. Denver, CO: Bureau of Reclamation History Program, 1998.

Sinykin, Dan. *Big Fiction: How Conglomeration Changed the Publishing Industry and American Literature*. New York: Columbia University Press, 2023.

Sisson, Henry T. "Temporary Binder." US Patent 18,994, issued December 29, 1857.

Sklarek, Norma M., and Wesley H. Henderson. *African-American Architects of Los Angeles: Norma Merrick Sklarek*. Los Angeles: Oral History Program, UCLA, 1994.

Slayton, William L. "Letter to Victor Khachooni," October 15, 1971. Papers of Vahe Khachooni. Private collection.

Slotten, Hugh. "Satellite Communications, Globalization, and the Cold War." *Technology and Culture* 43, no. 2 (April 2002): 315–50.

Smeins, Linda E. *Building an American Identity: Pattern Book Homes and Communities*. Walnut Creek, CA: AltaMira Press, 1999.

Smith, Adam. *The Wealth of Nations: Books I–III*. Edited by Andrew Skinner. London: Penguin, 2003 [1776].

———. *The Wealth of Nations: Books IV-V*. Edited by Andrew Skinner. London: Penguin, 2004 [1776].

Smith, Arthur. "The Transformation of Tientsin." *The Congregationalist*, February 1901, 173-76.

Smith, Doug. "Regional Water Authority Collides with Growth of Metropolitan Area." *Los Angeles Times*, January 27, 1977.

Smith, Douglas K., and Robert C. Alexander. *Fumbling the Future: How Xerox Invented, Then Ignored, the First Personal Computer*. New York: Morrow, 1999.

Smith, Elberton R. *The Army and Economic Mobilization*. Washington, DC: US Army, 1959.

Smith, W. B. "DMJM in Architecture." *DMJM Review*, September 1976.

Smith, William D. "Changes Salted at Storage Area." *The New York Times*, September 30, 1962.

Smithson, Alison, and Peter Smithson. *Italian Thoughts*. Self-published, Stockholm, Sweden, 1993.

Soja, Edward W. *Postmodern Geographies: The Reassertion of Space in Critical Social Theory*. New York: Verso, 1989.

Soules, Matthew. *Icebergs, Zombies, and the Ultra Thin: Architecture and Capitalism in the Twenty-First Century*. New York: Princeton Architectural Press, 2021.

Southern, Pat, and Karen R. Dixon. *The Late Roman Army*. New Haven, CT: Yale University Press, 1996.

Southwest Builder and Contractor. "Daniel, Mann, Johnson & Mendenhall: How Teamwork Has Built a Thriving Architect-Engineer Firm." September 27, 1957.

Space Design. "CRS: Design in a Process-Oriented Firm." March 1980, 22-23.

Special Commission for the Commonwealth of Massachusetts. "Final Report to the General Court of the Special Commission Concerning State and County Buildings." Boston, December 31, 1980.

Spellman, Catherine, and Karl Unglaub, eds. *Peter Smithson: Conversations with Students: A Space for Our Generation*. New York: Princeton Architectural Press, 2005.

Spencer, Brett. "Rise of the Shadow Libraries: America's Quest to Save Its Information and Culture from Nuclear Destruction during the Cold War." *Information & Culture* 29, no. 2 (2014): 145-76.

Spencer, Chelsea. "The Contract, the Contractor, and the Capitalization of American Building, 1873-1930." PhD diss., Massachusetts Institute of Technology, 2024.

———. "The Word Processing of Watergate and the Metaphysics of Information." *Grey Room*, no. 84 (August 26, 2021): 112–32.

Spencer, Douglas. *The Architecture of Neoliberalism: How Contemporary Architecture Became an Instrument of Control and Compliance*. New York: Bloomsbury Academic, 2016.

Sperling, John G. *Rebel with a Cause: The Entrepreneur Who Created the University of Phoenix and the For-Profit Revolution in Higher Education*. New York: Wiley, 2000.

Stanek, Łukasz. "Architects from Socialist Countries in Ghana (1957–67): Modern Architecture and Mondialisation." *Journal of the Society of Architectural Historians* 74, no. 4 (2015): 416–42.

Stengers, Isabelle. "Introductory Notes on an Ecology of Practices." *Cultural Studies Review* 11, no. 1 (2005): 183–96.

Stevens, Mary Otis. "Struggle for Place: Women in Architecture: 1920–1960." In *Women in American Architecture: A Historic and Contemporary Perspective*, 88–102. New York: Whitney Library of Design, 1977.

Stevens, Sara. *Developing Expertise: Architecture and Real Estate in Metropolitan America*. New Haven, CT: Yale University Press, 2016.

Stickler, K. D. "Letter to DMJM," July 22, 1958. Stanley Moe Papers. Huntington Library, San Marino, CA.

Stinson, Robert J. "The Money-Makers (and Some Losers): What the Reports Show." *Engineering News-Record*, May 1961, 212–13.

Stoler, Ann Laura. *Along the Archival Grain: Epistemic Anxieties and Colonial Common Sense*. Princeton, NJ: Princeton University Press, 2009.

Storper, Michael, and Susan Christopherson. "Flexible Specialization and Regional Industrial Agglomerations: The Case of the US Motion Picture Industry." *Annals of the Association of American Geographers* 77, no. 1 (1987): 104–17.

Stromseth, Jane E. *The Origins of Flexible Response: NATO'S Debate over Strategy in the 1960s*. New York: St. Martin's Press, 1988.

Stumpf, David K. *Titan II: A History of a Cold War Missile Program*. Fayetteville: University of Arkansas Press, 2000.

Sullivan, Louis H. "On the Historic Styles [1901]." In *Architecture in America: A Battle of Styles*, edited by William A. Coles and Henry H. Reed, 46–47. New York: Appleton-Century-Crofts, 1961.

Sutton, Antony C. *America's Secret Establishment: An Introduction to the Order of Skull & Bones*. Updated reprint. Walterville, OR: Trine Day, 2009.

Tafuri, Manfredo, and K. Michael Hays. "Toward a Critique of Architectural Ideology." In *Architecture Theory since 1968*, 6–35. Cambridge, MA: MIT Press, 1998.

Takeyama, Minoru. "Omni-Rental-Stores: Ni-Ban-Kahn." *The Japan Architect* 45, no. 8–166 (August 1970): 63–69.

———. "The Reinstatement of the Film Membrane." *The Japan Architect* 45, no. 8–166 (August 1970): 70.

Tarrant, John J. *Drucker, the Man Who Invented the Corporate Society*. Boston: Cahners Books, 1976.

The Temple Hoyne Buell Center. *The A&E System: Public Works and Private Interest in Architectural and Engineering Services, 2000–2020*. New York: Trustees of Columbia University, 2020.

Thomas, Amy. "Prejudice and Pragmatism: The Commercial Architect in the Development of Postwar London." *Grey Room* 71 (2018): 88–115.

Thompson, Scott A. *Douglas A-26 and B-26 Invader*. Marlborough, UK: Crowood, 2002.

Tobey, Aaron. "Drawing Management: Corporate Organization, International Practice, and the Making of Computer Aided Design." PhD diss., Yale University, 2024.

Toffler, Alvin. *Future Shock*. New York: Bantam Books, 1971.

Tombesi, Paolo. "Capital Gains and Architectural Losses: The Transformative Journey of Caudill Rowlett Scott (1948–1994)." *Journal of Architectural Education*, 2006, 145–68.

Touba, El Sayed. "Conservation in an Islamic Context: A Case Study of Makkah." Master's thesis, Durham University, 1997.

Traverso, Enzo. *Singular Pasts: The "I" in Historiography*. Translated by Adam Schoene. New York: Columbia University Press, 2023.

United Nations Population Fund. "World Population Dashboard." https://www.unfpa.org/data/world-population-dashboard. Accessed August 12, 2019.

United Nations Statistics Division. "National Accounts." https://unstats.un.org. Accessed June 12, 2019.

United States v. The American Institute of Architects. No. 92–72. US District Court for the District of Columbia, May 17, 1972.

University Extension, UCLA. "Course Catalog: Lifelong Learning." September 23, 1969. Papers of Vahe Khachooni. Private collection.

———. "Course Catalog: Lifelong Learning." March 30, 1970. Papers of Vahe Khachooni. Private collection.

———. "Course Catalog: Lifelong Learning." September 21, 1970. Papers of Vahe Khachooni. Private collection.

Upton, Dell. "Pattern Books and Professionalism: Aspects of the Transformation of Domestic Architecture in America, 1800–1860." *Winterthur Portfolio* 19, no. 2–3 (1984): 105–50.

US Bureau of Labor Statistics. "Current Population Survey: Employed Persons by Detailed Occupation," 2020. https://api.census.gov/data/2020/acs/acs5.

———. "Occupational Employment and Wage Statistics," May 2023. https://www.bls.gov/oes/current/map_changer.htm.

US Bureau of the Census. *Census of Service Industries, Subject Series.* Miscellaneous Subjects, 1987.

———. *Census of Service Industries, Subject Series,* 1970.

———. *Census of Service Industries, Subject Series,* 1972.

———. *Census of Service Industries, Subject Series,* 1977.

———. *Economic Census.* Subject Series: Professional, Scientific, and Technical Services, Establishments and Firm Size, 2012.

———. "Special EEO 2000 Tabulation, Detailed Occupations," November 2021. https://www.census.gov/topics/employment/equal-employment-opportunity-tabulation/guidance/2000-tabulation-data.html.

US Congress. Senate. Committee on Foreign Relations. *Foreign Assistance 1964.* 88th Congress, April 14, 1964.

US Department of Justice, Office of Public Affairs. "United States Joins Lawsuit against AECOM Alleging False Claims in Connection with Hurricane Disaster Relief." Press release, June 3, 2020. https://www.justice.gov/opa/pr/united-states-joins-lawsuit-against-aecom-alleging-false-claims-connection-hurricane-disaster.

———. "AECOM to Pay 11.8 Million to Resolve False Claims Act Allegations in Connection with Hurricane Disaster Relief." Press release, October 24, 2023. https://www.justice.gov/opa/pr/aecom-pay-118-million-resolve-false-claims-act-allegations-connection-hurricane-disaster.

US Department of the Army. *Surveying Computer's Manual: Department of the Army's Technical Manual TM 5-237.* Washington, DC, 1964.

US Federal Trade Commission. "Report of the Federal Trade Commission on the Merger Movement: A Summary Report." Washington, DC, 1948.

US Foreign Assistance Agencies. "Contract between the Government of Thailand and Daniel, Mann, Johnson and Mendenhall, Inc," 1958. US National Archives, US Foreign Assistance Agencies.

US Government Printing Office. *Congressional Record—Senate*, April 23, 1917. https://www.govinfo.gov/content/pkg/GPO-CRECB-1917-pt1-v55/pdf/GPO-CRECB-1917-pt1-v55-28.pdf.

———. "*Congressional Record—Senate*," October 3, 1963. https://www.google.com/books/edition/Congressional_Record/HD_Yq7en75IC?hl=en&gbpv=1&dq=%22this+Russian+empire,+held+together+by+force,+is+the+last+conglomerate+empire%22&pg=PA18741&printsec=frontcover.

———. "Government Procurement and Contracting." Washington, DC, 1969.

———. "Presidential Campaign Activities of 1972, Senate Resolution 60: Watergate and Related Activities, Phase I." Washington, DC, 1973.

———. "The Role of Giant Corporations in the American and World Economies: Automobile Industry." *US Senate, Subcommittee on Monopoly of the Select Committee on Small Business, Washington, DC*, July 11, 1969.

———. "Statement of Robert F. Hastings, President, American Institute of Architects; Accompanied by William L. Slayton, Executive Vice President, and Michael Barker, Director, Urban Programs." Washington, DC, August 2, 1971.

US National Labor Relations Board. "Decisions of National Labor Relations Board: Skidmore, Owings & Merrill," August 23, 1971. https://www.casemine.com/judgement/us/5c8b71b8342cca544f477337.

U.S. News & World Report. "Hoax of Horror? A Book That Shook White House." November 20, 1972.

US War Department. *Technical Manual: Maintenance Policies, Publications, and Forms*. Washington, DC, 1942.

Vaillancourt, Ryan. "The Quiet Giant: With a Massive Roster of Projects, AECOM, and Its 920 Local Employees, Are Poised to Shape the Future of Downtown." *Los Angeles Downtown News*, October 1, 2010. https://www.ladowntownnews.com/news/the-quiet-giant/article_78a5533a-f9bb-5cfa-a838-fd9cbebda5e5.html.

Vale, Lawrence J. *The Limits of Civil Defence in the USA, Switzerland, Britain, and the Soviet Union: The Evolution of Policies since 1945*. Basingstoke, UK: Palgrave Macmillan, 1987.

Vanderbilt, Tom. *Survival City: Adventures among the Ruins of Atomic America*. New York: Princeton Architectural Press, 2002.

Vernon, Raymond. "Multinational Enterprise and National Sovereignty." *Harvard Business Review*, April 1967.

Vine, David. *Base Nation: How U.S. Military Bases Abroad Harm America and the World*. New York: Metropolitan Books, Henry Holt, 2015.

The Wall Street Journal. "Defense Contracts Yield Higher Profits Than Private Work, Navy Study Says." November 29, 1985.

Wallerstein, Immanuel. *The Modern World-System*. New York: Academic Press, 1974.

Wang, Bing. *The Architectural Profession of Modern China: Emerging from the Past*. Beijing: Foreign Language Press, 2011.

Warnica, Richard. "Janet, the Mysterious Airline That Serves Area 51, Is Hiring." *National Post*, January 11, 2018. https://nationalpost.com/news/world/janet-the-mysterious-airline-that-serves-area-51-is-hiring.

The Washington Post. "Cabell Gwathmey: Director of DC Agency." January 9, 2002.

Watson, Andrew M., and Joel B. Dirlam. "The Impact of Underdevelopment on Economic Planning." *The Quarterly Journal of Economics* 79, no. 2 (May 1965): 167–94.

Weatherhead, Arthur C. "Architecture and Life." *Los Angeles Times*, April 22, 1928.

———. "Note on Education in Architecture." *Architect and Engineer* 123 (December 1935): 69.

Weber, Max. *From Max Weber: Essays in Sociology*. Edited by H. H. Gerth and C. Wright Mills. New York: Oxford University Press, 1946.

Weisman, Winston. "The Commercial Architecture of George B. Post." *Journal of the Society of Architectural Historians* 31, no. 3 (October 1972): 176–203.

Weiss, Ruth A. "Be Vision, a Package of IBM 7090 FORTRAN Programs to Draw Orthographic Views of Combinations of Plane and Quadric Surfaces." *Journal of the Association for Computing Machinery* 13, no. 2 (April 1966): 194–204.

Wellerstein, Alex. *Restricted Data: The History of Nuclear Secrecy in the United States*. Chicago: University of Chicago Press, 2021.

Wermiel, Sara E. "Norcross, Fuller, and the Rise of the General Contractor in the United States in the Nineteenth Century," 3297–3313. *Proceedings, Second International Congress on Construction History*. Cambridge, England, 2006.

Western Construction. "Missile Base Construction." April 1960, 47–52.

White, Hayden. *The Content of the Form: Narrative Discourse and Historical Representation*. Baltimore: Johns Hopkins University Press, 1992.

———. *Metahistory: The Historical Imagination in Nineteenth-Century Europe*. Baltimore: Johns Hopkins University Press, 2000.

———. "A Practical Past." *Historein*, no. 10 (2010): 10–19.

White, L. K. "Memorandum for Deputy Director of Central Intelligence Re: Case History on Buildings 213 and 213A," February 4, 1963. FOIA case no.

CIA-RDP78-04608A000400070005-2. CIA Special Collections. https://www.cia.gov/readingroom/docs/CIA-RDP78-04608A000400070005-2.pdf.

Whitehouse, Franklin. "Architect Fits Snugly into Owner's Role." *The New York Times*, September 28, 1969.

Whiteson, Leon. "Innovative Designs Can Enliven Even Those Difficult Buildings." *Los Angeles Times*, January 2, 1989.

Wickersham, Jay. "From Disinterested Expert to Marketplace Competitor: How Anti-monopoly Law Transformed the Ethics and Economics of American Architecture in the 1970s." *Architectural Theory Review* 20, no. 2 (2015): 138–58.

Williams, Raymond. "Experience." In *Keywords: A Vocabulary of Culture and Society*. New York: Oxford University Press, 1985.

Williamson, Oliver. *Markets and Hierarchies: Analysis and Antitrust Implications*. New York: The Free Press, 1975.

———. "The Modern Corporation: Origins, Evolution, Attributes." *Journal of Economic Literature* 19, no. 4 (December 1981): 1437–1568.

———. "The Theory of the Firm as Governance Structure: From Choice to Contract." *The Journal of Economic Perspectives* 16, no. 3 (2002): 171–95.

Williamson, Rebeca. "Degree Nomenclature." In *Architecture School: Three Centuries of Educating Architect in North America*, edited by Joan Ockman, 270–75. Cambridge, MA: MIT Press, 2012.

Wilshire Press. "More Reports from Women Successful in Man's World." August 16, 1973. Bakeman family papers. Private collection.

Wittman, Richard. *Architecture, Print Culture, and the Public Sphere in Eighteenth-Century France*. The Classical Tradition in Architecture. New York: Routledge, 2013.

Wolf, Eric R. *Europe and the People without History*. Berkeley: University of California Press, 1982.

Wood, Michael C., and John Cunningham Wood, eds. *Frank and Lillian Gilbreth: Critical Evaluations in Business and Management, vol. 1*. London: Routledge, 2003.

Woods, Mary N. "The American Architect and Building News 1876–1907." PhD diss., Columbia University, 1983.

———. *From Craft to Profession: The Practice of Architecture in Nineteenth-Century America*. Berkeley: University of California Press, 1999.

Woods, Shadrach. *The Man in the Street: A Polemic on Urbanism*. Harmondsworth, UK: Penguin Books, 1975.

———. "Stem." *Architectural Design*, 1960, 181.

The World Bank. "World Development Indicators." https://data.worldbank.org/indicator/NY.GDP.MKTP.CD. Accessed August 25, 2022.

Wrenn, Tony. "The Tenth Decade: 1957-1966." AIArchitect, August 2006. https://info.aia.org/aiarchitect/thisweek06/0804/a150_two80406.htm.

Wright, Gwendolyn. "On the Fringe of the Profession: Women in American Architecture." In *The Architect: Chapters in the History of the Profession*, 280-308. New York: Oxford University Press, 1986.

Xue, Charlie Q. L. and Guanghui Ding. *A History of Design Institutes in China: From Mao to Market*. New York: Routledge, 2018.

Yaneva, Albena. *Crafting History: Archiving and the Quest for Architectural Legacy*. Expertise: Cultures and Technologies of Knowledge. Ithaca, NY: Cornell University Press, 2020.

———. *The Making of a Building: A Pragmatist Approach to Architecture*. Oxford: Peter Lang, 2009.

Yoon, J. Meejin, and Eric Howeler. *Expanded Practice: Howeler and Yoon Architecture*. New York: Princeton Architectural Press, 2009.

Yoshida, Kensei. *Democracy Betrayed: Okinawa under US Occupation*. Bellingham: Washington University Press, 2001.

Young, Whitney M., Jr. "Keynote Address to 1968 AIA National Convention, Portland, OR." In *20 on 20/20 Vision: Perspectives on Diversity and Design*, edited by Linda Kiisk, 44-51. Boston: AIA Diversity Committee and Boston Society of Architects, 2003.

Zagore, Frank C., and D. Marc Kilgour. "Assessing Competing Defense Postures: The Strategic Implications of 'Flexible Response.'" *World Politics* 47, no. 3 (April 1995): 373-417.

Zimmerman, Claire. *Albert Kahn Inc.: Architecture, Industry, and Labor, 1905-1961*. Cambridge, MA: MIT Press, 2025.

———. "Building the World Capitalist System: The 'Invisible Architecture' of Albert Kahn Associates of Detroit, 1900-1961." *Fabrications* 29, no. 2 (2019): 231-56.

———. "The Labor of Albert Kahn." *Aggregate* 2 (December 2014).

Index

acquisitions: of architecture and engineering firms, 37–38, 52, 54–57, 78, 86–87, 93, 94*fig.*, 104–105, 113, 168; general theories of, 25, 42, 49, 116; news about, 37, 46–47; of publishing houses, 16, 49, 82–84
Adler, Dankmar, 29
AECOM: archives, 11–12, 17–19; leaders, 5, 11, 17, 70–71; origins, 12–13, 64–65, 94*fig.*, 104–109; prominence, 3–6
aesthetics: conglomerate theories of, 110–112, 122–123, 127–128; indeterminacy of, 79, 131, 135; postmodern theories of, 112, 129–131, 141
Air Force (US): architects in, 69–70; designs for, 147, 153–156, 171–177, 178*fig.*, 191, 210, 280n108, 281n114; educational collaborations with, 170. *See also* military
airplanes: used in architectural practice, 156, 163–166
American dream, 50
American Institute of Architects (AIA): code of ethics of, 27–28, 30, 38; contracts by, 158–161, 190, 277n62. *See also* handbook

ammunition, 155–156
annual reports, 12, 104, 106, 139, 186, 226
anonymity, 19, 53, 257n102
antitrust law, 30–39, 49, 159, 248n36. *See also* Sherman Antitrust Act
architects: as artists, 2, 8, 179, 185, 188, 251n16; authorial control and, 8–9, 26–27, 29, 140; as businesspeople, 8–10, 21, 31, 57, 73; design and, 112–115; entry-level, 66–68; as politicians, 1–3, 29. *See also* draftspersons
Architects Collaborative, The (TAC), 57, 73, 224, 236
architectural firms: control over profession, 31, 41–42; large, 3, 9–11, 25, 59, 83–84, 171, 197; revenue and employee size of, 40–41, 240–242. *See also* corruption; diversity
Architectural Forum: acquisitions of, 16, 88–83
architectural offices, 2–3, 9–11, 64, 68, 73–82, 88*fig.*, 97–100, 98*fig.*, 99*fig.*, 107, 207–209; diagrams of, 168; international, 34, 147–148, 153–154

[335]

architectural profession: corporate deregulation of, 26, 31–39, 49, 108, 159, 170; gentlemen and, 27, 41, 140; theories of, 38–42; US beginnings of, 27–30, 41, 251n16. *See also* American Institute of Architects (AIA)

Architectural Record, 33, 84–85; acquisitions of, 16, 82, 84

architectural schools, 66–69, 194, 234–235; corporatization of, 39, 170

archives: of architects' work, 224–225, 231; restricted access to, 12, 17–18, 31, 72–73, 89, 202–203; of states, 19–20, 203

Arendt, Hannah, 259n2

Army (US), 67, 69, 96, 146, 167–168, 183, 289n22, 291n40. *See also* military

Ashland Oil Inc., 104–105, 138–139

Associated Design, Planning and Art, 96

atomic bomb. *See* bombs

Austin, Field & Fry, 73

Bakeman, Carol Ann, 221–225, 229–230, 292nn58,60,61

Banham, Reyner, 128, 206

banks: architects' design of, 124–126, 129–131, 202; architects' use of, 15, 33, 34, 79–80, 100, 147, 153; bankruptcy, 147, 236; Manufacturers Bank, 125, 126*fig.*; World Bank, 144

black-boxing, 206, 219. *See also* deprofessionalization

Blau, Judith, 4, 38, 195

bombs, 156, 163–164; atomic, 1, 58, 65–66, 69, 206; bomb-resistant, 201; secrecy about, 219–220

books: architects' libraries of, 144, 155, 192, 221, 274nn9,10; architects' manuals, 87, 89, 139, 188, 192, 203; about architecture practice, 193–199; as metrics of value (of company shares), 184–185, 283n3. *See also* handbook

Booz Allen Hamilton (BAH), 75–80, 262n31

Bourdieu, Pierre: incorporation theories, 52; practice theories, 137–138, 195, 272n74, 286n52

branches: architecture offices as, 147–148, 153–154; banks, 129; corporate organization, 58, 116, 161; government, 221; military, 191. *See also* plant

bridges, 49–50, 55–56, 159. *See also* infrastructure

brochures: architecture firms', 71, 89, 91, 103*fig.*, 104, 147, 148*fig.*, 156, 226

Brooks Act, 59–60, 145, 274n10

bulldozers, 156

Bunshaft, Gordon, 35, 137

bureaucracy, 4–5, 7, 9, 33–39, 41, 50, 66, 214; designers within, 112, 140; protocols of, 146, 154–155

business: architectural effects of, 8–10, 206; cards, 207–208, 208*fig.*; creating new, 216–217; cycles of, 28–29, 203–204, 259n2; family-run, 68, 261n14; histories of, 16, 28, 50, 111, 140, 237; lack of knowledge about, 13, 262n25; leaders of, 226, 229, 265n65. *See also* manuals

Canadian Centre for Architecture (CCA), 224–225

Cape Canaveral, 156–157, 172

capitalism, 48–49, 61; corporate, 39, 108, 234, 238; disaster, 32; late, 15,

93, 111, 129, 138, 196, 254n68; monopoly, 8, 30, 39, 49-50, 58, 265n65; pastoral, 110-111. *See also* imperialism
Capitol (US): architects of, 32-33
Caudill Rowlett Scott (CRS), 157, 224, 236-237
Celler-Kefauver Act, 204, 248n36, 265n67
Chandler, Alfred D., Jr., 14, 25, 78, 111, 237
Charles, Abrams, 146
Charles Luckman Associates, 36-38, 62, 280n102
Chatelain, Gauger & Nolan, 37
China, 15, 35, 149, 150, 214
CIA, 207-213
cities. *See* urbanization
clerical workers, 18, 47, 203. *See also* secretaries
Coburn, William, 207-213, 214, 219
collaboration, 4, 23, 35, 57, 139-140
colonization, 5-6, 19-20, 24, 48-49, 55-56, 143, 236
Communications Satellite Corporation (COMSAT), 120-123
communism: spread of, 58, 114, 226
compensation: of architects, 68, 77, 271n66; cost-plus-fixed-fee method of, 60, 160-161; fixed-fee method of, 155, 162; in government work, 146, 152-153, 161-162. *See also* exploitation; labor
complexes: architecture of, 117-120, 281n114; military-industrial, 7, 42, 205, 210
computers, 38, 59, 72, 96, 100, 166-171, 173-177, 215*fig.*, 215-220, 278nn86,87,89; resistance to, 216
conflicts: in architecture firms, 57, 75-77, 227-229; of interest, 160, 188

conglomerates: architecture and engineering firms as, 3, 9-10, 13-14, 37-38, 54-56, 86-96, 182, 237, 253n51; buildings as, 115-132, 206, 267n7, 271n59; businesses as, 14-16, 46-49, 59, 156, 159, 181-182, 186, 248n36, 249n39, 265n67; countries as, 15, 214, 291n40; as economic portfolios, 185, 193; in postmodern discourse, 132-136; resistance to, 15, 92-93, 265n65. *See also* empire
Congress (US), 145. *See also* Senate (US)
conservativism, 21, 37, 57, 141
consultants: architects and engineers as, 12, 26, 55, 68, 70, 91, 158-159, 162, 179. *See also* management
contractors: architects working with, 38, 92; government, 146, 152-153, 182, 203, 225; government selection of, 60, 144-145; history of, 158-161; subcontractors, 91-92, 158-159
contracts, 17, 38, 59-61, 85, 142-144, 153-158; procurement of, 144-149. *See also* American Institute of Architects (AIA); contractors
controversy: about government spending, 151-153; about large architecture firms, 7-8; in public records, 31-34
Cooper, Rolland, 1952
cores: in buildings, 134-135; in business, 41, 50-51, 91; in relation to peripheries, 47-50
corporations. *See* incorporation
corruption, 1-2, 28, 59, 145-147, 234; professional effects of, 39-42; quid pro quo, 33-34, 203
Coxe, Weld (Group), 184

Crawford, Louis, 67; Crawford & Daniel Architects (firm), 67–68
Cuff, Dana, 4, 195, 234–235

Daniel, Mann, Johnson and Mendenhall (DMJM); acquisition of, 104–105; acquisitions by, 86–96; early beginnings of, 69–70, 73–85; office of, 73, 82, 97, 98*fig.*, 99*fig.*, 100; recognition of, 33, 63, 114–116, 229–230, 263n46; as urban system, 100–109. *See also* AECOM
Daniel, Phillip: death of, 72, 87; early career, 68–75, 70*fig.*, 112, 147; education, 66–67; role in corporate practice, 72, 73–75; work for the CIA, 209–213; work for the military, 112, 147, 155–156, 175*fig.*; work with computers, 96, 173–174, 174*fig.*, 215–217
Daniel Burnham & Co., 3, 9, 36
Dar Al-Handasah, 54–56, 257n110; Dar Group, 10, 54–55, 257n110
Davis, Arthur Q., 93, 271n66; Curtis and Davis Architects and Engineers (firm), 93, 271n66
Day, Kim, 230
Deamer, Peggy, 30, 59
death, 42, 71, 87, 204, 230; architects' anxiety about, 54; of builders, 29–30; of the profession, 31, 39–42, 233. *See also* deprofessionalization
Deaver, Michael, 1–2, 245n1
debt, 146–157
decentralization: of architects' firms, 90–96; military, 155, 175; office, 97–100, 116–123; urban, 65, 100–104
defense: contractors, 16, 49, 89; contracts, 59, 157, 218; national, 148, 153, 157, 160, 207, 289n25; strategies of, 167–168, 219. *See also* deterrence; military
democracy, 159, 214, 233
dependencies: of architects on the US government, 144–158, 215–216; of the US government on private companies, 100, 143, 232
Depression, Great: impacts on architects' careers, 13, 36, 66–67; impacts on architecture firms, 8, 58, 66, 73, 189, 194, 261n22
deprofessionalization, 40–42, 233–234, 254n59; corporations causing, 27–40
deregulation. *See* regulation
Derrida, Jacques, 204
Design Methods (company), 72, 167–168, 215–220
deterrence: military, 171–172, 179, 181, 207
development: of architects (and interns), 105, 170–171, 190; international, 55–56, 91–96, 142–151, 156, 214; as project, 157–158; real estate, 97–104, 125, 130, 253n51; tools used in, 163–171
diagrams: of architects' businesses, 44–52; in design, 175*fig.*
discrimination (in architecture), 205; gender-based, 87, 149, 226–229; price-based, 248n36
Disney, Walt, 69; the Walt Disney Company, 16; Disneyland, 97–98
distances: architects' calculations of, 163–164, 168, 174–175, 181, 193, 208–209, 218–219, 281n114
diversity: in architects' skills, 45–46, 73; in architecture firms (demographic), 204–205, 226–230; in

business offerings, 44, 79, 93, 96, 110, 132, 193
Dorman, Albert, 64–65, 70, 79, 86–87, 92–93, 100–101, 106
Douglas Aircraft Company, 163
draftpersons, 1, 2, 7, 205, 207–208, 225, 229, 261n15, 292n73
drawings: for construction, 66, 177; outsourcing of, 47; production in large firms, 44, 79, 99, 127–128, 173–174; renderings, 179, 180*fig.*, 181; signatures on, 292n68. *See also* labor
Drucker, Peter, 45–46, 56, 80, 89
DuPont, 46, 59, 110, 249n39

Eisenman, Peter: archival protocol of, 224–225, 292n68
empire, 54, 58, 147, 152–153; architecture and engineering firms as, 15–16, 182; conglomerates as, 15, 214, 249n43, 291n40; hiding of, 213–214. *See also* imperialism
enclosure, 111, 123, 134, 141; membrane as, 123–125, 127–131, 134, 136, 138. *See also* skin
Engineering News-Record: architecture firms ranked in, 46–47, 90
engineers. *See* integration
Escobar, Arturo, 158
ethics. *See* American Institute of Architects (AIA)
ethnography: of architects, 4, 186, 195–199; historical, 19–20, 230–231
experience: economies of, 145, 274n12; embodiments of, 106, 179, 195; fabricated, 182–183; project selections based on, 59–60, 144–145, 147; work-related, 104, 149, 170, 229

exploitation: of labor, 19, 89–90, 108, 161, 163; of resources, 14–15, 49, 55–56

façades, 97–100, 110–115, 123–132, 271n72
flexibility: in military strategy, 167–168; professional, 190–191; in work, 45, 50–52, 91, 106. *See also* post-Fordism
Ford, Henry, 44. *See also* Fordism
Fordism, 43; architecture firms and, 44–45, 45*fig.*, 47, 50, 84–85. *See also* post-Fordism
FORTRAN, 218
Fortune, 27–28, 83, 171, 265n65; Fortune 500, 83, 90, 116
freedom: in economics, 29, 30, 144; of information, 18, 220; practice of, 8; US ideals of, 159, 204
Friedman, Milton, 35, 193

Garcetti, Eric, 63, 183
Gehry Partners, 10, 247n29; Frank Gehry, 115, 268n18
gender. *See* men; women
Genge (company), 93, 184
genius, 7, 53, 66, 232, 245n5
genocide, 15, 57, 65
Gensler (company), 235; Art Gensler, 262n25
gentleman: architects as, 34, 225. *See also* architectural profession
geopolitics: of business, 108, 111, 134–135
Giedion, Sigfried, 119, 138
gig economy, 50
Gilbreth, Frank, 159–161
governance: firms and, 60–61, 258n129; shared, 52–53; urban systems of, 100–104

Index [339]

growth: business, 84, 86, 105, 135, 263n46, 264n58; designs for, 115–128, 269n25; economic, 28, 111, 170, 185; restrictions on, 92, 125–126; urban, 36, 63

Gutman, Robert, 4, 25, 38, 234–235

handbook, 188–189, 192–193, 196–197

Hardt, Michael, 54, 63

Harvey, David, 61, 129, 270

Hayek, Friedrich, 145

hegemony (American), 8, 143, 156, 163, 182

Helmuth, Obata + Kassabaum (HOK), 56–57, 236–237

Hitchcock, Henry-Russell, 9, 66

Hollywood: architects in, 67–68, 172, 179, 260n7, 281n123, 282n124; as metaphor for military weapons, 175–177, 178*fig.*

housekeeping: as federal privilege, 207, 221; as social reproductive labor, 222–224

IBM, 113, 230

immateriality. *See* labor

Immerwahr, Daniel, 213–214

imperialism: American, 54, 181, 205–206, 214, 232, 259n2; architects and, 3, 15, 25, 35–36, 42, 49, 64–66; statistics about, 241

incorporation: in architecture business, 43, 52–57, 80; of imperialist-capitalist tendencies, 3, 13–15, 143, 214; social theories of, 52, 137, 195; state charters permitting, 43, 72–73

indeterminacy: in aesthetics, 122, 128–132; in business, 110, 120–123, 134–136

individualism, 4, 15, 19, 25, 62–63, 106; in corporations, 53, 66, 140, 232, 145n5; in design, 136–140; evolution to imperialism, 64–66, 92; liability, 53–54, 80–86; limits to, 136–141. *See also* genius

Indonesia, 149–152, 154, 163

inequity, 4, 65. *See* colonization; discrimination

infrastructure: business, 111, 121, 125, 128, 132; redacted documents as, 211; urban, 49–58, 81–82, 108–109, 143, 156–158, 214; *See also* dependencies; military

integration: of architects and engineers, 78–79, 91; disintegration, 62, 100; horizontal, 44–45, 50, 123; vertical, 60–62, 100, 248n36

International Development, US Agency for (USAID), 142, 165*fig.*, 149–153

internationalization: of architecture firms, 26, 53, 57–60, 143–150, 155–164

interns: development program for, 170–171

Iron Mountain, 201–204, 225

Jameson, Fredric, 129–131

Jencks, Charles, 62, 112, 129–134

John B. Parkin Associates, 47–48, 48*fig.*

Johnson, S. Kenneth: childhood, 260n11; death of, 87; early career, 67–69, 70*fig.*, 75–78, 147, 154–155; education of, 68–69; roles in practice, 73, 98–99, 172, 175

Johnston, George, 188

joint ventures, 50, 78, 146, 159, 172–173, 208

journals, professional. See *Architectural Forum*; *Architectural Record*; *Engineering News-Record*; *Fortune*; *Progressive Architecture*

Kahn, Albert: Associates (firm), 10, 44, 47, 78, 83–84, 263n45, 280n106
Keating Mann Jernigan Rottet, 139, 272n79
Kennard, Robert, 225
Kennedy, John F.: administration of, 35, 149, 201; defense strategies of, 167
Keynes, John Maynard: Keynesian economics, 28–29, 61, 181
Khachooni, Vahe, 167–170, 215–220, 215*fig.*
Klein, Naomi, 17, 32

labor, architectural: as immaterial (nonmanual), 42, 45; as manual, 43–47, 84–85, 154, 161, 215; as unpaid, 68, 154. *See also* exploitation
Larson, Magali Sarfatti, 38–42, 195
Latour, Bruno, 52, 158, 195, 198
legacy: architects' as individuals, 24, 36, 224–225; family, 72, 225; files as, 202; firms, 12, 105, 205
liability, 52, 77, 80–82, 159
liberalism: architectural politics, 36–37; architectural profession, 21–22; economics, 28–29, 35, 145. *See also* neoliberalism
liberation, 66, 69. *See also* freedom
licensure: corporate control of, 8, 34, 37, 41–42; early debates about, 28–30
life, 199–200, 204, 230–233
Litton Industries, 16, 49, 59, 87–89, 115–116, 269n20
Logicomp, 72, 96, 100, 166–167
Los Angeles: architecture firms in, 2, 10, 36, 53, 61–62, 224, 265n63; growth and fragmentation of, 62, 125, 270n39, 276n37; projects in,

5–6, 114–115, 125–126, 166; school (of urbanism), 62–63, 115
Luckman, Charles, 280n102
Luckman, James, 36
Lumsden, Anthony, 22, 63, 97, 268n18; aesthetic theories of, 115, 123–132, 268n14; firing of, 139–140; roles in corporate practice, 113–116, 271n66; theories of individuals in corporate firms, 136–139, 271nn71,72

management: of architectural practice, 36–37, 45–47, 49–51, 59–60, 65–66, 106–107, 137–139, 170, 234; construction, 30, 57, 91–92, 96; consultants, 13, 26, 75–80, 184, 193; of debt, 152–153, 155; difficulties with, 55, 60, 75, 220; technologies for, 170, 224. *See also* computers; offices; records
Mann, Arthur, 13, 229; early career, 68–70, 70*fig.*, 78, 261n15
manuals. *See* books
Manzi, Albert, 33–34
market: construction, 26, 29, 101; disinterest in, 27–28, 41; economy, 8, 16, 23, 30–31, 39, 65; for services, 14, 46, 54, 55, 86; sheltered positions within, 39–41. *See* stocks
marketing, 45, 79, 85, 170, 234
Martin, Reinhold, 129–132
Mason & Hanger-Silas Mason Company, 172, 280n105
Massachusetts (state): lawsuits against architects in, 203, 252n32
McCone, John, 212–213, 221, 290n36
McCord, James, 220–221
McCoy, Esther, 114–115, 127
McKim, Mead & White, 9
McKinsey, 75
men, 57, 70, 108, 225–228

Mendenhall, Irvan: early work of, 68–70, 70*fig.*, 147; personal life of, 68, 261n14; positions on computers in architecture, 216; role in corporate practice, 73, 78, 82

mergers, 38, 57, 94*fig.*, 139, 266n87; Great Merger Movement, 8, 14

military: architects in, 69; architects' tools from, 163–170; bases, 147–153, 171; contracts, 157. *See also* war

mirror-glass, 4–5, 114–115, 128–131, 206

missiles (ballistic), 157; Atlas, 156, 172, 174, 280n102; Titan I, 156, 167, 171–179, 180*fig.*, 181, 280n108, 281n113. *See also* deterrence

modernity: of buildings, 99, 110, 116–118, 128–129, 177–179; of firms, 78–93, 111, 140, 224; in international development, 151–152, 158, 163–164; modernism, attachments to, 92, 114

Moe, Stanley, 71, 76*fig.*, 82, 155; archives of, 71–72, 274n9; international work of, 142–146, 149–150

money. *See* compensation; labor; profit

monopoly. *See* capitalism; Sherman Antitrust Act

Morgan, Julia, 226

Mountain, Barry, 32–34, 149–151

National Photographic Interpretation Center (NPIC), 209–212, 290n28

nationalism, 35, 149. *See also* development; internationalization

Navy (US): architects and engineers in, 69–70, 278n86; designs for, 147, 154–156. *See also* military

Negri, Antonio, 54, 63

neoliberalism, 7, 254n68; architects' contributions to, 42–60

Newman, Richard: work at AECOM, 70–71, 105–106; work at DMJM, 93–95; work at Genge, 93, 184

Nixon, Richard: administration of, 30, 35, 149, 252n39; efforts to reelect, 32–34, 220

nonprofits: architecture firms as, 41, 235

office buildings, 4, 22, 44, 110, 114, 123–124, 168, 169*fig.*

offices: cultures within, 19, 92, 215–216, 225–230; political, 34–35, 149; management of, 185–192, 202, 222–225, 230–231. *See also* architectural offices

oil companies, 14, 92, 104–105, 131, 138. *See also* Ashland Oil Inc.

oligarchs: businesses as, 63

organization: in architecture practice, 9, 18–19, 44, 47, 66, 83–99; charts, 44–45, 45*fig.*, 84*fig.*, 88*fig.*; of cities, 60–61, 72, 84–85, 272n72; "flexible," 50–51; industrial, 8, 44–46, 249n39

outsourcing, 51–52; of contractors, 91–92, 151; of drawing labor, 47, 89; of engineering work, 78. *See also* contractors

Owings, Nathaniel, 35–36, 44, 171, 252n39, 262n35

paperwork, 18, 71–72; in offices, 82, 83; storage of, 202–205, 213, 220–224

parents: architects as, 18, 72; businesses as, 10. *See also* patriarchy partnerships: as legal type of architecture firm, 9, 13, 27, 39, 43, 52–54, 73, 80–81, 84, 257n105, 261n14

patriarchy, 35–36, 220–221

Pelli, Cesar: theory of buildings as complexes, 118–120; theory of growth, 116–117; theory of spines in buildings, 119–120; work in corporate firms, 22–23, 112–115

peripheries: in architectural practice, 50, 85–86, 90–91; in building design, 100; in geography, 14–15; postcolonial theories of, 42, 47–49; in urbanism, 62–63

plants: buildings as, 119–120, 125–128, 171, 173, 233, 280n102; businesses as, 116–117

politics: architects and, 1–3, 27–42; parties, 8, 252n32; skirting by scholars of, 131–132, 141. *See also* imperialism; power

portfolios: design, 112, 191–192, 195; economic, 138, 185–186, 193; firms as, 193; military, 191

Portman, John, 129, 253n51

Post, George B., 9

postcolonialism, 15, 22, 26, 43. *See also* peripheries

post-Fordism: in labor, 43–52, 85–91, 108; in urbanism, 62–63, 89–91

postindustrialization: of businesses, 130; of cities, 61–62. *See also* post-Fordism

postmodernism, 22–23, 56, 111–112, 128–136, 130–143

postwar. *See* war

power: architects and political, 2, 13, 32–33, 213; masking, 214; militaristic, 208; professional, 14, 39, 44, 206

practice: architecture as, 4, 194–195; theories of, 137–138, 195

precarity: in employment, 47, 50, 91, 108, 154, 190

profit: architects and, 14–15, 28, 43, 52–57, 60–61, 77, 83–84, 87, 90–92, 104–106, 150–155, 160–162, 193, 262n31; lack of, 13, 74–75; as metric of success, 46–47. *See also* incorporation

Progressive Architecture (P/A): acquisitions of, 16, 49, 115–116; architecture firms featured in, 87–90, 98, 114, 121

projects, 150–158; of hegemony, 182; project-based jobs, 26, 50. *See also* development

proprietorship (sole), 9, 27, 43, 52–54, 73, 80

quid pro quo: between architects and politicians, 22, 33–34, 203

race-based, 225–226

Reagan, Ronald, 1, 252n30

real estate: architects in, 27–31, 37–38, 96–97, 103, 157–158, 185, 253n51

Real Estate technology Inc. (Realtech), 97–100

realism: theatrical, 67, 181

recessions, 23, 26, 38, 66, 73, 89–90, 193–200, 264n53; Great Recession, 3

records; falsification of, 182–183; management of, 24, 220–225; storage of, 201–205, 230

regulation, 29, 39, 196, 235, 284n17; deregulation, 32, 193, 197

rendering. *See* drawings

Republican Party, 1–2, 35; National Committee of, 32–33, 220, 252n32, 284n26. *See also* conservatism risk, 53–54, 58–60, 80, 97, 160–161, 193. *See also* uncertainty

Santa Maria (city), 67, 73–74
secrecy: in architecture and engineering practice, 205–226, 290n36; in government, 96, 201, 209, 213–218, 221–223; theories of, 204, 214
secretaries, 68, 216, 221–230
security: employment, 43, 69, 140; national, 144, 182, 205, 220–221. *See also* defense
Senate (US): debates about conglomeration, 15, 214; debates about foreign aid, 151–152; investigations of architects by, 220. *See also* Congress (US)
set designers: architects as, 68, 281n123. *See also* Hollywood
Shair, Kamal, 55–56
Sherman Antitrust Act, 30–31, 38, 49, 159, 248n36, 265n67
SHoP Architects, 10, 100, 247n30
Shope, Bill, 142–143, 151
Singleton, Henry, 115–117, 139
Skidmore, Owings & Merrill (SOM), 35–36, 44, 45*fig.*, 46, 78, 139, 255n72, 262n35
skin: façades as, 123–128, 131; as metaphor in practice theory, 137–138. *See also* enclosure
Sklarek, Norma, 226
Smith, Adam, 39, 58, 80
Smith, Hinchman & Grylls, 31–32, 37
Smith, Jack Martin, 68, 179–181, 282n124
Smith, Stanley, 213, 33, 245n1
Smithsons, Alison and Peter: theory of conglomerate order, 267n7

Soja, Edward, 50
sovereignty: US, 13, 43, 58, 66, 151, 205–206, 219–220
Soviet Union, 157, 204, 207
space: aerospace, 61–62, 116, 174–174; between buildings, 104, 157, 169*fig.*, 171, 173; designing for, 72, 171–172. *See also* distance
speculation, 53, 74, 114, 117–118, 129, 207, 259n2
Sperry Rand, 59, 167, 170, 215*fig.*, 218, 278n87
spines: in books, 184; in buildings, 119–120. *See also* Pelli, Cesar
stocks: architects', 31, 37–38, 53, 56; market, 4, 23–24, 35; publicly traded, 63, 93, 182–183
storage, 201–204, 224–225, 230
studios, 2, 139–140; in Hollywood, 16, 68, 104, 260n7
subcontractors. *See* contractors
subsidiaries: in architecture practice, 3, 10, 46–47, 58, 64–65, 89–96, 247nn29,30, 265n72; in building design, 100, 110, 116, 123
Sudan: development projects in, 165*fig.*, 166
system: architecture and engineering as, 42; building as, 120–122; capitalist, 35, 48–49, 55; computer, 96, 167–168, 278n86; façade as, 123–124; "Field System," 159–160; "Star-System," 136–137; studio as, 16; urban, 100–104, 157–158; weapons as, 155–156, 172, 280n108

Takeyama, Minoru, 132–135
Teledyne (corporation), 110, 115–116; laboratories designed for, 116–123, 117*fig.*, 118*fig.*, 121*fig.*

temporariness: of architectural labor, 19, 50–52, 91–92, 154, 191, 227; as military strategy, 185–186
Thailand: projects in, 142, 146, 150–151, 154, 161–162
Tillman Water Reclamation Plant, 125–128, 127*fig.*, 130. *See also* plants
Tokyo: architects' offices in, 147–149, 153; examples of postmodern architecture in, 132, 133*fig.*, 134

uncertainty: income-related, 146; job-related, 68–69; political-economic, 6, 56, 66, 140
unemployment: in architecture, 189; in the US, 28, 197
unions, 149, 194, 197, 233, 251n17, 285n38
Univac (computers), 96, 100, 166–168, 215*fig.*, 218
University of Southern California (USC): architects educated at, 66–68, 260n12; architecture school at, 67; art directors educated at, 68, 179, 260n13, 281n123; formation of, 66
urbanization, 36, 50, 61, 103–104. *See also* systems

value: of architects to the public, 27–28, 93, 107–108, 182, 189, 233; colonial flows of, 55–56; economic, 112, 141, 1773; of individuals within corporate practice, 139–140, 224–225; inflating, 182–18. *See also* books

vaults, 201–204, 213
Vietnam, 156

wages. *See* compensation
Wallerstein, Immanuel, 48–49
war: architectural practice after, 69, 75–80, 158–160, 190, 206; Cold War, 15, 26, 61–62, 140, 157, 167, 204–207; World War I, 147; World War II, 156, 185, 191, 202
Washington, DC: architects meeting in, 147, 151, 207, 209–210; architecture offices in, 35, 148
Washington Navy Yard, 209
Watergate: architects' involvement in, 220
Weatherhead, Arthur C., 67–69
Weber, Max, 39, 214
Welton Becket and Associates, 168, 169*fig.*
whiteness: in architectural practice, 19, 57, 82, 199–200, 225, 227–229; corporations and, 82, 108
William Pereira & Associates, 168, 224, 268n18, 280n102
Wilson, Zelma, 225–226, 230
women: in architecture, 96, 205, 221–230, 292n73, 293n76. *See also* discrimination
Woods, Mary, 4, 8, 31, 195
work. *See* labor
Wright, Ellen, 227–230

Yaneva, Albena, 36, 158, 198

Founded in 1893,
UNIVERSITY OF CALIFORNIA PRESS
publishes bold, progressive books and journals
on topics in the arts, humanities, social sciences,
and natural sciences—with a focus on social
justice issues—that inspire thought and action
among readers worldwide.

The UC PRESS FOUNDATION
raises funds to uphold the press's vital role
as an independent, nonprofit publisher, and
receives philanthropic support from a wide
range of individuals and institutions—and from
committed readers like you. To learn more, visit
ucpress.edu/supportus.

www.ingramcontent.com/pod-product-compliance
Lightning Source LLC
Chambersburg PA
CBHW021335230426
43666CB00006B/299